Gender and Violence
against Political Actors

Praise for *Gender and Violence against Political Actors*

"This ambitious and groundbreaking book provides a systematic gendered analysis of political violence across different countries and political contexts. It is based on solid theories and concepts and provides a broad coverage of the forms of violence that harm women's political participation. The rich case studies make the volume a rewarding read for scholars and students. The book is also highly recommendable as it provides suggestions for policy responses."—**Johanna Kantola,** Professor of European Societies and Their Politics at the Centre for European Studies at the University of Helsinki, Finland, and author of *Gender and the European Union*

"The editors and contributors to this book make broad contributions to our understanding of, and ability to conduct research about, gender and political violence. They examine various forms of violence—spanning physical to psychological violence—in diverse arenas, ranging from war to legislative chambers to political campaigns. This book's broad theoretical scope, paired with case studies in highly diverse contexts and with policy attempts to address political violence, makes *Gender and Violence against Political Actors* an indispensable resource for scholars and students in all areas of gender politics."—**Michelle M. Taylor-Robinson,** Professor of Political Science at Texas A&M University, and coauthor of *Women in Presidential Cabinets: Power Players or Abundant Tokens?*

"Whereas violence against women who take on political roles is as old as the witch hunts, it has only recently become the subject of systematic study. This book offers an important collection of perspectives from different subfields of political science that deepen and broaden our understanding of the phenomenon of gendered violence(s). Working with the notion of a continuum of violence spanning psychological and physical violence while attending to the gendered power relations that shape it, the editors and contributors highlight how multiple approaches are needed to fully explain and address violence against gendered political actors."—**Annick T. R. Wibben,** Anna Lindh Professor of Gender, Peace, and Security at the Swedish Defence University

EDITED BY ELIN BJARNEGÅRD
AND PÄR ZETTERBERG

Gender and Violence
against Political Actors

TEMPLE UNIVERSITY PRESS
Philadelphia • *Rome* • *Tokyo*

TEMPLE UNIVERSITY PRESS
Philadelphia, Pennsylvania 19122
tupress.temple.edu

Library of Congress Cataloging-in-Publication Data

Names: Bjarnegård, Elin, editor. | Zetterberg, Pär, 1975– editor.
Title: Gender and violence against political actors / edited by Elin
  Bjarnegård and Pär Zetterberg.
Description: Philadelphia : Temple University Press, 2023. | Includes
  bibliographical references and index. | Summary: "This edited volume
  brings together U.S. and European scholars within political science,
  comparative politics, international relations, and other related
  disciplines and practitioner fields to offer theoretical and
  methodological perspectives on gender and political violence and to
  encourage conversation across subfields and disciplines on the topic"—
  Provided by publisher.
Identifiers: LCCN 2022042168 (print) | LCCN 2022042169 (ebook) | ISBN
  9781439923306 (cloth) | ISBN 9781439923313 (paperback) | ISBN
  9781439923320 (pdf)
Subjects: LCSH: Women—Violence against—Political aspects. | Political
  violence. | Women—Political activity. | Women politicians—Violence
  against. | Sex discrimination against women—Political aspects. | Sexism
  in political culture.
Classification: LCC HQ1236 .G4613 2023 (print) | LCC HQ1236 (ebook) | DDC
  320.90082—dc23/eng/20230110
LC record available at https://lccn.loc.gov/2022042168
LC ebook record available at https://lccn.loc.gov/2022042169

Printed in the United States of America

9 8 7 6 5 4 3 2 1

Contents

PART III: CASE STUDIES

PART IV: POLICY RESPONSES

Preface and Acknowledgments

The idea for this book arose from a sense of confusion. We had the clear impression that discussions about gender and violence in different political settings were on the rise in the various academic and policy events we attended. Although similar experiences, events, and challenges were brought up, the discussions looked very different depending on the field of research or policy. The policy agendas invoked, language used, literature referenced, and methods used were all different. It was as if actors in the different fields were not aware of each other or did not see the relevance of each other. Yet, it seemed our understanding of gendered political violence would have so much to gain from increased interaction. So we began exploring what would happen if we brought people and organizations together. This book is a result of that process: a process of collective thinking, intellectually stimulating, sometimes frustrating, but very rewarding. We hope this book will provide a shortcut through the confusion for the reader interested in how political violence is gendered and how different subfields approach the question differently and thus make different kinds of contributions.

Research on gender and political violence is an emerging but burgeoning field—and the latter is particularly true if contributions made in different types of subfields are brought together, as this volume does. It is also a topic where different strands of research—feminist studies, political science, peace and conflict research—meet and contribute with different lenses, insights, and interpretations. Moreover, it is an area where many policy and practitioner organizations are engaged.

Collaboration between international organizations and research has been particularly prominent in this area. Most of the workshops and events that have, directly or indirectly, led to this publication have gathered both scholars and practitioners. Some of the early and highly influential publications came from international organizations, such as the Carter Center, International Foundation for Electoral Systems (IFES), the National Democratic Institute (NDI), Peace Research Institute Oslo (PRIO), and UN Women, to mention a few. The continued engagement from these organizations has been crucial. Events organized by some of these organizations have also been important both for putting this topic on the agenda and for providing platforms for discussions of experiences, methods, and prevention. The #NotTheCost events organized by the NDI, the Folke Bernadotte Academy (FBA) Policy Dialogue on Election Violence, the conference on Measuring Violence against Women in Elections at the Carter Center, the Expert Group Meeting on Data and Violence against Women in Politics at UN Women, and the FBA-PRIO-UN Women Research-Policy Dialogue on New Insights on Women, Peace, and Security for the Next Decade are all excellent examples of such important events.

Research funders of different kinds have also seen the importance of these questions and have contributed in different ways to different parts of the project. We are grateful to the Swedish Research Council as the main source of funding (project number 2015-03488). During the publication process, the Borbos Hansson scholarship and a grant from the Research Council of Norway also provided support. Uppsala Forum for Democracy, Peace and Justice provided funding for an early workshop held in Uppsala in 2016: Gender, Politics and Violence—Conceptual and Methodological Challenges (organized by Elin Bjarnegård, together with Gabrielle Bardall and Jennifer Piscopo). The ECPR Joint Sessions hosted a workshop in Mons in Belgium in 2019 on the topic of Violence against Political Actors: New Research Directions (organized by Mona Lena Krook and Elin Bjarnegård), and the Folke Bernadotte Academy provided funding for the final book workshop in Uppsala in December 2019. These meetings have been invaluable for moving forward and for increasing dialogue and improving the understanding of each other's starting points. Some of the events took place just before the pandemic made such meetings impossible, making them, in retrospect, seem even more valuable. The pandemic has taught us that many things can be done online, but we doubt this book would exist had it not been for the engagement and discussion during these live in-person workshops.

Last but certainly not least, we want to thank the authors of the chapters of this volume: they are the ones who took the engagement one step further and who have persistently worked together and with us toward the realization of this volume. A lot of the hard work also took place during challenging times, and we recognize the effort and dedication that made this book possible. Thank you! We hope that it will prove worthwhile and that this book will contribute to future important work on gender, politics, and violence.

Gender and Violence against Political Actors

1

Introduction

Politics, Violence, and Gender

ELIN BJARNEGÅRD AND
PÄR ZETTERBERG

Politics can be a dangerous business. In Mexico, Abel Murrieta was handing out campaign flyers when he was gunned down, making him one of the almost ninety Mexican politicians to be murdered in less than a year (Gallón and Rivers 2021). Other instances of violence that have reached the headlines and been met with public outcry include the plot to kidnap Michigan Governor Gretchen Whitmer in 2020 and the murders of the British MPs David Amess (in 2021) and Jo Cox (in 2016), to give just a few examples. While these illustrations emphasize politicians as targets of violence, voters and activists are also political actors who may be targets for people who are willing to use violence to achieve their political goals. For instance, intimidation of voters on election day is common in countries that hold contentious elections (Rauschenbach and Paula 2019; Thomas 2021), and in conflict-ridden countries, violence may be viewed as an everyday, inherent part of politics.

Violence against political actors is generally characterized as a twofold problem: it inflicts harm on the personal integrity of the victim, and it constitutes a challenge to the overall political system, as perpetrators do not respect the democratic rules of the game. This book adds a layer to the analysis of political violence by investigating how gender influences violence aimed at political actors. Gendered analysis of this topic is a fairly recent phenomenon, having emerged over the past twenty years. Because political actors constitute a heterogeneous group—as voters, supporters, lobbyists, activists, candidates, and elected officials, etc.—operating in different contexts—democratic, authoritarian, peaceful, and conflict ridden—research has been fragmented, divided among different research fields. But there are important commonalities. While women's participation in politics has increased all over the world, so have different forms of attacks against women as political actors. This book contributes interpretations of this phenomenon. For instance, while women's greater participation can clearly be seen as a sign of political empowerment, we cannot jump to the conclusion that discriminatory structures have been considerably weakened. On the other hand, political violence is an all-too-common phenomenon in many contexts, and we do not know to what extent women politicians are significantly more at risk than men politicians are. One thing is clear, however: the dynamics of violence against political actors have changed as a result of women's increased participation in politics. This book aims at introducing and discussing how a gendered analysis contributes to our understanding of political violence by bringing together knowledge from various subfields to jointly advance our conceptual, methodological, and empirical understanding of gender, politics, and violence. Importantly, it also contributes with a section on policy responses to mitigate the problem.

Being the first book to approach the problem from various perspectives, the book describes the specific vulnerabilities of women in politics, but it also points to how men and masculinities are part of a gendered analysis of politics and violence. In short, the book outlines some shared understandings of the gendered aspects of violence against political actors across research fields. In particular, the various contributions underscore the idea that a broad definition of violence, incorporating both physical and psychological forms, is crucial to unveiling gendered patterns. The book also outlines areas in which research fields can learn from each other, not least concerning the differences and similarities among organized, criminal, and domestic forms of violence and regarding intersectional analyses.

With respect to theory, the book is at the intersection of three different concepts: politics, violence, and gender. Employing these three concepts is important if we wish to deepen our understanding of various forms of attack on political and democratic participation as well as on gender equality. They are widely used in a variety of fields and have different meanings attached to them. Even when the concepts are brought together, as in this volume, they can be found in different configurations in which the emphasis may be on one or the other, depending on which scholars are asking the question and where they are coming from. Different fields have used these concepts, but with different foci and definitions, leading to different interpretations and analyses. For instance, conflict scholars are often engaged in an ongoing discussion about how violence is defined and measured. Researchers who come from a background of studying women and gender may be more interested in public manifestations of and reactions to masculinity and femininity. Comparative politics scholars will be interested in the conditions for carrying out politics within democratic institutions. These different starting points have an impact on how researchers approach the problem, what analytical lens they apply, what type of data they collect, and, ultimately, the answers they get.

None of these approaches is right or wrong; instead, they all emphasize different aspects of a common problem. They all come with advantages as well as trade-offs. They all come with unspoken assumptions and priorities that may not need to be clarified as long as they remain within their own field. But the problem of violence against political actors knows no disciplinary boundaries. That is why it is pivotal to engage authors from different fields in discussions with each other as well as with practitioners. The book urges authors to clarify where they come from and what kind of lens their perspective entails—it encourages them to learn from and engage in discussions with each other.

This introduction chapter starts by outlining the progress and setbacks seen in gendered power struggles in politics. It draws attention to the important contribution of global agendas and international agreements as well as to the impressive progress made, such as the increase in the number of women working in politics and as peacemakers. It also demonstrates how research has contributed to both documenting this progress and identifying remaining challenges. It then goes on to briefly account for the three concepts—politics, violence, and gender—and how they are used in this book. The importance of methodological plurality and how it is showcased by the variety of methodological approaches is then elaborated on. Finally, we present an overview of the book and its contributions.

Progress and Setbacks

The year 2020 marked the twenty-fifth anniversary of the Fourth World Conference on Women and the adoption of the Beijing Declaration and Platform for Action (1995), as well as the twentieth anniversary of the United Nations Security Council Resolution 1325 on women, peace, and security. These two important events have contributed to an unprecedented global push for gender equality in previously male-dominated areas such as politics and peace building.

The Beijing Declaration and Platform for Action has been crucial in advancing gender equality and empowering women at a global level, particularly with regard to increasing the representation of women in political decision-making worldwide. Often, the increase in women's representation has come about as a result of the introduction of electoral gender quota laws in around seventy-five countries (Hughes et al. 2019). This increase has been gradual but steady, and women now (as of October 2022) occupy 26.5 percent of the world's parliamentary seats, compared to just 10 percent in 1995 (IPU Parline 2022). This changed composition of parliaments around the world means that there are many more women in politics than there used to be.

In countries where political activity is dangerous, women's increased political inclusion means that more women have a highly unsafe occupation and are more likely to be the victims of political violence (Bjarnegård, Håkansson, and Zetterberg 2022; Piscopo 2016). The introduction of gender quotas and the increased presence of women in politics have, however, also been met with widespread misogynist resistance (Krook 2016), and recently the harassment, intimidation, and violence directed at women as political actors have received increased attention (Krook 2018). In 2011, the United Nations General Assembly called for a policy of zero tolerance for violence against female candidates and election officials (Resolution 66/130). The twenty-fifth anniversary is thus not merely a call for celebration, but it also highlights the continued need to focus on gender aspects of political activity and decision-making. Researchers have taken up the call, as described by Krook in her chapter in this volume. Krook has collaborated closely with international organizations such as the National Democratic Institute (NDI) to increase awareness of the phenomenon called violence against women in politics (VAWIP). While VAWIP has been a contested concept, there is increasing consensus that it should only be used to denote gender-motivated violence, when women are targeted specifically as women[1] (Krook and Restrepo Sanín 2020; Bardall, Bjarnegård, and Piscopo 2020).

The norm of including women and mainstreaming gender perspectives more broadly also entered the realm of conflict resolution and peace building with UN Security Council Resolution 1325 on women, peace, and security adopted in 2000. It brought about a needed focus on the specific consequences of armed conflict for women and girls, advocating for the need to include women in peacemaking and mediation processes. A number of follow-up resolutions have been adopted since then, followed by strong normative expressions and speeches (Olsson and Gizelis 2015). In addition, Nadia Murad and Dennis Mukwege were awarded the 2018 Nobel Peace Prize for their work against conflict-related sexual violence. The women, peace, and security agenda has contributed to the adoption of quota reforms in postconflict settings, to women's increased participation in peace agreements, and to some countries adopting feminist foreign policies. As Olsson describes in her chapter in this volume, the agenda has also contributed to increased research on gender aspects of armed conflict and peace building. Through her work at the Folke Bernadotte Academy and the Peace Research Institute Oslo (PRIO), Olsson has been involved in facilitating and coordinating data collection leading to empirical research.

While both these international agendas have been moved forward by international organizations such as UN Women (in collaborations with both Krook and Olsson), they have, to a surprising extent, operated alongside each other rather than in an integrated manner. Even though both use a gender perspective, they focus on different types of gendered dynamics in their study of violence and politics. This volume explicitly includes these dynamics, but it is limited neither to gender-motivated violence nor to the violence that affects women in conflict settings. Rather, it seeks to explore how gender dynamics are manifested in violent acts against political actors. Violent acts against political actors, broadly defined, include voters who experience violence when they are about to cast their votes, political candidates who experience increased abuse in the home as a reaction to their political activity, and politicians who receive threats on social media, to give just a few examples.

Political actors are targeted with violence in peaceful, democratic settings as well as in (post-)conflict contexts. The book thus paints a broad picture of the complex ways in which gender is at work in political violence in a variety of settings. Violence has been studied as a phenomenon that is either an aberration of the peaceful conflict resolution that democracy is supposed to be or a natural given that is constitutive of the armed conflict. In many contexts, however, it is something in between. While there may not be a full-scale war, politics may still be associated with violence. For a political actor faced with violence, the distinction between peace and conflict will not be particularly relevant. With this book, we argue that it is time to bring the different understandings together.

Discussing the Key Concepts: Politics, Violence, and Gender

The three key concepts of this book—politics, violence, and gender—are all widely used in a variety of disciplines, while at the same time, they are constantly being contested. This section serves as a very brief introduction to the concepts as they are used in the book. While there is no consensus about these concepts and what they imply, even among the chapter authors, all authors contributing to this book relate to the conceptualizations presented below.

Politics

The title of this book—*Gender and Violence against Political Actors*—indicates that primary identification of the political is made through the status of the victim of violence. If the victim is attacked when carrying out his or her political role, or because he or she carries out his or her political role, it is violence against a political actor (see, however, exceptions to this definition in the chapters by Eriksson Baaz and Stern, Kreft and Nagel, and Kishi, who also look at perpetrators of violence). According to the feminist slogan, the personal is political, and indeed, all acts are political in one sense of the word. We use a slightly narrower conceptualization of politics as our point of departure in this book, referring to political processes and formal political institutions. This means that the focus is on actors who are in some way related to the formal political process or who are acting within a formal political institution. Political violence refers to acts of violence that disrupt political processes (see Piscopo and Bjarnegård's chapter in this volume; Bardall, Bjarnegård, and Piscopo 2020), whereas this book focuses on the vulnerability of the actors operating within those political processes.

While most of the contributions in the book focus on violence against actors who are, in one way or another, connected to the formal political process, they also discuss the relationship between violence against political actors, on the one hand, and political violence as a disruption of the political process, on the other. A focus on political *actors* still enables a study that looks beyond the political *arena* and a broader investigation of when and where violence is carried out. Acknowledging that the distinction between public and private spheres is often artificial, we also include the private sphere and the online sphere as potential locations for violence against political actors (Bjarnegård 2018). If a woman candidate is abused in her home by her partner because he does not want her to speak in public, then she is abused as a political actor connected to the formal political sphere (as a candidate in an election) even though the violence is carried out in the private sphere.

The book also focuses on various political *contexts*, for instance, with respect to regime types that are likely to be important to understanding violence against political actors. Much can be gained from connecting violence to a particular political context. While most of the cases analyzed in the volume are considered democracies by most standard measures, we also include countries that are not, such as Sri Lanka and the Maldives (Zetterberg and Bjarnegård's chapter), Uganda (Schneider's chapter), and Papua New Guinea (Haley and Baker's chapter). Some analytical perspectives have been developed based on contexts in which war and organized violence dominate over peaceful, political conflict resolution (see the chapters by Olsson, Eriksson Baaz and Stern, and Kreft and Nagel). The gender dynamics of violence is a cross-cutting phenomenon in that experiences in the Global North and Global South often overlap. And when they do not overlap, what underlies the differences? By including different types of regimes and states, we can also discuss and compare gender dynamics in democracies and nondemocracies as well as in conflict, postconflict, and peace settings.

Violence

Studies of gender and violence against political actors have emphasized the need to incorporate different forms of violence, including physical and psychological forms (Bardall 2011; Krook and Restrepo Sanín 2016a). As a matter of fact, such a focus is included in the general definition of violence used by the World Health Organization, which emphasizes the consequences for feelings of well-being and security in both their psychological and physical forms (Krug et al. 2002). Therefore, we conceptualize violence along a continuum, our aim being to emphasize the commonalities between psychological violations of personal integrity and physical harm in attacks against political actors. While enabling a distinction between physical and psychological violence when necessary, a continuum conceptualization of violence does not disqualify psychological forms of violence from being part of definitions of violence. The psychological-physical continuum is thus more inclusive than definitions that are common in (often gender-blind) conflict studies and that only include physical violence (see, however, Kishi in this volume).

A few clarifications are needed with respect to the psychological-physical continuum of violence that is used as a joint framework for the various contributions in this book. First, the psychological-physical continuum encompasses some additional forms of violence that have been singled out as particular forms of violence elsewhere. For instance, as shown in Figure 1.1, sexual forms of violence can be positioned on either the physical or the psychological side of the continuum, whereas online forms of violence are, by definition, psychological. There is a section on forms of violence that includes physical forms (Kishi), psychological forms (Zetterberg and Bjarnegård), sexual forms (Kreft and Nagel), and online forms (Esposito). On the psychological-physical continuum, however, the former two are overarching types of violence that distinguish whether the perpetrator uses physical force or psychological intimidation.

Second, we do, however, leave out actions that some studies refer to as economic violence (Bardall 2011; Krook 2020). We do this mainly for reasons of

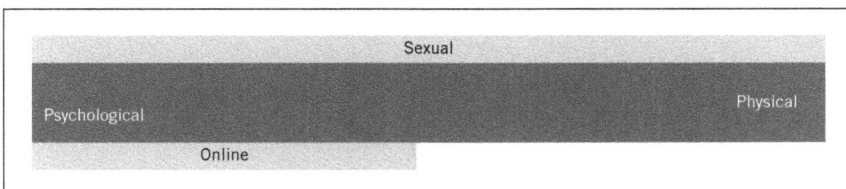

Figure 1.1 A continuum of violence

parsimony: this volume focuses on intentional physical and psychological harm against political actors, while recognizing that lack of resources and gender discrimination are crucially important questions that must be addressed. We see economic violence as distinctly different, as it pertains to structures rather than to particular acts aimed at specific individuals. Economic violence is not necessarily intentional and does not necessarily violate the personal integrity of the political actor.

Third, a conceptualization of violence on a continuum should not be interpreted to mean that some types of violence are more serious than others. They are simply different. We argue for a kind of continuum thinking (Boyle 2019b) that has its roots in feminist theory (Kelly 1988b). This thinking links experiences of violence together from a victim perspective, emphasizing the gray areas and the process of normalization (Lundgren 2002). In her studies of men's sexual violence against women, Kelly argues that women eventually make sense of individual events in relation to a continuum of related experiences. The continuum allows us, as a collective, to discuss a potential "basic common character that underlies many different events" (Kelly 1988b, 76). Here, it emphasizes the common denominator, which is that the victims referred to in this book are all attacked as political actors. As such, the source of oppression is similar even though the means used can be either psychological or physical. The book's focus on violence against political actors per se constitutes an attempt to merge insights and frameworks from different research fields to create a generally applicable analytical lens on the acts of violence. It emphasizes the need for clarity in the interpretation of the act of violence, and generally, the perspective of the political actor is in focus. This implies that if the aim is to assess the motive or the impact of the violence, physical attacks on family members can be understood as psychologically targeting the political actor, as the political actor is not physically harmed. In this case, the (physical) means used by the perpetrator are differentiated from both the intention of the perpetrator and the effect the act of violence has on the political actors. Thus, if a perpetrator uses physical force to destroy campaign material or property connected to a political actor, this would be classified as physical violence using an analytical lens that emphasizes the means used, while it would be interpreted as psychological violence against the political actor based on the type of impact it has. This perspective further underscores the need to view physical and psychological acts of violence as related.

Positioning violence along a continuum does not preclude the theoretical or empirical focus on a particular form of violence, but it does emphasize the need to position one form of violence in relation to other forms. It is important to be explicit, because different research traditions position themselves differently along the continuum and make different use of the word *violence*.

This book aims to facilitate communication across disciplinary boundaries, regardless of what is normally counted, or discounted, as violence.

Gender

Gender is a concept and analytical category that contributes a critical lens on power positions and hierarchies, particularly as they pertain to inequalities between women and men, but also to nonbinary individuals. A gender perspective implies constant attention to the socially constructed characteristics associated with ascribed gender identities, such as being seen as a woman or a man, as well as to the power relationships between the sexes. A gender perspective is not the same as a focus on women. Instead, a comparative analysis of gender relations illuminates, in the words of Weldon, "the *systematic* way that social norms, laws, practices, and institutions advantage certain groups and forms of life and disadvantage others" (2006, 236). Gendered power dynamics thus pertain to individual women and men, as well as to groups and societies more broadly. As such, applying a gender perspective is crucial to understanding power, and power is at the core of the dynamics of both politics and violence.

As alluded to above, gendered vulnerabilities and entitlements intersect with other social and economic inequalities, including (but not limited to) ethnicity and race, socioeconomic status, disability, sexual identity, and geographic location. These axes of advantage and disadvantage need to be contextualized, as they play out very differently in different countries and localities. This also implies that although gender is an important hub for understanding power, men and women are differentially positioned. Nonhegemonic men may well experience patterns of oppression that are similar to what the patterns some women experience. Intersectional studies allow for a greater degree of complexity.

It is understandable that in many disciplines, taking a gender perspective has come to imply an increased focus on women's perspectives and experiences, which have long been neglected in favor of implicitly male understandings and interpretations (Bjarnegård 2013). This can, indeed, be understood as a justified attempt to "recover" absent perspectives (Weldon 2006), and there are ample reasons for studying women as well as gender in politics and for doing so in relation to violence (Beckwith 2005). This book acknowledges the importance and impact of work that has focused on violence against women in politics (Krook 2020), but it sees the need to take a step toward gendering this field (Bardall, Bjarnegård, and Piscopo 2020). Important work in this direction has been conducted in studies focusing on political violence in conflict settings, and we hope that work on, for instance, masculinity and violence will serve as an inspiration (see Eriksson Baaz and Stern in this volume, but also Eriksson Baaz and Stern 2009; Bjarnegård, Brounéus, and Melander 2017; Cohen 2017). If we are to understand power hierarchies, we must analyze those who have more power as well as those who have less. Rigid notions of masculinity, often associated with toughness, risk-taking, and group cohesion, contribute to the fact that men are highly overrepresented as perpetrators of violence—in politics as well as in other spheres. When it comes to victims of political violence, such a gendered pattern is less well established. However, as we investigate and discuss in this volume, these patterns are likely to vary across type of violence.

The notion of gender that we put forward in this book is not new. Feminist research has long contributed to these understandings of gender, not least through its focus on masculinities in relation to violence and resistance (e.g., Connell 1995), intersectional approaches to power, privilege, marginalization, and vulnerability (e.g., Crenshaw 1989), and on queer perspectives and the inclusion of LGBTQ+ perspectives (e.g., Picq and Thiel 2015). Applying these feminist perspectives to mainstream analyses of politics and conflict is necessary, but it is also complex and challenging. This book does not claim to be successful in doing so, but it does strive to demonstrate several different ways in which feminist insights are useful for the study of violence against political actors.

Methodological Plurality

As this book will show, research on gender and political violence includes a large variety of methodological approaches. To some extent, these are dependent on the research tradition they come from. For instance, as Olsson shows in her chapter, research focused on including a gender perspective on conflict-related political violence has often drawn on established methods in the field, which have tended to be quantitative. Within this quantitative tradition, event-based (or incidence-based) data have been common. When adding a gender perspective, researchers have built on these traditions. To give a few examples, the ambitious Sexual Violence in Armed Conflict (SVAC) dataset (Cohen and Nordås 2014) identifies (with the help of reports from organizations such as Amnesty International) incidents of a type of conflict-related political violence that researchers long largely overlooked: sexual violence. The equally rich data on political violence targeting women from the Armed Conflict Location & Event Data Project (ACLED) (Raleigh et al. 2010) were also gathered using established strategies for incidence-based data collection (see Kishi's chapter in this volume).

Event-based approaches are also common in work on election violence targeting individuals (voters, party supporters, campaign staff, etc.), as brought up in Haley and Baker's chapter (in this volume). While this methodological approach can provide important information on election violence, its limitations cause scholars applying a gender perspective on election violence to face two challenges: First, event-based methods tend to focus specifically on physical violence, thus excluding other forms on the continuum of violence. Because women have been shown to experience psychological violence more often than men do, and because men experience more physical violence than women do, an exclusive focus on the latter generates an underestimation of women's experiences of political violence. A second challenge is that incidence reports are likely to focus mainly on incidents in the public sphere; however, women are more often than men targeted in the private sphere. Consequently, the magnitude of election violence targeting women is—even in this respect—likely to be underestimated.

Gender scholars working on election violence have therefore supplemented event-based data (often based on media reports) with other data collection strategies. For instance, Haley and Baker (in this volume) present an ambitious research strategy that includes trained observers who follow the entire election process on the ground, in the field. Observation reports are then combined with surveys and interviews to obtain a fuller picture of incidents of election violence that also includes psychological violence, such as threats as well as election-related violence that takes place in the home. In addition to these strategies, scholars have also made use of focus groups as a supplement to event-based data (see, e.g., Schneider's chapter in this volume).

Similarly, studies looking at election violence that targets the candidates themselves have used strategies that can capture both physical and psychological violence. Just like research that focuses on gender differences in violence against officeholders (e.g., Håkansson in this volume; Thomas and Herrick in this volume), a popular methodological approach has been to conduct candidate surveys with men and women candidates (see, e.g., Collignon's chapter in this volume). This strategy is suitable for scholars looking at the question of whether women are experiencing more and/or different types of violence than men are, but also whether the violence has different consequences for men and women candidates (dropping out, reluctance to run again, etc.).

Nevertheless, some have questioned whether conducting surveys with politicians is a fruitful strategy for investigating violence that specifically targets women politicians *for being women* (i.e., gender-motivated political violence). As noted by Krook (in this volume), women politicians may be attacked for both political and gender-motivated reasons, and established surveys rarely allow researchers to distinguish between the two. Thus, it is difficult to separate the former from the latter. As a consequence, Krook suggests an approach that has been used in research on hate crimes—a bias event approach—to collect evidence suggesting that the motive for the violence was related to the target's gender. Interestingly, the approach includes the use of surveys, provided that the questions specifically address the motive for the violence. Interviews and incident reports could also be used in this approach, employing questions that address the content of the violence, the actors involved, as well as the broader community's perception of the incident (e.g., did media or citizens interpret the incident as motivated by gender bias?).

Finally, as this book will show, a great deal of the violence targeting politicians takes place online (see, e.g., the chapters by Kuperberg, Håkansson, Thomas, and Herrick and Esposito). While surveys are also used to analyze online violence, as they address how targets interpret and are affected by online abuse, this form of violence even enables its own specific methodological approach: social media (or online) data analysis (Kuperberg, this volume). This type of method allows for an analysis of the magnitude (or quantity) of the violence (as each tweet, etc., is a data point), but also of the content or rhetoric of the violence (image manipulation included; see Esposito's chapter). Using this approach, scholars can identify the perpetrators' strategies. These are not only direct threats, but also more subtle strategies such as a variety of information disruptions (disinformation, etc.) intended to cause the victim (psychological) harm (see Bardall in this volume).

The diversity of methodological approaches used in the research on gender and political violence adds richness to this emerging field. It allows scholars to address various kinds of research questions as well as to identify different forms of and motives for violence. The chapters in this volume discuss methodological approaches and strategies in depth, including the limitations of different approaches in relation to different research questions. While the contributing authors differ in the methods they select, many of them have one thing in common: they suggest using multiple sources of data to get as good a picture as possible of the political violence that men and women experience. Ultimately, this picture needs to be adequately painted if it is to provide information about the problem and the particular dimensions that need to be targeted. We return to the use of research and different problem descriptions in the final chapters of the volume, where working methods intended to mitigate the problem of violence against political actors and its gender dimensions are elaborated on, thus bringing the theory back to practice.

Outline of the Book

The book is divided into four connected sections, each with its own focus. We start with a focus on theoretical approaches to demonstrate how different disciplinary starting points give rise to different lenses. None of them are wrong, but they determine what a researcher sets out to look for. The second section seeks to describe four different, but overlapping, positions along the continuum of violence, ranging from physical to psychological forms of violence, but also highlighting sexual forms of violence (which can be either physical or psychological) and online violence (which is, by its very nature, psychological, but which increases the speed and spread of such violence). The third section presents case studies from around the world, showcasing how different types of political actors have been targets of violence. The final section looks at different approaches to responding to the problem of gendered violence in politics.

The first, theoretical, section consists of four chapters introducing different theoretical approaches and research traditions. Two of these chapters, by Olsson and Eriksson Baaz and Stern, are written by international relations scholars, and two, by Krook, and Piscopo and Bjarnegård, are written by comparative politics scholars. While all are concerned with the central concepts—politics, violence, and gender—they come from different places and have different concerns. Olsson focuses on women's role as protagonists and victims in war and peace. Eriksson Baaz and Stern also look at conflict-related violence, but they focus on sexual violence and how it affects men. The two chapters clearly demonstrate how international relations have developed into a field where gendered concerns are much more prominent than they used to be, but also how core assumptions about armed violence and its perpetrators and victims are still present. Their perspective on the political can be described as "war as the extension of politics by other means" (see Eriksson Baaz and Stern citing Clausewitz in their chapter), and what such violent disruptions mean for gendered relations, in general, and for the categories of men and women, in particular. On the other hand, researchers working on comparative politics of gender have long been concerned with understanding the questions of when and why women participate politically, but in contrast to international relations, the issue of violence as an important factor in understanding women's motivations, patterns, and scope of action has entered the field quite recently. Here, the political process is the norm, and violence a distortion of that norm. Krook's chapter introduces the concept of violence against women in politics (VAWIP) and situates it in a broader framework of gender, politics, and violence. Piscopo and Bjarnegård's chapter explores what happens with the different theoretical perspectives if the primary focus is not on men or women as political actors, or on the context as one of either war or peace, but on the act of political violence and how it is gendered in its motives, forms, or impacts. Taken together, the four chapters demonstrate how, despite being concerned with politics, violence and gender, disciplinary boundaries—and perhaps even personal motivations—implicitly lead to different foci. The purpose of the section is to argue that we need to make our points of departure, and thus primary concerns as well as omissions, explicit if we are to enhance dialogue across disciplinary boundaries as well as with actors outside academia.

The second section consists of four chapters that each place one form of violence on the continuum of violence: physical, sexual, psychological, and online violence, respectively. The section is both theoretical and methodological, as each of the chapters engages with at least three questions: What constitutes the form of violence? How is the form of violence gendered? And how do we empirically investigate the form of violence? Each chapter presents and discusses some important features of the specific form of violence. For instance, in Kreft and Nagel's chapter on (conflict-related) sexual violence, the focus is not primarily on the targets of violence (both political actors and "regular citizens" can be attacked), but on the perpetrators. They argue that sexual violence as a form of political violence is perpetrated almost exclusively *by* political actors, specifically by armed actors in a political conflict. In addition, Kishi's chapter on physical violence compares the exposure between different groups of women political actors, ranging from women running for office to women belonging to state entities and political groups. By presenting new data on physical violence against women in politics, Kishi showcases what data that include a broader set of political actors can demonstrate. Finally, both Zetterberg and Bjarnegård's chapter and Esposito's chapter emphasize that the most common forms of (gendered) political violence are psychological violence, in general (Zetterberg and Bjarnegård), and online violence, in particular (Esposito), and that there are specific methodological challenges associated with investigating these less analyzed forms of violence.

The third section includes six country case studies, each investigating a certain set of political actors in a specific context. Two of them (Schneider's chapter and the chapter by Haley and Baker) focus on election violence targeting voters in nondemocracies where violence is widespread. Although both men and women are targets of election violence, the chapters pinpoint the gendered nature of the violent acts. The chapter by Schneider (on Uganda) also includes data on political candidates' experiences of violence. This type of political actor is the sole focus of the chapter by Collignon (on the United Kingdom). In both these contexts, women candidates experience more psychological violence than men do. Håkansson (on Sweden) and Thomas and Herrick (on the United States) analyze subnational elected representatives in two of the chapters. Again, there are some important similarities across contexts. For instance, in both countries, women mayors seem to be more targeted by violence than others are, suggesting that women's exposure to violence increases with higher levels of power. Finally, Kuperberg emphasizes the intersectional nature of online violence targeting women in politics. With illustrations from Israel, she shows how sexism is bound with other forms of discrimination.

The book's final section focuses on responses to violence against political actors, with four chapters that illuminate different ways of addressing violence against political actors and its gendered aspects. The lion's share of the book has focused on conceptualizing, defining, measuring, and assessing the phenomenon, but this is all done with the ultimate purpose of coming to terms with a serious problem. This section of the book is an account of what has already been done and an evaluation of different types of measures, operating at different levels. Ballington and Borovsky, from UN Women, highlight how UN Women has led efforts specifically to address gender-based violence against women in politics. As such, it shows how the UN has supported intergovernmental processes to address violence against women in politics normatively, providing the basis to assist states in devising and implementing mitigation policies and programs. Bardall tackles the specific problem of online political violence, arguing that because it is less clearly defined in time and place than offline violence is, it presents more challenges for mitigation and prevention. Her chapter differentiates between legal responses, platform responses, and community responses. The chapter by Nagel and Kreft looks at reactions and responses to conflict-related sexual violence at the international, state, and civil society levels, bringing the discussion back to the impact of the 1325 agenda, but also investigating what it actually means on the ground and for communities and women and men affected by conflict-related sexual violence. Restrepo Sanín's chapter assesses one of the front-runners when it comes to national legal responses: Bolivia, which has criminalized violence against women in politics. It compares the Bolivian law to a Mexican electoral protocol proposing measures to address violence against women in politics. The final chapter, by Raney and Collier, evaluates an institutional response: the MP Code of Conduct on Sexual Harassment in the Canadian House of Commons, which has subsequently been extended to all federal employees. Taken together, the final section discusses and evaluates policy responses at different levels and by different actors.

The book ends with a concluding chapter by the editors that seeks to be mainly forward-looking, but also summarizing. Because one goal of this book is to initiate a discussion that builds on the important insights of various research fields, the concluding chapter highlights what those insights are. It also distinguishes some points of agreement as well as some controversies that will be important to keep in mind moving forward.

In sum, we believe that the notion of building bridges is an important note to end this introduction chapter on and to remind readers of before they embark on reading the rest of the book. We hope that it will be clear how insights from different fields are needed to approach the complex problem of gendered aspects of violence against political actors. We may not be able to create a common language, but we do seek to increase interdisciplinary as well as external intelligibility. Different research fields will continue to engage with their particular interests and concerns, and controversies will remain—but it is an important step forward to identify irreconcilable disagreements as well as points of agreement and common agendas. This will help us build an agenda for studying politics and violence, as well as gender, in a more holistic manner.

PART I

Theoretical Approaches

2

Gender and Political Violence in Peace and Conflict Research

Louise Olsson

Introduction

There must be more to gender and war than women being incidental victims. It is January 1998, and I am trying to find a topic for my final student thesis in peace and conflict research. Prior to this, I had not really reflected on the lack of focus on women—let alone on gender—during my studies. Women had neither been recognized as actors nor as victims of political violence. The exception was a lecture earlier in the fall that included one sentence on civilian women being targeted by sniper fire in the besieged Sarajevo during the civil war in the 1990s. That one strong image had stuck in my mind, raising new questions about what I had previously learned about war. Why had the women been killed? They had not been in an apparent role of political agency. They had often been out to obtain food or water. Still, systematically targeting them seemed, by the actions of the perpetrators, to be serving a political purpose (see also Kishi in this book). This puzzle raised further questions regarding what role women can play in political processes that have escalated into organized large-scale political violence, that is, armed conflict. At this point, however, such questions were nonissues in most research and policy debates. It had only been a few years since Enloe had introduced the central research question, "Where are the women?" (Enloe 1989) and women and armed conflict had been formulated for the first time as a relevant international policy area in the 1995 Beijing Declaration and Platform for Action. The adoption of Resolution 1325 on women, peace, and security by the UN Security Council, the resolution that was to create a firmer foundation for recognizing women as actors for peace and for addressing the impact of war on women, was still over two years away (Gizelis and Olsson 2015; Davies and True 2019).

In my thesis, I finally opted for studying women's political roles in armed conflict by exploring under what conditions women were recruited as combatants (Olsson 1998). In the writing of that thesis and in my research since, this involved taking a position regarding two fundamental aspects. First, it quickly became apparent when reviewing the literature that there were several ways in which to approach the study of political violence and gender. I was interested in how gender dimensions could inform the study of armed conflict as understood by the Uppsala Conflict Data Program (UCDP); that is, as a "contested incompatibility that concerns government and/or territory over which the use of armed force between the military forces of two parties, of which at least one is the government of a state, has resulted in at least 25 battle-related deaths." That is, the definition shared the classical standpoint with Clausewitz of considering armed conflict as being the continuation of politics by violent means. Articulated in line with the approach of this book: violence toward political actors can be used to disrupt peaceful political processes to push an agenda by alternative means. Such violence can exist on a continuum in armed conflict contexts, from threats and other forms of psychological violence to direct physical violence, either in battle or directed toward more civilian settings.

Second, there existed several scientific methodological debates, running in parallel, on how gender and violence should be studied (see Cohen and Karim 2021; Eriksson Baaz and Stern in this volume). I come from a comparative and statistical empiricist research approach that seeks to systematically contribute to our understanding of what factors explain why armed conflicts appear, how we should understand their dynamics and effects, and under what conditions conflicts are possible to resolve, hereafter called mainstream peace and conflict research (see Svensson 2020 and Bjarnegård and Zetterberg in this book for a discussion of mainstream research).

In addition to positioning myself in relation to these fundamental aspects, there was a need to handle a combination of three challenges related to concepts, operationalization, and access to information that initially limited both my own research and scholarly progress when integrating gender into the mainstream. In the following decades, these challenges have been increasingly overcome by conflict scholars. Progress has entailed moving knowledge from an initial focus on women to a nuanced understanding of how gender plays into the manner in which violent conflict risk is instigated or hampered (Schaftenaar 2017; Forsberg and Olsson 2021; Dahlum and Wig 2020) and what roles masculinity and gender norms play in conflict dynamics related to recruitment and attitudes to violence (Melander 2005, 2016; Bjarnegård,

Brounéus, and Melander 2017). Furthermore, we now better understand how political violence during war targets men, women, or nonbinary individuals and when this violence can be considered as gendered (see Bardall, Bjarnegård, and Piscopo 2020; Johansson and Hultman 2019; see also Krook, Kishi, and Kreft and Nagel in this volume). Resolving conflict, we have learned that women's security and contributions are relevant for peace durability and quality but that gendered effects must be considered from the perspective of how gender intersects, or interacts, with other identities such as class, sexual identity, and ethnicity (Olsson 2009; Brounéus et al. 2017; Cohen and Karim 2021).

The aim of this chapter is to discuss what the study of gender and political violence has contributed to mainstream peace and conflict research and to exemplify what we have learned about gender and the continuum of violence in the context of armed conflict. To fulfill that aim, the chapter begins by discussing the three challenges on concepts, operationalization, and access to information that initially affected this process, including the importance of the exchange with more explicitly feminist approaches for scholarly progress. The chapter then outlines examples of how considering gender and political violence has contributed to research on three conflict phases: (1) preconflict factors affecting the risk of war, (2) conflict dynamics, and (3) conflict resolution. Finally, the chapter concludes with reflections on the path for future research.

Cross-Fertilizations and Contentious Dialogues with Feminist Research

From Caprioli's groundbreaking article "Gendered Conflict" in 2000 and Goldstein's book *War and Gender* in 2001, a growing number of mainstream scholars have used gender perspectives in their efforts to understand organized political violence, often basing their analysis on similar definitions of armed conflict as that used by the UCDP. In these efforts, scholars have drawn on hypotheses generated in feminist research in various disciplines, such as anthropology, ethnography, international relations, political science, and sociology. Hence, to understand progress in the mainstream, we need to consider the cross-fertilization and, at times, contentious dialogues with studies in the rich feminist traditions (henceforth called feminist research;[1] see Bjarnegård and Zetterberg and Eriksson Baaz and Stern in this book for a discussion). In fact, while much feminist research was rooted in different epistemological standpoints (i.e., different understandings about how you can examine and know the world) than mainstream research, the influence of feminist research has been substantial and has contributed to tackling three core challenges—concepts, operationalization, and access to information—to integrating gender into mainstream research (see Sjoberg, Kadera, and Thies 2018; Gizelis 2018; Cohen and Karim 2021).

First, conceptual limitations presented a core challenge. Neither women's involvement in conflict nor violence targeting women were considered relevant for understanding war (Gizelis and Olsson 2015). Feminist research pushed these conceptual boundaries by highlighting how the existing concepts used to capture peace, security, and war hid both gendered ideas and variations in men's and women's roles and experiences, resulting in an implicit exclusion of women and of the violence directed at them (Bjarnegård et al. 2015).

Second, at the time that interest in gender started to grow in academia, a substantial focus in conflict research was placed on explaining shifts and variations between peaceful and violent political processes. Here, there existed a limited understanding of how to operationalize "gender" as a variable and thereby how it could be relevant for explaining these fluctuations between war and peace. Feminist research played an instrumental role in overcoming these initial essentialist understandings of women and men as fixed categories and for recognizing the complexity of gender (see, for example, Caprioli 2000; Melander 2005). In addition, however, feminist research proposed an additional challenge through the introduction of a structural, apparently nonvarying, model of patriarchy as an explanation for war (Olsson 2009; Bjarnegård et al. 2015; Gizelis 2018).

Third, there was a severe dearth of gender disaggregated data and information. This meant that a limited number of questions could be systematically examined (see Bjarnegård et al. 2015). Although scholars associated with the mainstream empirical strand took an interest in gender already in the 1980s and 1990s (see Olsson 2000), about the same time as feminist research started to substantially progress (Davies and True 2019), the sparsity of data was to delay progress in the mainstream well into the 2000s.[2]

Gender and the Risk of Armed Conflict

Peace and conflict research starts from the understanding that there exist conflicting interests in all societies and all state relations. As a result, there is always competition for power and other resources. Such competition is normally pursued with nonviolent means or, at least, through political processes where violence is more rarely used or is used on a lower scale (see Krook in this volume). The need to understand under what conditions this state of affairs starts to change and actors begin to engage in more organized and large-scale forms of political violence is a foundational motivation for peace and conflict research (see Wallensteen 2013). Up until around 2000, the idea that gender could be relevant for understanding the risk of armed conflict was met with disinterest, if not outright disapproval (Bjarnegård et al. 2015). A dominant argument was that women were not "warriors," nor were they perceived to be decision-makers leading their states into war—Golda Meir and Margaret Thatcher being notable exceptions (see Goldstein 2001). A minor fly in the ointment of disinterest was the registered consistent gender gap in attitudes toward the use of armed force; women were found to be more negative toward armed force than men in attitude surveys in a range of countries (see, for example, Page and Shapiro 1992).

To come to terms with this disinterest, the feminist critiques of core concepts and how these were operationalized were central. Feminist scholars claimed that we might, by definition, exclude arenas where women could be more prominent actors and where violence targeting women might be part of an escalating political conflict, such as domestic violence, sexual violence, or online harassment (see Gentry, Shepherd, and Sjoberg 2019). Importantly, the Armed Conflict Location & Event Data Project's (ACLED) coding of violent events in which women constituted the dominant target group (see Kishi in this book) now provides new opportunities to explore gender in escalating conflicts.

A further contribution made by feminist studies was the arguments on the social construction of gender, which made the concept more nuanced and useful for exploration in relation to violent conflict risk. Based on such modes of thinking, Caprioli (2000, 2005) compared the explanatory power of existing biological arguments of women being more peaceful than men with an explanation relating to gender equality norms. What Caprioli found was that high levels of gender inequality appeared to increase the likelihood of armed conflict but that biology constituted a weak explanation (for progress in research, see also Melander 2005; Hudson 2012; Dahlum and Wig 2020).

While feminist research enabled a more fruitful understanding of existing concepts, it also presented a patriarchal structural explanation of war. Initially, this appeared to portray gender hierarchies as universal and resilient, if not as outright fixed and unchanging structures. While generating relevant explanations for mainstream research as well, a fixed, that is, nonvarying, concept is difficult to reconcile with explaining the great variations in the degree and forms of organized political violence that exist (Gizelis 2018). In this instance, mainstream research opted to focus on the idea of gender roles and power distributions between men and women as constructed—and thereby as potentially fluctuating and changing over time and space—combining it with existing models to collect granular data on gender inequality by international organizations. This was translated into using gender inequality as a scale from Caprioli (2000) onward and by adhering to ideas of disaggregating gender norms into different types of masculine ideals (see Bjarnegård et al. 2017). Bringing these two strands together, Forsberg and Olsson (2021) suggest there could be two potential pathways between gender and political violence: one pathway to peace that goes through investment in women, thereby improving societal capacity to handle conflict nonviolently, and a second pathway to war that goes through conditions that affect the probability of male recruitment to military organizations.

Gender and Conflict Dynamics

A growing theme in peace and conflict research has been the dynamics and effects of armed conflict. Considering gender, mainstream research originally focused on the proposition that women are more affected than are men by structural violence in terms of access to critical resources, such as food, health care, or education, during war (Plümper and Neumayer 2006; Urdal and Che 2013) and that mental health effects are gendered (Brounéus 2014). However, as Kishi points out in this book, it has not been until recent years that mainstream studies have really been able to start connecting the dots empirically between women's agency and how they are targeted by political violence. This gap stemmed partly out of women not having been viewed as agents in peace and conflict, an assumption that led to the associated fallacy that women are not deliberate targets of political violence. This assumption is the more interesting when one considers that on the flip side, the connection between agency and violence has almost constituted an axiom, that is, a given, in the understanding of political violence targeting men—a gendered assumption that constitutes an equal fallacy, as most men have been found *not* to be actors in war (see Bjarnegård et al. 2015). Still, the assumption of male agency has resulted in an increased risk of men becoming the victims of political violence (Carpenter 2005). From other forms of violence on the continuum that stereotypically are assumed to only target women, such as sexual violence, male victims have also long been overlooked (see Eriksson Baaz and Stern in this book). Likewise, women as perpetrators of violence tend to go against our gendered stereotypical assumptions, particularly when it comes to women being perpetrators of sexual violence during war (Cohen 2013). Using a gender perspective to understand political violence in war dynamics has thereby highlighted both the need to consider the role of stereotypes and constructions as well as the need to understand the varying repertoires of violence used to target different groups for various purposes. As articulated by Bjarnegård et al. (2015), "the gendered patterns of participation and suffering defy simplistic stereotypes that assign all men to the category of combatants and all women and children to the role of victim."

In terms of participation, recent studies further find that the level of gender equality appears to impact whether and how women come to be mobilized in political protests, something that, in extension, increases the risk of both physical and psychological violence. For example, Schaftenaar (2017) shows that higher levels of gender equality in a society offer a political movement improved opportunities for mass recruitment, as more people are available in the public space of society. Thereby, the movement has the option to choose a nonviolent campaign. Kishi, Pavlik, and Matfess (2019) and Chenoweth and Marks (2022) find that such mass movements are more successful when women participate. Given that this can entail that gender-mixed mass protests present a more substantial challenge, it is perhaps not surprising that the authors additionally find that such movements can be met with higher levels of violent repression by a state. This indicates that women can play a more direct role in an escalating conflict than previously thought. In an ongoing conflict, Thomas and Bond (2015) study 166 violent political organizations active across nineteen African countries (1950–2011) and find that women participated in 45 percent of the groups and in combat in more than half of these organizations, particularly in groups that had a gender equality platform.

In terms of the forms that political violence conducted by warring parties can take, research on gender has critically expanded our understanding, not least by bringing our attention to conflict-related sexual violence. This was long considered an unfortunate side effect of war and of little consequence for understanding armed conflict dynamics despite the fact that Brownmiller positioned sexual violence as important already in 1975 (Brownmiller 1975; see also Kreft and Nagel in this volume). For a long time, the lack of data prevented the ability to answer questions in mainstream research; however, today we know that there are trends and variations in the forms and degrees of such violence, not least through the groundbreaking Sexual Violence in Armed Conflict dataset (Cohen and Nordås 2014; Muvumba Sellström 2015). In later years, research on conflict-related sexual violence has been further influenced by research on military organizations, for example, related to the principal-agent dilemma on recruitment to, and personnel control within, armed groups. In turn, research on sexual violence has thereby unearthed important information about the internal dynamics and behavior of warring parties of importance for research on military organizations (Wood 2018).

Gender and Conflict Resolution

Understanding how a violent political process can be reversed into more peaceful politics constitutes a key theme in mainstream peace research. Earlier research focused on ending organized violence, but more recent debates have been expanded to include considerations into the quality of the peace, something that is critical for considering gendered consequences (see, for example, Joshi and Wallensteen 2018). Notably, women's inclusion is arguably central, as peace negotiations can be considered as a formative phase that sets the trajectory for postwar politics (Krause, Krause, and Bränfors 2018). Feminist research has efficaciously claimed that there might not even be peace for women if their concerns are not included; we cannot take for granted that women's situations will automatically improve to the same extent as men's. In empirical research, some representative surveys have also found that women tend to be more disillusioned about peace after war (Brounéus et al. 2017), and continued violence against women human rights defenders underline that this is about power and security. As Kishi, Pavlik, and Matfess demonstrate, there is a connection between preventing continued political violence against women and their ability to contribute to progressing into more "peaceful" politics (Kishi, Pavlik, and Matfess 2019). In seeking to understand this connection, we must then consider the intersection between identities, such as class, sexual orientation, or ethnicity, as women and men are not cohesive groups (Brounéus et al. 2017; Cohen and Karim 2021).

In addition to quality of the peace, ensuring women's participation is indicated as being related to durability, as Krause, Krause, and Bränfors (2018) suggest that women's involvement in peace negotiations could affect legitimacy and network resources, resulting in a higher durability of a peace. This is key, as many peace processes have been found to fail. Moreover, a growing trend in mainstream research perceives processes stemming from war as social ruptures with the potential to positively affect gender equality levels postwar and where change is argued to depend on women's active mobilization (see Berry 2015). In this tradition, Webster, Chen, and Beardsley (2019), using cross-national data from 1900 to 2015, find that political violence during long-term and intense armed conflicts improved opportunities for women's empowerment during the later stages of war and its resolution. However, they argue, for these changes to last, an integrated approach to gender equality by all actors involved is required (Webster, Chen, and Beardsley 2019). Building on that finding, other studies suggest that gender equality improvements primarily carry over to the postwar phase when the conflict ends through a comprehensive peace agreement (Joshi and Olsson 2021; Bakken and Buhaug 2021).

Conclusions

As this chapter has exemplified, integrating gender into mainstream peace and conflict research has presented novel insights relevant for progressing our understanding of conflict risk, dynamics and effects of political violence, and conflict resolution for more than two decades. This process of integration was propelled by cross-fertilization and exchange between mainstream conflict studies and the rich feminist traditions, as efforts for integration could draw on, and combine, concepts, knowledge, and insights generated in both. That said, while it has been over twenty years since Caprioli and Goldstein started to bridge the gap between mainstream peace and conflict research and feminist research, we could still benefit from an enhanced debate and exchange on data and operationalizations, requiring an openness by all affected fields (see Melander 2016). Finally, continued progress is dependent on international organizations and states expanding the collection and publicizing of gender disaggregated data and information over extended time periods. Recent studies have utilized time series of one hundred to two hundred years, thereby greatly improving the quality of research results (for example, Dahlum and Wig 2020; Webster, Chen, and Beardsley 2019). Improved survey methods add additional new opportunities for fine-grain analysis of complex concepts, thereby opening for nuancing our understanding of masculinity, nonbinary identities, and gender norms.

3

Violence against Women in Politics

MONA LENA KROOK

In recent years, politically active women have begun to speak out about physical attacks, rape threats, and other forms of sexist abuse connected to their
work in politics. These experiences first came to my attention during interviews with women in countries that had adopted gender quotas to increase
the share of women among political candidates and officeholders. Anticipat-
ing that quotas had transformed ideas about gender and leadership, I was sur-
prised to hear stories instead about resistance and backlash against women's
political participation. Although academic work had not yet named this problem, I discovered a nascent conversation in the policy world among practitioners who had confronted similar testimonies from women on the ground.
Global discussions to name this phenomenon eventually coalesced around
the term *violence against women in politics* to describe a broad range of harms
to attack and undermine women as political actors. In a recent book (Krook
2020), I trace the global emergence of this concept, illustrate what it looks like
in practice, catalog emerging solutions around the world, and consider how
to document this phenomenon more effectively. In this chapter, I summarize
some key findings, focusing in particular on how *violence against women in
politics* fits into larger conversations in this book—and political science more
broadly—on gender, politics, and violence. In the first section, I map how
actors around the world constructed this concept, drawing on women's experiences in the political world. In the second section, I distinguish two forms
of violence faced by political women: *violence in politics*, motivated by policy and ideological differences; and *violence against women in politics*, in-

spired by bias and discrimination. In the third and fourth sections, I consider how to measure this phenomenon in light of this distinction and outline a bias event approach as a way forward. I conclude by stressing that violence against women in politics is not synonymous with gendered political violence. Rather, it is a specific and underrecognized form of violence against women posing clear threats to democracy, human rights, and gender equality worldwide.

Constructing the Concept

Newspaper coverage in multiple languages and interviews with international practitioners active in different parts of the world reveal that the notion of violence against women in politics emerged in parallel across different parts of the Global South: in the late 1990s, locally elected women in Bolivia denounced "political harassment and violence against women"; in the mid-2000s, elected women across South Asia condemned "violence against women in politics"; and in the late 2000s, actors in Kenya decried "electoral gender-based violence." In the late 2000s and early 2010s, international practitioners linked these debates, opting for terms like "violence against women in elections" and "violence against women in politics." These debates gained further momentum in the mid- to late 2010s, as a series of developments in the Global North—including the "misogyny speech" of Australian Prime Minister Julia Gillard in 2012, the murder of British MP Jo Cox in 2016, and the rise of the #MeToo movement in 2017—drew attention to the global nature of this phenomenon.

As a result of this collective mobilization, the concept of violence against women in politics is increasingly recognized in global normative frameworks. In 2017, the UN CEDAW Committee issued General Recommendation No. 35, identifying "harmful practices and crimes against women human rights defenders, politicians, activists, or journalists" as "forms of gender-based violence against women" (CEDAW Committee 2017, 5). In October 2018, the UN Special Rapporteur on Violence against Women delivered a report to the UN General Assembly focused exclusively on the topic of violence against women in politics (United Nations 2018a). Two months later, the General Assembly approved Resolution 73/148, expressing deep concern about "all acts of violence, including sexual harassment, against women and girls involved in political and public life" (UN General Assembly 2018, 3).

Growing attention to violence against women in politics is largely the result of its collaborative and multistreamed construction as a concept by diverse actors across the globe (Krook 2019). Yet this inclusive, nonhierarchical process of concept formation has also given rise to vagueness regarding its contours, sparking debates as to the connection between violence against women in politics and the related concepts of gender, politics, and violence (see also Chapter 5). While there are some exceptions, in general this work starts from the perspective of *women*, not gender more broadly, due to an interest in barriers to women's political participation more specifically. Much of this work also focuses on women in *formal politics*. However, as seen in recent international frameworks, there are efforts to expand this concept to women in *public life*, recognizing that women may face violence while undertaking a wide range of political roles. Finally, all actors engaged in this work recognize a *spectrum of violent acts*, not limited to physical manifestations.

Two Forms of Violence

Academic debates on violence against women in politics have primarily revolved around two perspectives on gender and political violence.[1] One view privileges women's experiences and emphasizes the importance of gendered power relations as a driving feature of this phenomenon. This approach aligns with global advocacy on violence against women, which recognizes that women sometimes suffer the same abuses as men, but also notes that "many violations of women's human rights are distinctly connected to being female" (Bunch 1990, 486). According to this work, hostility and resistance to women's inclusion takes varied forms, ranging from physical and sexual abuse to verbal aggression and dismissal of women's political authority to deployment of highly sexualized gender stereotypes to minimize and degrade women aspiring to higher political roles (Krook and Restrepo Sanín 2020).

A second view questions the exclusive focus on women and highlights the possibilities of nongendered motivations for attacks on politically active women. These scholars argue that men's experiences must also be examined to "distinguish between instances of violence in which gender is part of the motive versus contexts in which violence is widespread and affects all political actors" (Bjarnegård 2018, 694). This work also suggests that activism and research on violence against women in politics have been overinclusive, "subsum[ing] general electoral or political violence" into the phenomenon of violence against women in politics, thus erasing any "distinction between gendered and non-gendered violence" (Piscopo 2016, 443).

These debates echo controversies that have long waged within the literature on gender-based violence. Feminist constructions conceptualized domestic violence as a form of patriarchal control exercised by male perpetrators over female victims. A counternarrative on family violence, however, reframed the problem as a case of human violence in which men and women were equally likely to be perpetrators and victims (Berns 2001). Yet Johnson (1995) questioned whether researchers were in fact studying the same phenomenon. Feminist studies tended to collect data from domestic violence shelters. Focusing on "patriarchal terrorism," they observed highly disproportionate gender ratios, with virtually all victims being female and nearly all perpetrators being male. Family violence scholars, in contrast, used data from national samples of women and men. Analyzing a wide range of domestic conflicts, this work uncovered only small gender differences in both the use and receipt of violence. Most incidents arose as everyday conflicts, shaped by the degree to which they were embedded within a broader violence-prone culture.

Giving these distinct starting points and research populations, Johnson (1995) concludes that a single research design might not suffice to study these two phenomena at the same time. Similarly, there may be *two types* of violence in the political sphere: *violence in politics*, targeting male and female political actors in gendered and nongendered ways; and *violence against women in politics*, directed specifically at women as a group to drive them out of the political realm. Both types of violence appear across the chapters in this book, with some authors interested primarily in gendered (and nongendered) violence in politics (see chapters by Piscopo and Bjarnegård, Schneider, Thomas and Herrick, and Håkansson, for example) and others focusing more squarely on violence experienced by women as women in the political realm (see chapters by Kishi, Esposito, Kuperberg, Ballington and Borovsky, Restrepo Sanín, and Raney and Collier). In addition to clarifying conceptual confusions, drawing this distinction avoids framing these phenomena as competing hypotheses—as well as opens up the possibility that these dynamics can coexist in the broader population of cases and in the context of a specific woman's own experiences.

Existing concepts in political science help elaborate how these two phenomena are related but distinct. In the case of violence in politics, hostility against political actors is rooted in what Phillips (1995) calls the "politics of ideas," or competition over political views. Men and women are vulnerable to this kind of violence, with risk levels varying depending on rates of violence in society more generally. In many instances, this violence affects women and men in similar ways, inflicting physical injury or displacement. In others, these acts take gender-differentiated forms, with women and men targeted for their political affiliations in different ways, for example, via politically motivated rape and forced circumcision. Affecting what Pitkin (1967) calls "substantive representation," this type of violence employs force to enable one set of political preferences to prevail over others. Seeking to punish or exclude on the basis of political opinions, it violates citizens' ability to make free and informed choices about political alternatives.

Violence against women in politics, in contrast, concerns the "politics of presence," or the inclusion of members of diverse groups in policymaking

(Phillips 1995). Rather than suppressing participation on the basis of political opinion, this type of violence promotes inequality, calling into question the rights of women to take part in politics at all. Expressing bias and discrimination, it is directed specifically at women, including in intersectional ways. Some manifestations, like sexual objectification, are clearly gendered, while others, like death threats, are not. By selectively targeting women, violence against women in politics seeks to shape what Pitkin (1967) calls "descriptive representation," the degree to which the composition of decision-making bodies reflects the diversity of the population. Infringing upon basic political rights, it seeks to exclude members of certain demographic groups *as group members* from participating in the political process.

Previous work has struggled to distinguish these phenomena for several reasons (Krook 2020). First, politically active women experience both forms of violence. Second, most of the data collected or available to study these dynamics captures both forms of violence simultaneously. Third, some women are attacked as women *and* in response to their women's rights advocacy, positioning them at the intersection between violence in politics and violence against women in politics. Clearer concepts, however, can help distinguish acts *directed at women* for political reasons from those seeking to *exclude them as women* from participating in public life.

Methodological Debates

Budding awareness of violence against women in politics has inspired a variety of efforts by scholars and practitioners to document and analyze this phenomenon. Reflecting ongoing theoretical debates, the literature espouses two measurement approaches, which closely align with the distinction between violence in politics and violence against women in politics. Scholars of gendered violence in politics emphasize the need to compare women's experiences alongside those of men (Bjarnegård 2018, 693). Yet focusing on male-female differences can only give insight into gendered patterns of violence in politics, for example, in its form and impact (Bardall, Bjarnegård, and Piscopo 2020). In contrast, comparing men and women provides little leverage for analyzing violence against women in politics, which—by definition—is only experienced by women.

Relying on male-female comparisons can also be misleading for at least two other reasons. First, not all individuals are equally vulnerable to attack: those who are more visible (Håkansson 2021; Rheault, Rayment, and Musulan 2019), hold leadership positions (Krantz, Wallin, and Wallin 2012), and promote controversial political opinions (Biroli 2018) tend to attract greater attention and hostility. If men are more likely to occupy top leadership roles, they may be more likely to face politically motivated attacks—in turn, depressing estimations of violence against women in politics as a separate phenomenon.

Second, gender may not be the only factor doing "added work" in shaping experiences of violence. Research on harassment of black elected officials (Musgrove 2012), as well as on the effects of race, age, class, sexuality, and religiosity in heightening vulnerability to violence against women in politics (Dhrodia 2017a; IPU 2016, 2018; Kuperberg 2018), suggests that attempts to exclude may activate multiple categories of political marginalization. These factors, moreover, may operate alternatively and simultaneously, collectively obscuring how much of this violence is issue versus identity based—as well as which identities, in particular, may be driving the results. Relying on male-female comparisons to ascertain the existence (and extent) of violence against women in politics is thus not an infallible approach—but, instead, one subject to serious estimation errors.

Research that focuses more explicitly on violence against women in politics, in contrast, places strong emphasis on women's lived experiences. Data collection by the Association of Locally Elected Women of Bolivia embodies this feminist ethos, treating the telling of women's stories as a form of resistance and empowerment by giving voice to women's realities (Rojas Valverde 2010). Yet relying on women to come forward with their testimonies has important limitations from a conventional social science perspective. Convenience sampling—drawing from population members who are available and willing to participate—can only provide insight into trends across the pool of people studied. Making claims about broader prevalence rates, in contrast, requires a random representative sample of the broader population.

While treated as a tenet of "good science," however, Johnston and Sabin (2010) point out such standards are difficult to achieve with "hard-to-reach populations," where respondents have strong incentives to remain hidden due to stigmas associated with the questions being posed. This is clearly the case for politically active women, who may hesitate to report incidents of violence against women in politics—or may simply normalize it as part of the political game. Absent traditional sampling opportunities, researchers can, nonetheless, aim to make their samples as representative as possible of the diversity of relevant explanatory features within the broader population. Reflecting this approach, two surveys by the Inter-Parliamentary Union (2016; 2018) sought interviews with female MPs from different regions, political parties, age groups, and other backgrounds to lend greater substance to their findings—even if the true generalizability of these trends may never be known.

While this body of research is closer to the concept of violence against women in politics, starting from the point of view of women's lives does not in itself resolve the issue of distinguishing between incidents of violence in politics and violence against women politics, as politically active women may experience both forms of violence. Conscious of these possibilities, some researchers take care to identify gendered content. Such a strategy does not necessarily succeed in differentiating between politically and gender-motivated acts, however. Data collected by IM-Defensoras (2015) on attacks against women human rights defenders records—when available—data on gendered components. Yet, without further details, it is not clear whether threats of sexual violence, for example, invoke a gendered trope against an ideological opponent or, alternatively, attempt to degrade and delegitimize women as legitimate participants in the political sphere. Focusing exclusively on women, therefore, does not automatically resolve the problem of identifying and measuring violence against women in politics—but may also, in fact, lead to significant distortions.

A Bias Event Approach

Ongoing debates thus indicate that identifying cases of violence against women in politics is not a straightforward task. The literature on hate crimes provides a means for overcoming this impasse and, in turn, for developing an empirical strategy to identify cases of violence against women in politics (Krook and Restrepo Sanín 2020). Hate crime laws impose a higher class of penalties when a crime targets a victim due to perceived group membership. These crimes are deemed to be more severe because, in addition to the crime, they involve group-based discrimination. While perpetrated against individuals, they target the group as a whole, seeking to send a message about the inferiority of the targeted group to members of the group as well as to society at large (Kauppinen 2015).

To facilitate the identification of bias, the U.S. Federal Bureau of Investigation (FBI) offers a list of potential sources of evidence that might be collected and analyzed to make these determinations. Reaching a finding of bias does not require that all categories of evidence be satisfied. Rather, investigators should consider the body of evidence as a whole to weigh whether, on balance, bias played a role in motivating the crime. Group-based bias need not be the sole motivation, however, but simply a substantial factor in victimization.

Five criteria are relevant for establishing the presence of gender bias in the political sphere. First, the offender made oral comments, written statements, or gestures indicating bias. This might include sexist or sexualized language objectifying or otherwise denigrating women. Second, the offender left bias-related drawings, symbols, or graffiti at the scene. Perpetrators might post degrading images of female politicians or paint sexist insults on campaign posters, homes, or constituency offices. Third, the victim was engaged in activities related to his or her identity group. Political women in this scenario might be outspoken feminists, but they may also simply have sought to speak up for women.

Fourth, the offender was previously involved in a similar incident or is a hate group member. The perpetrator might have harassed other female politicians or might participate in men's rights networks or other groups seeking to defend patriarchy. Fifth, a substantial portion of the community where the event occurred perceived that the incident was motivated by bias. Evidence might include speeches, opinion pieces, or demonstrations that explicitly attribute the attack to a woman's gender.

Not all acts of bias are so transparent, however. In cases of unconscious bias, people believe that they are not prejudiced—but nonetheless think or act in biased ways. To detect these forms of bias, a sixth criterion is required: the victim was evaluated negatively according a double standard (Krook and Restrepo Sanín 2020). In the context of violence against women in politics, double standards might entail attacking politically active women in ways and for reasons not used for men who are politically engaged (Price 2016).

A bias event approach is amenable to a variety of empirical research strategies. Most existing datasets of electoral and political violence, for example, are based on incident reports recording the type, location, perpetrators, and targets of violence. Incorporating a bias event lens might entail asking follow-up questions about the content of the incident (Did it invoke bias-related tropes?), the actors involved (Did the targets or perpetrators have a history of activism for or against the target's identity group?), and how the incident was perceived by the broader community (Did citizens or the media interpret the incident as motivated by bias?).

Similarly, surveys could integrate this approach into the design of questionnaires, as could individual case-based research. After survey or interview questions about online violence, for instance, respondents could be asked to estimate how much of the abuse was driven by political or gender reasons. Respondents could also be invited to give examples, which researchers could then analyze for bias-related content. Analyses of social media data, finally, often attempt to devise measures to capture the nature of content. Adapting these approaches in a bias detection–oriented direction, however, could help develop more nuanced typologies of misogynistic versus political issue content.

A bias event approach provides much-needed leverage in resolving current theoretical and methodological debates on violence against women in politics. Reserving judgment until further investigation, it advocates placing acts in their broader context, using information about their content, targets, perpetrators, and impact to determine in a more holistic manner whether bias was a substantial factor or played a driving role. This approach clarifies that violence against women in politics does *not* include *all forms* of violence faced by politically active women. Further, it may not be the *only* or even the *most common* form of violence they may experience. Rather, it is a *specific form* of violence that can, and often does, *coexist* with other forms of violence in the political sphere.

Conclusion

Violence against women in politics is increasingly recognized around the world as a barrier to women's political participation. It has received less attention to date, however, in comparison to political violence from a gender perspective (see chapters by Olsson, Eriksson Baaz and Stern, and Piscopo and Bjarnegård). Identifying instances of gendered violence in politics and violence against women in politics is important. Both involve violations of electoral and personal integrity (Bjarnegård 2018), undermining—in turn—both democracy and human rights. Yet violence against women in politics also merits its own attention, posing a third threat—to gender equality—that is not yet widely articulated or understood. Ignoring it—or accepting it as the burden that women must bear to have a political voice—perpetuates injustice and inequality with negative effects for society as a whole.

4

Conflict-Related Sexual Violence against Men

Maria Eriksson Baaz and
Maria Stern

The shroud of silence cast over sexual violence against men during war is quite frequently attributed to a 'general failure of feminist scholarship and activism to incorporate this issue' in the international agenda. By highlighting violence against women, some argue, feminist approaches continue to taint scholarly and policy circles with myopic narratives which men inhabit only as perpetrators. (Drumond 2019, 1283–84)

While feminist research and debates are more nuanced and theoretically informed than implied in the citation above, men/boys as victims of sexual violence have long been "uncomfortable subjects" in feminist research and particular in policy (Eriksson Baaz and Stern 2013). Yet, recently there has been a growing recognition that men and boys are also victims of conflict-related sexual violence (CRSV), and efforts to document and make sense of such violence have increased considerably within IR and political science research (see Zalewski et al. 2018 for an overview). However, a curious difference in explanatory framings between CRSV against women and men has emerged in much of these efforts: CRSV against men has largely been framed as more strategic and intentional and thereby somehow more "political" compared to CRSV against women (Schulz and Touquet 2020). This understanding of what constitutes "political" violence is indeed quite narrow and does not take into account how different forms of violence inform each other (see True 2012). In this chapter, we will provide an overview of the recent efforts to attend to, and make sense of, CRSV against men. Moreover, we propose that research on CRSV against men (like with that on VAWIP) would benefit from critically exploring various and intersecting motives and driving forces, resisting the tendency to conflate intentions with effects or the targets of violence by inferring motives from the identity of the victims, and assuming that violence against politicians always is politically motivated (see Schulz and Touquet 2020; Bardall, Bjarnegård, and Piscopo 2020).

Before continuing, let us first situate the chapter conceptually in relation to the key concepts of the book. First, similarly to Olsson (in this volume) but in contrast to many other chapters of the book, we address violence in a context in which physical violence is assumed as a defining feature, rather than an exception (see also Kishi in this volume; Kreft and Nagel in this volume). Moreover, we do not focus on actors connected to formal political processes, as is the case in most other chapters addressing violence against political actors in supposed "peace settings." Rather we focus on a context where all violence committed by armed actors tends to be construed as "political." All acts of violence by armed actors in war, including sexual violence, tend to be construed as "politically/militarily motivated." This reflects familiar (and deeply problematic) distinctions between war and peace, which posit "war as the extension of politics with other means" (Von Clausewitz 1976).

As we will argue in this chapter, this understanding and familiar distinctions between war and peace—which are deeply ingrained in explanations of CRSV against men/boys and women/girls—form part of the difficulty to think otherwise about CRSV (Eriksson Baaz and Stern 2018). CRSV against women was initially almost uniquely framed as the result of a pursuit of political goals through military means, as a weapon or strategy of war (see Eriksson Baaz and Stern 2013 for an overview). The familiar trope of "rape as a weapon of war" emerged as dominant globally following international recognition of mass rapes during the armed conflicts in Rwanda (1994) and Bosnia-Herzegovina (1992–1995). Hence, while recognized as dependent on and forming part of unequal gender relations outside of war, CRSV was to a large extent still construed as separate from sexual violence in peace settings. In light of this, a growing body of scholarship emerging in the last ten years (mainly focusing on CRSV against women) has not only come to emphasize the war-peace continuum more generally, but has problematized the weapon of war framing, arguing that it has created a reductionist and universalizing theory of wartime sexual violence that hinders us from paying attention to the particularities of conflict settings and other dynamics at play. Yet, a similar recognition is so far limited in relation to efforts to make sense of CRSV against men. Why might this be so? And what may we learn for our understandings about CRSV against men/boys from such recent research on

CRSV against mostly women/girls (see, e.g., Olsson in this volume; Kreft and Nagel in this volume)?

In an attempt to address these questions, the chapter proceeds as follows. After a short overview of what we know about who survivors and perpetrators are and where and how the violence is enacted, we provide an overview of the overarching explanatory framework for making sense of the motivation for the occurrence of CRSV against men. We then provide an overview of developments within the research field mainly addressing CRSV against women, highlighting the lessons learned and how they may be useful also in relation to the challenges involved in efforts to make sense of CRSV against men.

Men and Boys as Survivors of CRSV

CRSV against men/boys, like that against women/girls, comes in myriad forms. Research and policy texts tend to include the following forms: anal or oral rape, sexual humiliation, sexual slavery, genital violence, genital mutilation, forced nudity, and being forced to commit or to watch sexual acts, including forced incest. As reflected in this list, and in contrast to the broader definition of violence in this book (see Introduction), research and policy texts on CRSV tend to restrict violence to physical acts of violence, relegating the psychological to the effects of the harm. Current research also demonstrates that CRSV occurs in various public and private settings: for example, in detention or enslavement, upon arrest and during raids (Touquet 2018). So far most attention both in scholarly texts and in policy has been directed toward sexual violence in detention—until recently largely "de-sexed" under the label torture (see Gray and Stern 2019)—and anal rape. Sexual acts that do not involve penetrative anal rape are more likely to be overlooked and not reported (Leiby 2018; Schulz 2020).

The rapidly emerging literature documents CRSV against men from a range of conflict settings, including, for instance, Northern Ireland, the wars in the former Yugoslavia, DR Congo, El Salvador, Peru, Egypt, Sri Lanka, Liberia, Sierra Leone, Burundi, the Central African Republic (CAR), northern Uganda, Syria, Libya, and Myanmar (for an overview, see Touquet et al. 2020). This research shows how forms of violence, such as those mentioned above, vary between and within conflicts and also over time (ibid.).

The prevalence of CRSV also clearly varies between conflicts, and, we can surmise, much violence remains nonreported. Yet, recent data suggests that men and boys are victims of CRSV at quite high levels. For instance, the result of a screening and documentation of male refugees from the DR Congo conducted by the Refugee Law Project, Makerere University, and Johns Hopkins School of Public Health suggests that in some refugee populations, more than one in three men has experienced sexual violence in his lifetime (Dolan 2014).

Moreover, Leiby (2018), who conducted an analysis of more than two thousand testimonies of violence during the civil war in Peru and El Salvador, found that CRSV was widely unreported. Her data shows that approximately 30 percent of survivors of CRSV in Peru and around 50 percent in El Salvador were men, in contrast to the figures emerging from the truth commissions in the two countries, which suggest only between 1 and 2 percent.

Due to the focus on war and the familiar distinctions between war and peace, research and policy/advocacy addressing CRSV against men focus almost exclusively on sexual violence perpetrated by military actors/armed groups. Hence little is known about the proportion and forms of violence committed by civilian actors, and much of this violence is suspected to go unreported. In many conflicts worldwide, clear lines of demarcation between the civilian spheres and the active theater of warring either do not exist or are blurry at best; warring permeates all aspects of social life in conflict settings, rendering any tidy distinction between political violence and nonpolitical violence deeply problematic. Hence, it is also difficult to discern between what is CRSV and what is "only" SV. For instance, a recent report on sexual violence against men and boys among Rohingya refugees showed a tendency only to speak of sexual violence perpetrated by Myanmar military forces and not the abuse by family or community members, which, according to service providers, was more common (Chynoweth 2018).

While some sexual violence is committed by women, men are reported to be the main perpetrators and are often assumed to be heterosexual (Touquet et al. 2020). Limited scholarly attention has been directed toward sexual violence against military staff/combatants. This is both surprising and unfortunate, given the little existing research that reports high levels of sexual violence against military men (Belkin 2012) and studies that indicate that the levels of sexual violence against military men are often higher than that committed against male civilians (Johnson et al. 2008).

How then are the reasons for the committing of CRSV against men understood in dominant policy and academic conversations?

Making Sense of Why CRSV against Men Occurs

As noted above, while the framing of CRSV as a weapon of war previously mainly served to make sense of CRSV against women, it has become dominant in the more recent efforts to make sense of the motivation for CRSV against men (Touquet et al. 2020). The storyline that depicts CRSV as a weapon of war is, of course, neither monolithic nor static; there are different variants of and more nuances to the "rape as a weapon of war" narrative than we can capture in this short text (see, e.g., Eriksson Baaz and Stern 2013). In sum, this narrative explains the sometimes-wide occurrence of CRSV as a result of efforts to pursue military and political goals: CRSV is understood as a "military tactic, serving as a combat tool to humiliate and demoralize, to tear apart families, and to devastate communities" (UN-Action against Sexual Violence 2007, 5) and builds on familiar notions of how gendered power relations work in society.

Most research describes CRSV against men in two main interrelated ways: as a technique of interrogation that is particularly effective because of the symbolic meaning attached to it being "sexual" and/or as a political and targeted act, instigated to humiliate, demoralize, and punish men through "feminization" and/or "homosexualization." CRSV against men is seen as a tactic employed by the perpetrators to "feminize" their victims and thus render them weak and passive victims, stripped of their masculinity (Auchter 2017; Lewis 2014; Meger 2018). Some (e.g., Sivakumaran 2007) describe CRSV against men as being about emasculation, whereby the perpetrator asserts his power and robs the victim of his masculine status through violating him sexually. This has often been described with the terms *feminization* and attendant notions of *homosexualization*—both physically through penetrating another persons' body (in the case of anal rape) and symbolically, as the victim supposedly is diminished and loses his manhood and status. In short, the victim is stripped of his hetero-masculinity and is supposedly rendered a "woman" or homosexual with the entire negative and inferior gendered connotations implied.

Moreover, CRSV against men/boys is thus not only, or even primarily, understood as an individualized affront, but instead one against a collective. Violating one person's body sends a collective message to his "group" as a whole. For instance, in his exploration of castration as "messages" with particular audiences in mind, Myrttinen (2018) offers an account of CRSV against men that highlights it as a form of communication with specific, and highly political, intent.

While these explanatory frameworks surely reflect the particularities of many cases, recent research has come to problematize the idea that CRSV against men/boys has a one-size-fits-all or universal explanatory framework. Schulz and Touquet (2020) suggest, in a similar manner as we do in this chapter, that research focusing on men has much to learn from research on CRSV mainly focusing on women. Let us now attend to and provide a brief overview of some key lessons learned within that field.

Recognizing the Complexity of CRSV: Developments within Research Focusing Mainly on CRSV against Women

The framing of CRSV as a strategy and weapon, which has been dominant in policy, makes much sense from a range of perspectives. Perhaps most importantly, it broke with the previously dominant assumption that explained CRSV against women/girls as a tragic, yet "natural" consequence of war, which suspends the social constraints hindering men from being the sexual predators that they naturally are/can be (see Eriksson Baaz and Stern 2013; see also Kreft and Nagel in this volume; Olsson in this volume). Yet, as noted above, recent scholarship has also come to problematize the framing of rape as a weapon of war, arguing that it has created a reductionist and universalizing theory of wartime sexual violence that hinders us from paying attention to the particularities of conflict settings and other dynamics at play. When summarizing research from various conflicts and CRSV globally, for instance, Cohen, Hoover Green, and Wood (2013, 1) concluded that "wartime rape need not be ordered to occur on a massive scale" and that "wartime rape is often not an intentional strategy of war: it is more frequently tolerated than ordered."

Much of the initial and subsequent research problematizing the singular notion of CRSV as a strategy of war followed from an increased attention to military organizations, including both state armed forces and armed groups. This research showed that this explanation tends to confuse the consequences of wartime rape with the motives for it (cf. Gottschall 2004; Hoover Green 2018; Eriksson Baaz and Stern 2013; Cohen 2016; Wood 2018). Based on empirical studies of various military organizations, such research argues that the dominant narrative of CRSV as mainly/only strategic problematically assumes that military institutions are indeed the rational war machines they are meant to be. According to such logic, massive CRSV (or any other violence against civilians) must reflect orders or at least be somehow encouraged. While there have indeed been cases documented of CRSV ordered by military commanders as an explicit strategy of war, perhaps most infamously in the war in former Yugoslavia, this is clearly not always the case (Bassiouni 1994). Empirically based research on military organizations shows how such organizations often fail to operate according to the ideals of discipline, hierarchy, and control and that the occurrence of SV in warring contexts does not necessarily imply that it is promoted or construed as strategic by political or military leadership (and is thereby not political in a narrow sense) (see Eriksson Baaz and Stern 2013). Learning from empirical studies, it is also clear that CRSV is seldom perceived as strategic by military leaders. Military aims, contexts, and discourses diverge, and military commanders both presently and historically do not only discourage but also try to curb sexual violence (see Eriksson Baaz and Stern 2013; Wood 2018; Hoover Green 2018). This is not to say that individual perpetrators do not carry out acts of political violence, especially when we widen our notion of political violence to include acts that are informed by and inform myriad intersecting power relations.

Contributing to and building on other such critical research, Wood (2018, 514–15) proposes that CRSV should be classified in three broad categories: *strategic sexual violence*, which broadly refers to sexual violence "purposefully adapted by commanders in pursuit of group objectives"; *opportunistic sexual violence* "carried out for private reasons rather than organization objectives"; and sexual violence as *practice* in which sexual violence is not officially ordered, but nevertheless tolerated and perpetuated, and thus occurring regularly.

In short, research on CRSV has moved from conceptualizing CRSV only as purposefully adopted in pursuit of (formal) political and military organizational objectives to highlighting other motives and driving forces in relation to women. Research building on narratives from both perpetrators and survivors highlight a range of other potential dynamics, which in Wood's logic could be sorted both within the opportunistic and practice categories. For example, one motivation attributed to perpetrators is a wish to sexually "taste" individual or groups of women otherwise not available to them outside of conflict settings (Dolan, Eriksson Baaz, and Stern 2020); other explanations take into account the intermingling of violence and sexual desire as entwined frenzied "pleasures" of warring (Bourke 2008; Dolan, Eriksson Baaz, and Stern 2020). Some note how sexual violence is used as a means of settling various personal scores, which come in various forms and often cut across civil-military divides (for an overview, see Eriksson Baaz and Stern 2013). Moreover, many accounts complicate simple narratives about motivations and instead highlight multiplicity, complexity, and how driving forces may even "shift in the course of any single attack" (Bourke 2007, 409). Accounts of experiences of perpetrator's intermingling and shifting motives was also recurrent in interviews that we conducted among Congolese sexual violence survivors in Uganda. As one woman explained, "It can be [a result of] both sexual lust and [used to] to destroy—they go together [ezosangana]" (Dolan, Eriksson Baaz, and Stern 2020, 1159).

Furthermore, scholarship increasingly problematizes reductive notions of CRSV as only a tool for emasculation and feminization by highlighting analytical shortcomings in simplistic understandings of the symbolism of CRSV against men/boys.[1] However, a recognition of the possibly multiple and complex driving forces behind and varied contexts of CRSV against men/boys remains paltry indeed. Why might this be the case, and, if so, what might be avenues for further research?

Concluding Reflections

We begin this concluding reflection by training our reflexive and critical eye on the obdurate overarching storyline about rape as a weapon of war in relation to CRSV against men/boys. We propose that this singular and reductive explanatory framework must be understood in light of familiar ideas around heteronormative and patriarchal male heterosexuality that render sexual acts enacted between men as deviant. As Schulz and Touquet (2020, 1177) also conclude, the dominance of the strategic rape narrative in relation to CRSV against men/boys most certainly reflects unexamined heteronormative and homophobic assumptions in which "same-sex violations cannot be assumed ever to be opportunistic or linked to sexual pleasure, but must always and exclusively serve a strategic and military objective." Such framings are also common among many survivors. For instance, Congolese survivors of CRSV, whom we interviewed in Uganda, largely portrayed SV against men as explicitly political and, despite some hesitations, decidedly different from CRSV against women. While women (of a certain age) appeared as "always already rapable," following "rape scripts" based on a view of the immutable power of heterosexual male desire, men were not seen as similarly "rapable" (Dolan, Eriksson Baaz, and Stern 2020, 1165; see also Gavey 2005). As one male survivor concluded, "Sexual violence against men is planned, it is political, it does not just happen by accident, like it is for women" (Dolan, Eriksson Baaz, and Stern 2020, 1165).

It is clearly easy to dismiss such framings as reflecting the homophobic and backward worldviews of Others, thus constructing ourselves (as critical feminist scholars) as educated, liberal, open-minded, and free of such stale and politically unpalatable ideas. Yet, we suggest that we would do well to resist such temptations and instead engage in critical self-reflection around how also we, as scholars, are shaped by deeply ingrained ideas around heteronormative and patriarchal male heterosexuality that may limit our imaginations (see also Schulz and Touquet 2020).

Moreover, further recognition and exploration of various forms of continuance across "war" and "peace" (see, for instance, Boesten 2017; Kelly 2012; Eriksson Baaz and Stern 2018) are sorely needed, as these lines of distinction resonate poorly with the lived experiences of both war and peace in many contexts globally. Just as much more attention needs to be directed to shedding light on the dis/continuance between SV against women/girls across war and peace, the same applies to research on SV against men/boys. For instance, many of the forms of violence in warring contexts are also common in settings not marked by armed conflict, such as sex trafficking and exploitation (Frederick 2010; Moxley-Goldsmith 2005). In addition, sexual humiliation, genital violence, forced nudity, and being forced to commit or to watch sexual acts are also common in detention, in prisons, and in various initiation rites in sporting and educational settings also in peace (Finkel 2002; Westhead 2020). These acts can also be considered politically violent, and violently political, if one includes, for instance, the gendered workings of power, race, class, and sexuality as also political.

What then might the queries and arguments in this chapter mean for the general theme of this book on political violence against political actors more generally? As noted initially, we believe that research on VAWIP, similarly to research on CRSV against men/boys, could benefit from acknowledging various and intersecting motives and driving forces and refusing a conflation of intentions with effects or the sexual identity of victims. What both the research on VAWIP and research on CRSV against men/boys appear to have in common is that motives are inferred from simplistic understandings of the biological sex of the victims. Bardall, Bjarnegård, and Piscopo (2020) argue that in much of the VAWIP literature, the biological sex of the victim (female) (together with her position in formal politics) is often problematically considered enough to establish a political and strategic motive. Similarly, in much of the literature on CRSV against men/boys, assumptions about the biological sex of the victim that are informed by the ideas about heteronormative and patriarchal male heterosexuality highlighted above, appear to be enough to establish a clear politically strategic motive.[2] Yet, as the wider literature on CRSV against women has taught us, we need to better recognize the possibility not only of multiple, but of intersecting driving forces also beyond simplistic notions of strategic and opportunistic violence. We therefore join a growing cadre of academics and advocates alike that calls for further queries that remain open to both unexpected testimonies and explanatory frameworks and that thus explore how SV against men/boys is political and violent in varied and myriad ways.

5

Locating Politics and Gender within the Violent Act

JENNIFER M. PISCOPO AND
ELIN BJARNEGÅRD

The previous chapters offer different lenses into the relationship between gender, politics, and violence. Louise Olsson and Maria Eriksson Baaz and Maria Stern speak to international relations scholars, focusing on women's roles during war and peace and on how conflict-related sexual violence affects men, respectively. Mona Lena Krook speaks to comparative politics scholars who care about women's political participation. These are different conversations, given the authors' different subfields and research traditions. The authors all analyze women or men as political actors, but they link the three concepts—gender, politics, and violence—in ways that speak to their different audiences.

Another approach, articulated by us and Gabrielle Bardall in *Political Studies* (Bardall, Bjarnegård, and Piscopo 2020), starts not with actors, but with acts. We ask, *How is an act of political violence gendered?* To answer this question, we distinguish among three gendered facets: motive, form, and impact. This act-based approach sidesteps subfield boundaries and looks beyond conflict versus nonconflict settings. We begin by first assessing whether the violent act counts as *political violence*: Did the act intend to disrupt political practices or upset the balance of political power? If yes, we then ask whether gender appears in the act's motives, forms, and/or impacts. Gendered motivations identify attacks aiming to deter the political participation of those outside the hegemonic male group. Gendered forms mean using gendered scripts or tropes to carry out an attack (e.g., sexualized language or slurs). Lastly, gendered impacts capture how different stakeholders—from victims to activists to community members—read gender into an attack (e.g., perceiving the attack as harming a group's political rights). An act of political violence can be gendered in none, some, or all facets. Our approach demonstrates *whether* and *how* gender appears in each act of political violence, whether in conflict or nonconflict settings.

In this chapter, we show how an analytic framework distinguishing among acts' motives, forms, and impacts applies to various settings without losing analytic precision. We begin by identifying how conflict approaches and gender and politics approaches start in different places and reach different conclusions. Next, we explain how our own understanding of what is political, what is violence, and what is gender elevates certain acts for analysis, both within conflict settings and in peaceful settings, no matter the regime type. This framework lets the politically violent act reveal how gender operates, a precise approach that also captures Olsson's, Eriksson Baaz and Stern's, and Krook's concern with untangling women's and men's relationship to violence.

We illustrate our approach to gendered political violence by applying the Bardall, Bjarnegård, and Piscopo framework (2020) to different examples from the conflict literature and the violence against women in politics literature. We focus first on the separation between motives and forms and then on the notion of impacts. In separating gendered motives from gendered forms, we distinguish between political violence carried out for gendered reasons versus political violence carried out using gendered means. This distinction separates contestations over the gendered distribution of political power from other political struggles to conquer territory, impose one's views, or turf opponents from office. In separating the gendered impacts of political violence from motives and forms, we examine how victims, communities, and policymakers interpret and make meaning around violence. Such perspectives are essential for understanding how individuals and communities can stop abuse and heal.

Overall, we identify three contributions that our framework offers to studies of politics, gender, and violence, no matter the subfield, setting, or research question. First, starting with acts reveals how gender shapes political violence without grouping actors into fixed categories of "women victims" or "men perpetrators." Second, distinguishing among motives, forms, and impacts offers a careful accounting of when and where gender infuses political violence. Third, attending to audiences' and stakeholders' reactions to political violence shows how gendered social structures give meaning to violence.

Three Concepts, Two Subfields

The chapters by Olsson, Eriksson Baaz and Stern, and Krook link politics, violence, and gender in different ways, depending on the research agendas in each subfield. Olsson and Eriksson Baaz and Stern do not define "the political" explicitly, but their focus on armed conflict and postconflict suggests that, for them, "politics" is about how war and peace unfold. Olsson introduces gender by highlighting women, drawing out differences in women's and men's experiences with conflict-related violence and peace processes. Eriksson Baaz and Stern introduce gender by focusing on men, specifically men as victims of conflict-related sexual violence. Both tend to focus on the physical components of violence's continuum, namely, rape and sexual assault.

For Krook, "politics" looks quite different. Rather than an international relations perspective concerned with conflict and postconflict, Krook turns to everyday political activities, from citizens' turning out to vote to elites running for and holding office, whether in democratic, semidemocratic, or authoritarian contexts. Krook's subfields are comparative politics and gender and politics, and she builds on a well-established research question in these subfields: What forms of opposition do women encounter when participating in politics and running for and holding office? Krook expands this research tradition by reframing much of this opposition as violence. As such, she introduces gender through concentrating on women victims. On the one hand, she considers a broader continuum of violence, including psychological and verbal attacks, but on the other hand, she narrows the type of women actors: whereas Olsson considers women in all their conflict-related roles, from armed combatants to innocent bystanders, Krook is concerned with women who have political roles.

Each chapter encapsulates analytic approaches that break new ground. Studies of armed conflict traditionally overlooked gender, and studies of gender and political participation traditionally overlooked violence. Olsson exemplifies the first contribution: she takes violence and adds women's experiences and contributions. Krook takes the second perspective, arguing that gender and politics scholars had not fully conceptualized the obstructions to women's political participation: in Krook's view, this opposition is not just violence, but a specific form of violence that targets women in politics *because* they are women in politics. Importantly, Krook's approach erases the traditional boundaries between conflict and nonconflict settings since violence against women in politics can occur anywhere so long as the victim is a woman in politics targeted *as* a woman in politics. However, Eriksson Baaz and Stern—who share Olsson's commitment to gendering conflict studies—do caution against making gender synonymous with women, since men also experience sexual violence. Eriksson Baaz and Stern also start with violence, but they refute stereotypical assumptions about men as perpetrators and women as victims. As they rightly argue, such assumptions lock in narratives that sexual violence against men always aims to feminize them.

Taken together, the chapters remind scholars that the three concepts—gender, politics, and violence—take on different meanings in different research traditions. Two distinctions especially intrigue us.

First, we note that political violence designed to impede women's political participation differs from political violence that affects women and men differently. Krook's focus on bias events that aim to deter women from their political roles differs from Olsson's example about how wartime rape targeting women aims to provoke the enemy into escalation. Bardall, Bjarnegård, and Piscopo's (2020) separation between gendered motives, on the one hand, and gendered forms, on the other, offers clarity here. Gendered motives explain when political violence aims to suppress the political participation of individuals based on their gender or sexual identity, while gendered forms explain how gendered ideas, tropes, and narratives shape patterns of attack. In our framework, bias events to deter women from politics have gendered motives, whereas raping women to taunt the enemy is a gendered form. This separation accommodates each author, albeit differently: for us, Krook's violence against women in politics is about political violence with gendered motives, while Olsson's and Eriksson Baaz and Stern's gender and conflict research primarily analyzes political violence with gendered forms.[1]

Second, we distinguish between gendered effects and gendered intentions. Krook takes believing that gender bias was the motivation as evidence that gendered motives were actually present, letting an outcome demonstrate the motive. She notes that evidence of biased motives can be located in community members' interpretation of attacks as gender biased (see also Krook 2020, 95). By contrast, Eriksson Baaz and Stern caution against this conflation: just because men victims of sexual violence felt feminized does not mean perpetrators had the objective of feminization in mind. Eriksson Baaz and Stern argue that since perpetrators commit sexual violence against men for many reasons, the outcome *cannot* demonstrate the motive. Our framework follows Eriksson Baaz and Stern by separating intentions (motives) from effects (outcomes), but takes effects seriously through the notion of *gendered impacts*: What did the political violence mean to different audiences, including victims, and how should advocates respond? If audiences conflate effects with intentions, their understanding—even if technically imprecise—reveals something about how violence affects individuals, groups, and societies. In the next sections, we continue exploring how the Bardall, Bjarnegård, and Piscopo framework is well-suited for bridging research traditions from within conflict studies and gender and politics.

Locating the Political within Violent Acts

Our framework defines political violence by looking at the attacks' purpose. We foreground actors' intention to intervene in political life, meaning the use of violence to disrupt citizen engagement in politics, citizen mobilization, the carrying out of elections, and the tasks associated with governing, from convening parliament to passing public policy. Since our approach depends on the presence of political motives, any act along the continuum of violence—from psychological to physical—could potentially count as political violence.

At the same time, our approach ex ante excludes some violent acts important to conflict studies scholars. Language matters: when scholars talk about violence as *conflict related*, they include violence carried out in conflict settings but not directly aimed at the conflict itself. For instance, conflict scholars have documented increases in domestic violence during conflict periods, and this violence is gendered, in that women and girls bear the brunt of this violence (Østby, Leiby, and Nordås 2019). For us, this domestic violence is not political violence. Abusers may be responding to the normalization of violence in conflict settings or expressing their own conflict-related stress and anxiety, but they are not intending to disrupt politics when they carry out abuse in the home. (An important exception would be when domestic abusers use violence to control or prevent women's and girls' political engagement.) Certainly, the seriousness of domestic violence requires political redress, but domestic violence does not always constitute political violence.

By extension, not all violence carried out in conflict settings is actually political violence. Similarly, Eriksson Baaz and Stern note that sexual violence against men in conflict settings can resemble sexual violence against men in nonconflict settings: for instance, men prisoners during war and men prisoners during peace can experience similar forms of abuse. Eriksson Baaz and Stern therefore argue that framing sexual violence against men as *always* motivated by political goals obscures instances where sexual violence against men pursues other aims, such as hazing or team bonding (see also Cohen 2016, 2017). Like Eriksson Baaz and Stern, we distinguish between sexual violence carried out by armed combatants for political reasons and sexual violence carried out by perpetrators with personal or social objectives. Domestic violence, sexual violence, and other forms of violence remain important topics of scholarship, but they are not always relevant for studies of *political* violence.

The setting then, does not necessarily cue us about whether an attack constitutes political violence. The same holds true even when that setting is more narrowly construed, as in Krook's focus on violence against women *in poli-*

tics. For Krook, violence against women in politics is motivated by gender bias and consists of acts aiming to exclude women from participating in public life—which are distinct from acts that target women for other political reasons. So, to use a stylized example that we devised for ease of exposition: a U.S. congressman calling a congresswoman sexist names is violence against women in politics because he wants all women politicians to be quiet, whereas a congressman calling his woman colleague "stupid" in a committee debate simply wants to silence her political viewpoints. We concur with the distinction in theory but note that establishing certainty about gender bias versus political disagreement is difficult in practice. Additionally, our hypothetical congressman likely belittles and demeans women frequently. Does the occurrence in a political space (Congress as opposed to a restaurant) automatically make the derogatory language political violence? Or does the target automatically make the derogatory language political violence (a congresswoman as opposed to a waitress)? Verbal abuse of women is always unacceptable, but the question is whether and when scholars can confidently say verbal or other abuse is *political violence.*

The Bardall, Bjarnegård, and Piscopo approach shares Krook's concerns with separating gendered motives from political motives. Yet Krook sees violence against women in politics as separate from political violence (2020, 89–97), while Bardall, Bjarnegård, and Piscopo see violence against women in politics as a *subset* of political violence (2020, 925). Suppose certainty about the congressman's aims could be concretely established or reasonably inferred: he did intend to prevent the congresswoman's political speech. In the Bardall, Bjarnegård, and Piscopo framework, that intention interferes with political processes, and so *both* instances—the sexist slur and the insult of "stupid"—are political violence. The question then becomes, How is this political violence gendered? Forms are easy enough to detect: in the first instance, the use of sexist language is a gendered form.

Motives are trickier. In either instance, if the congressman verbally abused the congresswoman because he does not view politics as women's place, then gendered motives are present. But note that if the congressman has no particular feelings about women being *in politics* and simply behaves like a jerk to women colleagues and women waitresses alike, then we would consider him to be a misogynist and regard his behavior as reprehensible. Even so, if he is just expressing misogyny in its purest form, then he is not aiming to disrupt the process for political reasons and not even committing political violence, and so we would not take the next analytical step to assess whether he had gendered motives. Like domestic violence in wartime, sexual harassment in political workplaces is a *political problem* without necessarily constituting *political violence.* Similarly, not every act of misogyny occurring in politics is political violence.

What Krook calls violence against women in politics, we call *gender-motivated political violence* for two reasons. First, we want to use language that explicitly spells out the difference between violence faced by women in politics because of their gender versus violence women face for any reasons, like being in the opposition or being randomly attacked (e.g., having one's purse stolen). Second, we see women as not the only possible targets of political violence with gendered motives. When perpetrators aim to keep politics the preserve of hegemonic men, then nonhegemonic men and other gender and sexual minorities also experience political violence because of their gender and sexual identities.

Our approach consequently places tighter boundaries on "the political" than others. We view this narrowness as necessary, because the political setting—like the conflict setting—encapsulates myriad bad behaviors, abuses, and attacks, not all of which necessarily intend to disrupt political processes. While all types of violence are worth scholars' attention, we contend that political violence is discrete. By starting with the act, we begin with identifying whether we have an instance of political violence or not and then assess whether gender appears in the motive, the form, or the impact.

Impact captures how different stakeholders understand the event. In some cases, gendered impacts may classify some acts as political violence after the fact, changing the categorization of the act and leading to a reassessment of whether and how gender appears in all its facets. For instance, domestic abusers may not intend to keep wives and daughters from voting, or the congressman may be a boor who insults congresswomen and waitresses with equal abandon. Yet if audiences *understand* these acts as limiting the political participation of women and girls, or if women and girls actually do curb their political engagement to avoid the assault, then the acts have gendered impacts. We could still reach the conclusion that gender did not motivate the act, since victims' and stakeholders' interpretations and responses differ from perpetrators' intentions. Impacts explain how the congressman comes to symbolize how misogyny keeps women politically disempowered, no matter his intentions. Impacts further compel those who would otherwise discount him as a perpetrator of political violence (like we are initially inclined to do) to grapple with the broader consequences of his behavior. By analyzing impacts, researchers can identify how broader social structures imbue individual acts with meaning while avoiding the reduction of motives to the structures themselves.

Locating Gender within Violent Acts

We view the Bardall, Bjarnegård, and Piscopo approach as accessible to different research traditions. Scholars of gender and conflict, like Olsson and

Eriksson Baaz and Stern, and scholars of gender and politics, like Krook, all view gendered power structures as central for understanding men's and women's experiences. Our approach agrees and attaches gender to the acts *as well as* to the actor. As such, our framework avoids grouping men and women into essentialist categories.

Much gender research—including our other scholarly work—begins with actors. Scholars have examined the backlash women officeholders face (see, e.g., Piscopo and Walsh 2019; Wagner 2020) or the reasons men commit sexual violence in conflict (see, e.g., Solangon and Patel 2012; Cohen 2017). Similarly, Olsson, Eriksson Baaz and Stern, and Krook use the sex of actors as their point of departure. Olsson starts with women, considering their roles in conflict as combatants, peacemakers, and survivors; Krook starts with women politicians as victims of bias crimes; and Eriksson Baaz and Stern start with men victims. These researchers engage carefully with how gendered hierarchies shape men's and women's experiences, but the studies are often defined ex ante as about women or about men. Such actor-centered approaches are indeed valuable. For instance, our schema hinges on intentionality, but perpetrators' intentions are admittedly difficult to discern. Patterns wherein women politicians are consistently abused but men are not—meaning comparisons between groups of actors—provide important (albeit indirect) evidence toward gendered motives.

Nonetheless, gendered hierarchies do more than (re)produce men's dominance over women. Gendered hierarchies explain not just women's victimization, but the abuse of nonhegemonic men, members of the LGBTQ+ community, and other gender and sexual minorities. Gay, lesbian, queer, and trans politicians experience online abuse laden with gendered and homophobic tropes, for instance, and they understand these gendered forms as having gendered motives—as making the public sphere unwelcoming and hostile to those who are not straight or cisgendered (Wagner 2020). Here, gender explains both *who* was victimized—LGBTQ+ candidates—but also *how* the victimization occurs—through slurs that used sexualized and homophobic language.

In taking the act of political violence as the point of departure, our framework shows how gender shapes all facets of the act. At the same time, our approach may exclude how gender shapes larger social structures that pattern violence. Take men political activists in Thailand: researchers concluded that the men most likely to use violence (like throwing stones) during otherwise peaceful demonstrations are those who subscribe to masculine honor ideology, meaning those who hold patriarchal values and idealize masculine toughness (Bjarnegård, Brounéus, and Melander 2017). Here, gender explains why certain men resorted to political violence—in disrupting the otherwise peaceful demonstration, the acts "count" as political violence—but our framework would "see" gender in neither the motive nor form nor impact. The activists were not throwing stones to deter the participation of women, and throwing stones uses no gendered scripts and sends no gendered messages. According to the Bardall, Bjarnegård, and Piscopo framework, the Thai men are just committing "regular" (nongendered) political violence.

Of course, the fact that many acts of (political) violence are carried out by men shows that sex and gender are important determinants of violent patterns. Hegemonic masculinity fuels political violence in general. And as a principle that organizes society, gender writ large explains why domestic abuse increases during armed conflict and why the congressman is a boor in the first place. We do not discount gendered social structures. Rather, our point is that gendered structures cannot always say whether particular acts are motivated by, shaped by, or interpreted through the lens of gender. Just like we apply a narrow, but specific, definition of political violence that excludes many acts of violence, our framework may not capture underlying structural or behavioral causes of violence where gender plays a part.

The one exception appears in our concept of gendered impacts, insofar as certain audiences or stakeholders interpret the political violence by appealing to gendered social structures. In making effects separate from intentions, gendered impacts capture how people "read" violence through social structures that are infused with gender, but also with sexuality, race, class, and other identities. Recall the critique raised by Eriksson Baaz and Stern: researchers consistently interpret conflict-related sexual violence toward men by appealing to the idea that men are being subordinated and therefore feminized. In other words, sexual violence against men is consistently read through the gendered social structure of male dominance and feminine submission. We take this reading as a gendered impact: because gendered social structures place women as subordinate, audience members (including academics) interpret the sexual assault of men by men as replicating this submission. In other words, gendered hierarchies are not just scripts for the attacks (gendered forms), they are scripts for *understanding* the attacks (gendered impacts). Social structures may not always motivate the individual acts. Indeed, Eriksson Baaz and Stern tell us this particular script about subordinating men is often wrong. Nonetheless, social structures help people assign meaning to these acts.

Similarly, when women and LGBTQ politicians see online abuse using gendered and sexualized language as driving them from the public sphere, they see each tweet as producing and reproducing the gendered hierarchies where women and LGBTQ peoples are made inferior to straight, heteronormative men. Importantly, we do not view these understandings as wrong: individuals are authors of their own experience, and it is rational that individuals use social structures to understand what happened. Karen Boyle

(2019b) calls this "continuum thinking," wherein victims connect abuses of varied severity and at different moments in their lives by finding the common denominator, like their marginalized gender identity.

By viewing an act's impacts as meriting analysis separate from its motives and forms, the concept of impacts sets aside whether interpretations are "right" or "wrong." We believe this distinction can resolve the impasses in which stakeholders too often find themselves when seeking resolutions. For instance, a congressman may not understand why calling the congresswoman stupid has to become about gender when he thinks it is about her political views—but *she* views his comment as gendered because she engages in continuum thinking. Separating intentions from effects gives stakeholders language that help them speak to—rather than past—each other.

Meaning-making is further worthy of study in its own right because it reveals how different actors interpret violence to serve political goals. Consider instances of violence against women that have shocked and outraged national and international audiences and spurred mobilization from women and feminists, like gang rapes in India (Goetz and Jenkins 2018; Nigam 2014) and femicide in Latin America (Sandvik 2018; Wright 2010). These criminal acts were not carried out with political motives, but the specific acts become imbued with political meaning, particularly the state's disregard for women's and girls' human rights. In Mexico, for instance, activists and academics have read the epidemic of violence against women as caused not by criminal men, but by an impervious state (Monárrez Fragoso 2018). The state foments impunity by giving license to the abusers. By making social structures responsible for the violence, and then blaming the state for upholding these social structures, gendered arguments of this type transform certain criminal acts into political violence after the fact.

Gendered understandings thus affect collective interpretations about violence and are themselves fluid, contested, and constructed. Gendered impacts reflect the core analytic insights of the other approaches, from Krook's recommendation that bias should become central to prosecuting violence against women in politics, to Olsson's and Eriksson Baaz and Stern's point that societies must grapple with the full range of women's and men's experience as agents, perpetrators, and victims of violence.

Conclusion

Any analytic approach draws boundaries, some more expansive than others. In this chapter, we examined how the Bardall, Bjarnegård, and Piscopo (2020) framework engages and even bridges very different traditions in the study of gender, politics, and violence, from conflict studies in international relations to gender in comparative politics. Our framework opts for narrowness, both in terms of what acts count as political violence and where gender appears in acts' motives, forms, and impacts. This narrowness excludes certain instances of violence that occur within conflict settings but that are not directly fueling that conflict, as well as certain incidents that happen in political spaces or to political actors but that are not aiming to influence political processes. At the same time, our focus on (1) whether the act is one of political violence and then (2) whether gender appears in the motive, form, or impact applies to any setting, whether during conflict or peacetime or whether in democracies or nondemocracies.

Further, we push beyond actors' biological sex to examine how gendered social structures appear in political violence's motives, forms, or impact. Gender hierarchies permeate society and shape almost all human behavior. For this reason, we argue that we cannot stop with concluding that "gender matters" or that "gender is everywhere": we need to disentangle the myriad ways in which gender intersects with political violence. The Bardall, Bjarnegård, and Piscopo framework asks *How is political violence gendered?* and considers how gendered hierarchies and gendered social processes motivate violence, shape violence, and give meaning to violence.

PART II

The Continuum of Violence

6

Physical Violence

ROUDABEH KISHI

This chapter addresses physical forms of political violence targeting women in politics, relying on quantitative, event-based data from the Armed Conflict Location & Event Data Project (ACLED). It finds that the forms this physical violence takes, and the perpetrators of this violence, are numerous—with trends varying across regions of the world.

Women and girls, like men and boys, face a variety of forms of violations along a continuum, which manifest in physical and nonphysical ways. However, with the unprecedented numbers of women engaging in elections in recent years, both by seeking office (Berry, Bouka, and Kamuru 2017; Bottin and Young 2021) and by voting (Vaishnav 2018), they have faced heightened risks of specific forms of violence. This chapter specifically explores physical manifestations of political violence that target women in politics—which can include physical sexual violence (e.g., rape) yet would exclude psychological violence (e.g., threats) and online violence (e.g., hate speech). ACLED has long tracked political violence against both men and women and continues to do so (Raleigh et al. 2010), as well as political violence targeting women and girls specifically (Kishi, Pavlik, and Matfess 2019). *New* data from ACLED, however, explored here, offer a resource to allow for a focus on studying the subset of violations that women in politics face (i.e., political violence targeting women in politics) (Kishi 2021).

This chapter will begin with a conceptualization of physical political violence targeting women in politics, exploring specifically who the targets of such violence include. Next, methodological considerations are put forward, introducing the data while underlining what is and is not included within the data explored here. Next, empirical illustrations are explored to better understand both the types and the perpetrators of physical political violence targeting women in politics. In this section, the regional variation in these trends is explored along with examples and explorations of trends. Finally, the chapter ends with a concluding section, again underlining what the data presented in the chapter do and do not capture and, as a result, what types of conclusions, especially in regard to policy, can be gleaned.

Conceptualization

Physical violence is the most universally recognized as *violence*. Violence is defined as "the use of physical force so as to injure, abuse, damage, or destroy" (Merriam-Webster 2020). International humanitarian law recognizes the physical endangerment of civilians as a war crime. Outside of war, physical abuse of another tends to come with legal ramifications. This chapter, and the data presented therein, explore physical manifestations of political violence targeting women in politics. This subset of violations that women in politics face is positioned on the physical side of the continuum of violence explored in this book (see Chapter 1). Other forms of violations that women face, such as threats, intimidation, or bullying, are not explored in this chapter—all of which are incredibly more prevalent than physical violence. Yet a focus on physical violence here captures the most immediately life-threatening violations. Impunity for perpetrators of physical political violence targeting women is high, despite the fact that such crimes are legally enforceable. Better identification and monitoring of this subset of violence can help aid in legal enforcement and mitigation.

Yet even within the subset of physical political violence targeting women in politics, the conversation has often been narrowed. In discussions around physical political violence and gender, this violence tends to be understood as solely physical sexual violence (especially in a wartime context, such as conflict-related sexual violence discussed by Kreft and Nagel in this volume). While physical sexual violence disproportionately affects women at large, as well as women in politics specifically, other forms of physical political violence—such as abductions and forced disappearances—also disproportionately target women relative to trends in political violence writ large (Kishi 2021)—and this violence can occur both during and outside of wartime.

Physical political violence, such as attacks or targeting through the use of explosives, targets more women than solely those "women in politics" and can occur during and outside of election periods. Physical political violence targeting women in politics, explored here, can manifest in the same myriad of ways. Targeting of women in politics includes those actors who are somewhat related to the formal political process, in line with the focus of this book, including women candidates for office; politicians; political party members and supporters; voters; government officials, such as polling staff; and activists, human rights defenders, and social leaders. Table 6.1 (from Kishi 2021) introduces these categories, defines them, provides concrete examples from ACLED data, and points to the prevalence of such women in politics being targeted.

Methodological Considerations

This larger scope of types of physical violence, time periods, and contexts within which violence can occur and the perpetrators of this violence targeting women in politics specifically serves as the impetus for new data on physical political violence targeting women in politics (Kishi 2021).[1] There was a need for the systematic collection of comparable data across space and time and to capture a wider spectrum of physical political violence targeting women and that which targets women in politics specifically.

While in-depth country case studies have long existed, capturing some of the trends above, these data-collecting initiatives use different methodologies across countries and contexts as a function of different authors and mandates. This does not allow for making cross-country and -regional comparisons despite the benefit of adding nuance around a particular context. Further, many of these initiatives have also not been regularly updated, making it impossible to conduct continuous real-time monitoring.

The new data from ACLED can help to address the trends noted above, recording the various forms of physical political violence targeting women in politics and the perpetrators of this violence. Data are collected continuously over time (with no fatality threshold for inclusion) and include all women in politics, as introduced in Table 6.1. Physical political violence targeting women in politics is understood as "the use of [physical] force by a group with a political purpose or motivation" in the public sphere in which women in politics (e.g., women candidates for office; politicians; political party supporters; voters; government officials; and activists, human rights defenders, and social leaders) are the only, the majority, or the primary targets[2] (Raleigh et al. 2010; Kishi 2021). In this way, the data identify instances of gendered political violence, in line with that discussed in the previous chapter in this volume (by Piscopo and Bjarnegård). ACLED tracks physical political violence—both gendered and not—across the globe. Knowing which of these events have gendered *motivations* is difficult, as gendered scripts and tropes are not necessarily always used nor reported on (and hence cannot always be coded by data providers like ACLED); hence, the data examined here look specifically at events of physical political violence with a gendered *impact*, accounting

TABLE 6.1 WOMEN IN POLITICS WHO CAN BE TARGETS OF PHYSICAL POLITICAL VIOLENCE

Type of Target	Definition	Example	% of Targets of Women in Politics
Candidate for Office	A woman who is running in an election to hold a publicly elected government position; that position can be in local, regional, or national government. This includes, but is not limited to, incumbent candidates.	*A female candidate from the Mon Unity Party (MUP) was shot and killed by an unidentified gunman in the evening near Payathonzu town in Myanmar.*	8%
Politician	A woman who currently serves in an elected position in government, regardless of whether that government is at the local, regional, or national level.	*Mortar fireworks were fired at the balcony of a woman politician's parents in Corbeil-Essonnes in France while she was having dinner inside with several members of her family, likely triggered by political disagreements.*	12%
Political Party Supporter	A woman who contributes to, endorses, and/or acts in support of a political party or candidate that extends outside of voting, via membership, participation in party events, monetary donations, or other forms of support. This also includes women who refuse to act, endorse, or support a specific political party or candidate, regardless of whether or not their preferred party or candidate is listed.	*Two women, allegedly members of the Citizens' Movement (MC) party who were caught buying votes, were beaten by a group of people in Fraccionamiento Los Mangos in Mexico.*	24%
Voter	A woman who is actively participating in, has actively participated in, or attempts to actively participate in local, state/regional, and/or national elections or referendums. Active participation here refers specifically to registering to vote or casting a ballot in an election.	*A Communist Party of India (Marxist) (CPI-M) woman voter was attacked by suspected Bharatiya Janata Party (BJP) supporters in Matabari area in India after the results of the Parliamentary elections were released.*	2%
Government Official	A woman who works for the local, regional, or national government in a nonpartisan capacity. This includes public/civil servants, local authorities, or nonpartisan political appointments, such as judges. This also includes women who work to support the proper functioning of elections; electoral assistance groups include independent and/or nonpartisan poll workers or poll monitors.	*A group of locals beat up and injured a woman judge in Soavinandriana in Madagascar over a family court case.*	16%
Activist/ Human Rights Defender/ Social Leader	A woman who peacefully advocates for a specific social cause and/or actively promotes the expansion or protection of human rights. These rights can include women's rights, civic rights, environmental rights, and more. This also includes social leaders, who are often prominent, local activists known for their community advocacy.	*An Iraqi activist was kidnapped by unidentified men on her way to Tahrir Square in Baghdad in Iraq, though was later released.*	38%

Source: Kishi, Roudabeh. 2021. "Violence Targeting Women in Politics: Trends in Targets, Types, and Perpetrators of Political Violence." Armed Conflict Location and Event Data Project (ACLED), December 12. Available at: https://acleddata.com/2021/12/08/violence-targeting-women-in-politics-trends-in-targets-types-and-perpetrators-of-political-violence/.

for how stakeholders might perceive the attack based on who the victim(s) of the attack were. In this way, this chapter builds on the important work that has been done on violence against women in politics, by taking a step toward gendering the idea of political violence more largely, as put forward in the introductory chapter in this volume (see also Bardall, Bjarnegård, and Piscopo 2020).

Data collection is consistent across countries and regions to allow for comparison and is updated weekly for public use, allowing for analysis to be based on the most current information.[3] Information comes from a variety of sources: thousands of traditional media sources, ranging from national newspapers to local radio, in more than one hundred different languages; select new media, which constitutes vetted and trusted social media accounts; reports from international organizations and institutions; and partnerships with local conflict observatories. This can be an appropriate sourcing strategy when capturing information on *physical* political violence as such information tends to be well reported by these types of sources. This sourcing strategy would be less appropriate for data collection on other types of violations that women may face, such as intimidation or hate speech, which can often happen in private rather than in public reporting (as mentioned in the introductory chapter), making systematic coverage of such violations more difficult. As such, while the substantive distinction between public and private spheres is often artificial, as noted in the introductory chapter of this volume, there is a clear distinction made in this chapter as a result of the methodological tool (i.e., an event-based quantitative dataset) that is relied upon.

These data do not convey the totality of violence that women face; that is a much larger set of information. This subset of data captures *physical* political violence targeting women in politics. It does not include other nonphysical political violations women face, such as intimidations or threats (discussed elsewhere in this volume, such as by Schneider; Håkansson; Thomas and Herrick; Esposito; Zetterberg and Bjarnegård; and others). It also does not capture other physical violence that women may face—such as domestic or intimate partner violence (touched on by Kreft and Nagel in this volume as well). In this way, these data *do not* provide a gender disaggregation of the ACLED dataset by events nor fatalities and hence cannot be used to convey the total number of women who have been targeted.

An event-based data collection effort based primarily on secondary information gathering is distinct from a victim-based data collection effort based on primary information collection. Firstly, an event can involve one to many victims, so the number of events and victims should not be conflated—these capture different trends. Capturing events instead of victims may come at the detriment of being able to identify total numbers of victims; however, it can be important in ensuring that source reports do not introduce a bias into counts. A source may report an incident as "there were reports of rape"—while such reporting makes it impossible to know the number of victims, the number of "events" is clear from the location, date, etc. Such coding decisions help to ensure the data collection is systematic and therefore comparable.

Empirical Illustrations

Types of Physical Political Violence
Targeting Women in Politics

The data focus on five types of physical political violence. Political violence is perpetrated in the public sphere to achieve political goals and need not result in death to be included here. These types of physical political violence include the following: (1) sexual violence, (2) attacks that are nonsexual in nature, (3) abductions and forced disappearances, (4) mob violence, and (5) explosions and other forms of remote violence. The difference in the prevalence of these forms across different regions is depicted in Figure 6.1.

Physical *sexual violence* includes all physical violence of a sexual nature—such as rape, sexual slavery, forced sterilization, sexual torture, public nudity, etc. (and in this way is in line with the definitions put forth in this volume by both Kreft and Nagel; and Eriksson Baaz and Stern)—and disproportionately affects women. This type of violence, which is especially prevalent in North America (specifically the United States), is used one-third of the time

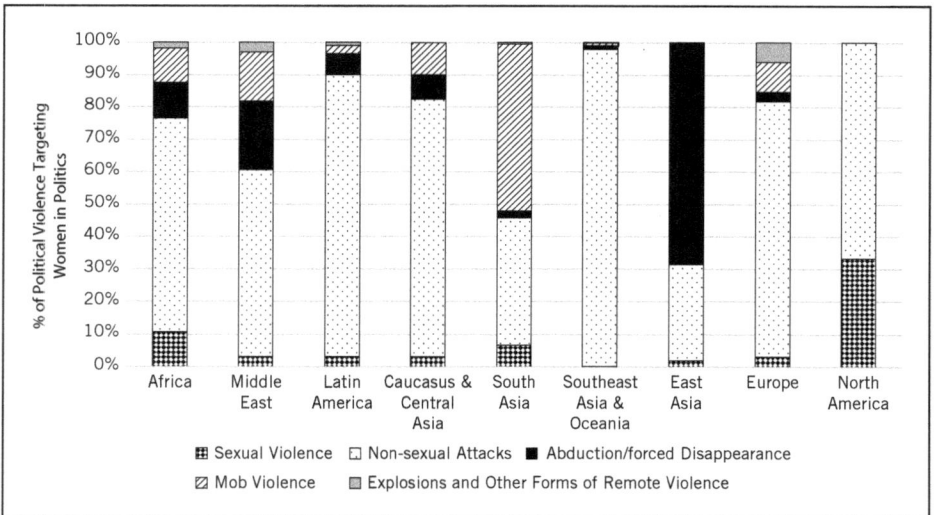

Figure 6.1 Regional variation in physical political violence targeting women in politics by violence type (Source: Armed Conflict Location & Event Data Project [ACLED])

to target women in politics, especially activists. For example, in July 2020, two Black Lives Matter activists were forced to strip by four officers at a correctional center in the United States after the officers learned that the women were transgender (Guirola 2020; Ceballos 2021). This differs from broader trends in the prevalence of sexual violence targeting women, which is disproportionately common in Africa and in Southeast Asia and Oceania.

Despite sexual violence often dominating discussions around physical violence against women, physical *attacks* of a nonsexual nature are the most prevalent form of political violence targeting women in general (Kishi et al. 2019); this trend holds for women in politics in particular as well, used nearly two-thirds of the time in the targeting of such women. Such violence is particularly common in targeting women in politics in Southeast Asia and Oceania, Latin America, and in Central Asia and the Caucasus. In Southeast Asia and Oceania, such violence is especially prevalent in the Philippines, with state forces and anonymous agents targeting opposition politicians and activists. In Latin America, activists in Colombia face heightened risks (Castro et al. 2020), as do nearly all types of women in politics in Mexico, especially at the hands of anonymous armed groups and gangs. In fact, Mexico is consistently home to the most physical political violence targeting women in politics in the world. In Central Asia and the Caucasus, women politicians and government officials face heightened risk in Afghanistan, both at the hands of the Taliban as well as anonymous agents.

Abductions and forced disappearances also disproportionately target women; this is especially the case in East Asia when it comes to women in politics, where it comprises over two-thirds of all such targeting in the region. This trend is driven primarily by the forced disappearance of human rights defenders and activists in China by the Chinese state.

Mob violence involves spontaneously organized mobs engaging in targeted physical violence. This violence is most prevalent in targeting women in politics in South Asia, comprising more than half of all such violence. Such violence is especially common in India, where violent mobs with connections to political parties target all types of women in politics, though especially political party supporters. The same is true also in Bangladesh, where physical violence both within and between political parties is often especially heightened during election periods.

While rarer given that the nature of this violence makes it more difficult to use it in gender-salient targeting, *explosions and other forms of remote violence* can also be used to target women in politics, making up just over 1 percent of all physical political violence targeting women in politics. For example, in February 2020, an IED exploded at the home of a woman member of parliament in Iraq, though it resulted in no reports of damage or casualties (Awla News 2020). Meanwhile, in July 2020, a "fire bomb" was thrown

at the home of an Iranian-Swedish politician in Sweden days after receiving
threats for criticizing the Iranian regime and speaking against honor violence
(Omni 2020; Dagens Nyheter 2020; SVT 2020).

Perpetrators of Physical Political Violence
Targeting Women in Politics

The primary perpetrators, too, of physical political violence targeting women
in politics vary across regions. The data focus on seven types of perpetrators
of this violence, both named actors—such as (1) state forces, (2) rebels, (3)
political militias and gangs, (4) identity militias, and (5) other/external forces—
as well as unnamed actors—such as (6) anonymous or unidentified armed
groups, and (7) violent mobs. While ACLED collects information on the activities of groups, an individual can carry out violence on behalf of a larger
group or movement. So, for example, an attack like the murder of British MP
Jo Cox would indeed be captured, as the individual perpetrating the attack
had far-right political ties.[4] The difference in the prevalence of these perpetrators across different regions is depicted in Figure 6.2.

State forces include groups such as the military and police; these agents
are responsible for large proportions of physical political violence targeting
women in politics in East Asia, where they perpetrate more than four-fifths
of all such violence. As discussed above, such violence often manifests as forced
disappearances targeting human rights defenders and activists.

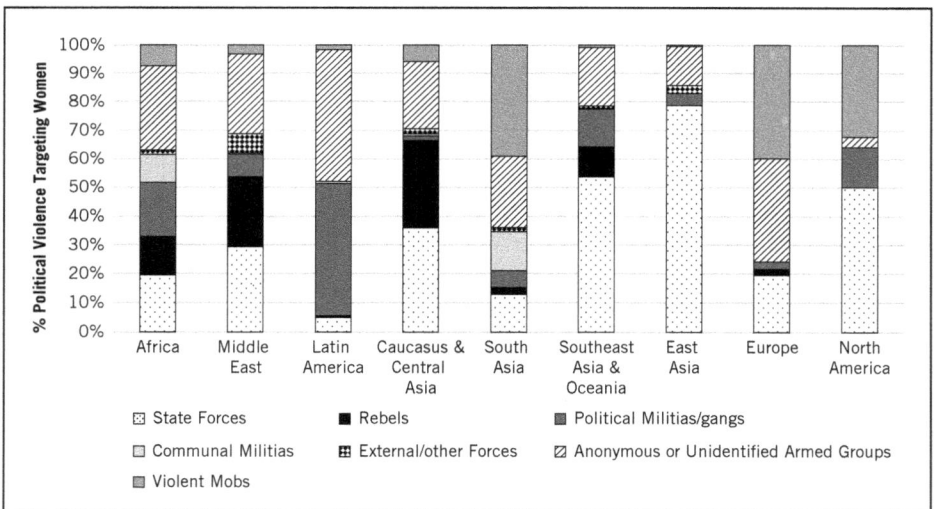

Figure 6.2 Regional variation in physical political violence targeting women in
politics by perpetrator (Source: Armed Conflict Location & Event Data Project [ACLED])

Rebel groups are armed, organized groups with a stated political agenda for national power, either through regime replacement or separatism. These groups are common perpetrators of physical political violence targeting women in politics in Central Asia and the Caucasus, where they are responsible for more than one-quarter of all such violence. This trend is specifically driven by the Taliban in Afghanistan,[5] who are responsible for both nonsexual attacks against women government officials and activists and abductions of women candidates for office and politicians.

Political militias are armed, organized gangs who may act on behalf of political elites. While these groups may be militias that regularly perpetrate political violence on behalf of politicians (e.g., the Imbonerakure in Burundi, the armed wing of the ruling party), they may also be armed gangs that are employed on an ad hoc basis to perpetrate political violence only under certain circumstances (e.g., the Mungiki militias in Kenya, employed by elites primarily around election periods). Criminal *gangs* are also included here under certain contexts; while such gangs may not have overt political ties, they may use violence for overt political goals or to challenge public safety and security (e.g., MS-13 in El Salvador).[6] ACLED also includes "sole perpetrators"—that is, physical violence that is carried out by a single "lone wolf" without an affiliation to a specific named group—in the U.S. context, where such attacks are more common; violence perpetrated by such actors is also included here. These actors (political militias, criminal gangs, and sole perpetrators) are especially active in the United States and Africa, where they make up approximately one-third of physical violence targeting women in politics in each region. For example, in the United States, in July 2020, a man, posing as a deliveryman, shot the family members of a woman U.S. district judge, killing her son and seriously injuring her husband (Russell 2020). The suspect was a self-described anti-feminist and was later found dead from a self-inflicted gunshot wound (Pantaleo and Chute 2020). In Africa, such violence is especially common in Burundi, where it is often carried out as nonsexual attacks by the pro-government Imbonerakure; as well as in Zimbabwe, where it is often perpetrated by militias associated with political parties, like the ZANU-PF, who engage in often nonsexual attacks, especially around contentious periods like election cycles.

Identity militias are armed groups that are organized around a collective, common feature, including community, ethnicity, region, religion, or, in exceptional cases, livelihood; these violent groups often act locally in the pursuance of local goals, resources, power, security, and retribution. Such groups are responsible for 5 percent of all physical political violence targeting women around the world and less than 2 percent of all physical political violence targeting women in politics specifically. Such actors are often more active in the "periphery" and are far more removed from engagement in the national political arena (Raleigh 2014), so such low rates of involvement in the targeting of women in politics is no surprise.

External or other forces refer to actors such as: state forces active outside of their home country, multilateral coalitions, and private security forces. Such groups are not very active in the targeting of women, including the targeting of women in politics too. Such perpetrators make up about 3 percent of all physical political violence targeting women in politics in East Asia, where such violence occurs in China at the hands of private security forces acting on behalf of the government, targeting activists and human rights defenders.

Mobs can have links to political parties or religious groups, or they can be vigilante groups taking what they perceive to be justice into their own hands. These groups are especially active in South Asia, where they are responsible for more than half of all physical political violence targeting women in politics in the region. As described in the last section, such violence is common in India especially, as well as in Bangladesh, targeting all types of women in politics, though especially political party supporters.

Anonymous or unidentified armed groups are the primary perpetrators of physical political violence targeting women in politics; about one-third of all such violence has been perpetrated by such agents, and they represent the primary threat to women in nearly all regions of the world. These agents can be unknown due to insufficiently detailed reporting or as a result of strategic anonymity—doing the bidding of others who have "outsourced" violence to them (Kishi 2015). These groups are responsible for nearly three-quarters of all such violence in Latin America as well as in Europe. In Latin America, such agents are often known to be members of criminal gangs,[7] with activists, human right defenders, and social leaders most often the targets of this violence. In Europe, this violence most often manifests as nonsexual attacks, occurring in a wide variety of countries. For example, in August 2019, unknown individuals sabotaged the brakes of the car belonging to a mayor in Moldova, causing her to have an accident in which she broke a leg (Moldova .org 2019).

Conclusion

Women face a continuum of violations; physical violence is a subset of that continuum that has been narrowly explored, with foci often being on physical sexual violence during wartime. There has been a need for a more nuanced and substantiated understanding of physical political violence targeting women in politics, which is what ACLED data presented in this chapter strive to do. The variance in the types, perpetrators, and targets of physical political violence targeting women in politics across geographic space points to the importance of understanding that one size will not fit all when it comes to specific policy recommendations to confront this violence (Kishi and Olsson 2019, 2022).

While these data from ACLED present an important step toward having a more complete picture of the physical threats and risks to women in politics around the world, the picture is not yet complete, so to speak. Users should consider the factors below[8] to couch the conclusions they draw from the data.[9]

Firstly, users should remember that women face violence beyond political violence alone. Domestic, interpersonal, or intimate partner violence is not included within ACLED's mandate. Personal physical violence, however, significantly impacts the lives of women around the world (Stark and Ager 2011; UNODC 2018; WHO 2017). Further, women are also the targets of violence beyond that which is physical[10] in nature; intimidation and psychological threats, such as online violence, extend beyond ACLED's mandate and are covered elsewhere in this book. This type of harassment can indeed play a crucial role in thwarting women's political participation through fear (IPU 2016; Amnesty International 2018; IFES 2019; NDI 2018b). In short, the total sum of violence (broadly defined) that women face stretches far beyond the subset of violence captured in the data by ACLED.

Secondly, coverage of the data is also limited to the temporal coverage of the ACLED dataset, which varies and is nonuniform. ACLED began as an African data project, and hence data covering the African continent span back the farthest (to 1997). Since then, other regional expansions have taken place, with each expansion extending back only as far as funding resources have allowed. It is imperative to keep this in mind when reviewing trends across regions over time so as not to introduce an artificial spike into the data with the introduction of new regions into the timeline.[11] For the latest information on ACLED's temporal coverage by region, see the ACLED website.

Thirdly, the ACLED data capture physical political violence *targeting* women in politics—by definition, this includes cases in which women are the *victims* of physical violence. But women, as political actors, can of course also be *perpetrators* of physical violence. While reporting will often note the gender of victims (which is what is used by ACLED to capture trends in physical political violence targeting women in politics), the gender makeup of armed groups (and often many other details, too, of armed groups) is not often noted and so could not be collected systematically as part of event data collection by ACLED.[12] The role of women as political actors should hence not be reduced to the subset of physical violence captured by ACLED, which focuses on women as the targets of violence explicitly.

7

Psychological Violence

PÄR ZETTERBERG AND ELIN BJARNEGÅRD

This chapter addresses psychological violence—a type of violence that is nonphysical in nature, but that may have causes and consequences similar to those of physical violence (see, e.g., Bardall, Bjarnegård, and Piscopo 2020). Psychological violence differs from physical violence in that it aims to cause emotional rather than bodily harm. For example, perpetrators may use psychological violence, such as threats, to inflict fear in the victim. In politics, many actors—elected representatives, candidates, voters, etc.—are (potential) victims of psychological violence. In our empirical illustrations below, we zoom in on one of these actor categories: political candidates.

By placing psychological violence on a continuum of violence, we can elaborate on its distinct gendered features. Doing so is important, for various reasons: First, until recently, research on gender and political violence has mainly focused on physical violence—particularly in wartime situations. Research has shown that women are less likely to experience deadly violence—on the battlefield and as civilians—during armed conflict (Bjarnegård et al. 2015; Goldstein 2001). On the other hand, research on violence outside the political sphere has shown that women are more likely than men to experience different forms of psychological violence, such as harassment, threats, libel, etc. (Kellermann and Mercy 1992; Tjaden and Thoennes 2000). Thus, to obtain a more comprehensive picture of the political violence that women and men experience, it is important to look at psychological violence as well. Second, men and women seem to experience violence in partly different settings. Putting it simply, men are more often attacked (physically and psychologically) in the public sphere, whereas women are commonly targeted in the private sphere. This means that men's experiences are more often publicly observable, whereas women's experiences of violence tend to remain private and unseen. Thus, conducting research on and identifying violent psychological attacks require different empirical approaches compared to research on physical violence, which commonly relies on event-based approaches using newspaper data, observation reports, etc. (see Kishi's chapter in this volume).

This chapter addresses these issues, first, by conceptualizing psychological violence and discussing its gendered features and, second, by elaborating on how this type of violence could be empirically analyzed. Finally, we look briefly at psychological violence targeting men and women candidates in two neighboring South Asian countries: the Maldives and Sri Lanka. We suggest that the context needs to be considered when trying to understand and assess men's and women's vulnerability to psychological violence, in general, and gendered forms of psychological violence, in particular.

Conceptualizing Psychological Violence

Violence is an essentially contested concept. Various fields and bodies of literature have defined violence in different ways. One main controversy concerns whether violence should be restricted to physical violence (i.e., a minimalist definition) or whether it should rather be characterized as a multidimensional concept (DeKeseredy 2000; Kilpatrick 2004). As mentioned in Chapter 1, we draw on the work of scholars who employ a broader definition and place different forms of violence along a continuum of violence. From this perspective, it is important to complement a focus on physical violence (which is brought up in Kishi's and Kreft and Nagel's chapters in this volume) with a focus on the other end of the continuum: psychological violence.

Psychological forms of violence have been included in various scholarly definitions of violence—both within and outside the political sphere. Within the political sphere, for instance, research on election violence has included in its conceptualization of violence nonphysical acts such as harassment, intimidation, and threats (Fischer 2002; Höglund 2009). This body of research has often focused on organized forms of psychological (and physical) violence that political leaders use strategically as a means to achieve electoral ends (Birch, Daxecker, and Höglund 2020). Similarly, the bodies of literature on interpersonal violence, intimate partner violence, and violence against women have emphasized the emotional harm perpetrators cause their victims through different forms of nonphysical violence, such as threats and stalking. While it is very difficult to measure and compare levels of pain, many victims perceive certain psychological acts of violence to be as painful as (or even more painful than) certain physical forms of violence because these acts inflict trauma on individuals' mental state (Krook 2020). Ill mental health can be long-lasting and sometimes takes longer to heal than physical wounds. Psychological abuse can also cause physical harm (just as physical harm can have psychological consequences). In addition, physical and psychological violence frequently go together (DeKeseredy 2000). Thus, it is important to emphasize that psychological violence should not be characterized as a "milder" form of violence than physical violence. Rather, as suggested in Chapter 1 and elsewhere (see also Boyle 2019b; Kelly 1987), they should be seen as different violent manifestations along a continuum.

As indicated above, psychological violence includes a range of acts, and different studies have emphasized different acts. To give an example, Bardall (2011) distinguishes between five types of (social-)psychological violence in her pioneering study on gender and election violence: psychological intimidation, social sanctions and punishment, familial pressure, child abuse, and domestic violence. What all these types have in common is that they, broadly speaking, focus on means of control. Psychological intimidation refers to acts such as degrading talk or terrorizing of a political actor (such as a candidate). Social sanctions and punishment refers to acts such as systematic ridicule, exclusion, and shaming. Familial pressure, child abuse, and domestic violence are, in an electoral context, specific forms of intimidation, as they attempt to put pressure on family members to support a specific party or candidate or to prevent family members from voting. Other studies, focusing specifically on violence targeting elected representatives or political candidates, emphasize acts such as different kinds of threats, libel, degrading talk, uninvited behavior, verbal contact, and photographing (e.g., Håkansson in this volume; Thomas and Herrick in this volume; Bjarnegård, Håkansson, and Zetterberg 2022).

As societies have become more digitalized, the arenas in which different acts of psychological political violence take place have changed. Previously, most discussions about where psychological violence takes place focused on the public sphere (political rallies, the streets, parliament, etc.) and on the private sphere (households, etc.). However, as discussed in Esposito's chapter in this volume, and as empirically shown in the chapters by Håkansson, Collignon, Kuperberg, and Thomas and Herrick, a substantial amount of psychological violence has moved online, for instance, to social media platforms such as Facebook and Twitter. In fact, threats or intimidation on social media constitute the most commonly experienced acts of psychological violence among political candidates in the United Kingdom (Collignon in this volume), local elected representatives in Sweden (Håkansson in this volume), and state senators and mayors in the United States (Thomas and Herrick in this volume).

Gender and Psychological Violence

Given the fact that psychological violence is such a widespread form of political violence, an important question is whether there are any gender differences in exposure to this form of violence. In research on wartime violence,
psychological aspects such as traumatization and stigmatization have largely been connected to conflict-related experiences of physical and sexual violence (Brounéus 2010; Edström et al. 2016; Koos 2018). Researchers have been
paying increased attention to this issue in non- or postconflict situations. For
instance, Bardall (2011) analyzes electoral violence in six countries in Africa
and Asia, revealing that women are more exposed to psychological violence
than men are. The largest group of targets is political parties' candidates and
their supporters, followed by voters. Scholars working on the Global North
have also found gender differences. Among elected representatives in countries such as the United States (Thomas and Herrick in this volume) and Sweden (Håkansson in this volume), women are more exposed than men are to
this type of violence. Overall, psychological violence is the most common type
of political violence among women (Bardall 2011; Krook 2020).

There is a difference not only in the prevalence rates of psychological violence between men and women, but also in the type of act they are targeted
with. For instance, Krook (2020) shows how women politicians are being targeted with rape threats—often online—in an attempt to instill fear in and
disempower them. Thomas and Herrick (in this volume) add to that picture
by showing that women politicians in the United States are more exposed to
online psychological violence (such as disrespectful images) than are men
politicians. In addition, Håkansson (this volume) finds that women in local
bodies in Sweden are more likely to be targets of harassment and threats than
men in similar positions are. Below, we nuance this picture by discussing the
role of context in understanding the manifestations of psychological violence
targeting men and women.

When employing a gender perspective on psychological violence (and on
political violence in general), one contested issue is whether perpetrators target men and women for different reasons. In other words, is there a difference in the motive for the attack? This question is discussed in Part 1 of this
volume. Krook's chapter on violence against women in politics emphasizes
violence that women in politics experience because they are women. This is
a type of violence in the political sphere that stems from gender bias, misogyny, and discrimination and that aims to drive women as a group out of the
political realm. In other words, a gendered motive is embedded in the concept of violence against women in politics. Piscopo and Bjarnegård, on the
other hand, argue in their chapter that while it is theoretically important to

single out violence that women experience for gendered reasons, it is in practice difficult to establish such a gender bias and differentiate it from other motives.

Analyzing Gender and Psychological Violence

The challenge of establishing a gender bias brings us to a discussion about empirically analyzing gender and psychological violence. As indicated in Kishi's chapter in this volume, research on *physical* violence—especially in conflict situations—has been active in complementing case study research with large-scale cross-national datasets containing incidents of physical political violence. Kishi presents new data from ACLED (the Armed Conflict Location & Event Data Project). Other similar datasets, but with a specific focus on election violence, include the Countries at Risk of Electoral Violence dataset (Birch and Muchlinski 2017a) and the Electoral Contention and Violence (ECAV) dataset (Daxecker, Amicarelli, and Jung 2019). These event-based datasets usually collect information from several sources, such as traditional media sources (e.g., newspaper articles), observation reports, and trusted social media accounts.

The established data collection strategies for researching physical violence are not always suited to analyzing psychological violence. One challenge is that this type of violence does not necessarily take place in the public sphere. In addition, victims rarely speak out about it, partly because many political actors believe that tolerating a certain level of intimidation is simply part of the job. To circumvent the limitations of event-based data, scholars wishing to measure psychological violence have looked for alternative sources of data. One clear trend is to make use of self-reported data gathered through interviews and/or surveys. This research strategy explicitly addresses the challenge of underreporting by asking political actors (e.g., elected representatives, candidates, and voters) about whether they have been victims of different types of psychological (and commonly also physical) violence. Thus, the focus has been on the victims and their exposure to, and experiences of, psychological violence.

One advantage of conducting (semistructured) interviews is that they have good internal validity: they capture the nuances by focusing on the narratives of victims and thus on the victims' lived experiences. This helps researchers better understand what victims perceive as violence, including the range of acts of psychological violence that victims are exposed to. In addition, interviews give opportunities to ask follow-up questions, thus allowing researchers to gain a deeper understanding of how victims perceived the attack, the type of harm it caused, and the potential impact it had on the victim, etc. This testimonial approach has been popular in early work on violence against women in politics (see, e.g., Albaine 2016). It has helped researchers—as well as women's groups—call attention to a specific type of (gender-based) violence that women confront in politics and that was not previously characterized as a political problem (see Krook in this volume). In addition, and for the same reasons, semistructured interviews have been popular as complements to surveys (see, e.g., Haley and Baker as well as Schneider in this volume).

However, one limitation associated with (semistructured) interviews is that they are not well suited to analyzing prevalence rates, and gender differences, in a larger population. Large-scale survey data can be employed to address this limitation. The past few years have seen a rapid increase—from low levels—of survey data on violence against elected representatives or candidates in multiple settings, such as the United States, Sweden, the United Kingdom, and Uganda (see chapters by Thomas and Herrick, Håkansson, Collignon, and Schneider in this volume). Thus, there has been a recent surge in this direction.

However, event-based approaches are used in some types of analyses on psychological violence, namely, those examining psychological violence that takes place online. These approaches use machine learning, or manually conducted content analysis (see also Kuperberg in this volume), to identify acts of online psychological violence (such as threats, libel, etc.). Whereas manual coding is suited to smaller samples, machine-learning techniques enable analysis of a very large number of tweets or posts. One advantage of these approaches (in relation to interviews or surveys) is that researchers can define a priori what qualifies as political violence, thus reducing the risk that an act of nonpolitical violence will be wrongfully counted as political violence (or vice versa).

Another strategy suggested in the literature is a bias event approach (see Krook in this volume). This strategy attempts to address a specific challenge in the literature: the identification of gendered motives in research on violence against women in politics. This approach draws on the literature on hate crimes to establish the presence of gender bias in the political sphere. To determine whether gender bias is part of the reason for a violent attack, Krook suggests that scholars include a bias event approach in an event-based analysis by posing follow-up questions to the data (e.g., about the context of the incident, the actors involved, etc.). Alternatively, surveys and interviews could integrate the approach into the design of questionnaires, for instance by inviting respondents to give examples, which researchers could then analyze from a bias event perspective.

Finally, a few words should be mentioned about a research strategy that has not received much attention in research on gender and political violence but that has become increasingly popular in political science and international relations: survey experiments. Survey experiments could be potentially useful in this literature, which deals with a sensitive issue such as gendered violence in politics. Respondents may not want to provide the details of the intimidation they have experienced, for instance, in cases where it is sexual in nature. In such cases, survey techniques in the form of list experiments may be useful strategies. List experiments typically include questioning techniques in which individual responses to sensitive questions are not directly revealed (Blair, Imai, and Lyall 2014). Thus, we encourage researchers to consider using survey experiments in future work on gender and political violence.

An Illustration: Gender and Election Violence in South Asia

Hitherto in the chapter, we have presented some of the conceptual and methodological challenges associated with analyzing gender and psychological violence against political actors. In this last section of the chapter, we illustrate these challenges through research we have conducted on election violence targeting political candidates in two neighboring island states in South Asia: the Maldives (Bjarnegård 2021) and Sri Lanka (Bjarnegård, Håkansson, and Zetterberg 2022).

Theoretical Issues

Starting with theoretical issues, one conceptual challenge concerns what counts as psychological violence as well as what types of psychological violence should be included in an empirical analysis. While we acknowledge that psychological violence in the context of election violence can include a large number of acts (as exemplified by Bardall 2011), we decided to include only a limited number of acts, such as threats (see, e.g., chapters by Schneider, Håkansson, Collignon, and Thomas and Herrick in this volume), libel, and degrading talk. These types of psychological violence are well suited to an analysis of political candidates, whereas other types, such as social sanctions, are better suited to an analysis of voter intimidation (see, e.g., Haley and Baker in this volume).

Another challenge is theorizing the motives for using psychological violence on men and women candidates and whether the reasons differ for the two groups. On the one hand, a focus on election violence implies, by definition, a focus on politically motivated violence. On the other, as suggested by Krook (this volume), women in politics may also be targets of violence because they are women. In the case of election violence, this means that perpetrators may be attacking women to push them out of not only elections, but also out of politics as such. However, Piscopo and Bjarnegård (this volume) emphasize that capturing intentions and motives is inherently difficult. Thus, any gender differences found in men's and women's experiences of psychological election violence do not necessarily mean that the violence is gender motivated.

To address this issue, and thus understand what political gender motives may look like, we compared gender patterns of election violence in the Maldives and Sri Lanka. We suggest that the extent to which gender is politicized in a given context will affect whether women are primarily targeted *as women* or *as politicians*. A comparison between the two countries illustrates how gender roles are highly politicized and sensitive in the Maldives, but less prominent in the political debate in Sri Lanka, and how this seems to affect the violence and intimidation that candidates face. Even though religion plays an important role in both electoral contests (with Islam being the mandated state religion of the Maldives, and Buddhism being embraced by the majority of the population in Sri Lanka), gender is a more salient feature of the discussion on religion in the Maldives than it is in Sri Lanka.

Methodological Issues

When considering the methodological challenges associated with analyzing gender and psychological violence, the first such challenge concerns the number of cases to analyze. We believe that a comparison between two contentious elections in the Maldives and Sri Lanka highlights the need for a comparative agenda on gender and election violence. Such comparisons help us discern the different roles that gender can play in politics. To reiterate, we can distinguish between a context in which women are clearly targeted *as women* and where gender roles are highly politicized—the Maldives—and a context in which gender roles are not as central to the postconflict political debate—Sri Lanka. These differences are interesting, as the countries in other respects share some characteristics, such as low levels of women's political representation and relatively high levels of election violence (for a more thorough presentation of each of the country cases, see Bjarnegård 2021, and Bjarnegård, Håkansson, and Zetterberg 2022).

The second challenge concerns which political actors to analyze. In elections, various important actors are involved in the process: candidates, campaign workers, party supporters, voters, etc. While analyses that use public incidents of election violence as the starting point commonly include voters and party supporters as victims (Hafner-Burton, Hyde, and Jablonski 2014; von Borzyskowski and Kuhn 2020), we chose to focus on political candidates, who are obvious targets of election violence. Violent activities are often perpetrated to prevent candidates from actually standing for election or to stop them from campaigning. Importantly, we focused on the experiences of women *and* men. If research on incidents of election violence has unintentionally excluded the experiences of women, research on women in politics has sometimes rather intentionally excluded the experiences of men. What is needed to assess to what extent election violence is gendered is an explicit comparison between men and women, including victims and nonvictims as well as winning and losing candidates.

The third and final challenge we wish to address here concerns choosing the methodology to use as well as strategies for data collection. One possible methodology is to analyze reports of public incidents and pay explicit attention to incidents where candidates are among the victims. We believe such a strategy would give us a partial picture. For instance, when we analyzed public incidents in the preelection stage of the 2018 local election process in Sri Lanka, we found that there were women candidates who had received death threats just outside their house, while men candidates had received such threats at marketplaces, etc. (Centre for Monitoring Election Violence 2018). Thus, we saw that women were attacked closer to their private sphere than men were, which is in accordance with research showing that women are more often targeted in their homes than men are. However, we argue that reports of public incidents exclude a great deal of nuance and important information. For instance, in the Sri Lankan case, the main form of psychological violence included in these reports was the death threat. We know that other forms of psychological violence can be just as effective as death threats. Therefore, in both countries, we opted for a research strategy that would allow us to analyze various manifestations of psychological violence: small-scale surveys targeting candidates coupled with interviews with a sample of the surveyed candidates.

The survey method is useful for gaining access to a larger sample of candidates than we would be able to include in an interview study while focusing on individual experiences, which would be impossible in an incident study. Our experience from the two studies is that surveys provide reliable answers. Politicians have a vested interest in telling us their stories. Researchers have often expressed surprise at how willing candidates are to share the problems they have encountered. However, politicians want to point out flaws in the system, particularly flaws they feel have disadvantaged their own political campaign. For women experiencing unequal treatment, contributing to research is also a way of getting these issues on the agenda. On the other hand, the anonymity that a survey can offer can also be seen as security in a context of violence and intimidation. Research on sensitive issues such as intimate partner violence and rape in the Asia Pacific has suggested using self-administered surveys to address sensitive questions (Fulu et al. 2013a; Fulu et al. 2013b). People tend to answer more honestly when they are not asked questions by another person, but they feel they can give their responses while remaining anonymous.

Regarding the data, collecting separate data for a project is both advantageous and disadvantageous. One advantage is that it gives the researchers some control over the data collection process—the survey questions included. One disadvantage is that data collection is costly and time-consuming. In our case, we did not have the financial resources to contract a polling firm to collect the data. Thus, we used a strategy that relied on collaboration with an international organization working on electoral support: the International Foundation for Electoral Systems (IFES). When collecting data in both countries, first in the Maldives (April 2015) and then in Sri Lanka (June 2018), we received ample support and advice from each of the two country offices. This collaboration was useful for many reasons. First, the credibility of IFES and its large local networks made it easier for us to identify and access our respondents as well as to credibly carry out the project without being previously known. Second, the comments from local staff were invaluable for elaborating on the questionnaire and for making sure the survey questions as well as the accompanying interview questions were formulated in appropriate and intelligible ways. The assistance from local staff also included a process of initial translation of the questionnaire from English to the local language, as well as an independent back-translation to English, pilot surveys, and then a final revision of the local language version. This was done to ensure, to the greatest extent possible, that the questionnaire was culturally suitable and that there were few opportunities to misinterpret the questions asked. Finally, our collaboration can also be of importance to the organization. As researchers, we can design data collection and analyses in a manner that can generate useful and evidence-based knowledge about the very issues these organizations are working with. A close collaboration between researchers and practitioners also makes it more likely that the results will be relevant and followed up on in future activities. As a researcher, it is problematic when you enter a context, raise (potentially traumatic) issues, and then walk out. While we can certainly work to ensure a better continued presence, it is difficult to take responsibility for maintaining long-term work. Collaboration with locally established organizations alleviates these problems. As long as our findings are relevant to these organizations, they will use their new knowledge in designing and implementing their future activities.

One specific challenge associated with data collection in comparative studies concerns how to deal with the lessons learned in one context when designing a study in another context. Obviously, we learned a great deal in the Maldives that was useful for the Sri Lankan study we conducted three years later. Thus, there was a fine balance between using lessons learned to improve the Sri Lankan study and maintaining the comparative aspect. We decided to adapt our survey questionnaire to the respective contexts. More specifically, we included a fairly large number of questions in Sri Lanka that we failed to ask in the Maldives. To enable a comparison, we concentrated one analysis to questions that were similar or identical in the different cases. This enabled us to compare three manifestations of psychological violence: libel, threats, and sexualized psychological violence (rumors, degrading talk, rape threats, etc.). For instance, the questionnaires included questions such as, "Have you experienced *threats* meant to dissuade you from running in the election, prevent you from campaigning efficiently or to decrease your chances of winning?" Thus, we explicitly mentioned a variety of forms of psychological violence so that we could properly document them. This strategy was important because even experts on the issue of election violence disagree on what to include in the definitions, meaning that it was safe to assume that political candidates would not all interpret the meaning of a more general formulation of election violence in the same way. How the questions are interpreted also depends on the context and political climate in which the candidates operate. Where election violence is widespread and normalized, even specific questions about whether the candidate had experienced threats may not result in an affirmative answer. In the Maldives, some candidates commented on the survey after having taken it, saying that they did not consider it relevant to note that they had been threatened because this was nothing out of the ordinary. Instead, they said it happens all the time in politics. Thus, learning from this experience, we explicitly encouraged candidates in Sri Lanka to record everyday experiences as well.

Conclusion: Some Lessons Learned

Let us conclude the chapter by sharing some main findings and lessons learned from this illustrative comparative case study (for a comprehensive presentation of the results of the respective cases, see Bjarnegård 2021 on the Maldives; and Bjarnegård, Håkansson, and Zetterberg 2022 on Sri Lanka). One overall discernible pattern is that women in the Maldives are disproportionately affected by psychological violence, particularly threats and sexual harassment. In Sri Lanka, there are fewer clear gender differences in the reported experiences. Taking a gender perspective and including psychological forms of violence are thus important strategies for understanding the situation of women (and men) candidates in either of the contexts, but in the Maldives, being a woman candidate seems to entail being more vulnerable to violence, which is not necessarily the case in Sri Lanka.

One important distinction is the extent to which candidates are targeted for their politics or as a private person. In the Maldives, the debate about gender roles and the perceived dangers of globalization have come to blur the boundaries between the public and the private: criticizing women's lifestyles in derogatory ways is part of the political debate in the Maldives. Interview data show that rumors were often spread with a view to questioning the morality or the private lives of women candidates rather than their political standpoints.

Another important lesson learned from the Maldives is the importance of focusing on online election violence attacks (see also Esposito's chapter and Kuperberg's chapter in this volume). In the Maldives, women candidates were more aggressively attacked online during the campaign—and the attacks were more often sexual in nature—as compared to the negative online experiences of Sri Lankan women candidates. The rumors that were spread online in the Maldives demonstrate a strong trend of attacking women's morality by suggesting that they have sexual affairs, often using techniques such as photoshopping.

More broadly speaking, these differences between the two cases highlight the benefit of using a research design that is suited to comparative analysis, that captures a variety of manifestations of psychological violence, and that includes a broad range of candidates (both men and women, both victims and nonvictims, and both winning and losing candidates). By using a comparative approach, researchers can identify the extent to which gender differences in election violence are context specific. They may also be able to address the question of *why* there are distinct gender patterns in different contexts. In our case, we tentatively suggest that the role of religion may (partly) explain the observed differences between the Maldives and Sri Lanka. While religion in Sri Lanka seems to play a role in the postconflict context, religion in the Maldives has come to concern gender roles. This means that violence may be more gender motivated and involve gendered forms in the Maldives, while the violence that women candidates in Sri Lanka face is generally quite similar to that experienced by their male colleagues. A broader research agenda on gender and psychological violence should look more closely at contextual differences, thus enabling a better understanding of men's and women's experiences of psychological violence in a variety of empirical settings. Given that the analyzed elections in our two case study countries did not occur at the same level of government, such an agenda should also consider the possibility that gender differences are greater—and women more exposed—at higher levels of government (see also Håkansson in this volume). Finally, this chapter has shown that such an agenda will also have to include various manifestations of psychological violence (including psychological violence of a sexual nature), target different kinds of political actors (e.g., women and men candidates at both the national and local levels), and concern different sites (online, at public events, or in the private sphere).

8

Sexual Violence

Anne-Kathrin Kreft and Robert U. Nagel

This chapter introduces the concept of sexual violence with a focus on conflict settings. We deviate somewhat from the definition of political violence advanced in the Introduction in that we focus not on violence *against* political actors, but on violence perpetrated *by* a subset of political actors (state militaries, nonstate armed groups, paramilitary forces, or armed gangs) against civilians. Conflict-related sexual violence (CRSV) is political because it can be used strategically in pursuit of conflict goals and because it (re)asserts gendered power structures permeating societies, as discussed in the Introduction and outlined below. In this chapter, the focus is on sexual violence against women (Eriksson Baaz and Stern discuss CRSV against men in Chapter 4).

With respect to the continuum of violence discussed in the Introduction, we engage here primarily with coerced sexual acts and encroachments on individuals' sexual or reproductive autonomy that are *physical* in nature (for psychological violence of a sexual nature, see Chapter 7). In doing so, we follow the established definition of CRSV in the academic literature as well as in policy circles. However, throughout the chapter, we also highlight how CRSV has distinct psychological dimensions in drawing on preexisting gendered fears and entrenching gendered relationships of power and subordination, thus demonstrating how CRSV has diverse impacts on the psychological-physical continuum of violence. We organize this chapter into four sections, in which we discuss the concept of CRSV, its place on the continuum of violence, its gendered and political nature, and some of the methodological considerations of researching CRSV. Throughout the chapter, we rely on the empirical case illustration of Colombia, based on interviews carried out in 2017 and 2018 with women civil society activists (Kreft 2019, 2020).

What Is Conflict-Related Sexual Violence?

We understand sexual violence as a distinctly gendered form of political violence, in terms of how this violence is perpetrated, how it is anchored in social and structural conditions, and what this violence signifies to the victims and perpetrators (for a perspective that is more critical of understanding sexual violence as a gendered violence grounded in heteronormative norms, see Eriksson Baaz and Stern in Chapter 4).

The standard definition of CRSV denotes it as a physical assault on an individual's sexual or reproductive autonomy through the use or threat of force by an armed actor, that is, members of state forces (e.g., military, police, and paramilitary organizations) and nonstate groups (e.g., rebel groups, progovernment militia, and/or vigilante groups) in the context of an armed conflict. CRSV can take many different forms. The International Criminal Court lists five forms of sexual violence as crimes against humanity: rape, sexual slavery, forced prostitution, forced pregnancy, forced sterilization, and forced abortion (International Criminal Court 2011). Building on these five forms, the most comprehensive cross-national quantitative data collection effort of CRSV—the Sexual Violence in Armed Conflict dataset (Cohen and Nordås 2014)—records a total of seven forms, adding sexual mutilation and sexual torture based on work by Elizabeth Wood (2009). The threat of rape or other forms of sexual violence is usually excluded (for an example that includes threats of rape, see Schulz 2020).

CRSV on the Continuum(s) of Violence

As is the case for violence against women in politics (see Chapter 1 by Bjarnegård and Zetterberg), sexual violence is violence that targets women *as women*: "What can happen to one woman can also happen to you and generate a situation of horror." (For more expansive discussions, see Piscopo and Bjarnegård in Chapter 5 and Kishi in Chapter 6.) Armed actors often perpetrate sexual violence because it communicates gendered power and dominance (Alison 2007). It draws on and entrenches existing fears. The result is a distinctly *gendered fear* of sexual violence, that is, of a violent manifestation of masculine power over women. One interviewee suggested, "The risk is not the same for men. That is not to say that men do not get raped, [but] it is not the same . . . belonging to a collective that holds power as belonging to a collective that exists in a relationship of subordination and oppression."

This performative violence thus works across the psychological-physical continuum to subordinate those perceived as female/feminine. How sexual violence is feared, understood, and anticipated depends on the social relationships and gendered hierarchies that exist in society, and it shapes also how women in private and public spaces relate to men (Sjoberg 2016). This is where sexual violence generally, and CRSV specifically, emerges as a form of violence that, by virtue of its gendered nature, assumes *social and political significance*. Sexual violence simultaneously emerges from and upholds patriarchal power relations—it is a political form of violence playing out in a context of gendered power imbalances.

CRSV as a physical form of harm is inseparable from its psychological harms. Humans' perception of identity and self are inherently intertwined with our physical bodies, which is why certain forms of violence, like CRSV or torture, attack the body and "[destroy] a person's self" (Scarry 1985, 35). The intimate nature of CRSV exacerbates these damaging effects. As Agger and Jensen explain regarding sexual torture: "The victim experiences the torture as directed against his or her sexual body image and identity with the aim to destroy it. Thus, the essential part of sexual torture's traumatic and identity-damaging effect is the feeling of being an accomplice in an ambiguous situation which contains both aggressive and libidinal elements of confusing nature" (1993, 687). The psychological harm is also not always limited to the direct victim. In several conflicts, fighters have forced men at gunpoint to rape or sexually abuse family members (Carpenter 2006, 95). In such cases, victim and perpetrator of the act experience it as torture. As Charli Carpenter emphasizes, "It is likely that such acts are deeply humiliating, violating private space, the sanctity of family relationships, and other cultural norms" (2006, 96). Even if physical wounds heal, the psychological pain often endures (see interviews with survivors in Skjelsbæk 2012).

CRSV has an additional psychological dimension that extends its harm beyond the direct victim. Early on, Ní Aoláin (2000) identified these "connected" harms in situations where armed actors force men to watch as they rape (primarily female) family members. Benard writes about how Serbian fighters intended to demoralize Bosnian men by raping Bosnian women in front of them (1994). Chris Coulter recounts similar connected harms in Sierra Leone. The Revolutionary United Front (RUF) had abducted a young man (John), his mother, and his aunt. RUF fighters raped and abused his mother and aunt in front of John, who "said this all happened in his presence and that it hurt him immensely, but most of all, he said, he was 'shamed' by the sexual violation of his mother in his presence; perhaps also he was ashamed on a more personal level as he could do nothing to protect her" (Coulter 2009, 145). These cases demonstrate that while perpetrators wield the direct physical (and psychological) violence against women and their bodies, perpetrators also intend to hurt men psychologically and emotionally. Carpenter describes this as "rape of women as psychological torture of men" and calls for greater recognition of such trauma (2006, 96).

Besides the psychological-physical continuum of violence, two other continuums of violence are central in the literature on CRSV: one spanning war and not-war and one spanning the public and private spheres (Cockburn 2004; Swaine 2015; Gray 2019). To illustrate, Harriet Gray notes "dividing [sexual and gender-based violence] in conflict spaces into the categories of war and not-war closes down space for recognising how war is (also) enacted within 'private' spaces and through 'private' experiences within warzones—how the 'private' is, itself, a space in which war (also) takes place" (2019, 190). In line with this, research shows that armed conflict and specifically exposure to CRSV increases the risk that women become victims of intimate partner violence even years after a war has formally ended (Østby, Leiby, and Nordås 2019). Other research examining sexual violence by armed actors in years considered postconflict (or not-war) shows that it is associated with a higher likelihood that battle-related violence escalates again, demonstrating that the conflict/postconflict dichotomy is untenable (Nagel 2021a). Several women activists in Colombia evoked these multiple continuums when discussing the patterns and significance of sexual violence.

A recurring notion among civil society activists was that sexual violence is but one—albeit an extreme and especially gendered—manifestation of the devaluation of, and discrimination against, women. It occupies one spot on the continuum that encompasses different types of psychological and physical violence, as elaborated in the Introduction (see Kishi, Chapter 6, for a discussion of other prevalent forms of violence against women). Many of the activists pointed to links between (conflict-related) sexual violence, domestic violence, different forms of violent and coercive control over women's lives (for example, men policing how women dress and whom they can meet), and feminicides. These different forms of violence extend over time and space and, in the perception of many interviewees, characterize the daily, lived experiences of many women. One interviewee summarized this continuum of violence thus:

> All the women in the world, since we are born, at the very moment we are born, we already have the shadow [*sombra*] and the possibility of being victims of violence; in fact, I think that all women at one point will experience it, we are experiencing it or we will experience it at one point in our lives—any type of violence—for the sole reason that we are women.

The existence of many forms of gendered violence along the psychological-physical continuum has prompted Hilary Matfess to call for researchers to pay more attention "to the full spectrum of violence that women face during conflict and the conditions under which this violence takes different forms than violence targeting civilians generally" (2020, 12).

Another frequent theme among Colombian civil society activists was that sexual violence against women preceded the armed conflict in the country, and it will persist after it is resolved because the roots of CRSV are prevailing patterns of violence against women entrenched in society:

> No, I wouldn't say that [sexual violence] is a product of the war. It's the product of a pattern of generalized violence against women that already exists in society and that in the context of war exacerbates, it becomes more evident and it is used a lot more.

War amplifies sexual violence that is already a daily reality for women. This exacerbation of existing violence blurs the lines between war and not-war and also between public and private. One activist, for example, discussed how uncertainty about whether a perpetrator is affiliated with or acting in his capacity as a member of an armed group may leave some cases of sexual violence in the gray area between conflict related and "personal," with complicated implications for legal jurisdiction. CRSV is commonly viewed as a distinctly political form of violence due to its real or assumed political objectives, as Eriksson Baaz and Stern problematize in Chapter 4. Whether an act of sexual violence is classified as CRSV has politico-legal significance for perpetrators (e.g., Is it a war crime?), victims (e.g., Is the victim entitled to redress from the state?), and other (political) actors such as governments and nongovernmental organizations (see Nagel and Kreft's discussion of responses to CRSV in Chapter 18).

Conflict-Related and "Everyday" Sexual Violence: Parallels and Differences

Despite these continuities across war and not-war, the activists also noted the ways in which CRSV is exceptional—as some scholars have emphasized (Cohen and Wood 2016). The parallels and differences between conflict-related and "everyday" sexual violence (i.e., sexual violence not perpetrated by armed actors) fall into four dimensions: logics, prevalence, manifestations, and functions of CRSV (Kreft 2020, 471–74). Being anchored in patriarchy, CRSV and everyday sexual violence share the same *logics* as—in the words of several interviewees—an extreme expression of gender inequality. As one interviewee put it, sexual violence "does not have to do with war, but it has to do with being a woman." This does not mean that women in any way invite, provoke, or are to blame for sexual violence; it means that it is precisely their womanhood that is under attack with the aim to assert masculine power (see Eriksson Baaz and Stern in Chapter 4 for a critical discussion of sexual violence as a gendered violence grounded in heteronormative norms). This assertion of masculine power can be an underlying, subconscious factor—rather than an express objective—in the perpetration of sexual violence, as Krook discusses in the case of bias crime (Chapter 3 in this volume).

Despite shared logics across everyday and conflict-related sexual violence, there are nonetheless distinctions in *prevalence*. In Colombia, sexual violence perpetrated in the private sphere—by intimate partners, other family members or acquaintances—is more prevalent than CRSV, even in the areas affected by the armed conflict (Sanchez et al. 2011). The risk of being victimized in any form of sexual violence certainly increases in conflict-affected territories, due to the accumulated risk of everyday sexual violence and CRSV, but the numbers show a clear preponderance of the former.

Simultaneously, armed conflict and the presence of arms transform the *manifestations* of sexual violence. In the words of some interviewees, war "dehumanizes" the perpetrators, who are prone to commit more cruel forms of violence than they ordinarily would. CRSV is, for example, often exceptional in the frequent perpetration of gang rape, which is less common in everyday sexual violence (Cohen 2016). War also amplifies militarized masculinities; that is, it glorifies what one interviewee called the ideal of the *varón guerrerista*, who expresses his strength and power through embracing violent masculinity. This may result in what Leatherman (2011) refers to as gender polarization, in which sexual violence becomes a "runaway norm" that becomes rampant in a context of impunity. Sexual violence that in the private sphere is primarily hidden now turns outward and becomes more visible.

This visibility of CRSV, then, is closely linked to the distinct political *functions* that CRSV may fulfill. While interviewees insisted that much of the CRSV is a direct continuation of everyday sexual violence, they also pointed to a more instrumental use of sexual violence. Armed actors exploit the gendered fear associated with sexual violence in their pursuit of specific conflict goals. They instrumentalize the domestic, nurturing, and caregiving roles women traditionally play in Colombian families and communities. The activists also mentioned the use of CRSV as a form of punishment for women defying traditional gender roles or engaging in political or civil society activism (compare here the discussions, e.g., by Krook in this volume). An important caveat is that observers often deduce the function of CRSV from perpetration patterns and from the impact this violence has on its victims, while evidence of an articulated strategy or intent by the perpetrating actors is rare. This means that strategic CRSV is likely a lot less prevalent than commonly assumed, as Eriksson Baaz and Stern discuss in Chapter 4.

Regardless of what motive underlies the large-scale perpetration of CRSV, it spreads fear among women and communities, intimidates those who might otherwise challenge the legitimacy of the armed actors, and allows armed groups to maintain territorial control, either by terrorizing women and communities into submission or by displacing them altogether. Ethnicity and race are crucial factors in this, and white supremacy has frequently manifested itself through sexual violence. As Angela Davis noted in 1971 about the role of sexual violence during slavery: "In its political contours, the rape of black women was not exclusively an attack upon her. Indirectly, its target was also the slave community as a whole" (Davis 1971, 12). Part of the mechanism at play, particularly in conflicts, is the targeting of the male opponent and his honor by perpetrating sexual violence against "his women," whom he is unable to protect (Sjoberg and Peet 2011). In other contexts, such as in the wars in former Yugoslavia or with the Rohingya minority in Myanmar, sexual violence targeted at certain communities has been part of ethnic cleansing campaigns (Alison 2007). Besides this "symbolic rape of the body of [the] community" (Seifert 1996, 63), the Colombian women activists also mentioned the use of CRSV as a form of punishment for women defying traditional gender roles or engaging in political or civil society activism (compare here the discussions, e.g., by Krook in this volume).

Sexual Violence, Gender, and the Political

Colombian activists situate CRSV in a patriarchal societal context, that is, in "a system of social structures, and practices in which men dominate, oppress and exploit women" (Walby 1989, 214). As per the interviews, a sense of men's entitlement to women's bodies, the objectification of women and a general sense of women as extensions of, or belonging to, men are commonplace (elaborated more extensively in Kreft 2020). Surveys suggest that such patriarchal norms are widely held in Colombia and other Latin American countries, especially by men but also by women (Ruiz and Sobrino 2018).[1] Rape in intimate partnerships is so common, several women argued, that it is *normalized* and the women who are subjected to it often do not even recognize it as violence but rather as part of conjugal life. This normalization of sexual violence, the activists suggest, then facilitates widespread sexual violence also in the armed conflict: sexual violence that is perpetrated in the private sphere and CRSV perpetrated by armed actors are two sides of the same coin. This is where the gendered nature of sexual violence and its political significance converge.

Figure 8.1 visualizes the cases of CRSV included in the National Registry of Victims (Registro Único de Víctimas). Even though it is plausible to expect that underreporting among men is even higher than among women, due to an even greater stigma (Schulz 2020), the gender-differential trend is

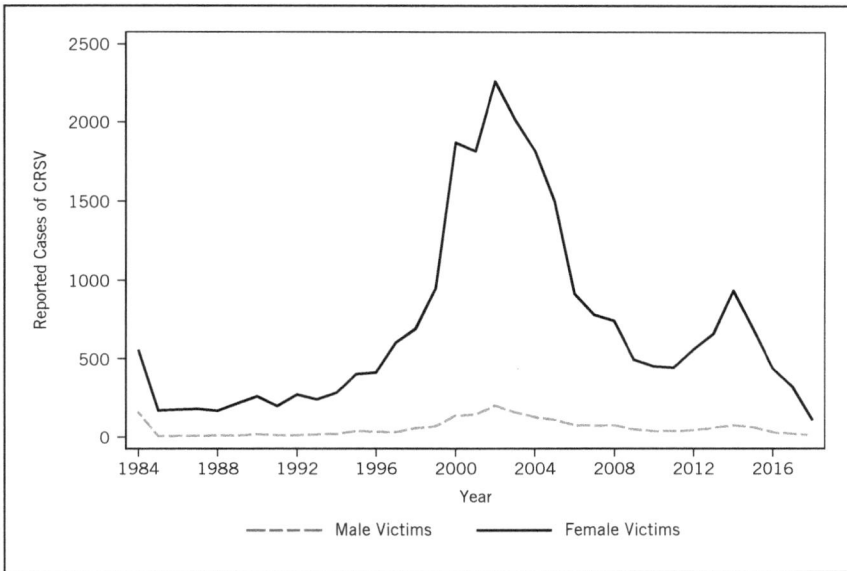

Figure 8.1 Male and female victims of CRSV as registered in the Registro Único de Víctimas (Source: Registro Único de Víctimas)

clear. However, gender is not binary and does not comprise a world divided into men and women. Gender and gendered hierarchies also operate along the axes of sexual orientations and gender identities. Armed actors also perpetrate CRSV against LGBTIQ+ people to assert cis-heteronormativity. Accordingly, several interviewees pointed out that individuals with diverse sexual orientations and gender identities, including trans and nonbinary people, are at heightened risk of being targeted in sexual violence by armed actors.[2] Finally, intersectional identities certainly play a role, with those belonging to minority ethnic groups, having a lower socioeconomic status, or living in rural areas—all those, in other words, furthest removed from the center of (sociopolitical) power—are particularly exposed to sexual violence. That said, no context is exactly like another, and the patterns observable in Colombia are not necessarily universal.

The gendered power imbalances that enable sexual violence are structural. There are men who actively challenge and resist patriarchal norms and practices, just as there are women who perpetuate them. Interviewees mentioned women who do not report or challenge their partners if they perpetrate sexual violence (often, of course, out of fear of repercussions to themselves or their children), women in power who refuse to fight against sexual violence for fear of losing their jobs, women journalists who do not pick up stories on CRSV and sexual violence, or women who uncritically adopt language that legitimizes narratives about women and war. One interviewee, herself a victim of CRSV, made this striking statement:

> Many of us women still have not been able to learn how to speak, when they say, "We are the spoils of war." No, I am not a tank, I am a territory. My body is a territory, which they [the armed actors] entered and invaded without my permission.

Living in a patriarchal context means having been socialized into certain gender roles, and unlearning these is difficult. Another interviewee's critical reflection summarized the struggle: "It is very difficult to get rid of our inner patriarch"—a statement that resonates well beyond Colombia and applies beyond sexual violence. The pervasive nature of patriarchal practices means that individuals are often unaware of them, that they go unquestioned, and that women not only accept them but are unwittingly co-opted into perpetuating them against other women or even their daughters.

Methodological Considerations

Understanding the patterns of how much, how, and when armed actors commit CRSV helps improve prevention and accountability efforts. Jelke Boesten, for example, highlights the efforts of researchers and investigators in truth commissions, UN investigative committees, and elsewhere to provide evidence and estimates of patterns of sexual violence to facilitate understanding who perpetrators and victims might be and why (2017). Quantitative data also help challenge the notion that CRSV is ubiquitous in war.

Dara Cohen and Ragnhild Nordås (2014) created the Sexual Violence in Armed Conflict (SVAC) dataset, which constitutes the most comprehensive data collection to date. The dataset covers all state-based conflicts (inter- and intrastate) in the period from 1989 to 2019. It presents a numerical prevalence score for each armed actor and year: 0, no reports of CRSV; 1, isolated reports of CRSV; 2, reports of widespread CRSV; and 3, reports of systematic CRSV. This approach helps navigate the inherent difficulties in establishing accurate estimates because of biases, stigmatization, and underreporting. The SVAC dataset has enabled researchers to detect and illustrate patterns associated with CRSV as they relate to conflict dynamics, socioeconomic conditions, as well as domestic and international responses (as Nagel and Kreft discuss in Chapter 18).[3]

Cohen and Nordås recognize, despite a clear coding manual, a conservative coding approach, and well-trained and supervised coders, there are limitations and biases inherent in the data, primarily because of underreporting and data collection bias that vary across contexts. Even establishing temporal trends is difficult, as international advocacy and attention has reshaped the information landscape over the last two decades, incentivizing exaggerating accounts of CRSV to drive fundraising and international awareness (Cohen and Hoover Green 2012).

Given the limitations of quantitative data on CRSV, many scholars advocate for and use qualitative methods, usually based on interviews or document analysis. Using qualitative methods allows scholars to move beyond (sanitized) abstractions of numbers into deep description and contextualized narratives. While quantitative studies, too, have contributed to illustrating the links between conflict-related and domestic sexual violence (Østby, Leiby, and Nordås 2019), qualitative methods are particularly fruitful for teasing out the complex, and gendered, sociopolitical contexts in which CRSV occurs (Davies and True 2015; Boesten 2017) and in which ostensible dichotomies between public and private and war and peace become blurred (Swaine 2015; Gray 2019). In addition, qualitative research has provided insight into perpetrator behavior (Eriksson Baaz and Stern 2013; Skjelsbæk 2015; Cohen 2016) and experiences of victims of CRSV (Maedl 2011; Porter 2015; Schulz 2020). Qualitative research thereby often foregrounds the lived experiences of those exposed to sexual violence.

Much of the qualitative research on CRSV relies on fieldwork. Such fieldwork raises a number of ethical concerns, such as exploitative dynamics between researchers extracting data from (traumatized) victims without providing tangible benefits in return, research fatigue among interviewees in extensively studied contexts, and the risk of retraumatizing research participants or otherwise exposing them to harm through some element of the research process (Wood 2006; Lake and Parkinson 2017; Boesten and Henry 2018). On the other hand, Skjelsbæk (2018) reminds us that avoiding research topics such as CRSV altogether can also be considered a form of silencing. Rather, qualitative researchers need to exercise care in formulating their research questions, developing their research designs and interview guides, and selecting their research settings and interviewees. Reusing publicly available qualitative data is also a viable but often overlooked research approach (notable exceptions are Skjelsbæk 2015; Schulz 2018). Particularly fruitful ways of studying CRSV are research designs that combine quantitative and qualitative methods, thus leveraging their respective strengths (excellent examples are Cohen 2016; Hoover Green 2018).

Conclusion

Sexual violence is a highly gendered form of violence, in terms of the gendered power relations and hierarchies that facilitate it and that it subsequently reinforces and also in terms of the dominant patterns of perpetration and victimization. Neither its gendered nature nor the assertion of gendered power relations is unique to sexual violence of course. As per the premise underlying this volume, sexual violence exists on the physical end of a continuum with other forms of gendered violence, but it is also inherently intertwined with traumatic, psychological pain for individuals and women as a collective because it is rooted in gendered power relations.

In the case of CRSV, when various forms of sexual violence are perpetrated by armed actors in war, the political nature of sexual violence becomes most obvious. It is sexual violence in conflict that has therefore attracted the attention of political scientists first and foremost. As we discuss in this chapter, CRSV elicits gendered fears among women—gendered fears that armed actors may instrumentalize to hurt, intimidate, subjugate, control, or displace communities during war. Yet, this chapter emphasizes—drawing on the views expressed by civil society activists in Colombia—that sexual violence that occurs "in the private sphere" is grounded in the same gendered power relations that permeate societies and, as such, affects the behavior of women, including in the public sphere. Sexual violence, in other words, has sociopolitical significance in a context of gender inequalities and should therefore be considered political in general.

The stigma and fear associated with sexual violence poses challenges for researchers seeking to collect data and establish prevalence, an endeavor that becomes even more difficult in the uncertainty of armed conflict. We discuss the merits and drawbacks of different methods used to record and analyze CRSV. Despite the challenges associated with data collection, quantitative research has greatly improved our understanding of the patterns and variations in CRSV and responses to it. Qualitative research, by contrast, has situated these patterns in the lived experiences of those immediately affected by CRSV, and it has allowed insights also into perpetrator motivations and perceptions of those targeted. Different methodological tools are useful for answering different research questions and for filling in different parts of the puzzle that is the crime of CRSV.

9

Online Violence

ELEONORA ESPOSITO

When Professor Liz Kelly conceptualized the existence of a "continuum of violence" in 1988, her groundbreaking new idea was to deal with a vast and diverse range of forms of violence as cumulative lived experiences, largely informed by the same gendered relationships and power structures. She asked key questions about the categories we use, who decides what is abusive and what is not, which actions count as abuse, and what the connections are between different acts of abuse. By exploring these complex connections (e.g., the connection between sexual and domestic violence), Kelly aimed at unveiling the most subtle and distorted forms of everyday gender-based control, abuse, and silencing to finally reveal their physical, psychological, and material consequences (also see the Introduction to this volume).

In 1988, people's life-worlds were very different than they are today. Much has changed in little more than thirty years, but few aspects have been revolutionized as much as our daily practices of communication and interaction. Supported by the diffusion of smartphones and tablets (the so-called mobile web), the participatory and social nature of Web 2.0 has contributed to configuring what we now define as "constant connectivity" (Keipi et al. 2017, 2): immediate access to global news, friends, interests, new contacts, and modes of expression as an assumed part of life in most societies.

The Web 2.0 revolution has also deeply transformed political communication. The current generation of political leaders is faced with the unique challenges of ascending to power in "profoundly mediated contexts" (van Zoonen 2006, 288), in which politics is being "mediatized," "spectacularized," and "personalized" (Mazzoleni and Schulz 1999) at unprecedented levels. Digital affordances play such a pivotal role in sharing political information and engaging and building relationships with the electorate (especially in reaching younger voters or during fast-paced election campaigns) that having an established presence on the principal social media platforms is now indispensable for any politician. Unfortunately, this digital visibility comes at a cost, as the cybersphere has come to represent an authentic new frontier of violence: a breeding ground for the expression and dissemination of insults, defamation, and threats against various political actors, including elected leaders, candidates running for election, and policymakers.

Coming to represent yet another "digital divide," online violence against political actors is also a profoundly gendered phenomenon. Statistics show that women in politics are targeted disproportionately in comparison with their male counterparts (Atalanta 2018). Nowadays, online violence is one of the most prevalent forms of violence against women in politics: six MPs and parliament staff out of ten across Europe have faced online violence in their workplace (Inter-Parliamentary Union 2018). At the same time, gender is not the only factor at play; online violence is profoundly intersectional and is exacerbated by factors encompassing racial, ethnic, and religious identity (Kuperberg in this volume); sexual orientation; a young age (<40); and being more or less outspoken on topics such as equality and human rights.

The prominence of the digital in our daily lives poses renewed challenges in the definition and conceptualization of a continuum of gender-based violence. In fact, new forms of violence are being encountered as our life experiences unfold between "offline" and "online" spaces. In particular, social media platforms have come to play a crucial role in the perpetration of violence, which is only maximized by their embeddedness in our daily life rhythms and activities. Unfortunately, it has often proven difficult to distinguish the forms and pinpoint the tangible consequences of actions that are initiated in digital environments; often, the perceived disembodiment that characterizes the digital sphere has allowed a quick dismissal of online violence as an insignificant, virtual phenomenon, which hinders the full development of mitigation and prevention measures (see Bardall in this volume).

This chapter is informed by "continuum thinking" (Boyle 2019a; also see the Introduction in this volume), which is aimed at addressing online violence on an equal footing with other forms of (sexual and nonsexual) violence, such as physical (Kishi in this volume), psychological (Zetterberg and Bjarnegård in this volume), and conflict related (Kreft and Nagel in this volume). When explored along a physical-psychological continuum of gender-based violence, online violence against political actors can be problematized as yet another form of abuse and silencing that is embedded within the existing gendered power structures, whose tangible consequences are often ignored. In particular, since gender-based online violence is too often dismissed as an internet phenomenon and normalized as the cost of inhabiting an unregulated cybersphere, theory and methods for its investigation should aim at connecting the dots between such instantiations of violence and the profoundly gendered nature of both the digital and the political contexts.

As such, this chapter has two main aims. Firstly, it delimits the field of gender-based online violence, conceptualizing the phenomenon and identifying its main forms with specific reference to political actors. Secondly, it gives a brief overview of some methods available for the investigation of gender-based online violence, discussing the related advantages and trade-offs. It also includes empirical illustrations of the application of these methods, as well as some best practices in social scientific research employing social media data.

Conceptualizing Online Violence: Politics, Gender, and Web 2.0

One of the most difficult tasks in understanding online violence is to establish a useful definition of the concept. Defining violence in the nondigital, physical world presents similar challenges, but these challenges are taken to a new level of complexity when dealing with the digital realm. In part, defining online violence is difficult because it entails confronting a well-engrained, dystopic perception of the internet as an alternate, simulated, and disembodied virtual environment within which humans can engage in a vast number of daily activities without these being regarded as "real." One of the main challenges is the fact that digital acts of violence more rarely lead directly to physical harm, which is traditionally regarded as the most visible and indisputable form of violence (Kilger 2016). In this respect, conceptualizing violence along a continuum is a useful starting point in acknowledging the harm of online violence. In line with the broader definition of violence proposed in 1996 by the World Health Organization, a "continuum thinking" makes it possible to encompass different forms of violence beyond the physical (e.g., verbal and psychological abuse) and to identify common ground between them (see Introduction in this volume).

While certain instances of online violence, such as youth cyberbullying (and cyberracism), have managed to capture considerable public interest in recent years (Harmer and Lumsden 2019), online violence against political actors has not received the same degree of attention. Generally speaking, the political arena has been discursively constructed as a public space that is not for the squeamish, thin-skinned, or fainthearted and where violence is largely normalized. Violence is typically regarded as the cost of doing politics—as one of the prices to pay to have that degree of power and public visibility—although it rapidly turns into blatant exposure in the era of Web 2.0. In 2016, the tragic murder of the British Labour MP Jo Cox resparked the debate on online violence against political actors: when online death threats from one of the many white supremacists inhabiting the cybersphere turned into a "real-life" murder, the issue of online violence suddenly became much more newsworthy and urgent (Saner 2016).

A difficulty in defining online violence against political actors is that such violence is situated at a very complex intersection of existing patterns of violence, well-established gendered social structures, politics "as we know it," and new digital technologies as facilitators (see Krook in this volume; Piscopo and Bjarnegård in this volume). The targeted victims experience violence both in the political arena and in the cybersphere; furthermore, online violence can take on so many different and evolving forms that producing a complete taxonomy proves to be very challenging. Also, threats and abuse are both posted publicly on social media profiles and sent privately (e.g., via email, instant messaging), which poses issues in a comprehensive assessment of both the quantity and quality of online violence. Below is an overview of some of the most widespread forms of violence that political actors encounter in the cybersphere.

Death threats affect politicians' activities to the point of forcing them to suspend their campaigns or move their offices to different and more secure locations, as shown by the recent experiences of LGBTQ+ candidates in the United States (Stack 2018). It has been observed that the increasing polarization in the political sphere—especially during heated debates over key issues such as the Brexit campaign—contributes to death threats (as well as other threats) against political actors reaching unprecedented levels (Sabbagh 2019). Regrettably, although MP Jo Cox's murder raised some urgent questions about politicians' security in the U.K. and beyond, death threats are often not taken seriously, are not always investigated, and do not necessarily translate into stricter security measures, such as being granted a police escort (Fitzpatrick and Grierson 2019).

Rape threats are another form of online violence against political actors in which digital media act as a force multiplier for both quality and quantity. For example, British MP Jess Phillips has reported receiving more than six hundred rape threats on her social media profiles in a single night (Rawlinson 2018). As social media platforms support a vast range of multimodal data, forms of rape threats that are indigenous to the digital environment also proliferate, such as "virtual rape" or "rape memes," in which images are manipulated and/or animated to portray a forced sexual act with the victim

(Powell and Henry 2017). Violence often extends to the family members of targeted MPs, such as in the case of rape threats made via Twitter against the ten-year-old daughter of Indian politician Priyanka Chaturvedi (News18.com 2018). These attacks on family members are a form of violence that targets political actors indirectly and holds strong potential to affect them psychologically (see Introduction in this volume).

Gender-based abusive/hate speech against political actors encompasses a vast range of sexist and sexually charged insults. These are often aimed at "slut-shaming" the victim, as an immediate and successful strategy of social stigmatization and exclusion (Manne 2017). Far from being just words, this form of online violence is framed as a "harmful speech act" (Langton 2012, 80) and has the potential to annihilate certain groups, legitimate their discrimination, and shift attitudes and behaviors toward them. British MP Diane Abbott has highlighted the highly intersectional nature of this form of online violence by recounting how frequently she is body-shamed, slut-shamed, and racially insulted in one short sentence labeling her a "fat b***h n****r" (Levesley 2017). Similar patterns of abuse are exemplified by the digital attacks occurring at the intersection of race, ethnicity, and gender against U.S. Congresswomen Alexandria Ocasio-Cortez, Ilhan Omar, Ayanna Pressley, and Rashida Tlaib. Intersectional violence also characterizes the experience of many LGBTQ+ political actors, such as Italian MP Vladimir Luxuria or British MP Mhairi Black.

Image-based sexual abuse against political actors is a new form of violence that capitalizes on the primacy of visuality across digital media and is paired with established strategies of gender-based sexual objectification (Nussbaum 2010). Strategies of digital visual misogyny (Esposito, 2022) are particularly frequent on social media. These include image manipulation, in which the head or face of the victim is inserted onto an existing picture of a (little-dressed or naked) woman, often retrieved from an adult content website. Manipulation may also entail altering textual messages in the picture in a sexist and degrading way. Another very common strategy is fake identity attribution, which entails the viral circulation of an unaltered image of a (again, scantily dressed or naked) woman with a more or less close facial resemblance to the targeted politician and accompanied by a persuasive caption aimed at a deliberate misattribution of identity.

As exemplified by this nonencompassing overview, online violence is a complex techno-social phenomenon characterized by a wide array of different instantiations, whose spread, consolidation, and salience have certainly been amplified by specific features of the participatory web. The continuum thinking advanced in this chapter (and, more broadly, in this volume) is relevant in navigating this complex phenomenon at the intersection of gender, politics, and violence without falling into reductionism. As such, physical-psychological continuum thinking also fosters a (felicitous) departure from some established tendencies in both academic and lay debates on online violence, which have hindered the acknowledgment of online violence as an actual, full-fledged form of violence and the consequent development of adequate responses (see Bardall in this volume).

The first tendency to avoid is indulging in a digital deterministic narrative of online violence. The increasing incidence of violence has been directly connected to the democratization of access to digital recourses in the absence of gate-keeping practices, as well as to key features of computer-mediated communication, such as perceived anonymity and the lack of face-to-face context, to name a few (for an overview, see KhosraviNik and Esposito 2018). In this view, online violence would be largely rooted in the negative impact of the horizontal context of social media platforms on human communication and would be regarded as an internet phenomenon rather than a social issue.

A second, infelicitous tendency is the "gamification" of online violence; that is, framing digital violence and harassment as episodes of "hate-play," "signviolence," or "recreational nastiness" (Jane 2014, 531–32), which are portrayed as playful rather than harmful (Hardaker 2013). Assigning a juvenile, goliardic, and virtually harmless nature to these phenomena has contributed to preventing them from being framed within a narrative of criminal aggression with social, material, and ethical relevance and has played a key role in their normalization as an integral act of digital citizenship (Sarkeesiaan 2015).

A third dangerous tendency to depart from draws on a libertarian ethos of free speech, which too often results in an exculpatory narrative that justifies online violence. Online violence, abuse, and hostility have even been celebrated as a liberating, anti-hegemonic act of free speech, a "laudable and savvy resistance to mainstream media norms" (Jane 2014, 539) and to political correctness. This refusal to acknowledge online violence as a violation of cultural norms (Lange 2006) inevitably weakens the definition of hate speech as a legal term and as a crime that victims may want to redress (see Bardall in this volume).

These three tendencies can prove to be particularly dangerous when dealing with a specific type of online violence: that is, gender-based hate, harassment, and violence, which have been largely invisible or deemed to be intractable in most legislations (Barker and Jurasz 2018), if not "trivialized, mocked, regarded as a personal matter" (Jane 2016, 287). If online violence is "deliberately abusive and/or insulting and/or threatening and/or demeaning" and largely "directed at members of vulnerable minorities" (Waldron 2012, 8–9), then the taxonomy of these vulnerable minorities and of who could or should be included in such groups remains very much open to individual interpretation. Overall, we are witnessing a widespread institutional failure to acknowledge gender as a social factor that, per se, is enough to trigger hate, especially when compared to race, ethnicity, or religion.

Under the cloak of "innocent gossip" or "harmless humor," terabytes of content that delegitimize, objectify, shame, and sexualize political actors are being consumed on social media platforms. This has a tragic impact on equality and diversity in the political realm, which is particularly relevant, since the digital sphere was initially regarded as a very promising low-cost resource for visibility, especially for underrepresented groups (Patterson 2016).

In fact, online violence has been functioning as a fairly effective gate-keeping practice for the silencing and exclusion from the public and political arena of less-represented political actors and the (re-)establishment of power as a white, cisgender, male property. For example, research from Australia found that 60 percent of women aged eighteen to twenty-one and 80 percent of women over thirty-one said they were less likely to run for political office after seeing the digital and media violence endured by PM Julia Gillard (NDI 2018a). Other shortcomings include political actors withdrawing from digital dialogue and reducing their presence online, with detrimental effects on their political career (Lumsden and Morgan 2017). At the same time, political actors are starting to question whether social media are actually contributing to advancing their political career: they are becoming increasingly vocal about the digital abuse they endure and have started mobilizing against the phenomenon and against social media entrepreneurs themselves (Wong 2017).

Investigating Online Violence: Methods and Best Practices

While the value of investigating the cybersphere as a site for the (re-)formation and consumption of information, values, and worldviews is recognized, the unprecedented volume, variety, and velocity of social media data may prove intimidating for researchers in the humanities and social sciences. Although knowledge of programming language (e.g., the open-source Python or R) provides an advantage, researchers today can make use of a wide array of new and emerging user-friendly (but not always free of charge) software for data collection, visualization, and analysis.[1] Many options are available when it comes to methodological approaches (and related software); this section illustrates three different methods and their empirical application to online violence in recently published studies. This section also presents an overview of best practices for scholars and practitioners who are starting to approach social media to investigate online violence and other complex social phenomena.

Sentiment Analysis

Sentiment analysis shows considerable potential for the investigation of online violence, as it allows researchers to detect the polarity (i.e., more or less "positive," "neutral," or "negative") of a given message, which may range from a single word or sentence to an entire document (Liu 2015). Existing software (e.g., Datasift, Crimson Hexagon, SentiStrength) supports the fast analysis of large corpora and allows comparisons of the quantity and quality of abusive messages targeting political actors of different genders, ethnicities, or party affiliations.

There are currently two leading approaches to sentiment analysis. One is the lexically based (LB) method, which makes use of natural language-processing tools to associate each word or phrase with a specific sentiment, usually employing a predefined list of words. The other is a machine learning (ML) method, in which a training (labeled) dataset is used to train the algorithm to build classifiers that make it possible to identify sentiments (see Verma and Thakur 2018 for an in-depth comparison). Although they are constantly being improved and refined, both methods still have limitations when processing complex, ambiguous, or culture-specific material such as colloquialisms or sarcasm. For example, a sexist insult against a woman politician such as "Go back to the kitchen!" would be unlikely to be deemed as "negative" by a basic sentiment analysis tool. However, wordlists and training datasets can be customized to identify online violence in a more effective way, although doing so may prove to require more time and/or cost than expected.

A recent large-scale study by Amnesty International used sentiment analysis to shed light on the means and measures of online violence against women MPs on Twitter (Dhrodia 2018). Employing the social listening tool Crimson Hexagon in the six months preceding the 2017 U.K. general elections, the study identified the women MPs that received the most negative sentiment in the form of harassment and abuse as follows: Diane Abbott (Labour), Emily Thornberry (Labour), Joanna Cherry (SNP), Jess Phillips (Labour), and Anna Soubry (Conservative). Thus, the study showed that online violence is a bipartisan issue that does not pay heed to political boundaries. Moreover, the analysis found that black British MP Diane Abbott alone received almost half (45.14 percent) of all the abuse against women MPs on Twitter, confirming the strong intersectional nature of online violence (Stambolieva 2017).

Social Network Analysis

Social network analysis (SNA) methodology allows an investigation of social structures that is grounded in networks and graph theory (Scott and Carrington 2011). By means of dedicated visualization and exploration software (e.g., Node XL, Gephi) aimed at the identification of "nodes" (individual actors, people, or things within the network) and "edges" (relationships or interactions that connect them), SNA can yield insights into how connections networks are built and how information circulates on social media. As such, it can be employed to understand how online violence goes viral and the ways in which abusive content (but also misinformation and fake news) spreads across the cybersphere.

For example, SNA makes it possible to track the online communication channels of violent and extremist groups and provides a direct window into their online leadership and global relationships. These relationships are often regarded as reflecting and shaping the offline behavior of such groups while at the same time being easier to access and survey (Veilleux-Lepage and Archambault 2019). However, although this approach is valuable in offering a macro perspective on the patterns and shapes of social networks and the role of influential members, it may be fruitfully integrated with more in-depth, qualitative approaches examining the content of these social relations and their underlying ideological values to encompass both outsider and insider views of the social structure (Nooraie et al. 2020).

While not specifically focused on abuse against political actors, Boyle and Rathnayake (2019) employed SNA to investigate gender-based online violence against the #MeToo movement. In particular, they mapped and investigated actor centrality and connectivity on Twitter with a focus on #HimToo, a Twitter-backlash to #MeToo that emerged around the Brett Kavanaugh hearings. The study integrates the quantitative SNA approach with a qualitative investigation of media representations of men's sexual violence against women. This focus enabled an exploration of how #HimToo discursively developed across two key periods, characterized by an actor-centric conservative engagement with a subsequent response, both serious and satirical. On a more macro level, the analysis showed that while #MeToo has had a global reach, the backlash(es) seemed to have taken on a more regional character. On a more micro level, it also showed how the #MeToo counter-backlash managed to contain #HimToo, but was characterized by persistent gendered and generational patterns with a potentially negative impact on women's political expression.

Social Media–Critical Discourse Studies

Grounded in the focus on the dialectical relationship between language and society and related power relations, social media–critical discourse studies (SM-CDS) aim to provide an emerging critical discursive model that is specifically designed for digital data (KhosraviNik 2017). The model is characterized by the immersive, digital, ethnographic observation of social media communicative events, which makes it possible to account for the ways in which they are shaped and scaffolded by both the digital ("horizontal") and social ("vertical") contexts (KhosraviNik and Esposito 2018). In parallel, the model features a social semiotic perspective, which is able to account for the new and emerging audiovisual communicative resources that are typical of social media, including emojis, GIFs, or memes. Such a qualitative, in-depth analysis can prove time-consuming and is more easily performed on smaller, down-sampled datasets. The use of supporting software (e.g., AntConc, Wordsmith Tools, Sketch Engine) allows a faster, quantitative identification of discursive patterns, such as "key keywords" (words with higher or lower frequencies), collocations (frequent co-occurrence of words), and semantic prosody (the consistent "aura of meaning" of a given word), among others (Baker and Egbert 2016).

Using the SM-CDS approach, Esposito and Zollo (2021) analyzed a corpus of the most-viewed and commented-on YouTube videos featuring British women MPs. They identified the proliferation of videos consisting of mashups of different snippets of interviews, TV shows, or other public appearances of the targeted politician. The modification and montage of these user-generated videos, which included the addition of several meaning-making resources (e.g., a new title and description or overlay messages with different styles, colors, pictures, and sounds), marked a shift from an informative (and more or less unbiased) message to content aimed at derision and abuse. The study also identified a wide range of discursive strategies used to enact digital misogyny in the related comment sections, encompassing body-shaming, gender stereotyping, moral degradation, and direct threatening, among others. The study gave insight into the role played by YouTube as a horizontal digital context for video- and comment-sharing in the absence of gatekeeping practices; it also explored what the multimodal instantiations of online violence reveal about gender and politics in the vertical sociocultural context of the U.K.

Social Media as Data: Tips and Best Practices

Based on our experiences in conducting research with social media data, this section presents some tips and best practices to address the main practical challenges posed by dealing with the inherent nonlinearity and fleeting nature of Web 2.0.

- *Inhabit the cybersphere:* To be able to capture the interactivity, connectivity, and "always-on" nature of social media communication, being an active user of various social media platforms is likely to be helpful. Regardless of the specific aims and methods of research, immersive ethnographic observation of the actual processes of production and consumption of social media content will support the identification of its volatile debates and discourse concentrations.

- *Define your scope of research:* The cybersphere is an incommensurable and potentially dispersive realm that is likely to provide a too-wide scope for the investigation of social phenomena within it. A clear research design, with a definite scope of research and well-developed research questions, can act as a useful compass. The research design is likely to have an impact on the choice of specific platform(s) where the data collection and analysis will take place in order to ensure a clear focus of the specific features and technicalities of Facebook, Twitter, Instagram, or YouTube, to name a few. The design should determine key choices such as the amount of data to be retrieved (e.g., complete or sampled datasets), timeframes of collection (e.g., collecting current data or retrieving historical data), and methodology to be employed in the analysis of the corpus of data collected.

- *Look out for triggers:* Very often, online violence is unleashed by a more or less related critical incident, "a 'trigger' or galvanizing event" (Williams and Burnap 2015), which would be helpful to monitor closely for its potential to catalyze attention and generate a considerable response on social media platforms. Online violence against political actors more specifically can include elections and related campaigns, lawmaking (especially around highly debated topics such as migration, economics, or women's rights), public declarations, and aspects or events related to a politician's private life. At the same time, online violence pervades the everyday digital experience of many political actors and is not necessarily bound to a particular event.

- *Check your pockets:* Although researchers are not always aware of this, funding availability can make all the difference between success and failure when it comes to digital data. In fact, social media data is a commodity, and funding may be needed to purchase access to existing or custom datasets from the social media platforms themselves (e.g., the Historical PowerTrack for Twitter). Moreover, funding may be useful in seeking the support of consultants on data management or in buying access to paid software for data collection, visualization, and analysis.

- *Be ethical:* The quantity and quality of social media data that can be collected, stored, and published largely depends on the ethics of the topic or situation under study. Current social science ethical guidelines are not always fit and/or updated for dealing with digital data satisfactorily, and a situational, case-by-case approach is considered to be best practice. Aspects to be considered include the general principles of anonymity, confidentiality, and risk of harm avoidance, as well as terms of service and privacy policies (varying across different social media platforms) and type of research (e.g., observational vs. interactional) (see also Beninger 2017).

Concluding Remarks

The cybersphere is far from being a neutral space, and the lived experiences of internet users can vary considerably according to their gender, as well as their sexual orientation, race, ethnicity, mother tongue, age/generation, and dis/ability, among others. Online forms of violence replicate and extend the power relations that preexist digital communications technologies and should not simply be trivialized as internet phenomena. The continuum thinking advocated in this chapter—and more broadly in this volume—fosters a conceptualization and critical explication of the phenomenon that is rooted in a profound awareness of the gendered nature of the political realm. As such, it lays the foundation for a more comprehensive analysis of online violence against political actors, which is able to pinpoint the specific gender-based motives, forms, and impacts (Bardall, Bjarnegård, and Piscopo 2020). The development of a systematic approach to the investigation, mitigation, and prevention of online violence would respond to an urgent global agenda, addressing gender-based violence, digital security, and, ultimately, gender equality.

While the pathways, levels, and areas of analysis are intimately connected to the scope and design of a research project, continuum thinking in the investigation of online violence is best operationalized by means of an integrated approach. For example, the methodologies illustrated here could be combined in a two-phase analysis, in which a sentiment analysis or SNA could be performed at an entry level and an SM-CDS analysis could be performed at a subsequent stage on a down-sampled dataset. More compelling results, in fact, are likely to emerge from the synergic incorporation of more quantitative (macro) views on the magnitude and spread of online violence and more qualitative (micro) approaches that can critically explicate it as a techno-social and cultural phenomenon.

PART III

Case Studies

10

Electoral Violence Targeting Voters in Papua New Guinea

NICOLE HALEY AND KERRYN BAKER

This chapter takes the question of electoral integrity as its starting point. Electoral integrity is fundamentally important as it relates to public faith in electoral processes, the legitimacy of institutions and elected governments, and the prevalence of internal state violence (Norris 2014). International standards provide the baseline for our understanding of electoral integrity, yet simplistic measures—whether elections are deemed to have "failed" or not—are not wholly adequate. We argue that violence that disproportionately affects women voters can have the effect of disenfranchising women, producing unequal and delegitimized political outcomes. If male and female voters are participating unequally in electoral processes, this poses a profound threat to electoral integrity and therefore to democracy, albeit one that is underacknowledged by international actors.

Electoral violence, involving coercive, intimidative, and retributive acts against people, property, and communal infrastructure, "is levied by political actors to purposefully influence the process and outcome of elections" (Birch, Daxecker, and Höglund 2020, 4). It seeks to restrict political participation by preventing or discouraging eligible citizens from registering to vote, casting ballots according to their personal preference, or otherwise engaging with the election process (Bardall 2011). Threats, intimidation, and election-related violence can occur publicly and privately and across the electoral cycle, and as such they are subject to different reporting biases (Birch, Daxecker, and Höglund 2020). The scant attention afforded the gendered nature of electoral violence targeted at voters is in part because violence against women in elections tends to be less visible than other forms of electoral violence and is significantly underreported (Ballington, Bardall, and Borovsky 2017). Increased attention to women's leadership and political participation in recent years is helping to ensure the gendered nature of electoral violence becomes more visible (IFES 2017).

Using a continuum of violence approach and focusing on a case study of Papua New Guinea (PNG), this chapter explores the gendered nature of violence targeting voters. PNG is the largest country in the Pacific Islands region, with a population of between eight and ten million people. It is the most ethno-linguistically diverse country in the world, with more than eight hundred languages spoken, and despite a wealth of natural resources faces severe developmental challenges. Human Rights Watch (2017) has labeled PNG "one of the most dangerous countries in the world to be a woman"; rates of gender-based violence are extremely high, as are maternal mortality rates, and women are disproportionately the targets of sorcery- and witchcraft-related violence. Since independence in 1975, when a Westminster unicameral system of government was adopted, PNG has had an unbroken record of regular elections. Yet PNG elections are hyper-competitive, administrative capacity is relatively weak, and electoral malfeasance and politically motivated violence are commonplace. Freedom House (2021) characterizes the country as "party free," noting key issues in terms of political rights, including electoral violence and malpractice, widespread corruption, and the restricted political participation of women and LGBTQI+ groups.

Drawing upon data from a large-scale research-based election observation project conducted in 2017, as well as comparative data from 2007 and 2012, we offer insight into how violence targeting voters is perpetrated and its gendered dynamics. We argue that gendered violence targeting voters in PNG effectively alienates women from the political process and poses a serious threat to electoral integrity. Yet it is a pervasive and inherently politicized issue, which hampers efforts to mitigate it. The chapter is structured in four parts: first, we look at violence targeting voters as an element of political violence, how it is gendered and how it might be measured; second, we outline trends in electoral integrity in PNG elections; third, we use a case study of the 2017 PNG election to highlight the gendered forms, motives, and impacts of violence targeting voters; and finally, we conclude by examining the impacts of gendered violence targeting voters and attempts to address the issue.

Violence Targeting Voters

Electoral violence targeting voters seeks to restrict and stifle political participation with a view to subverting the electoral process or manipulating election outcomes. Electoral violence can take many forms, and while it has a particular electoral focus, it can intersect with other common forms of violence and societal inequalities, perpetuating vulnerability for women and other marginalized groups. Conceptualizing violence as a physical-psychological continuum allows for full consideration of gendered dynamics (see Bjarnegård and Zetterberg's Chapter 1 in this volume).

The gendered nature of election-related violence is underexplored, although it has been argued that women are particularly vulnerable to violence targeted toward voters. According to Bardall (2011, 16), women voters are around four times more likely than their male counterparts to be victims of election violence. Research on political violence as it relates to other political actors shows similar patterns: women candidates and politicians are especially vulnerable to political violence, particularly if they are in highly visible positions of power and if they seek to challenge social norms of leadership (Collignon in this volume; Håkansson in this volume; Schneider in this volume; Thomas and Herrick in this volume). In the Pacific Islands region, emerging research has highlighted violence against women in politics as a pervasive issue that perpetuates male dominance of politics (NDI 2020). Yet the violence and intimidation women face can be substantively different and thus harder to quantify; women disproportionately experience psychological abuse, intimidation, and verbal harassment, while men are more likely to experience physical violence of a kind that is more likely to be documented (Ballington, Bardall, and Borovsky 2017; Bardall 2011; Bjarnegård 2018).

Getting a clear picture of the forms and impacts of electoral violence that targets voters is hampered globally by a lack of data. Existing datasets concerning electoral violence, including the Countries at Risk of Electoral Violence dataset (Birch and Muchlinski 2017a) and the Electoral Contention and Violence (ECAV) dataset (Daxecker, Amicarelli, and Jung 2018), are based on media reports and include events considered causally and temporally connected to the electoral process. They are biased in favor of particular countries and publicly observable events, obscure the identity of actors, and are not nuanced enough to reflect what is happening locally (Daxecker, Amicarelli, and Jung 2019, 716, 718; Birch and Muchlinski 2020, 219), meaning they are of limited utility when seeking to examine the gendered nature of electoral violence.

Voter intimidation and gender-based violence often take place in the private sphere, which makes data collection difficult (Bardall 2011) and diminishes the likelihood that such events are captured in comparative datasets. As such, collecting and coding data on violence targeting voters is difficult. So, too, is determining what is election related and what is not and how different forms of violence might be interrelated and informed by gendered motivations. Getting this right often relies on in-depth knowledge of a particular context, including its culture and history. Large-scale projects that draw on a depth of local expertise and cultural knowledge can supplement existing datasets to more fully interrogate the continuum of violence targeting voters and its gendered dynamics.

In this chapter, we draw upon data collected as part of a large-scale research-based observation of PNG's 2017 national general elections, undertaken by the Australian National University (ANU) and its research partners (see Haley and Zubrinich 2018). The same methodology was also employed during the 2007 and 2012 national general elections, allowing for comparative analysis of PNG elections over time. In 2017, the ANU observation team comprised 258 observers from academia and civil society, including 224 locally engaged Papua New Guinean observers. Observers mobilized in thirty-five teams, conducting observations in sixty-nine of PNG's 111 electorates, and detailed studies of forty-four electorates. To capture the whole electoral process, observers were engaged for up to three months. The project employed a mixed-methods approach involving observation of the campaign, pre-polling, polling, counting, and postelection periods; key informant interviews; and two citizens' surveys, one conducted pre-polling and the other postpolling. Overall, 7,510 citizens were surveyed.

Through engaging domestic observers, including many with close connections to the areas in which they were observing, the observation was designed to take advantage of local knowledge and expertise. The research design also allowed for observations over a significantly longer period than traditional election observations, meaning election-related issues arising before and after the formal election period were captured. Overall, ANU's 2017 observation was the most comprehensive study of PNG elections ever undertaken.

As part of the project, observers were asked to collect data about all facets of the election process, including questions on election-related violence and the security context, in a specially designed journal. Conducting the observation itself involved serious security challenges. A number of observers reported threats of violence, including some who had to be relocated as a result, and others were assaulted in the course of their work. In 2017, new questions were added to the journal to assess election-related sorcery and witchcraft allegations and violence.

Collecting data on election-related violence and particularly violence targeting voters is difficult. Violence does not occur in a vacuum; it is heavily influenced by context, histories of conflict, and underlying power dynamics. Election-related violence can be opportunistic, with the election giving perpetrators a chance, while tension is high and they are protected by powerful patrons, to settle old scores. In contexts where violence is normalized—either within the family or community—tracing incidents definitively to elections poses challenges, both conceptually for victims and perpetrators and methodologically for data collectors.

These are ongoing issues in the study of election violence generally and violence targeting voters specifically. Yet data gathered on violence and security in elections through the 2017 election observation project provides both insight into the gendered dynamics of violence targeting voters and lessons for future research in this space. In this chapter, we draw on Bardall, Bjarnegård, and Piscopo's (2020) typology of gendered political violence, distinguishing between gendered motives, when violence is used as a means to specifically exclude women from politics; gendered forms, where violence is expressed in different ways when directed toward male or female voters; and gendered impacts, when responses to violence targeting voters play out in gendered ways.

Elections in PNG

PNG is among the most expensive places in the world to conduct elections, with the 2012 general election costing an estimated USD$60 per voter (DFAT 2013). There is a myriad of challenges to electoral administration at play, including poor transport infrastructure, weak government capacity, extreme cultural and linguistic diversity, and high rates of illiteracy. Elections in PNG also take place in a complex security environment. In some areas of the Highlands region, tribal fighting regularly leads to death, injury, and displacement, and violent crime is commonplace in the major cities of PNG (Haley and Muggah 2006).

The 2002 general elections, which saw serious issues with the electoral roll, dozens of election-related deaths, and failed elections in five provinces, were generally considered PNG's worst elections ever (see CS/PIFS 2007, 2). Following the 2002 polls, increased investments were made in security for elections. The next general elections, in 2007, also marked the shift from a first-past-the-post electoral system to limited preferential voting (LPV). The introduction of LPV—in which voters rank their top three candidates in order of preference—was intended to facilitate the election of candidates with broader mandates; to foster more cooperation between different candidates and voting blocs; and to reduce election-related violence. The move to LPV was also seen as beneficial for female voters, as it was hypothesized women would have more freedom of choice to allocate their second and third preferences to their preferred candidates, even if they were pressured by their family or community to give their first preference to a certain candidate (Haley and Dierikx 2013).

The electoral environment in 2007 was deemed much improved in terms of security, and while the 2012 elections saw setbacks, it was not considered as bad as 2002. The 2017 PNG general elections, however, represented a marked deterioration in the electoral environment. These elections saw "unprecedented levels of violence and insecurity which punctuated the elections from start to finish" (Haley and Zubrinich 2018, xi; see also TIPNG 2017). Fewer than half of all citizens surveyed by ANU observers in the postpolling period reported being able to exercise their vote freely (Haley and Zubrinich 2018, 60).

Observations of elections in Hela province (Highlands region) across the 2007, 2012, and 2017 elections by one of the authors of this chapter (Haley) illustrate this change. In 2007, the large security presence compared with the previous election was welcomed, and voters turned out in large numbers. Yet significant irregularities were noted, including the absence of a secret ballot, the buying and selling of votes, premarked ballot papers at some polling stations, multiple voting, and underage voting. For the most part, voters considered 2007 a good election, describing it as "democratic" (in that everyone got to vote, even children) and "transparent" (in that everyone got to see how others voted). Weapons, though present in the community in large numbers, were largely absent from polling stations, unlike in 1997 and 2002. Women turned out at polling stations in large numbers, and it seemed that those who wanted to vote did so largely unhindered. Importantly, women voters were observed to mark their own ballot papers, although often under the watchful eye of male minders. While all but a handful of Hela women surveyed postpolling in 2007 had voted in the election, nearly half (49 percent) reported having experienced intimidation with respect to voting.

The situation encountered in 2012 was considerably different, with threats and intimidation more widespread. Fighting disrupted polling at one-third of the polling stations in which observations were made, and observers witnessed seven ballot boxes forcibly hijacked and four ballot boxes destroyed. They also witnessed violent assaults on polling officials and bystanders and the destruction of property (Haley and Zubrinich 2013, 78). Bribery, personation, and multiple voting were widespread, and premarked ballot papers were issued to voters at many polling stations. At a small number of polling stations, groups of young men were seen filling out entire books of ballot papers. A third (35 percent) of all Hela women surveyed postpolling reported that they had not voted, and only two in five (44 percent) reported being able to vote freely.

The 2017 elections in Hela were marred by serious irregularities of various kinds. Throughout much of the province, systematic manipulation of the electoral roll was evident, resulting in serious underenrollment and overenrollment at the ward level. This led to heated polling day standoffs, fights over ballot papers, and, in some cases, the eventual destruction of the ballot boxes in question. At some polling stations, compromise agreements were reached, including that no one would vote or that the available votes would be split or shared on some agreed basis. Where agreements were reached, they rarely included women voters, but instead saw the available ballot papers distributed to men representing different sections of the community or among candidates' scrutineers. Such ballots were invariably filled out by small groups of men sequestered behind locked gates or fences; the few women who turned out seeking to vote were not permitted to enter the polling place. Only 10 percent of women surveyed postpolling reported that they had been able to vote freely, while 58 percent reported that they did not vote.

We share these reflections from Hela because they are indicative of a broader trend in PNG elections whereby the deterioration of the electoral environment and increased violence have distinct gendered impacts. While PNG's unbroken record of postindependence elections is often noted, the prevalence of electoral malfeasance and election-related violence pose significant electoral integrity concerns. These issues were particularly pronounced in the 2017 elections and are reflective of broader democratic decline.

Violence in the 2017 Elections

Violence was a clear and defining feature of the 2017 PNG elections. The ANU observation team documented 204 election-related deaths between the issue of writs and the immediate postdeclaration period. By way of contrast, the ECAV database records twenty-two deaths in relation to the 2002 general elections (see Daxecker, Amicarelli, and Jung 2018). Incidents of election violence resulting in serious injury, the large-scale destruction of property, and the hijacking and destruction of numerous ballot boxes were also observed. In sixty-three of the sixty-nine constituencies in which observation were made, observers witnessed violent altercations leading to death, serious injury, or major property damage (Haley and Zubrinich 2018, 32).

Gender and Voter Intimidation

Gendered power dynamics within communities and families come into play during PNG's highly competitive elections. Women are often viewed not as individual voters, but as part of a voting bloc controlled by a family member or community leader. Family voting as a practice is a gendered form of coercion (Ballington, Bardall, and Borovsky 2017). Women in PNG are regularly pressured by male relatives or community members to vote a certain way, with such practices enforced by threats—implicit or explicit—of violence or social ostracism (Baker 2018). In 2017, voter intimidation was widespread.

Family voting and coerced collective voting can take many forms, including a voter allowing another person to vote on their behalf or being issued with premarked ballot papers (Haley and Zubrinich 2018). One observer in

Chimbu province, Highlands region (quoted in Haley and Zubrinich 2018, 81), noted the prevalence of forced assistance:

> Many women here know how to read and write and don't need assistance but when it comes to voting the men and boys just come and take control of women's votes. They take away their democratic rights through forced voting.

Forced assistance at polling stations was more likely to be imposed on women than men, similar to past elections (see Haley and Zubrinich 2013).

Bloc voting practices tend to be far less overt. Pressure to bloc vote is fueled by widespread skepticism about the existence of a secret ballot. Observers of the 2017 elections determined that few voters had the opportunity to cast a genuinely secret ballot, with candidates, candidates' agents, and community members employing various means to ensure voters' choices were made known. Fear of postelection retribution is a key motivating factor in the enforcement of bloc voting.

In the 2007, 2012, and 2017 elections, in each electorate surveyed, more women than men reported experiencing intimidation while voting or being denied the right to vote. The extent to which women voters experienced intimidation in 2017, however, was far more pronounced than in previous elections. For example, while 29 percent of women surveyed in Koroba-Lake Kopiago Open electorate (Highlands region) in 2012 reported having experienced intimidation, this figure was 83 percent of women in the same electorate in 2017. The proportion of Koroba-Lake Kopiago men reporting having experienced intimidation was also up, from 20 percent in 2012 to 66 percent in 2017. Tellingly, close to three-quarters of women surveyed in 2017 (73 percent) also reported that they did not vote. By contrast, fewer than one in five (18 percent) had not voted in 2012 (Haley and Zubrinich 2018). In each case the proportion of men who did not vote was significantly lower: 47 percent in 2017 and only 5 percent in 2012.

Across PNG, local supporters of candidates were the principal agents of intimidation for both men (52 percent) and women (47 percent). Much of the intimidation experienced by women voters was also attributed to family (32 percent) and community leaders (23 percent). Only 10 percent of women reporting intimidation identified candidates and their campaign teams as the source of that intimidation, and even fewer attributed it to polling officials (9 percent) or security personnel (7 percent). By contrast, men were 50 percent less likely to experience intimidation from family and 50 percent more likely to be directly intimidated by candidates and members of their campaign teams.

Gender-Based Election Violence

Where observers directly witnessed incidents of gender-based violence during the campaign and polling periods, the perpetrators were often the husbands or domestic partners of the women involved. In East Sepik province, observers saw a man severely injure his wife with a spear at a polling station after she had voted for a candidate he did not support. Another observer group in the Highlands witnessed a man shoot his wife with a bow and arrow after she had voted for a rival candidate (Haley and Zubrinich 2018). Elsewhere, observers reported women being threatened with divorce should they choose to vote against their husbands' wishes.

In PNG, political alliances are often forged and strengthened through marriage. In the context of recent elections, observers reported marriages being arranged in exchange for votes and the "gifting" of young women to candidates, key officials, or security personnel. Observers were of the view that most of the women involved were being forced or coerced by male family members (Haley and Zubrinich 2018).

In Western Highlands province, observers reported that women—euphemistically referred to as "coffee ladies"—were providing sexual services in exchange for votes. This activity was conducted in "campaign houses," sites for the supporters of particular candidates to gather and often where vote buying and gifting takes place. Observers noted that many of these women were in vulnerable positions, usually widowed, divorced, or separated and reliant on local strongmen for financial support and protection (Haley and Zubrinich 2018). As such, they were considered duty bound to "work" for the benefit of the group and contribute to the election effort.

Gender-based violence and the strict enforcement of gender roles that emphasize female subservience are issues by no means confined to the election period in PNG. Yet accounts from observers suggest they can be weaponized for political ends during elections. In Hela province, observers witnessed one polling official, defying instructions to establish gender-segregated polling booths, asserting: "We have bought these women. We own them and we own their votes." Similarly, the coercion of women into marriages and sex work to secure campaign access, political alliances, and electoral support is another clear example of perpetrators using "violence to preserve men's hegemonic control of politics" (Bardall, Bjarnegård, and Piscopo 2020, 2).

Sorcery- and Witchcraft-Related Election Violence

In PNG, the "belief that illness, death and misfortune of all sorts is frequently caused by the deliberate interventions of individuals with special powers or magical knowledge is pervasive" (Forsyth and Eves 2015, 1). This belief is often the source of significant community tension, which can then be exacerbated by the high-stakes environment of a national election. Sorcery and witchcraft were of greater concern to observers and voters in the 2017 elections than in previous general elections (Haley and Zubrinich 2018). In different parts of PNG, citizens expressed their concern that magic had been used to alter election results. In various locations, the deaths of candidates or their close family members during the election period were attributed to sorcery.

Sorcery accusations in PNG are directed toward both men and women and are instigated by both men and women. Yet women are particularly vulnerable to sorcery accusation–related violence (Eves and Kelly-Hanku 2014). While women can also be perpetrators of sorcery accusation–related violence, the primary perpetrators are young men (Gibbs 2012). The gendered forms in which sorcery accusation–related violence is enacted were obvious in observer reports of incidents during the 2017 national elections. In the Western Highlands, four women were tortured and killed after being accused of poisoning a young girl at a campaign event. In the Eastern Highlands, the death of a candidate during the campaign period sparked sorcery accusations against two women, who were then killed in retribution.

Women's De Facto Disenfranchisement

The deterioration of the electoral environment in 2017 had serious impacts on the integrity of the election, with implications for democracy more broadly. While the disenfranchisement of women was not necessarily the main goal of those who sought to disrupt electoral processes, women disproportionately felt the impacts. This is not a new development in PNG's political history. Dickson-Waiko (2013, 193) has examined how gendered colonial policy that subordinated women was perpetuated by the postcolonial state, arguing: "The full enjoyment of citizenship in PNG—that is, the full range of social, legal and political rights—is experienced only by men."

Across the Highlands in the 2017 elections, observers witnessed men—usually young men—controlling the vote at polling stations. Again, this was not necessarily a deliberate strategy to disenfranchise women, but rather a show of force and a means to secure the vote for a particular candidate or candidates. Yet where this happened, very few women voted, and even fewer voted freely.

In a context where voter intimidation is rampant and strongmen seek to control large voting blocs, gender gaps in political participation will inevitably widen. While there were votes cast on behalf of women in Hela province in 2017, very few votes were actually cast *by* women. Many did not even present at the polling station. One counting official in Hela (quoted in Haley and Zubrinich 2018, 90) articulated how women were marginalized from the election process:

> Elections in Hela are only for young, strong and energetic men and boys. The determining factor in this election was how effectively candidates mobilised the boys. You don't need to appeal to women, old people or those living in remote places. They are of no concern. Few of them vote and they do not influence election outcome in any way.

An observer in the same province (quoted in Haley and Zubrinich 2018, 95) agreed: "This election was just for the young and the strong. Women were totally excluded from the voting process. It must be that they are no longer citizens of this nation." While 179 female candidates contested the election, no women were elected to Parliament in the 2017 general elections.

Gendered Violence Targeting Voters in PNG: Addressing the Problem

The 2017 elections in PNG were experienced fundamentally differently by women and men voters. While violence and insecurity were widespread and affected both men and women, violence targeting voters was often expressed in gendered ways and generated gendered impacts. Ultimately, the main impact of gendered violence targeting voters is alienation from the electoral process. This can manifest in a variety of ways: lower voter turnout for women; lower levels of voter registration; and ramifications for women's political participation in other aspects of the political process, including as candidates and electoral officials (Ballington, Bardall, and Borovsky 2017). Our case study of the 2017 general elections in PNG shows how widespread gendered violence targeting voters can have profound effects on the integrity of an election and the strength of democracy in general.

Gendered electoral violence is a recognized issue in PNG, but there is little clarity on how best to address it. The Electoral Commission has taken some steps, including the introduction in 2007 of gender-segregated polling in an attempt to improve the franchise of women voters. Implementation has been patchy, and observers in 2017 noted declining adherence to the policy, with no teams reporting separate queues or voting compartments for women being consistently provided in the constituencies in which they were observing (Haley and Zubrinich 2018).

Institutional measures such as gender-segregated polling also fail to tackle the root of the issue. If voter intimidation experienced by women primarily takes place in the home or community, then such measures will have a limited effect on the ability of women to vote freely (Baker 2018). During the 2017 elections, some local observers suggested that the gender-segregated polling policy actually makes women voters more vulnerable to violence, especially in highly competitive and volatile environments. It effectively offers a false sense of security to women wanting to vote, fueling men's suspicions that women seeking to vote in secret are doing so with the intent of voting against the wishes of their husband, family, or community (Haley and Zubrinich 2018).

It has been recommended that violence against women in elections (VAWE) monitoring be integrated into the practice of election observation (Ballington, Bardall, and Borovsky 2017). Election observations do indeed provide a unique opportunity to systematically collect data on the gendered experience of elections, including in relation to election violence, as this chapter has demonstrated. There is a tendency, however, for international observation missions to moderate adverse findings, especially when they cannot be systematically corroborated. Thus, reports of violence are often dismissed as anecdotal or isolated incidents.

Take, for example, the report by the Commonwealth Secretariat (2017, viii), which acknowledged serious incidents of election-related violence in the 2017 PNG elections, but concluded that the campaign period was "broadly peaceful." The report noted low turnout for women in the Highlands region; that their observers had seen aggressive tactics used to dissuade women from voting at polling stations; and incidents of presumed forced assistance and violations of voter secrecy when women were casting votes. Yet the executive summary claimed the following:

> Voters who were able to participate were generally free to exercise their democratic right, and in most provinces women, the elderly and young people appeared largely unhindered in their participation in the process (Commonwealth Secretariat 2017, viii).

This contrasted with the report from Transparency International Papua New Guinea (2017, iii), a local nongovernmental organization, which asserted that "the 2017 elections were flawed to an unforgiveable extent." The Pacific Islands Forum (2017, 1) observation team noted the following:

> There were significant and widespread challenges observed in all aspects of the 2017 Elections. . . . The common view shared by the majority of people the Team spoke to was that the 2017 National Election was chaotic and challenging and that the reported incidences of election related violence, deaths and destruction of property are higher than recorded in previous elections.

The Australian government—the largest aid donor to PNG, including substantial support through its electoral program—sent a team of four members of Parliament to observe the election. While this report was never publicly released, Foreign Minister Julie Bishop released a statement following the return of writs, saying, "The Australian Government congratulates PNG, one of our closest friends and partners, on its successful election" (quoted in Armbruster 2017).

The apparent contradictions in observer groups' assessments of the 2017 elections reflect the challenges in addressing violence targeting voters, an inherently politicized issue. For developing countries like PNG, there is significant pressure to present to the world a "good," and by inference violence-free, election. Any attempts to collect data on election-related violence will be affected by these dynamics.

Yet in PNG we see a vibrant civil society seeking to bring a spotlight to issues of election-related violence and electoral integrity issues more broadly. Domestic election observers, including the majority of the ANU observation team and those from other organizations, including Transparency International, were a core part of these efforts; their data collection and observations, often undertaken at high personal risk, ensure we have a clear picture of what kinds of election-related violence happened and where, the perpetrators and victims, and the enabling factors behind the violence. These efforts were bolstered by the use of mobile phones and social media to share information among the public of voting irregularities, electoral law violations, and election-related violence, including police brutality (Haley and Zubrinich 2018). Working alongside local civil society organizations to track incidents of election-related violence and find local solutions to mitigate this violence is a clear area of opportunity.

This chapter highlights the opportunities presented by large-scale mixed-method election research projects that are embedded in local context to illuminate, firstly, the extent of election violence across a continuum from physical to psychological violence and, secondly, the gendered dynamics of election violence. In the case of PNG, the data tell a story not only of the particularities of gendered violence targeting voters in the 2017 elections, but also the enduring exclusion of women from full citizenship. Future research on gendered violence targeting voters could adopt a similar mixed-method approach. Accurately researching gendered political violence requires creative data collection methods (Bardall, Bjarnegård, and Piscopo 2020), including those that examine voter experience. Both quantitative data gathering and the use of qualitative methods, including ethnographic approaches, are important in capturing the full scope of gender violence targeting voters.

11

Election Violence in Uganda

PAIGE SCHNEIDER

On election day, voters supporting the woman candidate were physically beaten and property was destroyed. The perpetrators said things
such as "*Can a skirt stand in front of a man and lead?*" These slogans
were meant to denounce her because she was a female. (Case 40, female, Moroto, Uganda)

This chapter considers the relationship between gender and election violence in Uganda through the experiences of female and male political
actors in their roles as candidates, agents working for candidates, party
leaders, elected officials, and voters. Uganda is characterized as a multiparty
authoritarian regime and, as such, is more likely to experience election violence than the democratic countries analyzed in this volume (Wahman, Teorell, and Hadenius 2013, 27; Norris, Frank, and Coma 2015, 134–37). Election violence poses a serious threat to the stability of a country, as it instills
fear in voters, breeds cynicism around democratic processes and procedures,
and impedes the ability of citizens to hold government accountable through
the ballot box. Moreover, many if not most of the countries at risk for election violence have also struggled to extend full and equal political rights to
women. Challenges at the intersection of the conduct of democratic elections
and the struggle for women's equal political rights are central to this chapter.

Uganda is an east African country of about thirty-five million people that
utilizes a plurality, or "first past the post," electoral system. Current president
Yoweri Museveni and his political party, the National Resistance Movement

(NRM), began consolidating power in the 1990s. Over the last few decades, it has grown increasingly difficult for opposition parties and their candidates to campaign freely and without fear of retaliation by the NRM (Schedler 2006; Tripp 2010, 4). Ironically, while the NRM has undermined the integrity of Uganda's elections by crippling the opposition, it has generally been supportive of the expansion of women's rights and the incorporation of women into the political process. For instance, it first adopted gender quotas to increase women's political representation in 1986—long before many other countries— and in 1995, it institutionalized a 30 percent reserved seat quota system for women at all levels of government (Tripp 2019, 579). As of 2019, women comprised 35 percent of the Parliament of Uganda and held at least 33 percent of local council seats in all districts (Women in Local Government 2018, 11).

The reserved seat quota system, along with efforts by women's rights groups to recruit and train women candidates, has increased the number of women running for and winning elective office in Uganda. Yet women are far from reaching parity with men due to at least three important factors.

First, women candidates are often discouraged from competing for the much more numerous direct (nonquota) seats. So pervasive are expectations that women stay "in their place" and leave to men the direct seat competitions that direct seats are referred to simply as the *man seats* (Edgell 2018). When women do choose to run for a direct seat, they may face overt hostility from men and sometimes even from other women. Consequently, women hold *less than 1 percent* of the directly elected local councillor positions nationwide (Women in Local Government 2018, 12).

The second significant challenge that women candidates face is a scarcity of funds to run their political campaigns (FOWODE 2018, 8). The monetization of electoral politics in Uganda means that it is difficult to mount a viable campaign, even at the local level, without the resources necessary to sustain a patronage network. Women generally have less wealth than do men, and this, compounded by the fact that political parties favor male candidates in the distribution of campaign funds, leaves women at a distinct disadvantage in direct seat races (ibid.).

Third, in what the organization UN Women-Uganda describes as sexualized political space, women face significant levels of election-related violence, threats, harassment, and expectations of sexual quid pro quo if they seek to participate on equal footing with men (Ahikire 2015, 34; FOWODE 2018, 40–41). It is this third factor—election-related violence—to which I now turn.

Studying Gender and Election Violence in Uganda

In conventional political violence scholarship, election violence is defined as acts perpetrated to control the electoral process or election outcomes. It is assumed that the motivation behind the violence is political or factional in nature (Bekoe 2012; Straus and Taylor 2012; Taylor, Pevehouse, and Straus 2017; Söderberg and Bjarnesen 2018). However, as noted by Piscopo and Bjarnegård, and Krook (both chapters in this volume), the motivation behind an act of political violence may be gendered, with the intent to dissuade or deny to women, gender-nonconforming individuals, or nonhegemonic men the ability to participate in the political process. For researchers working at the intersection of political violence and gender, discerning the motive behind an act of violence is essential to differentiate acts motivated by misogyny or gender discrimination from acts motivated by purely political or factional disputes.

Scholars and practitioners working in the arena of women's human rights have documented a wide range of gender-based harms experienced by women attempting to exercise their political rights as citizens during elections (Kellow 2010; Bardall 2011, 2013, 2016; Cerna 2014; Ballington 2016; Bjarnegård 2018; IPU 2016; Piscopo 2016; Krook 2017; United Nations 2018a, 9–10). In their research on election violence in the Maldives, Zetterberg and Bjarnegård (this volume) found that women were more likely than men to be targets of psychological violence. Haley and Baker's chapter on election violence in Papua New Guinea (in this volume) reports widespread violence against women voters perpetrated by close family members who seek to control the votes of their female relatives.

Election violence targeting women in their political roles falls along a continuum of violence that ranges from incidents of psychological violence, such as verbal harassment, intimidation, or threats, to physical acts of bodily harm. Economic harm in the form of destruction of property, the loss of a job, or similar may occur during highly contentious elections. In fact, findings reported below from elections in Uganda attest to the widespread occurrence of both *threats* and actual economic harm during elections.

As is mentioned in Chapter 1 in this volume, scholars continue to debate the utility of including economic violence along the continuum of political violence. Economic harm that results from structural processes, such as discriminatory legal practices that deny landowning rights to a disfavored group over successive generations, can be diffuse and difficult to measure. This type of structural economic violence is much different in kind from the type of economic violence we see perpetrated during an election. Acts of economic violence that occur during elections are frequently perpetrated by the political opponents of the target of the violence during one or more episodes of contention. For this reason, I include economic violence in the following definition of electoral violence:

Election violence constitutes any purposeful or calculated act of physical, sexual, psychological or economic harm against an individual or group, including threats, harassment, intimidation, or deprivation that occurs at any point throughout the election cycle, with the intent to discourage or prevent an individual or group from participating, or to alter an election process or outcome. (Schneider and Carroll 2020)

This definition guided the collection of data for this project and provides structure to the reporting of findings below.

Methodological Approach: Focus Groups and Microlevel Data

As the chapters in this volume attest, important insight about the relationship between gender and political violence requires a multiplicity of methodological approaches. Findings reported below are informed by both qualitative and quantitative data collection methods. Data gathered by the author and Ugandan research assistants reflects the experiences of politically active Ugandans from scores of municipalities, towns, and villages in three regions of the country during local councillor (LC) elections in 2016 and 2018. Given the dearth of data about women's experiences of election violence, women from a variety of ethnic, religious, and socioeconomic identity groups were oversampled to capture the widest possible range of experiences along the continuum of violence.

Collecting data on hard-to-reach populations, such as rural populations in lower income countries like Uganda, can be challenging (Lupu and Michelitch 2018). Recruiting respondents required methods different from those used in general population studies. We employed purposive sampling techniques identifying *seeds*, or initial contacts in a social network, to assist us in recruiting participants for the study (Johnston and Sabin 2010; Greiner et al. 2014). Two methods of data collection are utilized in our research.

The first is focus group discussions (FGD).[1] We recruited local council candidates, elected officials, and campaign mobilizers—or agents—for our focus groups. Focus groups are an ideal method to learn about the social and political attitudes and behavior of marginalized groups like rural women because the researcher can ask follow-up questions in real time, clarify responses, and thereby decrease the likelihood that questions are misunderstood (Cyr 2016, 232). This increases the validity of the data and findings. The main limitation of data gathered from FGDs is that findings may not be generalizable to other populations of interest. Unless the participants are selected by strict adherence to scientific sampling methods, the researcher cannot assume that the views and opinions expressed by participants represent the general tendencies of the entire population from which the participants are drawn. For this reason, findings should be interpreted as suggestive, as respondents were not randomly selected from the population of Ugandan adults and women were overrepresented among respondents.

The second method of data collection was administration of a survey instrument. The survey is in the form of an election violence incident report (EVIR) developed for this study. All focus group participants completed an EVIR survey, but not all respondents to the EVIR survey were part of a focus group discussion. For analyses using the EVIR data, the episode of violence is the unit of analysis. Survey questions yielded data on the type and context of the violence, gender of the target and the perpetrator, and the motivation driving the violence, among other factors.

Gender Differences in Election Violence:
Types and Targets

Table 11.1 displays results from the EVIR survey on the most frequently reported *types of violence*, by the *gender of the target(s)*. Note that respondents can report multiple forms of violence experienced during a single conflict event or episode. For instance, if a candidate was meeting with supporters and experienced an attack, that was recorded as a single episode, and all acts of violence perpetrated during the episode would be coded as such. Respondents identified 274 acts of violence across ninety-eight distinct episodes.

Results show that individuals were much more likely to be targeted than groups. A total of seventy-one male and female targets were alone when targeted, while in twenty-seven cases, groups were the targets of violence. When groups were targeted, mixed male/female groups comprised 70 percent (n=19) of all group targets. Experiences reported in the EVIR survey comport with information shared by focus group participants, who stated that groups comprised of candidates and their male and female agents and supporters were often targeted at night during campaign activities.

Candidates alone and in groups were the most commonly targeted type of political actor, comprising sixty-seven of the ninety-eight intended targets. Women alone or in groups were more likely to be targeted than men. In an analysis of this data not included in the present study, we found that a majority of women who were targeted when alone were, in fact, women candidates (Schneider and Carroll 2020). The remaining targets in Table 11.1 are primarily agents or supporters of candidates. A small number of voters are represented in the data, including women who experienced domestic violence due to familial conflict around the elections.

TABLE 11.1 DISTRIBUTION OF TYPES OF VIOLENCE BY GENDER AND STATUS OF TARGET

Type of Violence, Intimidation, or Harassment	Acts of Violence across All Episodes, by Form of Violence N=274 (Column Percentages)	Episodes of Violence across Gender and Status of Target (Row Percentages), by Form of Violence (N=98)		
		Female (47) or All Female Group (5) N=52 (53%)	Male (24) or All Male Group (3) N=27 (28%)	Mixed Male/Female Group N=19 (19%)
Physical Violence against Individual(s) and/or Family Member	44 (16%)	16 (36%)	18 (41%)	10 (23%)
Property Destruction and/or Other Economic Harm, Deprivation, Banishment	22 (8%)	8 (36%)	9 (41%)	5 (23%)
Verbal Harassment, Intimidation, Emotional Distress	69 (25%)	41 (60%)	15 (22%)	13 (18%)
Threats of Physical Violence, or Threats of Property Destruction, Deprivation, or Other Economic Harm	100 (36%)	48 (48%)	27 (27%)	25 (25%)
Incidents of a Sexual Nature				
Rape/Penetrative Sexual Assault; Forced Unwanted Sexual Contact	5 (2%)	4 (80%)	1 (20%)	0
Sexual Propositions, Coercion, Harassment, or Use of Sexual Language or Insults of Sexual Nature	34 (13%)	28 (82%)	3 (9%)	3 (9%)

Note: Respondents can report *one or more* acts of violence, intimidation, or harassment in a single episode with a discreet target(s) and perpetrator(s). A target may experience multiple forms of violence over the period in which a single episode occurred.

Along the continuum of violence, the most commonly reported category of violence is the *threat* of physical violence, or the *threat* of economic harm such as property destruction, job loss, or banishment from a village. This category of violence represented 36 percent (n=100) of all reported acts of violence. A closer examination of targeting around threats shows that 48 percent of the targets were individual females or all-female groups, while 27 percent of the targets were individual male or all-male groups. The remainder of targets were mixed male and female groups.

After threats, instances of verbal harassment and intimidation are the second-most cited type of violence in the sample, with sixty-nine reported cases. Women alone and in groups were by far the most frequently targeted for this form of violence. Verbal harassment and intimidation are considered a form of psychological violence along the continuum of violence (Zetterberg and Bjarnegård in this volume) when the abuse has the effect of publicly humiliating or shaming the target or the magnitude of the harassment causes serious emotional duress. Bjarnegård et al. (2015) also found that women are more likely than men to experience psychological violence.

Psychological violence can be an effective method for exerting power and control over others because the likelihood of a threat progressing into an actual act of physical violence is unknown. One respondent from our study, a young woman candidate running against a male candidate for a direct seat in the city of Gulu, reported that during fireside campaigning with her supporters (known as the tradition of *wangoo* among the Acholi people), she was constantly berated and harassed by the agents of her male opposition. They would yell deflating or demeaning comments, such as, "You are too young," and "Why does a mere woman think she can run against a man?" The agents would then often follow the woman and her supporters as they walked home at the end of the night, leaving the candidate feeling increasingly threatened and vulnerable to harm (EVIR case 156, female, Gulu, Uganda).

Incidents of physical violence directed at the target or their family members occurred forty-four times and represent 16 percent of all reported acts of violence. Violent fights between gangs of individuals supporting opposing candidates were commonly reported, but rapes and deaths also occurred. One respondent had direct knowledge of an abduction that resulted in the rape and death of one woman at the center of a feud between two male candidates.

Men alone or in groups were slightly more likely than women to be the targets of physical violence. Our findings corroborate the findings of Bardall (2011) and Bjarnegård et al. (2015) in that men and male gangs/groups are at higher risk for physical violence committed in public spaces. This is likely a function of the fact that individual men and all-male gangs or groups are disproportionately represented in street-level violence so much so that discussions of such violence in scholarly work rarely even mention the gender of the actors.

A novel finding of the present research is that women alone and in groups did report instances of physical violence that occurred during quota seat races between two or more women candidates. The perpetrators were most often men serving as agents for women candidates, but there were instances in which females alone or in groups perpetrated the violence. A female candidate respondent detailed how in a quota seat race, one of her female opponents would throw rocks at her and her supporters during campaign rallies (EVIR case 4, female, Gulu, Uganda).

Property destruction, or other types of economic harm, including withholding food or shelter (deprivation) or banishing someone from the community, also occurred at high rates in our sample. Respondents spoke of how support for a candidate disfavored by the majority of the community could result in the loss of a job and refusal to hire anyone in the family (EVIR case 17, female, Soroti, Uganda). One female candidate who had experienced persistent threats and harassment from the agents working for an opposing female candidate escaped to a male friend's house after receiving a death threat. The agents "burned the house to the ground and my friend lost everything" (EVIR case 12, female, Gulu, Uganda).

Turning now to reported incidents of violence and intimidation of a sexual nature, five respondents reported that they either experienced, observed, or had direct knowledge of an election-related rape or other form of forced sexual violence that occurred during campaigning. In four of the five instances, females were targeted by males in groups. In one of those cases, a woman candidate was raped in a car by the chairman of her own political party while out campaigning with other candidates. A number of male party members stood watch outside while the attack occurred (EVIR, case 7, female, Gulu, Uganda). The one male target of sexual violence in the sample was attacked by other men who opposed his candidacy because he was running as a candidate under the Forum for Democratic Change party label in an area dominated by the ruling NRM party. The men grabbed and attempted to twist his testicles (EVIR, case 167, male, Soroti, Uganda). All of the reported incidents of a sexual nature occurred in a public or outdoor space (not in a private residence).

There were thirty-four reports of inappropriate or unwelcomed propositions, sexual coercion or harassment, insults of a sexual nature, or the use of sexual language. Insults and other types of sexualized language were the most commonly reported type of sexual violence. Women were the targets of sexual harassment or sexualized language in twenty-eight out of thirty-four (82 percent) instances, while men were targets in only three cases (the other targets were mixed male/female groups). This is a remarkably high level of harassment against women in political roles and demonstrates how different forms of violence may be highly gendered. Intentionally spreading rumors about female candidates—that they had loose morals, were sexually available, or were engaged in a sexual relationship with a party leader to gain favor—emerged as common themes in the stories of women candidates in focus group discussions.

Two Primary Motivations for Election Violence

Understanding the intentions behind violence, or the motivation to perpetrate such violence, can be difficult to discern, as the target of violence may perceive the motivation behind the attack differently than the perpetrator(s) (Piscopo 2016, 446). Conventional election violence research has typically assumed that political or factional conflict drives all election-related violence. However, scholars of gender and political violence argue that election-related violence may be motivated by at least one other important factor—sex discrimination or misogyny. Feminist scholars maintain that violence driven by sex discrimination or misogyny can manifest in the full range of types of violence along the continuum and serves to depress or dissuade the electoral participation of women (Bardall, Bjarnegård, and Piscopo 2020).

To untangle the complex interplay between intent and action and determine whether an attack was motivated by political conflict, gender discrimination, or perhaps some of both, respondents to the EVIR survey were asked to provide detailed descriptions of episodes of violence, including the relationship between the target and the perpetrator. Understanding the relationship between target and perpetrator, and the context in which the violence occurs, can increase the reliability and validity of the data documenting acts of election violence.

Table 11.2 displays two main types of motivation for violence, distributed across the gender of perpetrators. While a large majority of incidents of violence were motivated by political or factional conflict (71 percent), a sizable percentage of reports (29 percent) attribute violence to sex discrimination or both sex discrimination and political factors (mixed motives). The distribution of motivation by gender characteristics of the perpetrator reveals some important, if not unexpected, gendered patterns. Almost all group-perpetrated violence was motivated by political or factional conflict. However, all-male groups were implicated in five cases of violence motivated by sex discrimination and another five cases in which the motive was perceived as "a little of both" sex discrimination *and* political factors. Individual males alone (n=12) represented the single largest category of perpetrators motivated by sex discrimination.

Motivation for Violence (N=97*)	Gender of Perpetrator(s)					
	Female Alone	Male Alone	All Female Group	All Male Group	Mixed M/F Group	
Political/Factional	5	6	4	30	24	69 (71%)
Sex Discrimination/ Misogyny	0	12	0	5	1	18 (19%)
Mixed Motives	0	1	2	5	2	10 (10%)
Total	5	19	6	40	27	97 (100%)

TABLE 11.2 MOTIVATION FOR VIOLENCE BY GENDER OF PERPETRATOR

* Note that in Table 11.2, the gender of the perpetrator in one case is missing from the dataset. This explains the decrease from N=98 in Table 11.1 to N=97 in Table 11.2.

Cases of violence in which women were the targets, males were the perpetrators, and sex discrimination the motivation were widely discussed by women participants in focus groups. Women who ran against men in open seats reported the greatest amount of violence motivated by sex discrimination, including serious incidents of extrajudicial arrest and detainment. A respondent from Pader in the Gulu region relayed how a female candidate she supported in 2016 ran for an open seat, but had little money so could afford no security. The other male candidates colluded and coordinated with the police to arrest her and her agents because she was a woman. The respondent claimed, "This is when women experience violence because they are seen as going out of their role and infringing on men's rights to seats" (FGD, Muslim women's group, Gulu, Uganda).

There were many mentions of *intraparty* violence in the context of sexualized political space, where women candidates and activists are vulnerable to pressure or attacks by members of their own party. One focus group participant shared that party leaders "expect that women party candidates will have sex with not just one, but many!" (FGD, candidates, elected officials, agents, Soroti, Uganda). Another woman who was part of the same focus group stated, "It is pervasive that women candidates are expected to sleep with party leaders. That is why some husbands do not want their wives to run, because they assume that they will have to sleep with the male politicians" (ibid.).

Single women, and young women in particular, appeared to be disproportionately targeted with sexual innuendo and slurs, as the assumption is that if she is young, unmarried, and involved in politics (a "man's game"), then she must be sexually promiscuous and sleeping her way into positions of power. For instance, a thirty-two-year-old female local council speaker from Gulu shared an incident from her 2016 campaign to win a direct seat in which a male from within her own party spread rumors that she was sleeping with the husband of another candidate. Her status as a single woman left her particularly vulnerable to being labeled *malaya*, or prostitute (FGD, Women councillors LC3, Gulu, Uganda).

Some women candidates faced derision and threats that were not of a sexual nature, but were still sexist, with the intent to dissuade the woman from running for a direct seat. For instance, one female candidate from a focus group in Soroti stated that she ran against five men for a direct seat and that campaigning door-to-door was very intimidating, as she frequently encountered men who would badmouth her: "You are not fit for this post. Why are you contesting this post? Why don't you contest the woman's seat? This is a stupid woman!" (FGD, candidates, elected officials, agents, Soroti, Uganda).

Conclusion

While women in Uganda report a wide range of experiences with violence during elections, they demonstrated resolve in exercising their political and civil rights. One of the most encouraging trends suggested by the findings from this study is that women in Uganda are feeling empowered to participate in all aspects of local campaigns and elections. Even in rural areas with historically low levels of socioeconomic development, women have assumed roles as candidates, agents, party activists, and voters. This differs from what Haley and Baker report in their chapter on Papua New Guinea, where election observers noted high levels of voter intimidation and harassment targeting women in the Highlands regions. The gendered impact of this violence resulted in low turnout among women voters in the 2017 elections.

Women reported a wide range of abuse at the hands of male candidates, party leaders, and voters, especially when they ran against men in direct seat contests. In particular, women were more likely than men to be targets of verbal harassment and intimidation—yet the line between verbal harassment and the threat of serious violence may be thin. Women were particularly susceptible to inappropriate or unwelcomed propositions of a sexual nature.

The extent to which women in their political roles as elected officials, candidates, activists, or voters experience sexual violence or harassment is of particular concern to scholars of gender and politics. The phenomena of violence against women in politics *because they are women* can have a pernicious effect and depress rates of women's political participation because acts that dissuade one woman from participating may be perceived by other women as a warning that engaging in political activity could result in harm to themselves, their families, or their property. Acts of violence motivated wholly or in part by sex/gender discrimination—or what might be more appropriately termed misogyny when acts are perpetrated by men alone or in groups—were found in 29 percent of the episodes of violence. Given that conventional election violence scholarship overlooks sex discrimination as a motive for violence, these findings suggest that the current state of knowledge fails to account for a significant driver of violence that disproportionately harms women political actors.

The failure to consider sex/gender as a variable in research on electoral violence can lead to important gaps in our understanding of patterns of perpetration, targeting, and harm, including instances when women are perpetrators of violence. Incidents such as these demonstrate that analyzing election violence through a gendered lens exposes gaps in our knowledge of the causes and consequences of electoral violence. These gaps must be addressed both to develop more comprehensive theories and to construct more effective policies aimed at mitigating violence and securing electoral integrity for all citizens.

12

Harassment and Intimidation of Parliamentary Candidates in the United Kingdom

SOFIA COLLIGNON

The murder of Labour MP Jo Cox during the European Union referendum campaign shocked the United Kingdom (U.K.). This event sparked concern about the personal safety of politicians. Later, in 2017, Sheryll Murray, MP for South East Cornwall, was the first member of the Conservative Party to speak out about her treatment during the campaign, saying it involved someone urinating at her office door and death threats on social media. She was not the only one experiencing aggressive behavior; the online "trolling" of prominent female politicians, such as Diane Abbott, attracted major attention during the election campaign. While all these events are different, all of them affect politicians' feelings of safety. The concern was shared across parties, and once the new Parliament was formed, PM Theresa May was urged to take action and the Committee on Standards in Public Life (CSPL) started an inquiry to determine the magnitude of the problem.

The publishing of the CSPL report in 2017 was important because it established a set of recommendations for action to the government, social media companies, political parties, the police, broadcasters, the media, and MPs, and parliamentary candidates themselves (Collignon et al. 2017; CSPL 2017). But despite the publication of the Online Harms White Paper (U.K.-DCMS-Committee 2019), the political pressure, and media attention to the problem, the situation did not improve in the following years. When a new general election was called in 2019, a string of politicians—among them Heidi Allen, MP for South Cambridgeshire, and Nicky Morgan, MP for Loughborough—

stepped down, citing abuse, harassment, and intimidation as their main reasons not to stand for reelection. Just two years later—in October 2021—Sir David Amess, a Conservative MP, was tragically stabbed to death during a regular surgery in his constituency, prompting discussions about MPs' security and the urgency of taking more effective action.

These events show firstly that the harassment and intimidation of political elites in the U.K. has been going on for a while, reaching levels that make politicians fear for their security and their families. Secondly, it shows that violence is increasingly becoming an additional barrier for political participation, which can make it even harder for women and other underrepresented groups to stand for office.

Using surveys of sitting MPs, researchers have determined that the frequency in which parliamentarians suffer from violence while performing their duties is alarming. In the U.K., 81 percent of parliamentarians in the office between 2010 and 2015 suffered some form of abuse (James et al. 2016). A later survey of British MPs on their experience with online trolling conducted in 2018 found that 100 percent of respondents had experienced this form of harassment (Akhtar and Morrison 2019). Other academic studies of tweets sent to MPs come to similar conclusions (McLoughlin and Ward 2017; Gorrell et al. 2018; Southern and Harmer 2021). Current research shows that female MPs are not always subject to more frequent abuse than men but that there are distinctive ways in which they are abused. The differences manifest in the content and type of abuse. However, since the majority of studies focus on sitting MPs, they conclude that the visibility and prominence reached by the politician are what put them in risk. Moreover, other than the victims' status as MPs, current research does not look at the gender and power dynamics behind the abuse.

Building on previous research (Collignon and Rüdig 2020, 2021; Collignon, Campbell, and Rüdig 2021), this chapter goes beyond the current focus on MPs and representatives to a focus on candidates in general. The focus on candidates offers a unique opportunity to look at the experiences of women and men *seeking power*. Their experiences are different from the experiences of men and women *in a position of power (MPs)* because they respond to different power hierarchies and have different structures that protect them. For example, being in Parliament can make MPs subject of cyclical violence driven by partisan alignments, budgetary constraints, or policy positions. However, in the case of women candidates, they can be targeted by individuals willing to prevent them from reaching power either because they are supporters of other parties or candidates, because their condition of women makes them disruptive in a traditionally male-dominated sphere, because of the policies and ideology they advocate, or for all these reasons simultaneously. Thus, this chapter asks: Are women participating in elections, as candidates, in the U.K. more likely to suffer harassment and intimidation than men? What type of experiences do women suffer the most? Why is harassment carried out?

This chapter refers to the terms *harassment, intimidation*, and *abuse* instead of *violence* because these terms are often used interchangeably in the U.K. context (James et al. 2016; Collignon et al. 2017; Nadim and Fladmoe 2019; Collignon and Rüdig 2020). In the U.K., the Protection from Harassment Act 1997 indicates that someone's actions amount to harassment when they make feel the victim distressed, humiliated, threatened, or fearful of further violence; aim to persuade them not to do something that they are entitled or required to do; or direct them do something that they are not under any obligation to do. Actions listed under the Protection Act include (but are not limited to) phone calls, letters, emails, visits, abuse on social media, stalking, verbal abuse of any kind, threats, damage to property, and bodily harm.

The broad definition of harassment present in the U.K. legislation provides an umbrella for different manifestations of physical and psychological (including online) violence as defined in Chapter 1 in this volume. By taking the view that harassment, intimidation, and abuse constitute forms of violence in a continuum that manifest in different and often intertwined ways (Kelly 1988a), this chapter explores violence perpetrated against women and men candidates in the U.K. In concrete, this chapter looks at physical violence, such as bodily harm (i.e., kicks or punches) and sexual assault, and psychological violence, including sexual harassment, threats, having people loitering around, damage to property, and online violence (emails and social media).

Drawing on lessons learned from the Representative Audit of Britain (RAB) survey of all 2017 general election candidates standing from any of the main parties in England, Wales, and Scotland,[1] I argue that women in the U.K. are distinctively affected by harassment and intimidation in at least two ways: frequency and motivation (Bardall, Bjarnegård, and Piscopo 2020). Women who stand for office suffer from more frequent physical and psychological violence—online and offline—than men. As a result, they experience higher levels of fear while campaigning. The harassment is motivated, to a great degree, by their visibility and leadership, the distinctive political ideology they advocate, and the degree in which they do not abide by mainstream politics.

In the next section, I go into more detail into the approach taken to empirically address harassment and intimidation of political elites in the U.K. and how this approach is useful to understand gender-motivated political violence (see Chapter 5 by Piscopo and Bjarnegård). This chapter contributes to the field in at least two ways. First, I provide evidence of the targeting of women in politics (Krook 2020). Second, by showing the emotional consequences of harassment and the political motivation behind it, I show that the targeting of women in politics is gender motivated (Bardall, Bjarnegård, and Piscopo 2020).

Approaching Harassment and Intimidation of Political Elites in the U.K.

A first challenge encountered in the U.K. is the ambiguity in which the words *harassment* and *intimidation* have been used. In a British context, the term *inappropriate behavior* is understood as conduct that is unwarranted and is reasonably interpreted to be demeaning or offensive. Persistent inappropriate behavior constitutes a form of harassment. Thus, much of what would be regarded as *political incivility* in the United States would probably be termed *harassment* in the U.K. (Stryker, Conway, and Danielson 2016). Until recently, the term has been mainly used to refer to sexual harassment, but the increasing interest in abusive online behavior, such as trolling, and evidence of widespread abuse has led researchers to use the term to refer generically to a wide range of phenomena (Collignon and Rüdig 2020, 2021; Collignon, Campbell, and Rüdig 2021). Following Chapter 1 in this volume, this chapter understands harassment and intimidation to be part of a continuum of violence that includes psychological (including online) and physical violence. It recognizes that individuals do not deal with experiences in isolation but that those experiences accumulate and are linked to specific gender, racial, and power dynamics (Kelly 1988a) and, therefore, all experiences can be equally damaging.

Empirically, one problem to study how gender influences violence targeting political elites relates to men's and women's normalization of certain types of violence. In the case of political elites, men and women are hesitant to speak about their experiences of harassment and intimidation due to fear of being labeled as "snowflakes" that need to "toughen up" to be worthy of participating in the "hard business" of politics. Later, their own understanding of what is and what is not acceptable behavior is faced with a reality in which society presents victims with the forced choice to disregard or excuse certain experiences that have not been typified as serous by the law (Halder and Jaishankar 2011). Therefore, an empirical strategy that presents victims with a normative definition of harassment will be very limited in its scope and most likely will produce biased results.

In consequence, to empirically observe how harassment and intimidation in the U.K. manifests in different ways for men and women, I follow a victimology approach in which it is up to victims to define themselves if the behavior experienced should be or should not be classified as intimidatory. The term *victimology* refers to the scientific study of crime victims. It focuses on identifying the elements that make certain victims more vulnerable than others and the most frequent forms of victimization among certain groups (Mendelsohn 1976). This approach recognizes the uniqueness of their experiences, the shared characteristics that may put them at risk, and the importance of their voices to design mechanisms to prevent crime.

In particular, a feminist victimization approach was born from the realization that victims do not always report crimes because of fear or shame. The women's movement emphasized, for example, that women cannot be blamed for sexual assault and domestic violence, as they are a by-product of misogyny (Daigle 2017). The approach should not be understood as victim-blaming, as modern victimology offers an alternative to empower victims and vulnerable groups to protect themselves (Romano et al. 2011). Thus, modern victimology emphasizes the innocence of the victim and the need to *understand* the causes of victimization to tackle them (Doerner and Lab 2017). By focusing on victims, the approach is suitable to study how their gendered life experiences shape their understanding of the harms suffered.

Under this perspective, instead of looking at perpetrators, the characteristics of the victims studied—candidates—can provide information about the *motivations* behind the attack (Bardall, Bjarnegård, and Piscopo 2020; Collignon and Rüdig 2021). In the context of gendered political violence, patriarchal attitudes and institutions may play a role in facilitating the victimization of women by providing perpetrators with the justification to intervene to prevent women from achieving a position of power (Crittenden and Wright 2013; Crittenden and Policastro 2018; Collignon and Rüdig 2021). At the same time, women in politics may not always report the aggressions suffered, either because these structures of power dismiss women's claims attributing the violence they suffer to the competitive nature of politics or because they need to protect their image of leadership (Aaldering and Van Der Pas 2020).

This approach focuses on victims and not on perpetrators. It steps up to the challenge of underreporting violence against women because of hesitations of being identified as a victim or because the system does not provide victims with the legal framework to do so. It recognizes that gender dynamics play a role in how men and women are positioned in the electoral process. This approach also allows me to look at some elements proposed by Bardall, Piscopo and Bjarnegård—motives, forms, and impact—in the analysis of gendered political violence, specifically, by addressing how gender shapes men's and women's understanding of their experiences of violence when they participate in politics (Bardall, Bjarnegård, and Piscopo 2020).

Findings

In this section, I look at men and women candidates standing in the 2017 U.K. general election. I show evidence of gender-motivated political violence by demonstrating that women in politics in the U.K. are targeted because of their visibility, leadership, and political ideology.

Women in Politics in the U.K. Are More Likely to Suffer Abuse and Intimidation Than Men

As discussed above, presenting candidates with a survey question using a stringent definition of harassment will prompt responses to refer only to widely recognized forms of abuse, leaving out other more subtle, but equally harmful, experiences. In consequence, the RAB 2017 questionnaire included a question that was deliberately formulated in a way that it required candidates themselves to define what they consider to be harassment and intimidation before answering.[2] The formulation of the question recognizes that the same act of intimidation can be interpreted as serious or not by the victims depending on many factors, such as their gender, age, or life and political experiences (Doerner and Lab 2017).

Of course, there are advantages and disadvantages associated with this empirical approach. The main strength lies on the fact that it gives a voice to victims who can self-define what they consider to be abusive behavior independently from the intentions of the perpetrator. This approach also recognizes that for some candidates, it is the accumulation of experiences of microaggressions that takes the toll on their mental health. The main disadvantage of the approach is that since the questionnaire does not provide victims with a clear definition of harassment, it is difficult to determine exclusively from this question the nature of the experiences. I address this shortcoming later in this chapter when I look in detail to further questions in the survey where candidates are asked about the type of physical and psychological abuse suffered.

The survey analysis indicates that 38 percent of candidates affirm to have suffered harassment or intimidation while campaigning, suggesting that about four in every ten candidates are victims of abuse. A simple cross-tabulation with a Pearson's x^2 test shows that women are being particularly targeted. Forty-five percent of women candidates suffered harassment and intimidation, compared with 35 percent of men ($p<0.05$) (Collignon and Rüdig 2020).

Figure 12.1 presents graphically the coefficients of a logistic regression using a binary measure of harassment as the dependent variable and sex, ethnicity age, incumbency, and position in the electoral race as independent variables. Controls include party and nation in which the candidate stands for election. Full details of the models are available in Collignon and Rüdig (2020). Marginal probabilities obtained after the logistic regression indicate that women are about 9 percentage points more likely to be harassed than men, even when other sociodemographic and political factors are controlled for.

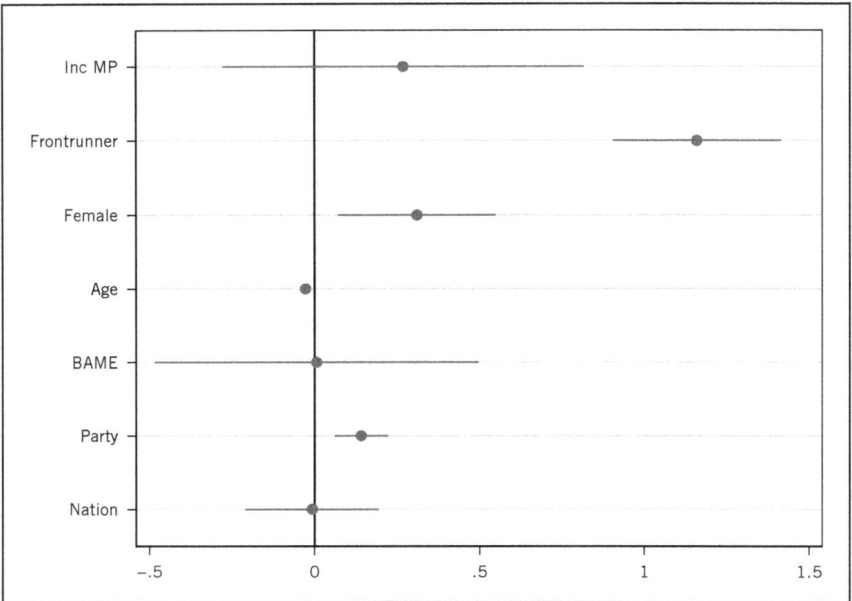

Figure 12.1 Coefficients of logistic regression explaining harassment (Model 1)

In a country where parity is still way off and only 29 percent of candidates were women in 2017 and 37 percent in 2019, it is particularly worrying to observe such levels of violence toward women in politics.

Looking closer at differences between candidates, I first compare incumbents and nonincumbents. One hundred sixty-eight of sitting MPs responded to the survey. This corresponds to a response rate of 26 percent among parliamentarians.[3] A simple cross-tabulation with a Pearson's x^2 test shows that incumbent MPs are significantly more likely than nonincumbent candidates to be harassed; 62 percent of them affirm to have suffered harassment while campaigning compared with 34 percent of nonincumbents ($p<=0.05$). The proportion of women and men MPs being harassed is very similar, 62 percent and 63 percent, respectively ($p>=0.05$). However, as Figure 12.1 shows, incumbency loses its explanatory power once other factors are taken into consideration. Thus, it is possible to say that incumbency status is not one of the main reasons behind the harassment of candidates in the U.K.

Looking at the position of the candidate in the race, it is possible to observe that leading candidates who finished the race in first or second place suffer from significantly more harassment (53 percent) than candidates who are not front-runners. Fifty-eight percent of women leading the race affirm to suffer harassment while in the campaign, and 52 percent of leading men affirm the same. Figure 12.1 shows that the coefficient of this variable is positive and significant. In terms of predicted probabilities, a woman who is a front-runner is 7 percentage points more likely to be harassed than a man in the same position.

Looking at intersectionality, the sample includes seventy-eight candidates from a black, an Asian, and another minority ethnic origin (BAME). Fifty-three of them are men, and twenty-five are women. Numbers are too low to infer anything from a simple cross-tabulation. But a logistic regression shows no evidence that candidates from an ethnic minority are being targeted. Differences in predicted probabilities between women candidates from an ethnic minority background and white men candidates show that the former are 7 percentage points more likely to be harassed than the later. But again, the number of BAME respondents is too low to generalize.

Younger candidates are also more likely to suffer harassment than older candidates. The mean age of candidates in the sample is fifty-one years old (SD 13.84). On average, younger candidates of twenty years of age are 18 percentage points more likely to be harassed than a fifty-year-old candidate. Female candidates of twenty years of age have a probability of being harassed of about 58 percentage points, 7 percentage points larger than a man of the same age.

The severity of the abuse is reflected in the consequences of concerns about safety expressed by the candidates. Perhaps the most striking finding is that 32 percent of candidates affirm to feeling either moderately or very fearful as a result of their experiences of harassment and intimidation. Women feel significantly more fearful (44 percent) than men (25 percent). Together, these findings indicate that women are not only attacked more frequently than men but also that the attacks they suffer harm their sense of safety, as almost one in two women campaigns for election in fear.

Women Suffer from Different Types of Abuse

As I mentioned before, one of the main caveats of a general question on harassment and intimidation is that it does not offer punctual information on the nature of the experiences of abuse. This book approaches violence as a continuum (Kelly 1988a) that includes different kinds of violence ranging from psychological violations of personal integrity to physical harm. The approach here taken allows differentiating by type of abuse while comparing the experiences of men and women. I do so by analyzing different items of a question in the survey asking candidates to indicate the frequency in which they suffered different forms of psychological—including online (see Esposito's chapter for a definition)—and physical violence.

Starting with online experiences of abuse (digitally facilitated violence), the analysis of responses shows that 29 percent of the total number of candidates affirm to have suffered of improper communications on Twitter and/ or Facebook at least once during the campaign. Twenty-five percent did so three times or more. The data shows significant differences by sex, as 34 percent of female candidates were targeted compared with 26 percent of men. Twenty-three percent of candidates received inappropriate emails at least once during the campaign. This percentage is significantly higher for women (28 percent) than it is for men (20 percent).

Regarding other psychological abuse, women suffer significantly more threats to harm (5 percent affirm to have suffered three or more during the campaign) and from individuals loitering around their homes or other places they frequent (4 percent three or more times) than men (3 and 2 percent in the same categories). They also suffer significantly more experiences that involve interference with their property (6 percent of women and 5 percent of men).

Regarding physical abuse, 5 percent of women and 4 percent of men indicated having suffered some form of body harm or the intention of it; no significant differences between men and women were observed in this regard. Three percent of women candidates suffered from sexual harassment (including unwanted invitations and rape threats). No men reported any instance of sexual harassment. No evidence was found that candidates in the U.K. suffered any sexual assault during the 2017 GE campaign. Figure 12.2 shows graphically the frequency of online, physical, and psychological abuse suffered by women and men candidates.

Women Who Speak Out or Do Not Conform with Mainstream Politics Are Targeted

Taken together, these findings suggest that the harassment and intimidation of women candidates presents particular characteristics related to the type and frequency of the abuse. Now I look into the motives of such acts of violence, showing that while men and women suffer from harassment and intimidation during campaigns, women candidates are targeted because of their political views. Here I test three possible links behind the harassment, intimidation, and abuse of women candidates and their political views: abuse because of their ideology, abuse because of their polarization, and abuse because of distance to voters in their constituency. They are tested with a series of logistic models that use the binary measure of harassment as the dependent variable and measures of ideology as independent variables and adds the same controls as in model 1. Coefficients are graphically presented in Figure 12.3. Model tables are available in the appendix at the back of this chapter.

The RAB 2017 survey asks candidates to note their position and the position of voters in their constituency in a left/right ideological scale.[4] The closer

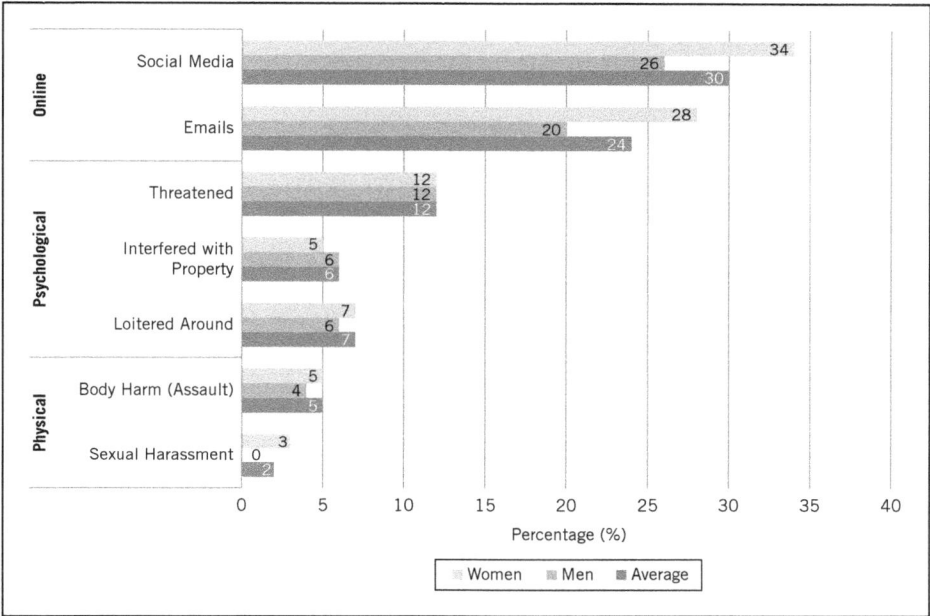

Figure 12.2 Forms of abuse, harassment, and intimidation suffered by candidates standing in the 2017 general election

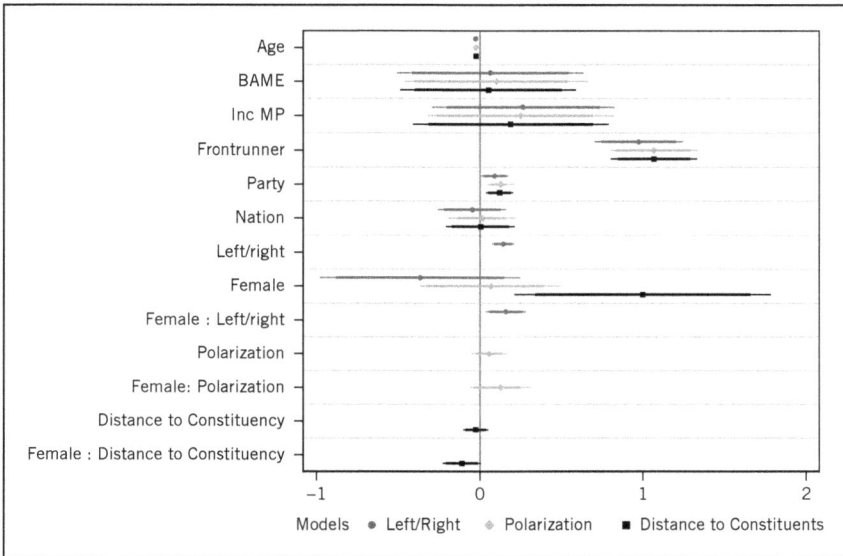

Figure 12.3 Coefficients of logistic regression explaining harassment (Models 2–4)

the candidate scores themselves and voters to zero, the more left wing they are considered to be. The closer to ten, the more right wing. Looking at the self-position of candidates in the ideological scale, female candidates are, on average, significantly more left wing than male candidates (means of 4.7 and 5.3, respectively), but in both cases, it is possible to observe a tendency to express moderation in their views.

The black dots and lines in Figure 12.3 represent the coefficients and confidence intervals of a model that includes the left/right self-measure of ideology as a predictor for harassment and interacts it with the binary measure of sex of the candidate. The coefficient for the sex of the candidate is not significant, indicating that women and men candidates are as likely to suffer from harassment when they are close to zero in the left/right ideological scale. The coefficient for left/right ideology is significant and positive, indicating that, on average, candidates on the right are significantly more likely to be harassed. However, the effect of ideology on the likelihood of harassment is stronger for women, as the coefficient of the interaction between ideology and sex is positive and significant, indicating that female candidates on the right side of the political spectrum are significantly more likely to be harassed than women on the left and men in general. Together, these findings indicate that women candidates are targets of harassment, intimidation, and abuse when they express or represent a particular ideology.

For example, Figure 12.4a shows how two left-wing (score of zero in the scale) candidates—male and female—will have a similar probability of being harassed (20 percent and 19 percent, respectively). The probability increases progressively for both, but not at the same rate. A very right-wing man (score =10) will have a probability of experiencing any form of intimidation of about 50 percent. A woman with the same characteristics has a likelihood of 80 percent. That is, a right-wing woman is 30 percentage points more likely to suffer abuse than a man with the same characteristics. Together, these results support the notion that the abuse sustained by women candidates is motivated by ideology.

Now, to look further into the argument that women are targeted when they do not conform with the mainstream political views, I analyzed the effects of polarization and ideological distance to citizens in the constituency, as they reflect two different processes that may lead to the abuse. The first indicates that the further apart the opinion of a woman is from the opinion of *other candidates*, the more likely it is that she will suffer from intimidation or abuse. Alternatively, the second link suggests that women can be victims of abuse if they do deviate from the mainstream political views in their constituency. That is, the further apart the opinion of a woman is from the opinion of the majority of voters in her constituency, the more likely it is that she will be harassed.

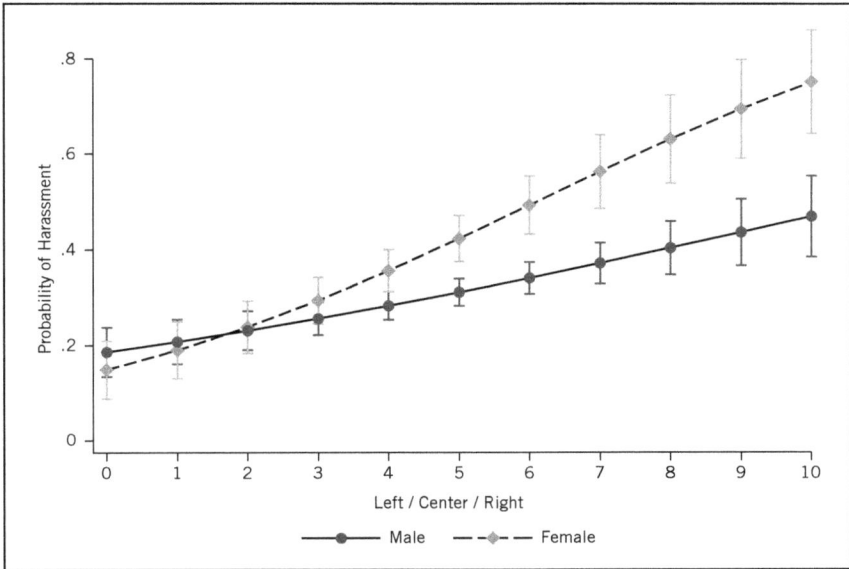

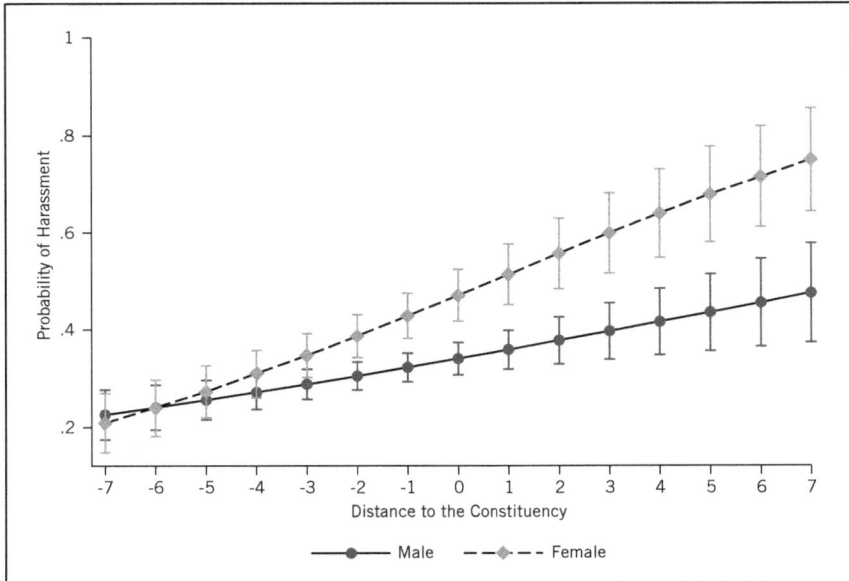

Figure 12.4 Predicted probabilities of harassment motivated by ideology
Figure 12.4a Predicted probability of harassment of men and women candidates based on their left/right ideological position
Figure 12.4b Predicted probability of harassment of men and women candidates based on their distance to voters in the constituency

To test the first mechanism, I used a simple measure of polarization calculated by taking each candidate's distance to the median left/right position in the sample. A simple test of differences in means shows that female and male candidates are, on average, equally polarized. The coefficients of the model represented with the blue dot and line in Figure 12.3 indicate that neither the measure of polarization nor its interaction with sex is significant. Thus, candidates—women and men—holding polarized views are almost equally vulnerable.

The next link is tested by including a measure of the candidate's ideological distance to the constituency. This variable is calculated by taking the distance between the self-position of the candidate in a left/right ideological scale to the perceived position of the voters in the constituency on the same scale. When the distance takes a value of zero, it indicates that the candidate and voters in the constituency are perceived to be aligned by the candidate. Values smaller than zero indicate that the candidate is more left wing than voters in the constituency. Positive values indicate that the candidate expressed to be righter wing than he or she perceives the voters in the constituency to be.

The coefficients of the model, represented by green dots and lines in Figure 12.3, suggest a positive and significant effect of the distance to voters and the interaction term. As it can be observed in Figure 12.4b, the probability of harassment increases for both men and women the larger the distance to the constituency. However, this effect is larger for women, indicating that they are more harshly penalized for expressing views that do not conform with the views of the constituency and, in particular, if these are right-wing views. Take, for example, a woman expressing extreme left-wing views in a constituency that is perceived as very right wing (value of −10). She will present a probability of harassment of 13 percent, which is 6 percentage points smaller than the predicted probability of a man with the same ideological distance to the constituency. When the distance to the constituency is zero, indicating congruence between candidates' views and the views of the constituency, the difference in the predicted probabilities between female and male candidates is 13 percentage points (34 percent for men and 47 percent for women). The likelihood of harassment keeps increasing the more they move to the right but at a higher rate for women. A woman who locates herself in the extreme on the right in an extreme leftish constituency has a probability of harassment of 83 percent, 30 percentage points larger than that of a man in the same position (53 percent).

Taken together, both women and men candidates are penalized for expressing right-wing views. However, women are penalized in a larger magnitude. A possible reason behind these differences is that women may be penalized for deviating from mainstream politics. This would suggest that the abuse may be coming from individuals who feel threatened by their opposing views or believe that women need to advocate the values and views of the left. Further support for this statement is found in the source of harassment. The survey asked candidates if they have suffered any form of harassment, abusive behavior, or intimidation *by supporters of other parties or candidates.* Seventy-one percent of candidates who suffered harassment answered affirmatively to the question. Unsurprisingly, women are significantly more likely to suffer this type of abuse than men.

Conclusions

The issue of the harassment and intimidation of political elites in the U.K. is a source of concern for the quality of public life in the country. This chapter aimed to answer the questions: Are women in the U.K. more likely to suffer abuse and intimidation than men? How and why is violence carried out?

This chapter follows Piscopo and Bjarnegård's multifaceted approach. It applies a victimology angle to the empirical study of gendered political violence. It does not look at perpetrators but focuses on the victims and lets them define what they consider to be harassment and intimidation based on their own experiences and the consequences that such experiences have had in their lives. By letting the victims themselves define the abuse, its causes, and its consequences, this approach recognizes that men and women have internalized different vulnerabilities and entitlements, which position them differently in a context of electoral politics.

This chapter offers evidence from the RAB 2017 general election candidate survey. The survey results and evidence presented throughout this chapter show that harassment and intimidation toward women candidates is substantively different in form and motives from abuse toward men candidates. Findings suggest that women candidates in the U.K. are particularly affected by psychological and physical violence in at least four ways. Firstly, they are affected by the frequency of the abuse. Women candidates are 7 percentage points more likely to experience any form of intimidation than men. Secondly, they are affected by the particular ways in which the abuse is conducted. Women are more likely to be harassed on social media and over email than men. Echoing Kuperberg's chapter, online abuse toward women candidates is also the most frequent form of abuse observed in the U.K. Thirdly, there is also evidence of significantly higher psychological harm, as almost one in every two women indicated having experienced some fear as a result of the harassment suffered during their electoral campaigns.

Fourthly, and perhaps more importantly, this chapter showed evidence that harassment and intimidation of candidates in the U.K. is gender motivated. Women candidates are affected by intolerance. They pay a larger cost than men for expressing distinctive political views, especially when these views do not correspond to what is socially expected from them. Women who suffered abuse did so by the hands of supporters of other candidates and parties in larger degree than men.

This chapter provides evidence that women participating in politics in the U.K. suffer, indeed, from targeted and gender-motivated political violence. The frequency, motivation, and impact of the physical and psychological violence analyzed impose a higher price for women than men who want to participate in politics. The U.K. is still a long way away from gender parity in Parliament. Future work urgently needs to be done to look into the long-term effects of violence into the demographic diversity in the pool of candidates standing for elections, not only in terms of gender, but also in terms of race and sexuality.

Appendix: Model Tables for Chapter 12

TABLE A12.1 LOGIT COEFFICIENTS REPRESENTED GRAPHICALLY IN FIGURE 12.1	
	(M1)
Variables	Harassed
Inc MP	0.27
	(0.28)
Front-Runner	1.16***
	(0.13)
Female	0.31**
	(0.12)
Age	−0.03***
	(0.00)
BAME	0.01
	(0.25)
Party	0.14***
	(0.04)
Nation	−0.01
	(0.10)
Constant	−0.33
	(0.27)
N	1122

Standard errors in parentheses.
*** p<0.01, ** p<0.05, * p<0.1

TABLE A12.2 LOGIT COEFFICIENTS REPRESENTED GRAPHICALLY IN FIGURE 12.3

Variables	(M2) Harassed	(M3) Harassed	(M4) Harassed
Age	−0.03***	−0.02***	−0.03***
	(0.00)	(0.00)	(0.00)
BAME	0.06	0.10	0.01
	(0.29)	(0.29)	(0.28)
Inc MP	0.27	0.25	0.21
	(0.28)	(0.29)	(0.30)
Front-Runner	0.98***	1.07***	1.01***
	(0.14)	(0.14)	(0.14)
Party	0.09**	0.13***	0.11***
	(0.04)	(0.04)	(0.04)
Nation	−0.05	0.02	−0.07
	(0.11)	(0.11)	(0.11)
Left/Right	0.15***		
	(0.03)		
Female	−0.36	0.07	0.51***
	(0.31)	(0.22)	(0.15)
Left/Right: Female	0.16**		
	(0.06)		
Polarization		0.06	
		(0.06)	
Polarization: Female		0.13	
		(0.10)	
Distance to Constituency			0.09***
			(0.03)
Distance to Constituency: Female			0.10**
			(0.04)
Constant	−0.89***	−0.51*	−0.07
	(0.32)	(0.30)	(0.30)
N	1034	1034	1034

Standard errors in parentheses.
*** p<0.01, ** p<0.05, * p<0.1

13

Physical and Psychological Violence among U.S. Mayors and State Senators

SUE THOMAS AND
REBEKAH HERRICK

I'm not here to be kissed. I'm here to lead this city and
to create policy for the people in this community.
—San Luis Obispo, California, former Mayor HEIDI HARMON

In 2020, San Luis Obispo, California, former Mayor Heidi Harmon, recounted an experience that still reverberates. At a public event, she introduced a male public figure. The man started his remarks by saying: "Wow, how great it must be to live in a town with a kissable mayor." Mayor Harmon knew that the speaker was trying to compliment her, but the message his words sent was undeniably sexist and condescending. They said to everyone that even if women win elections and lead cities, their worth is based on their appearance rather than their professional status and accomplishments. To this day, she thinks about this event and its effects (Wick 2020).

Mayor Harmon's story about being "kissable" emerged in the aftermath of a Facebook comment she posted after reading a *New York Times* article about research we report in this chapter: "The amount of cruelty, rudeness, threats, sexism, stalking, body shaming, rude/threatening comments towards my children, etc. I receive are unbelievable" (Harmon 2020).

Later the same day, a man tried to force his way into city hall to get to Mayor Harmon and pushed a city staff member to the ground. The police were called, and the man was detained. Instead of being concerned with her safety and the safety of all those in city hall, some members of the public responded on social media with the opposite reaction. One said that Mayor Harmon "deserved to be sexually assaulted."

This story makes clear that some officeholders experience violence. What is less clear from former Mayor Harmon's story is the extent to which women's experiences differ from those of men and whether some women—and some men—are more likely to face violence than others. To illuminate the gendered experiences of elected officeholders in the United States, we explore the degree to which women and men mayors and state senators face psychological, physical, and sexualized violence, and we do so at two of the three levels of U.S. government for legislative and executive positions. In addition to reporting gender differences in frequency, correlates, and effects of violence against women and men officeholders, we report on whether party, power, and race intersect to explain experiences of violence more deeply. In all, our research spans the continuum of violence against political actors outlined in Chapter 1 in this volume and uses quantitative survey methodology to reveal gendered experiences.

Overall, we find that U.S. mayors and state senators face meaningful levels and varying types of violence. Most centrally, women mayors were more likely than men to experience violence—and gender was the only factor that was associated with all types of violence. In contrast, the findings pertaining to state senators showed fewer overall gender differences. It is possible that weaker gender differences among state senators than mayors may be attributed to variations in power between the two types of offices. Looking more deeply into intersectional identities, we also found that women senatorial leaders faced more violence than women of the rank and file; strong women mayors suffered more violence than weak women mayors; women mayors and state senators reported more sexualized violence than their counterparts; and the rates of violence experienced by women of color state senators often exceeded those of others. In contrast, among mayors, there was mixed evidence of the effects of race and gender on experiences of violence.

Understanding these episodes and their patterns is critical for the people who are exposed to them and because they may affect both political processes and public policy.

U.S. State Senators and City Mayors in Context

In the United States, state senators are legislators who work in upper chambers of the legislative bodies of the fifty states and are elected by district.[1] There is general uniformity of the roles of members, which primarily entails introduction, consideration, and passage or rejection of legislation. However, within each senate are leaders who hold more power over policy proposals than rank-and-file members: committee chairs who direct advancement or failure of legislative bills and party leaders who have power over the entire chamber, including scheduling bills for floor debate. However, state senates in the United States differ from each other in several ways. Most critical for this research are differences in levels of professionalization. Some senates meet year-round, and others meet only a few months every year or every other year.

More professionalized legislatures have personal and committee staff, whereas less professionalized ones have few staff members to assist them. Finally, some senators are paid considerable salaries, and others get paid very little.

In contrast, mayors in the United States hold executive positions and preside over city councils—which, in turn, take on the legislative function. However, mayors differ a great deal in the extent of their power. First, some are elected directly by voters, while others are selected by city council members from within their ranks. Second, some mayors are considered "strong" mayors and others "weak" mayors. The distinction refers to differences in the power to veto decisions of city councils and the power to perform executive-level city hiring.

Key distinctions between mayoral positions in the United States and state senate positions are visibility and accountability. As singular executives, mayors tend to be more visible than state senators, who are one among many. That means that mayors tend to be more well-known by constituents, garner more media attention, and be seen around town more than senators, whose primary work is in state capitols. As singular officeholders and executives, mayors tend to be held to higher levels of accountability than legislators (senators), who are one vote among many. Consequently, it may be that mayors face more violence than state senators—particularly women who hold those positions.

Conceptualizing and Defining Violence

Those who study violence against officeholders and its gendered nature tend to think of the subject from two different but related perspectives. The first examines the subject through the lens of violence against women generally and all the ways and places in which violence is triggered and manifested. The second perspective pertains to violence against officeholders and candidates specifically and the ways that violence can be gendered. Our work is grounded in the second perspective—which facilitates inquiries about how the wider political environment perceives who belongs in political power, how they should behave in office, and how those traditionally in power respond to newcomers. Further, as the introductory chapter of this volume illuminates, violence is situated on a continuum ranging from psychological violations of personal integrity to physical harm. In our work, we explore both physical and psychological violence perpetuated by the public against U.S. mayors and state senators. Specifically, we define experiences of violence as follows:

> *Psychological abuse* involves acts likely to harm the psychological well-being of individuals or their families by inducing fear or harm to their sense of self-worth or well-being. These include exposure to insistent

and uninvited behavior, attention, or verbal contact; seeing oneself or one's family in images of or experienced disrespectful comments in social media, traditional media, or at a public meeting; and threats of death, rape, beating, abduction, or similar acts.

Physical violence involves activities that directly harm one's physical well-being or property—or the physical well-being or property of one's family. These include being slapped, pushed, or subject to projectiles, shot, assaulted, or otherwise injured; and violence against property.[2]

Sexualized abuse/violence is physical, psychological, or both. In our work, this concept is measured by whether respondents to our surveys indicated that any of the negative experiences reported were sexual in nature.

Using these definitions allows us to provide a broad view of violence among U.S. mayors and state senators—with specific focus on gender differences. However, our research is not designed to shed light on motivators for or the characteristics of the people who perpetrate violence, as we have not collected data on those who attack.

How We Studied Violence and Study Results

To estimate the levels of violence faced by United States mayors and state senators, we conducted mixed mode surveys using both mail and internet survey options.

The survey of mayors was sent out in 2017 to all mayors and asked them whether, in the course of their careers, they faced the types of violence introduced above. For the survey of state senators, we asked the same questions, but we asked respondents to limit their answers to the first six months of 2019. We made the timing change between the two surveys so that in the latter, we could assess current episodes compared with career-spanning encounters (see also Håkansson in this volume for discussion of the costs and benefits of survey research of officeholders). In the senate survey, we made it easy for respondents to indicate the frequency of violence by using a five-point scale that ranged from never to more than four times a month.

For both the mayoral and senatorial surveys, we report results for experiences of physical, psychological, and sexualized violence separately, as frequency, correlates, and effects may differ from each other. For the mayoral results, we report whether women or men were more likely to experience violence than their counterparts, and we did so with separate summary measures for physical and psychological violence. For the senate results, we analyze whether women or men faced more violence and report differences using two indices. The first is a dichotomous index for episodes of physical violence, and the second is an additive index for episodes of psychological violence. For both mayors and senators, we also report whether any of violence was sexualized. For more details about the surveys, please see our previous publications from this project: Thomas et al. 2019; Herrick et al. 2019; and Herrick and Thomas 2022.

Mayors: Overall and Gender Differences

The results of our survey demonstrate that Mayor Harmon's experiences are not unique. Over the course of their careers, 78.8 percent of mayoral respondents experienced some type of psychological violence, and 13.4 percent faced some type of physical violence. The most cited conveyors of violence were social media, with 71.7 percent of mayors reporting such episodes. In addition, 7.0 percent of mayors indicated that they had experienced sexualized violence. The finding that social media are the dominant form of psychological violence is consistent with the work of Håkansson in this volume with respect to local officeholders in Sweden as well as Collignon's chapter pertaining to candidates for Parliament in the U.K.

Our results also show that, overall, women mayors faced more violence than men. They were more likely to report each type except general harassment, disrespectful content in traditional media, and threats to family. Approximately three-quarters of women and two-thirds of men encountered disrespectful content in social media; 47.2 percent of women faced disrespectful content in public meetings compared with 41.6 percent for men; 16.4 percent of women and 14.3 percent of men suffered threats of death, rape, beating, or abduction; and 18.8 percent of women experienced violence against property compared with 9.4 percent of men. Additionally, 5.9 percent of women faced minor physical violence compared with 2.0 percent of men.

Our summary indices, as displayed in Figure 13.1, show that 22.7 percent of women faced physical violence of some type compared with 10.2 percent of men, and 90.3 percent of women experienced psychological violence of some type compared with 80.9 percent of men. These two differences were statistically significant.

Women mayors were also significantly more likely than men to face sexualized violence. Approximately 21 percent of women mayors and 2.5 percent of men mayors who encountered violence reported that it was sexualized. And these experiences appeared to be of a more disturbing nature. For example, in an open-ended portion of the survey, one man reported accusations of an affair, and another noted that a sex offender gave him a vile picture. Of the women who commented on these types of experiences, one reported that she had been stalked; one was called a whore; and a third had a blogger make sexual comments about her.

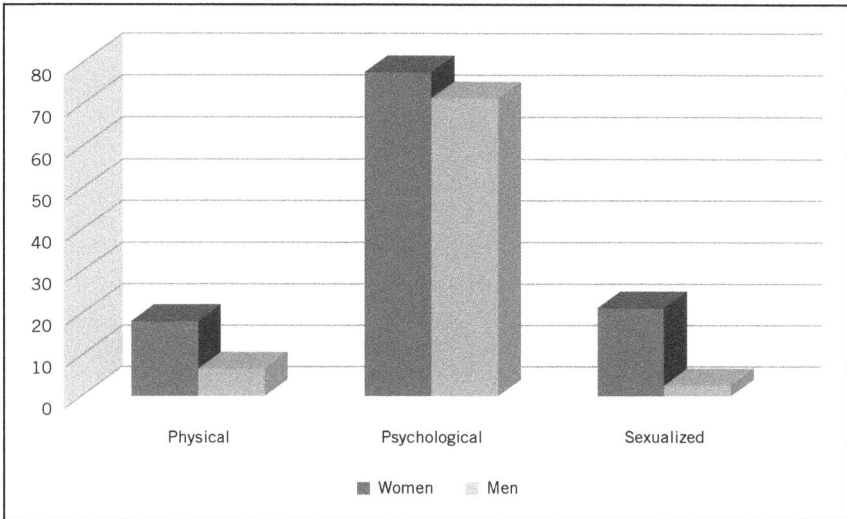

Figure 13.1 Proportion of mayors who experience violence: by gender

In addition to assessing the differences in types of mayors' experiences of violence, we created statistical models to test whether the relationships between gender and violence held in the face of other possible intervening explanations—that is, were caused by another factor. In our models of physical, psychological, and sexualized violence, we controlled for several individual mayoral characteristics, city characteristics, and political factors. The results affirmed the initial findings. In fact, gender was the most consistent statistically significant factor explaining mayors' experiences of violence and sexualized violence in particular. In short, women mayors were more likely to face all types of violence than men.

U.S. State Senators: Overall and Gender Differences

State senators also report having faced violence. For example, in 2019, Senator Cathy Osten of Connecticut was subjected to death threats while she campaigned (NBC 2019). Our survey of senators demonstrates just how common this violence has become. During the first six months of 2019, 83.7 percent of senators reported encountering psychological violence. Data on the types of psychological violence show that 77.6 percent of senators observed disrespectful content via social media. Of those who did, the average was once or twice a month. Further, 60.6 percent encountered harassment, with an average of once or twice a month; 54.4 percent experienced harassment via the traditional press, with an average less than monthly; and 46.8 percent of senators faced such behavior at public events, also with an average less than month-ly. Finally, approximately one-quarter of senators suffered threats of death, rape, beating, or abduction; 10.4 percent of senators' families faced similar threat.

Additionally, 10.3 percent of state senators encountered some type of phys-ical violence. Eight percent of senators suffered violence against property; 4.4 percent faced minor violence; and 0.4 percent encountered significant phys-ical violence, such as being injured, shot, or assaulted. Those who experienced physical violence did so less than once a month. Additionally, approximate-ly 12 percent of senators experienced sexualized violence.

For state senators, the gendered patterns that emerged were somewhat different than the mayoral results. Although the bivariate data analysis shows that women senators faced more of each type of violence than men senators— except being disrespected by the traditional press—the differences were very small. Only two of the gender differences were statistically significant: women faced more harassment and significantly more types of major physical vio-lence than men.

Figure 13.2 depicts the proportion of women and men senators who faced any physical, psychological, or sexual violence. It shows that women were sig-nificantly more likely to experience physical violence of any type than were men (18 percent for women compared with 8 percent for men) and sexual-ized violence (25 percent for women compared with 7 percent for men). How-

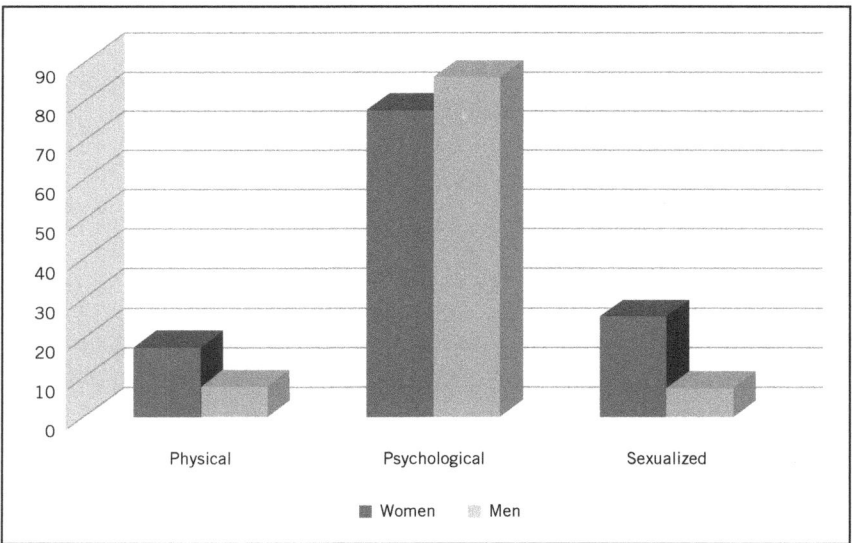

Figure 13.2 Proportion of state senators who experience violence: by gender

ever, women state senators were not more likely than men to face psychological violence than men.

As we did for mayors, we also created statistical models to test whether the relationships between gender and violence held in the face of other possible intervening explanations. The results show that holding other factors constant, women senators were not significantly more likely than men to face psychological or sexualized violence. This means that although women experienced more psychological and sexualized violence, gender was not the factor that explains the relationship. However, even after accounting for other influences, women senators were more likely to experience physical violence than men.

The disparate findings of gender differences between mayors and state senators may be explained in three ways: (1) constituents are much less familiar with their state senator than with their mayor; thus, contact with senators and displeasure or anger toward their actions may be less common; (2) mayors are executives, and theories of gender and status disruption suggest that role incongruity distress is higher for the executive than the legislative function (Eagly et al. 2003); and (3) the mayoral survey asked about experiences of violence over the course of their careers, including their campaigns and their service as mayors. The state senate survey asked about experiences as senators during the first six months of 2019. Thus, if the gender gap in violence was stronger in the past, the mayoral survey answer would reflect that situation.

Intersectional Analyses of Mayoral/Senatorial Findings

As discussed by several authors in this volume, not all women officeholders are equally likely to experience violence. In her chapter, Kuperberg explains that the concept of intersectionality, which has its roots in race relations, suggests that the experiences of women of color are likely to differ from white women because race and gender result in two related forms of oppression. Additionally, the Håkansson chapter shows that in Sweden, women politicians in positions of power are subjected to more violence than those in less powerful positions and that this may be because women are threats to the status quo. Similarly, Kuperberg reviews evidence that advocating for feminist or leftist issues may also make women more vulnerable. To test these findings in a U.S. context, we examine how the intersection of gender with race, power, and party affects violence faced by women and men mayors and state senators.

Race

As discussed in Kuperberg's chapter in this volume, race may intersect with gender to affect violence. Our ability to compare women and men of color with white woman and men is limited because only 7 percent of our state senate sample were officeholders of color and only 11 percent of the mayoral sample were officeholders of color. With that caveat, analysis of the data by race suggests that race interacts with gender for state senators but not for mayors. For mayors, 89 percent of white women faced psychological violence compared with 90 percent of women of color. For sexualized violence, the percentages were 16 and 20. Among women mayors who suffered physical violence, the differences were 21 percent for white women and 30 percent for women of color. Among men mayors, the differences were smaller.

Among state senators, analysis of the intersection of race and gender shows that women of color experienced much more psychological and sexualized violence than white women. In fact, women of color faced more violence than any other group, and white men faced the least. On the psychological violence scale, women of color averaged 7; men of color averaged 4.9; white women averaged 4.7; and white men averaged 4.2. On the physical violence variable, 28 percent of women of color suffered physical violence compared with 18 percent for men of color; 16 percent for white women; and 7 percent for white men. This finding is consistent with theories of "multiple jeopardy" faced by women of color in politics and society. As articulated by Buchanan and West (2009, 449): "Women of Color are multiply marginalized due to race, gender, and often social class, which places them at increased risk of victimization."

Power
To explore whether power affected the likelihood that mayors reported experiences of violence, we examined the degree to which the strong mayor/weak mayor dichotomy mattered. We found that strong women mayors were statistically significantly more likely to experience psychological and sexualized violence than weak ones. Every strong woman mayor reported psychological violence compared with 84.0 percent of weak women mayors. In comparison, the results for men mayors were similar in direction, but slightly weaker than the ones for women: 83.6 percent of strong men mayors faced violence compared with 72.8 percent for weak ones. The difference among men was 13 percent and 16 percent among women. We also assessed the relationships between gender and experiences of violence among women and men mayors directly elected by the people versus those elected via city councils. The results mirror those of strong mayors, with those who were directly elected reporting more violence.

For women state senators, the effects of leadership positions (either a committee chair or a leadership position in a party) were even more stark. Women senate leaders were significantly more likely to have suffered each type of violence: physical, psychological, and sexualized. For example, women leaders averaged 5.7 on the psychological violence scale compared with their counterparts, who averaged 4.4. In contrast, leadership positions among men state senators did not affect their levels of violent episodes. In sum, women officeholders with the most power in their realms suffered the most violence, but having power did not differentiate among men's experiences of violence.

Party

In the United States, the Democratic Party is the more liberal party and more likely to support women's rights measures. Because research suggests that women who are more supportive of women's issues are more likely to face violence (in this volume, see, for example, the Krook chapter), it is important to assess the differences in experiences of violence between women and men Democratic and Republican mayors and state senators.

Analysis of the interaction of party and gender show that among mayors, Democratic women were the most likely to face physical violence and sexualized violence. For example, 28 percent of Democratic women mayors reported episodes of physical violence compared with 18 percent of Republican women. Regardless of party, approximately 11 percent of men mayors faced physical violence. The party difference among women was even larger for sexualized violence: 25 percent of Democratic women mayors reported encountering sexualized violence compared with 5 percent of Republican women, 3 percent of Democratic men, and 2 percent of Republican men. There were no gender/party differences in psychological violence.

Among state senators, we found that the intersection of gender and party also mattered. Democratic women reported more sexualized violence than other senators: approximately 27 percent faced sexualized violence compared with 11 percent of Democratic men, 5 percent of Republican women, and 3 percent of Republican men. For physical and psychological violence, there were small differences between Republican and Democratic women and men senators. For example, Republican women averaged 5.2 on the psychological violence scale compared with 4.6 for Democratic women and Republican men and 3.7 for Democratic men. Overall, the clearest intersectional pattern pertains to sexualized violence. That it is mostly Democratic women who reported sexualized violence may mean that liberal women are particular targets. This finding is consistent with Krook's (2017) work that women who speak from a feminist perspective are more likely to experience violence.

Effects of Encounters of Violence

On both the mayoral and the state senatorial surveys, we asked respondents if their negative experiences with violence made them consider leaving office. The results were generally the same for the two sets of officeholders. For mayors, among those who reported at least one act of violence, 15.61 percent considered leaving office. Additionally, despite their generally greater exposure to violence, women's considerations were not affected more than men's considerations. In our interview with Mayor Heidi Harmon, she provided insight into why this may be. Harmon said that she vacillated between feeling like quitting because of the effects of abuse and feeling more committed than ever in the face of those experiences (Harmon 2020). In the context of the discussion, her implication was that it was important for women to stay in elected positions to combat efforts to deter them.

Among state senators, approximately 18 percent who experienced violence thought about leaving. Again, there were no meaningful differences between the proportions of women and men senators. Although there was similarity between women and men in the types of violence that led them to consider leaving, there were also some gender differences. One woman senator reported specific gendered language that caused her concern: she was called a cunt and told to "die, bitch." No similar comments were reported by men. Further, although only one women senator commented about the detrimental effects of violence on her family, six men reported that such threats led them to think about leaving. This result may be gendered in that it reflects a type of masculinity. A key sociocultural role for men is that of family protector (Person 2006). The relative lack of comment among women senators about the effects of violence on their families may be a function of self-selection. Women who consider running for office may opt out due to family concerns (see Lawless 2012; Shames 2017) and may be protective of families earlier in the process than men. It may be that men's concern emerges after threats rather than before. Indeed, Mayor Harmon commented that her exposure to abuse because of her job is "definitely a concern for my children because they worry that my safety is implicated in these kinds of comments" (Harmon 2020). Whatever the reasons for this gendered finding, it is intriguing.

Conclusions

Among the strengths of this research is that our surveys of mayors and state senators are, to our knowledge, the first in the United States that address violence directed to officeholders by the public. Further, our research is among a small body of literature that compares violence between women and men officeholders (see also Håkansson, Schneider, and Collignon in this volume).

Overall, we find that mayors and state senators in the United States face meaningful levels and types of violence. Most central to our research though are the findings of gender differences among officeholders and the fact that the level of office affects the extent of those differences. Women mayors were more likely than men to experience violence. In fact, gender was the only factor in our multivariate model that was associated with all types of violence. In contrast, the findings pertaining to state senators showed fewer overall gender differences. It is possible that weaker gender differences among state senators than mayors may be attributed to variations in power between the two types of offices. Senators work in more collaborative institutions, whereas mayors are the top executive of a hierarchical bureaucracy, often the most powerful political actor in town.

We also found some evidence of intersectional vulnerabilities. Power of positions in combination with gender had effects on encounters of violence in the ways noted just above. Additionally, analysis of the interaction of gender and race indicated that the rates of violence experienced by women of color state senators, but not mayors, often exceeded those of others, and men of color state senators often faced violence on par with or at higher rates than white women. Together, these findings suggest that women mayors and state senators, especially those who hold the most power in their institutions, may face more violence than their male counterparts because they are perceived as transgressing gender norms and upending the status quo. This may be particularly true for women of color who not only may threaten male power but may also threaten white dominance of power (Eagly et al. 2003; Okimoto and Brescoll 2010; Buchanan and West 2009).

The implications of having some mayors or senators leave office due to violence include the possibility that the number of people who might consider future runs for office is reduced, which, in turn, raises serious questions about the quality and diversity of future representation. It is possible that more women than men may avoid running for office because they are more likely to experience more and more types of violence. Coupled with research that suggests that women state legislators are less likely than men colleagues to seek higher office (Einstein et al. 2017, Fulton et al. 2006; Maestas et al. 2006) and that women are more affected than men by the high costs of running for and serving in elective office (Lawless 2012; Shames 2017), women's underrepresentation may not be alleviated in the near future. This matters for reasons of descriptive and substantive representation. Indeed, Mayor Heidi Harmon noted that after her Facebook post about her gendered experiences as mayor, the reactions she received most were from women in general and young women in particular who said that they "could never do my job, and that they would never be able to withstand these types of personal attacks" (Harmon 2020).

Diversity in representation also matters in terms of policy and process: for example, a wealth of research shows that women mayors are more likely than men to identify women's issues as germane to the business of local government and are more willing to change budget processes, be more inclusive, and seek broader participation by the public (Boles 2001; Tolleson-Rinehart

2001; Holman 2014). Similarly, women state legislators tend to vote for, sponsor, and enact more women's issues legislation than men and are more successful passing their legislative priorities (Barrett 2001; Barnello and Bratton 2007; Epstein et al. 2005; Hogan 2008; Thomas 1994).

In sum, violence against women in politics is likely to have broad and lasting effects for individual politicians, for representative diversity, and for public policy. To understand the full implications of those effects, more work is needed to deepen our knowledge of gender differences in types, amounts, and correlates of these behaviors. In particular, future research must focus on differences among groups of women, especially those pertaining to race and ethnicity and other groups who lack power. This is a particular concern, as minority women may be especially likely to encounter violence (Kuperberg 2018; IPU 2016). Finally, additional insight is needed into violence against officeholders from colleagues (other officeholders, staff, the media, or lobbyists) and the motivations of those who perpetrate violence against officeholders.

14

Violence against Swedish Local-Level Politicians

SANDRA HÅKANSSON

One morning, Swedish municipal politician Kristina Axén Olin found that her home had been spray-painted with the words, "You might also become homeless." During the same time, she received threats concerning her children, detailing which school they went to and explicitly stating that they might not live the next day (Wrede 2017). This example highlights an utterly intolerable cost to holding political office: the fact that politicians face risks of physical, and perhaps even more psychological, violence because of their roles as such.

In line with Bjarnegård and Zetterberg's definition of political violence as violence that disrupts political processes (see Chapter 1), I consider any form of violence that targets a politician when carrying out their political roles or because of their roles, regardless of where it takes place, a violation of the political system. Being forced to consider personal risks in relation to activities such as publicly stating one's stance on a certain issue, participating in a public meeting, or engaging in dialogue with constituents online disrupts the political process. Just like the chapters by Collignon as well as Thomas and Herrick in this volume, I highlight the gender dimensions to violence against politicians by comparing women's and men's violence exposure. The chapter provides an empirical analysis of a central question regarding the project of gendering political violence: Are women targeted with more violence as politicians than men?

Previous research in political science and political psychology provides several theoretical reasons we should expect women to be targeted with more violence as politicians than men. Power spheres, such as politics, are imbued with gendered norms privileging men by tying leadership ideals to male stereotypes. Decades of psychological research has demonstrated that gender-biased attitudes influence candidate evaluations to the detriment of women: women are assessed as poorer leaders, less qualified, and less likable than men exhibiting the same characteristics, qualifications, and behavior (e.g., Bohnet 2016; Carli and Eagly 2001; Eagly and Karau 2002; Okimoto and Brescoll 2010; Rudman and Fairchild 2004; Rudman and Glick 1999). This scholarship shows that agentic leadership qualities, for example, assertiveness, independence, ambition, and confidence, are associated with men, and women who demonstrate these qualities are disliked and punished. Agentic women challenge the gender hierarchy: they exhibit what is stereotypically understood as masculine competencies and thereby "undermine the presumed differences between the genders, and discredit the system in which men have more access to power and resources for ostensibly legitimate reasons" (Rudman et al. 2012: 166).

Hence, the prevailing negative, and not seldom hostile, attitudes to women politicians motivates an expectation of more violence against women in politics than male counterparts. Furthermore, executive women can be expected to receive even more political violence relative to male counterparts than women at less powerful positions. The political hierarchy is a key dimension to consider in research about the gendered nature of political offices (Carli and Eagly 2001; Folke and Rickne 2016; O'Brien 2015; O'Neill, Pruysers, and Stewart 2019). VAWIP motivated by negative attitudes to female politicians (Krook and Restrepo Sanín 2016a) is more likely to target the most visible women in politics, and the most agentic leadership is required from executive women and men.

This chapter focuses on Swedish municipal politicians. Sweden represents an advantageous case for comparing women's and men's exposure to political violence across the political hierarchy. Statistical comparisons of women's and men's violence exposure are possible in Sweden since women are present in politics in relatively high numbers, nationally as well as locally. Furthermore, women are present in the top layer of politics.[1] Moreover, women politicians are comparable to men in the sense that they are not newcomers. Women have had a marked presence in Swedish politics since the 1970s. This makes the country somewhat unique in terms of gender equality in politics as one of the countries with the highest historical representation of women. These features are advantageous for comparing how women and men are treated in politics: women as a group are not newcomers in politics, and there are enough women at top positions to be able to compare men and women who hold as much power. Differences in how women and men are treated in politics are less expected in Sweden than elsewhere due to the history of relatively high equality. The Swedish case can hence be perceived as a "hard test" for the hypothesis that women face more violence than men in politics.

Some features specific to local politics are worth noting. As opposed to national-level politicians, local-level politicians are often known personally in their communities. They live their everyday lives close to their constituents and frequently interact with them, for example, when grocery shopping, picking up their children from school, or taking a walk. Consequently, when local politicians receive threats or harassment, the perpetrators often live in the same community and might be people that they frequently run into. Another important feature of local politics is that concrete service provision, such as schools, hospitals, and road construction, typically is organized locally and that political decisions directly impact individuals in highly tangible ways. Swedish municipal politicians even apply the law in individual cases and make decisions on, for example, removing children from their parents' care. Such sensitive decisions create specific sources of frustration for individuals and, coupled with the geographical proximity to local politicians, set the stage for attacks on politicians being particularly personal for perpetrators as well as targets compared to the violence faced by, for example, MPs.

This chapter makes a case for survey research when examining gender differences in violence against politicians. Drawing on three waves of survey data on eight thousand Swedish municipal politicians, I analyze the statistical relationship between politicians' sex and exposure to violence. In short, I show that women are exposed to more violence than men, particularly at higher levels of power.

Survey-Based Violence Research

From interviewing politicians, I have learned that they tend to have a perhaps surprisingly high tolerance for aggression against them. Politicians seem to fully accept what many would consider problematic behaviors, such as being screamed at or being called an idiot, because they think it is fair that citizens should be able to express their views toward those who hold power and responsibility. Nevertheless, threats and intimidation, especially against family members, crosses a line and is viewed as inacceptable (see also, e.g., James et al. 2016).

Following WHO's definition (Krug et al. 2002), the present study defines violence as actions intentionally designed to cause physical or psychological harm. Hence, this conceptualization includes violations of personal integrity as well as physical harm (see description of the "continuum of violence" in the introductory chapter). Other studies put less emphasis on intentionality. Which conceptualization of violence is most suitable will vary depending on the research question and purpose of each study. What is important to keep in mind is that prevalence rates will not be comparable across studies that do not use the same conceptualization of violence. Furthermore, I categorize violence as psychological or physical based on the means used, rather than the impact on the victim (c.f. Chapter 1), which also naturally impacts how the prevalence rates of these two forms of violence are understood.

Using Survey Data

My study primarily relies on the Politicians' Safety Survey (PTU), collected by the Swedish government.[2] I use three waves (2012, 2014, and 2016) of responses from about eight thousand municipal politicians per wave, corresponding to a response rate above 60 percent. As a form of self-reported data, where it is up to respondents to report what they have experienced, concerns are sometimes raised regarding the reliability of surveys as a data source. However, compared to other possible sources of data on violence against politicians, self-reported data, in fact, has several advantages.

An argument against using police statistics on crimes against politicians as a measure of prevalence is that victims have many reasons not to report crimes. Crimes are more likely to be reported if the victim believes it can result in conviction or remuneration from insurance companies, if the crime is not stigmatizing for the victim, and if the victim is not acquainted with the perpetrator (Sporre and Standar 2006). Many politicians refrain from reporting attacks on them since they do not think it will lead to anything (Frenzel 2017). Moreover, politicians' need to present themselves as strong and capable candidates to voters might indeed make official records of crime victimization stigmatizing and likely even more so when it comes to, for example, sexual violence. Being acquainted with the perpetrator, furthermore, could plausibly be a source of underreporting pertaining more to women than men. Many testimonies of abuse coming from colleagues in politics were revealed during the #MeToo movement in 2017. The very likely underreporting of many relevant experiences, hence, makes crime statistics a flawed measurement of violence against politicians.

Another alternative might be using media reports, often used by political violence researchers to estimate when and where violence has erupted or count the number of violent events, for example, during an election. This type of data has several biases: for example, it tends to underreport violence in rural areas and less public forms of intimidation (Bjarnegård 2018; Borzyskowski and Wahman 2021; Fjelde and Höglund 2016; McCarthy et al. 2008). As demonstrated throughout this book, including in my chapter, most violence targeting politicians is psychological in nature and not publicly visible unless politicians themselves speak out about them (see, e.g., Thomas and Herrick's chapter). While media reports are important tools to describe incidents of violence, they are less reliable sources to assess the frequency of (certain) attacks.

Since many events are not publicly visible, self-reported data is better equipped to capture a fuller range of relevant experiences. Within the family of self-reported data, interviews are undoubtedly better tools to shed light on the multiple varieties of violence used against politicians and better suited to getting at the most fine-grained differences in women's and men's experiences of violence. Compared to interviews, surveys normally paint a more simplified picture. To avoid ambiguity, survey questions need to be precise and delimited, which entails a risk that some relevant experiences will not be covered by the predefined survey items. Advantages of surveys compared to interviews, on the other hand, are that they can capture large-scale patterns, for example, how frequently politicians are exposed and to which types of event. While survey data cannot capture all nuances relating to the gendered nature of attacks, they can establish statistical differences between women's and men's exposure to violence. In a new research field such as this one, the broad picture of who is exposed and how frequently it happens to various groups is important to establish a basic understanding for the empirical contours of the problem.

Designing Survey Questions on Violence Exposure

When designing survey questions about violence exposure, in addition to the choice of how to conceptualize violence, key aspects to consider are what time period to cover and whether to ask open or specific questions. These aspects are also highly important to keep in mind when interpreting studies relying on survey data.

Most often, the time period covered by survey questions on violence exposure is either lifetime victimization (e.g., *"Has any of the following ever happened to you?"* or *"During your time as an elected official, has any of the following happened to you?"*) or a restricted time period (e.g., *"During the last election campaign, did any of the following happen to you?"* or *"During the past year, did any of the following happen to you?"*). By design, these survey questions will give different prevalence rates. It is sometimes recommended by survey methodologists to reduce recall bias by limiting the time period covered (see, e.g., Groves et al. 2009). The survey design should depend on the research aims, and lifetime victimization can serve distinct research purposes. However, it is important not to draw comparative conclusions based on sets of survey data that cover widely different amounts of time. The time period covered can also potentially have implications for analyzing gender differences in exposure. If more women than men are newcomers in politics, men will have accumulated more years when they might have been exposed to violence. Hence, lifetime exposure means different things for different groups of politicians. It is also possible that as many women and men are exposed to violence at some point of their political career but that women are attacked more times than men over the course of a political career. This can become evident when comparing exposure rates during a more confined time period. While similar shares of women and men report lifetime victimization to violence as politicians, more women than men report being exposed during the previous year in the PTU data.

Another key dimension when designing survey queries on exposure to political violence is how to phrase the question: mainly, whether it should be phrased as an open or a specified question (see also Collignon in this volume). The PTU survey asks about violence exposure in the following way: *"Did any of these incidents happen during the previous year?"* Respondents are then presented with a list of incidents, and they tick the boxes of the incidents they were exposed to, leaving the rest blank. This can be compared to another survey, KOLFU, that targets the same respondents (Karlsson and Gilljam 2014). The KOLFU survey asks: *"Over the last 12 months, have you been exposed to violence or threats because of your political office?"* and only those who reply yes are asked which forms of violence they experienced as a follow-up question.

The KOLFU and PTU surveys have both been collected in 2012 and hence cover the same respondents, Swedish municipal politicians, during the same year. Both have high response rates. Given the unspecific nature of the KOLFU survey's violence query, it is not surprising that this data reports a substantially lower frequency of violence exposure: 7 percent compared to 19 percent in the PTU data. Interestingly, the relative frequencies of psychological and physical violence are similar between the two surveys.[3] Hence, both psychological and physical violence become underreported if the question is phrased in an imprecise way.

Physical violence is somewhat less underreported among male respondents (see Table 14.1). Overall, however, women and men underreport exposure to both physical and psychological violence to a similar extent, suggesting that gender does not affect what is perceived to "count as" violence to a significant degree. This is also an argument against interpreting higher self-reported violence exposure among women than men as a result of gender differences in perceptions of what violence is. If women had been more "all-inclusive" in their understanding of violence than men, we should expect women to report more violence exposure when asked about it with an imprecise question as in the KOLFU survey. If anything, women underreport physical violence more than men and underreport psychological violence to a similar extent.

TABLE 14.1 A LIST-BASED VS. AN OPEN SURVEY QUERY ON VIOLENCE			
	PTU 2012	KOLFU 2012	Relative Difference
Survey Query	"Did any of these incidents happen during the previous year?" [Incident types listed, see figure 1]	"Over the last 12 months, have you been exposed to violence or threats?" If yes: "In what way were you exposed?"	
Sample of Respondents	Swedish Municipal Politicians	Swedish Municipal Politicians	
Response Rate	68%	79%	
Prevalence of Violence			
All Respondents			
Any Form of Violence	18.50%	7.46%	0.40
Physical	2.08%	0.99%	0.48
Psychological	18.18%	6.47%	0.36
Men			
Any Form of Violence	17.98%	7.11%	0.40
Physical	2.31%	1.25%	0.54
Psychological	17.70%	6.13%	0.35
Women			
Any Form of Violence	19.22%	7.94%	0.41
Physical	1.76%	0.63%	0.36
Psychological	18.86%	6.93%	0.37

Notes: Data from PTU 2012 and KOLFU 2012. The relative difference between the share of politicians exposed to violence according to each survey dataset is expressed as the ratio of KOLFU relative to PTU.

Based on findings such as these, it is advisable to phrase survey queries on violence exposure in a way that asks about as concrete examples of incidents as possible. The risk of recall bias as well as the research interest should guide the choice of time period covered by the survey query. The most important thing is, again, being transparent about how questions on exposure are phrased to make it possible to assess to what extent it is comparable to other studies.

Gender Differences and Similarities in Violence against Swedish Politicians

Having established the appropriateness, and limitations, of using the PTU survey data to study violence against politicians, I next turn to analyses of the data. This section of the chapter summarizes findings from Håkansson (2021).

Forms and Sites of Violence

First, I find that both female and male politicians experience far more psychological than physical violence in the Swedish context.[4] The most common form of attack in 2016 against both female and male politicians is on social media, followed by verbal threats in person, threatening emails, and threats communicated on the phone (see Figure 14.1). On average, 25 percent of Swedish municipal politicians experience political violence in a year. Physical vio-

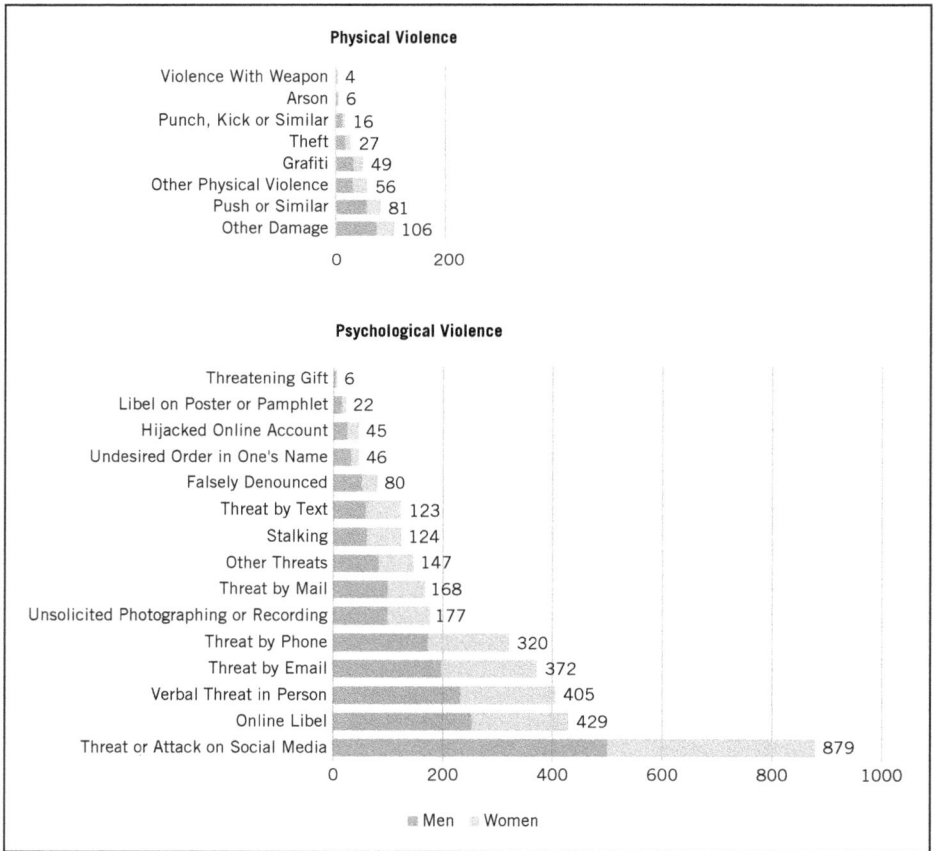

Figure 14.1 Number of victims per violence type in 2016. *Notes*: Data from PTU 2016. The graph reports the number of respondents who report having experienced each form of violence as a response to the query, "Did any of these incidents happen during the previous year?" Some respondents have experienced several forms of violence. (Source: Sandra Håkansson, 2021, "Do Women Pay a Higher Price for Power? Gender Bias in Political Violence in Sweden," *Journal of Politics*, 83, no. 2, University of Chicago Press. Used with permission.)

lence is experienced by 3 percent, whereas 24 percent experience psychological violence. Luckily, very few experience the most severe and potentially life-threatening forms of physical violence, but a large segment of Swedish politicians are affected by psychological violence, such as online abuse.

My study further suggests that the problem of violence against politicians has increased over time. The share of politicians targeted increased between 2012 and 2016, and these trends apply to both women and men. The increase is driven by an increase of online abuse. This should not be understood as the online space constituting a cause of increased violence, but as constituting the context of violence, as Esposito writes in this volume: an expanded online space constitutes an expanding arena for perpetrators where they can carry out violence.

In terms of the most common forms and sites of violence, there are some small differences in the forms of violence used against women and men. Whereas men are slightly more exposed to property damage, women are more exposed to threats and harassment. This corresponds to studies from other countries that similarly find that physical force is more commonly used against men and/or their property, whereas psychological violence is more commonly used against women (Bardall 2011; Bjarnegård 2018). However, one needs to keep in mind that all forms of physical attacks are very rare against women and men alike in Swedish politics. At the level of the types of events women and men experience, there are more similarities than differences. The following quotes, from interviews I have conducted with municipal politicians, illustrate what psychological violence can entail:

> They emailed and sent letters to my home and to everyone on the social committee, demonstrating that they had found out the names of our children and our partners. This makes you feel really sick. (Woman 1)

> A lot is about immigrants, "you are a Muslim and you are one of them and you don't get anything and you think that women should be raped" /. . ./ and then they of course hope that the same should happen to me, that someone should shoot me or that I should be raped. (Man 1)

These two quotes also illustrate that threats are often implicit rather than direct, clearly intended to harm the target's psyche without overtly committing the crime of an unlawful threat.

Who Perpetrates?

The PTU survey contains a question about who respondents believe was behind the most recent attack against them. An analysis of their replies demonstrates vast similarities between the most common types of perpetrators targeting women and men (see Figure 14.2). The most common reply among both female and male politicians is that they believe citizens to be behind the attack: around 60 percent respond "aggravated citizen" or "querulant." The second-most-common reply is elected politicians from another party (12 percent). Members of one's own party are rarely believed to be behind attacks against either women or men.[5] The same holds for business owners.

The survey also asks about group characteristics of perpetrators (see Figure 14.3). In relation to this question, the politicians believe perpetrators to be right-wing or left-wing extremists in 17 percent versus 11 percent of the attacks, respectively. Perpetrators are believed to be members of local action groups in 9 percent of the cases and criminal groups in 2 percent of the cases. There are some statistically significant, but small, differences in the perpetrators attacking women and men politicians. Right-wing extremists and anti-

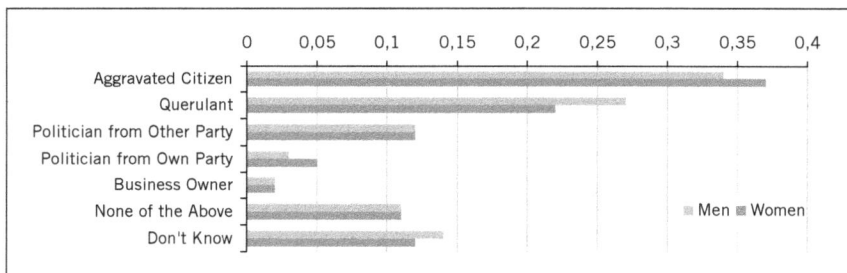

Figure 14.2 Perpetrator types. *Note*: "Who do you think the perpetrator of the most recent attack against you was?" (Source: Sandra Håkansson, 2021, "Do Women Pay a Higher Price for Power? Gender Bias in Political Violence in Sweden," *Journal of Politics*, 83, no. 2, University of Chicago Press. Used with permission.)

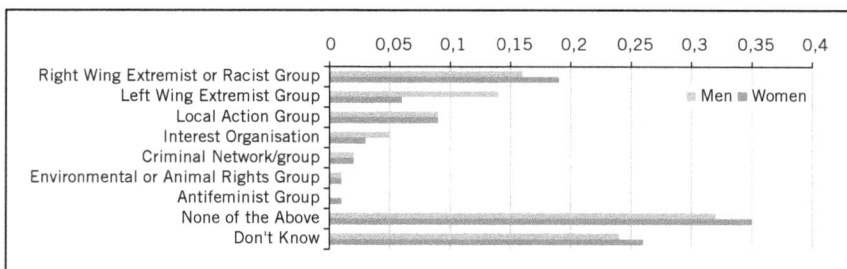

Figure 14.3 Perpetrators' group characteristics. *Note*: "Do you think the perpetrator was a member of any of the following?" (Source: Sandra Håkansson, 2021, "Do Women Pay a Higher Price for Power? Gender Bias in Political Violence in Sweden," *Journal of Politics*, 83, no. 2, University of Chicago Press. Used with permission.)

feminists are perceived as more common perpetrators targeting women, and left-wing extremists as more common perpetrators targeting men. However, all in all, similarities rather than differences dominate the pattern when comparing women's and men's perceptions of who perpetrates violence against them.

A Persistent Gender Gap in Politicians' Violence Exposure

Municipal councils in Sweden are elected in direct, proportional elections, and the executive branch, the municipal board, holds a lot of power (Montin 2014). The mayor is selected by the majority party or coalition and chairs the board. Municipalities are responsible for various policy areas, such as education, housing, infrastructure, and social welfare, usually organized in municipal committees chaired by a representative of the political majority (Karlsson 2006). Hence, this structure consists of three clear hierarchical levels: rank and file, committee chairs, and mayors.

Looking at the average share of politicians targeted per year (Figure 14.4), it is first of all clear that the risks increase with the level of power. At the lowest level of power, that is, rank-and-file politicians, about 20 percent are exposed to violence per year. Among committee chairs, this number is at least 10 percentage points higher, and among mayors around 60 percent experience violence each year.

Further scrutinizing the gender pattern illustrated in Figure 14.4, it can be concluded that the gender gap in violence exposure is small at the lowest

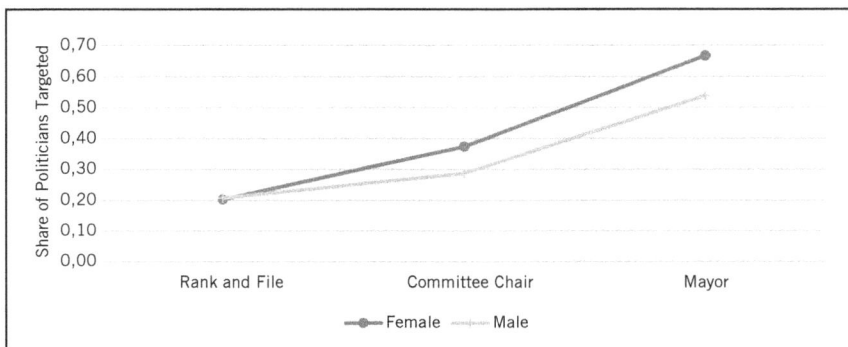

Figure 14.4 Share of politicians exposed to violence by gender and level of power. *Notes*: Data from PTU 2012, 2014, and 2016. Estimates show the share of politicians exposed to at least one form of violence in a year. (Source: Sandra Håkansson, 2021, "Do Women Pay a Higher Price for Power? Gender Bias in Political Violence in Sweden," *Journal of Politics*, 83, no. 2, University of Chicago Press. Used with permission.)

level of power. Since the overwhelming majority of politicians are found in this type of role (i.e., political office carried out in one's spare time without much visibility), the average gender gap in violence exposure among all politicians, though statistically significant, is not larger than around 1 percentage point. Hence, without disaggregating the analysis into different levels of power, one could conclude that the gender gap in violence exposure is rather small. However, the disaggregated analysis shows that that the gender gap becomes increasingly large the higher the level of power. At the chair level, women experience around 8 percentage points more violence than men and around 12 percentage points more among mayors. In other words, while the risks of exposure increase with the level of power for all politicians, it does so more dramatically for women than for men, resulting in a gender gap in violence exposure that increases with the level of power. Executive women violate gender norms of the gendered political hierarchy, and just as, for example, Collignon, Kuperberg, and Schneider find in their respective chapters, these norm-violating women face the most violence.

More in-depth analyses including controls for party, year, municipality, foreign background, status as newcomer in politics, age, level of activity on social media, and perceived sexual minority motive can be found in Håkansson (2021). These analyses demonstrate that the gender gap in violence exposure is unaffected by these factors. Furthermore, while the gap in violence exposure is more affected by certain forms of violence, no single form of violence is driving the result.

These findings are in line with the theoretical expectations outlined in the beginning of the chapter. Perpetrators seem to be biased toward directing political violence at women, and the results demonstrate that having political power entails higher risks for women than for men.

Political Violence Disrupts the Democratic Conversation

What are the consequences of the violence Swedish municipal politicians face? While very few PTU respondents report considering leaving politics or altering a political decision as a consequence of violence against politicians, 25 percent of politicians exposed to violence in the previous year report refraining from making public statements. Free text answers in the PTU data as well as my interview data suggests that this often applies to migration issues:

> There are periods that are very intense, and one of these periods was during the refugee crisis in 2015. I was then responsible for [migration related issues] /. . ./ and I was rather attacked by the other side. It actually made me subdue myself for a while. /. . ./ I didn't partici-

pate in public debates for example, where I would be present physically. But it also meant that I didn't take the debate on my own Facebook page. I posted something and there was a lot of hate and I actually didn't reply. (Woman 2)

Hence, violence against politicians disrupts the democratic conversation. Dropouts do not appear to be widespread, and the formal components of political processes seem to remain intact. However, representatives are severely constrained when they refrain from debates with constituents or from presenting their views in public. Women and men report being impacted in similar ways, but a larger share of women representatives report, in the words of the woman in the quote above, "subduing themselves." This unequal impact is to be expected given the fact that more women than men are targeted with violence, and the ramifications deserve further attention in future research.

Conclusion

In conclusion, an increasing share of municipal politicians in Sweden is targeted with violence each year, particularly psychological violence, and women mayors are targeted far more than any other politician. It all comes down to the fact that perpetrators of political violence seem to be more prone to choose female targets, and this pattern is even stronger for mayors and committee chairs.

Using the PTU survey data, I was able to demonstrate that women get targeted more frequently than men, especially powerful and visible women. Furthermore, this type of data made it possible to show both similarities and differences between women's and men's violence exposure as politicians. In terms of similarities, women and men in politics are mainly targeted by the same types of perpetrators (ordinary constituents), and the same types of incidents (psychological, social media) are the most common against both women and men. But women are exposed more than men, especially powerful and visible women. The largest gender gap in exposure is found in the most common violence form (attacks on social media), but the gap is not entirely driven by this form of violence.

A limitation of significance to using this kind of data is the inability to learn about the nature of attacks. A key question in the research field is whether psychological violence against women, or other groups of politicians, is nastier than psychological violence against hegemonic men (see, e.g., Erikson, Håkansson, and Josefsson 2021; Kuperberg 2018). The level of detail on specific events will always by definition be limited in surveys, especially in comparison to interviews or in-depth analyses of a limited number of abusive events. It is important not to interpret results relating to gender differences in the frequency of violence exposure as encompassing all aspects of how gender impacts and interplays with the risks of violence that politicians face.

In addition, there are several important avenues for future research to explore relating to the (gendered) impact of violence against politicians. There are a few studies that look into ambition in terms of dropouts (Herrick and Franklin 2019) and opt-outs (Daniele 2017), but more research is needed on the gendered nature of opt-outs, as well as on the demand side of ambition. Are women deterred from running in face of risks of exposure to physical and psychological violence differently than men? How are parties' recruitment patterns and framings of desirable candidates shaped by the violence that targets politicians? Moreover, the impact on psychological well-being and state of health of those targeted needs to be studied further. Herrick and Franklin (2019) make a valuable contribution in this regard, and an extension could be to compare effects of different forms of violence. Sexual harassment in the workplace has been shown to have a demonstrably worse impact on targets than other workplace bullying (Fitzgerald and Cortina 2018). The often-sexualized nature of attacks on women politicians can therefore be expected to have another impact on the health of those targeted than the targets of other forms of political violence.

15

Intersectional Online Violence against Women in Politics in Israel

G lobal politics are changing. As a result of political gender quotas and international legal reforms, women and other historically underrepresented political groups are increasingly entering politics. Simultaneously,
the "sites" of politics are expanding, from the traditional halls of Parliament
to the online space. Acts of gendered political violence, our conceptions of
this violence, and the tools to measure and understand violence have shifted
with this global landscape.

During the early years of the web, optimists believed that individuals could
overcome the limitations of society and social division in the online space.
Moving from the physical to the virtual, we could replace racism and sexism
with a discrimination-free, democratic, and equal internet (Loader and Mercea 2011). Instead, as many feminists and critical race scholars feared, and
as Esposito writes in this volume, offline and online oppressions, including
racism and sexism, exist on a shared spectrum reinforced by the other. As
Bardall adds, also in this volume, the anonymity and fast pace of internet
exchanges can exacerbate violence and challenge both our understanding
and response.

Even individuals with substantial privilege, such as elected representatives, can be subject to debilitating abuse in the online space. The differences
between politicians—to what extent they challenge existing power structures,
what issues they support, and what identities they hold—impact the types
and severity of abuse they receive. Because of these differences, we can and
should use theories of intersectionality—which argue that forms of discrim-

ination cannot be "analyzed or understood separately from each other" (Weldon 2006, 196)—to better understand online violence against politicians. This violence can silence, force political actors offline or out of politics, deter potential aspirants from engaging in political activity, and send explicit and implicit messages about who "belongs" in the public sphere.

There are a number of ways in which online political violence is gendered. Focusing on online violence against women in politics (VAWIP)—related to but distinct from gendered violence against politicians, as Krook argues in this volume—in this chapter, I concentrate on the intersectional discriminations targeting women politicians. Women politicians are diverse, and the online violence targeting them is not homogeneous; sexism is bound with other forms of discrimination. Perpetrators target political officials when their presence and voices defy existing political norms. Other differences—such as political party, visibility, and leadership—can also exacerbate sexism and other forms of discrimination online. At the end of this chapter, I illustrate this intersectional nature of online VAWIP through a qualitative Twitter analysis of Israeli women members of Parliament. Israel is a suitable case to analyze due to the salience of identities including race and religion.

Situating This Research

This chapter is informed primarily by political science research, particularly research on violence against women in politics, but incorporates research on intersectionality, violence against politicians, and online abuse. As Krook writes in this volume, VAWIP and violence against politicians are separable, distinct forms of violence. I use gender-based political violence to describe both forms of violence. Gender-based political violence can target men and nonbinary individuals. However, the focus of this chapter is on VAWIP, gender-based violence targeting political women because they are women.

Though gender differentiation, comparing men and women, is one means of understanding the unique violence facing women in politics, this chapter starts with the assumption that women face distinct quantities and forms of violence, including online violence, illustrated in this volume by Collignon, Håkansson, and Thomas and Herrick. From this assumption, I aim to complicate the prominent emphasis on sexism in VAWIP, asking: How do multiple forms of discrimination—including but not limited to sexism—intersect in acts of VAWIP? How can an intersectional approach be used to understand VAWIP?

Research on intersectionality and online abuse is especially multidisciplinary, and debates have emerged in both fields over conceptual definitions and methodological best practices. To ground this chapter more concretely, I will use specific theoretical frameworks and conceptual definitions even though some of these ideas are contested. I understand intersectionality as a frame for analysis. Intersectionality is attributed to Kimberlé Crenshaw, building from decades, if not centuries, of communities—particularly Black American women—discussing their intersecting identities and discriminations (Tormos 2018). This chapter, which brings together empirical studies from across the world and adds a case study on the Israeli Parliament, utilizes an understanding of intersectionality that social scientists, including political scientists, have often employed. That is, I will highlight the ways in which the differences among women contribute to their different political experiences, in this case with online violence. I use *intersectional online violence* to describe how online VAWIP contains discriminatory tropes in addition to sexism that should be incorporated in an analysis of VAWIP and gender-based political violence.

What makes an analysis intersectional—whatever terms it deploys, whatever its iteration, whatever its field or discipline—is its adoption of an intersectional way of thinking about the problem of sameness and difference and its relation to power. This framing—conceiving of categories not as distinct but as always permeated by other categories, fluid and changing, always in the process of creating and being created by dynamics of power—emphasizes what intersectionality does rather than what intersectionality is (Cho, Crenshaw, and McCall 2013, 795).

Regarding online abuse, I align with the near consensus of feminist, online violence scholars, and Esposito in this volume, who argue that the online space is gendered. Megarry (2014) describes the internet as a "new public space" and that like street harassment, which serves to punish women for their presence in public space, online harassment threatens women who are visible online (51–52). This is echoed by many other feminists analyzing experiences of online abuse (Mantilla 2013, 568; Penny 2014, 163). Because perpetrators of violence are motivated by marking the internet as male and masculinist space, it makes sense that "norm-violators"—including feminists, elected politicians, and feminist elected politicians—are frequent targets of abuse (Eckert 2018; Sarkeesian 2012). This echoes findings from Håkansson that powerful women politicians in Sweden experience disproportionate violence as well as Collignon, both from this volume, that U.K. women politicians are especially targeted when defying political norms through voicing distinctive political positions.

This chapter focuses on the experiences of women elected political officials. Because women MPs serve as representatives for constituents, the violence they face shares similarities in form but can have different implications compared to the violence faced by other political actors, such as human rights defenders. Political violence is understood as violence that disrupts political processes; violence against elected officials contributes to distinct disruptions within processes of representation and governance.

That said, intersectional analysis asks us to reflect on power. Elected officials often have more social and political power than other political actors, such as voters. In addition, certain groups—younger, poorer, disabled, and/or other marginalized groups—are often unrepresented or underrepresented in electoral politics. While the insights gleaned from elected representatives may extend to others, a focus on formal politicians in this chapter may overlook forms of discrimination crucial in our understanding of the violence facing a broader set of actors.

Defining Violence: Online Violence as and on the Continuum

Existing studies on online political violence vary greatly in their categorizations of online abuse; they range from studies that do not indicate classification metrics to those that classify profanity as uncivil (Rheault, Rayment, and Musulan 2019) and those that individually investigate each instance of abuse to determine its appropriate classification (Southern and Harmer 2019). In this volume alone, Esposito defines online violence to incorporate, but not overstate, the role of technology in violence, while Bardall, describing online political gender-based violence, considers the offline space but emphasizes a spectrum of online harms. In this chapter, focusing on VAWIP and distinguishing between this violence and online violence against politicians (Krook in this volume), my focus overlaps with components of both Bardall and Esposito's conceptualizations.

I define individual posts as abusive if they are derogatory—meaning unkind, demeaning, or disrespectful—and directed at an individual or nonpolitical group. I do not classify contentious debate over policy or political ideas as online abuse unless they delve into personal characteristics; some public policies, such as feminist issues, muddy this distinction. As Bardall writes in this volume, online incivility is part of a broader continuum of aversive online speech (Chen 2017), one that can complicate emphases on both free speech and freedom from violence. Abuse, as I define it here, does not overlap entirely with incivility but instead requires targeted, non-policy-related derogation. VAWIP is even more specific, including identity-based abuse bridging gender-based incivility, hate speech, and criminal acts (Bardall in this volume) as well as cyberracism and gender-based abuse/hate speech (Esposito in this volume). In the penultimate section of this chapter, I draw further distinctions among abusive Twitter posts for a typology I used to classify tweets directed at Israeli MPs.

Online violence is not uniform and can constitute a spectrum of violence in and of itself (Lewis, Rowe, and Wiper 2016). Under the continuum of violence outlined in the Introduction of this book, it might be tempting to place online violence exclusively under psychological violence, as it is causes psychological harm by provoking anger, anxiety, and fear among recipients. This depends, in part, on whether we see the continuum as referencing the form or impact (Bardall, Bjarnegård, and Piscopo 2020), the content of abuse or harm suffered.

Distinguishing between the form and impact, I place online violence as primarily semiotic—largely text and image based and with the goal of demeaning not just a single woman but women as a group (Krook and Restrepo Sanín 2020, 5; Krook 2020)—as well as psychological in form, though it can cause physical, psychological, and economic harm (Kuperberg 2021). I also recognize that online violence is not fully separable from offline violence (Esposito in this volume) but instead defined as such because the online space can exacerbate injury (Citron 2016).

Where studies of physical and political violence often focus on the target or victim of violence, the reach and speed of online violence (Bardall in this volume) requires that we consider both the (1) target of abuse, but also the (2) audience. For an elected official with a social media staff, the MP may never even see egregious accounts of online violence directed at them. The audience, from the staff to the general public viewing the message, must also be taken under consideration.

Intersectional Violence against Women in Politics

An intersectional approach underscores that individuals are not the product of a single identity, nor are we impacted by isolated forms of discrimination. Intersectionality encourages researchers to reflect on the dangers of analyzing women as a relatively homogeneous group but also identifies new possibilities for solidarity.

Marielle Franco's assassination in March 2018, almost certainly an act of political violence (Funari 2018), exemplifies what is illuminated with an intersectional framework. Franco, a city councilwoman in Rio de Janeiro, was assassinated after she attended an event on Black women's empowerment. Franco was an LGBTQ Afro-Brazilian woman, a *favelada*, the only Black woman representative in Rio's city council, and she was an outspoken critic of inequality and discrimination in Brazil. Her attackers have not been brought to justice, and their motives have not been definitively determined. However, her political activity was informed by her ideological commitments, sexuality, race, and gender identity. It is challenging, if not impossible, to "separate" the extent to which this attack was gendered, as opposed to racialized or homophobic. Furthermore, women, leftists, feminists, Afro-Brazilians, LGBTQ activists—and individuals and groups at the intersection of these identities, particularly Afro-Brazilian women—have invoked her memory as a political catalyst under which to mobilize (Haynes 2018; Froio 2019; Tucker and Camara 2020).

When we consider empirical cases, such as Marielle Franco's above, sexism and gender alone are insufficient to understand violence that affects women, particularly those whose identities encompass multiple marginalized groups. Intersectionality also illuminates the way that power operates and is maintained in the public space. Political power has not only been historically vested in the hands of men, but in the embodiment of heterosexual, majority-ethnicity, upper-class men. If women are the targets of violence (even just in part) because they are "space invaders," entering a predominantly and historically male space, considering other dimensions of privilege and oppression, disaggregating the women we study, and expanding beyond "just women" will further illuminate our understanding of political power (Puwar 2004).

Women who identify with groups historically underrepresented in the public space experience qualitatively and quantitatively distinct violence online. However, it is not as simple to say that women with multiple marginalized identities experience "more sexism." Women may experience other forms of discrimination or sexism that intersects with other forms of abuse.

Methodological Approaches (and Challenges) to Online Intersectional Violence

Existing research is varied in its methodologies, providing a series of useful templates for how to conduct online and intersectional research. Intersectionality has not been incorporated into many studies of online political violence. As such, I will note strategies by which researchers can incorporate an intersectional lens into survey and social media data analyses.

Several questions are particularly useful in defining an intersectional method: (1) How do you choose which groups to study; and (b) who do you compare? In her 2011 piece on Uruguay, Townsend-Bell advocates an approach that uses interviews to determine "relevant" or salient structures of discrimination for analytic study. Townsend-Bell (2011), as well as Yuval-Davis (2006), confirms that analysts do not need to consider *all* identities at all times, but can prioritize the study of some identities or discriminations according to the case context, subjects of analysis, and project scope. In addition, McCall's (2005) intracategorical and intercategorical methodological approaches are useful for studying gendered political violence. An intracategorical approach focuses "on particular social groups at neglected points of intersection" centering marginalized identities within a broader category, such as Black women in the United States (McCall 2005, 1173). An intercategorical approach, by contrast, compares relationships between multiple social groups across categories. For instance, a study on race and gender may require comparing ethnic majority men, ethnic majority women, ethnic minority men, and ethnic minority women. Depending on the scope of the question, an intercategorical or intracategorical approach may be the more effective methodological choice. In the following case study on Israeli women in the Knesset, I use a modified intracategorical approach. Due to the relatively small numbers of political women, I gathered data on all Twitter-using women members of the Knesset, but focused my qualitative analysis on politicians at intersections of multiple forms of discrimination and abuse.

The two primary methods used by scholars of online political violence are the following: (1) surveys; and (2) social media data analyses. These methods can incorporate intersectionality both in their design and interpretation. Survey questions can ask about the rhetoric and discriminations present in social media abuse as well as if the respondent believes the abuse to be motivated by discrimination. Surveys should try to avoid asking respondents to choose *between* different identity or discrimination "options," which assume that the respondent can or should separate axes of oppression (Bowleg 2008, 316). These choices can make statistical or quantitative analysis more challenging but remain true to intersectionality's precepts. Researchers can also interpret results using intersectional frameworks. As with design, measuring which groups receive more abuse is likely to essentialize women and other groups. This reduction is more likely, and harder to overcome, in larger studies. Pairing larger studies with more qualitative work, such as asking survey respondents to expand on answers or following up surveys with selected interviews, can offer a more nuanced perspective.

Social media data analysis of online violence makes use of the billions of social media posts, tweets, or responses that are generated every day. To design a social media[1] study that considers intersectionality, researchers should be attuned to difference. Deep knowledge of a case, including which identities or axes of discrimination are salient, is crucial. Researchers, such as those at the International Foundation for Electoral Systems (IFES), have used keyword banks to "mine," or search, online data. To set up an intersectional study, researchers should consult communities and different internet spaces to collect a repository of abusive words that incorporates multiple discriminations. In interpreting results, as with surveys, analysts should refrain from just classifying abuse quantitatively. While aggregating data is useful, researchers should aim to disaggregate larger groups to consider multiple categories of

difference. In addition, including and analyzing text—whether directly cop-
ied to illustrate the viciousness of the messages (Jane 2014; Megarry 2014) or
altered to protect the identity of the author[2]—demonstrates the language used
in abusive posts.

Social media data presents an important, accessible, and constantly growing dataset. It offers opportunities for researchers: there is constantly new,
low-cost (or free), public data from around the world. However, there are also
limitations. Public officials experience abuse on multiple platforms and
through private, as well as public, messages. Analyzing data on one platform
presents an incomplete picture. Relatedly, it is likely that public data *under-
estimates* the amount of violence, as it does not include many posts that have
been removed due to their violent content. The successful removal of violent
posts demonstrates that social media platforms are responding to concerns
of online hate, but researchers should qualify that their findings may be limited as a result.

There are pros and cons to both surveys and big data analyses. Importantly, both can provide answers to different questions. Survey data can help
us understand how politicians experience and are impacted by online abuse.
On the other hand, data from social media platforms illustrate the quantity
and forms of violence to which viewers—including targeted political actors—
are subject online. Both methods can incorporate an intersectional framework to make visible additional layers in the quantity and content of online
abuse.

Empirical Research on Intersectional, Online Violence against Elected Representatives

Intersectional empirical analyses of online VAWIP have traditionally investigated the intersections between racism, classism, and sexism. However, as
mentioned, salient forms of discrimination differ across countries and communities. In addition to intersectionality broadly (#ToxicTwitter 2018) and
race (Dhrodia 2017b; Thomas and Herrick in this volume), analysts have highlighted the role of ability (Southern and Harmer 2019; Zeiter et al. 2019), religion (Kishi in this volume; Kuperberg 2018), and age (Erikson and Josefsson 2019; Thomas et al. 2019). Alongside multiple forms of discrimination,
others have considered the effects of partisanship (Kuperberg 2018; Rein Venegas 2019), feminist affiliation (Krook 2017), and visibility (Rheault, Rayment,
and Musulan 2019; Håkansson 2021) on online abuse.

This research has generated some important findings. For instance, Amnesty International's 2019 report on U.S. and U.K. women politicians and
journalists found that women of color were twice as likely to be targeted with

problematic or abusive tweets than white women in the sample; this disparity was even greater for abuse that mentioned race or ethnic background. Similarly, Thomas and Herrick in this volume find that women of color in U.S. state senates face more violence than their white female and male of color colleagues. In addition, in my own research, using both big N and text analysis, I have found that sexist, Islamophobic, and antisemitic tropes have been levied against Jewish and Muslim British women MPs (Kuperberg 2021). In addition, religious-minority women are targeted with posts that were *both* sexist and racist, such as being described as a "terrorist-supporting whore" or "Soros-funded tits" (ibid.).

The internet and politics are not only historically male spaces; they also hegemonize other forms of power. Men of minority ethnicities and religions and other nonhegemonic men, such as LGBTQ men and nonbinary individuals, are also likely to be targeted by violence and abuse that seeks to reestablish norms of power (#ToxicTwitter 2019). Even when individuals *do* conform to hegemonic norms, they may still be targeted with homophobic and sexist abuse. By using feminizing or LGBTQ "slurs" to demean political actors, perpetrators are contributing to the continued subordination of marginalized groups in public space.

Finally, researchers have found that political party, feminist ideology, and visibility or leadership motivate, inform, or contribute to the effects of online discrimination for women parliamentarians. My research on Israel (Kuperberg 2018), which I detail below, and research by Rein Venegas (2019) find that in Israel and Chile, respectively, women from centrist parties are impacted by online abuse less vociferously than women from the left and right parties. Scholars of online violence, including political online violence, have also considered the role of feminist ideology in online violence. For example, British parliamentarian Stella Creasy received continuous rape threats after advocating for a seemingly innocuous "feminist" position: the placement of Jane Austin's picture on a British banknote. And lastly, researchers have found that visible women, including party leaders and political actors with greater online presence, are uniquely targeted with abuse and violence online (Rheault, Rayment, and Musulan 2019, 5; see Håkansson in this volume).

The ways that ideology, political party, and visibility interact with gender in the online space are illuminating for understanding online political violence and VAWIP. First, these characteristics are explicitly bound with politics. These affiliations indicate that online violence against politicians cannot simply be understood by applying frameworks and conceptualizations of online violence against everyday citizens to women in politics. Second, each of these indicators demonstrates that women are subject to increased violence when they upset the status quo. Entering politics as a woman is already unsettling traditional power hierarchies, but these characteristics, as well as identity-based factors described above, further disrupt discriminatory power norms.

Online Violence against Israeli, Women Members of the Knesset

As an illustrative case study, I analyzed online, intersectional VAWIP of Israeli, women members of Parliament (the Knesset) from 2017 to 2018. Israel is undoubtedly a country with salient identities. As a result of the multidecade conflict between Israel and Palestine as well as Israel's constructed identity as a Jewish state, the most obvious of these salient identities is religion. Within religion, level of religiosity among Israeli Jews is a source of polarization. In addition, though Jews of many races and ethnicities are recognized as Jewish citizens of the state, Jews of color (particularly Mizrachi and African Jews) experience discrimination in Israeli society (Zak 2015).

I relied on both a close-reading thematic analysis of Twitter data and interviews. The Twitter sample, collected between January and February 2018, comprised 2,601 tweets directed at thirty-one women members of the Knesset. I closely read each post and thematically categorized the tweets. The interviews, conducted in June 2017, comprised eleven MPs, former MPs, and staff of the Knesset. Though a small sample of interviewees, due to the size of the Knesset, I was able to interview 17 percent of nonministerial women MPs.

Through these data, I found that VAWIP in the Israeli case is influenced by sexism, ageism, discrimination due to national origin, Islamophobia, and political polarization. Interviewees described differences between the language and harassment that takes place in public—whether in open sessions of the Knesset or publicly on the internet—and that which occurs "privately," in closed sessions or in private messages. Women MPs indicated that the latter tends to be more severe. Similarly, interview and Twitter data reveal some similarities, such as an emphasis on political party, but these data significantly diverge, particularly on the role of age and national origin. This divergence could indicate that (1) the two arenas of violence—in person and online—are not identical but also that (2) public online data (particularly taken from a short period of time) does not reflect the most impactful abuse targeting politicians.

Interviewees detailed VAWIP that crossed the online and offline spaces. A Knesset staff member described harassment of women in politics by other politicians, damaging comments on social media, and sexual harassment of staff members within the Knesset. She noted that the tenor of abuse against women is different than that against men. Often, harassment against women is sexual or related to women's appearances. Women parliamentarians also described being "attacked in the comments section" when they write articles related to gender-based issues, with an emphasis on how they look rather than their policies. These experiences mirror those of women in many contexts, who have described that men are often critiqued for policy positions while women are subject to personal attacks, including those about their looks and sexuality (Southern and Harmer 2019; Ward and McLoughlin 2020). This distinction maps onto the difference between VAWIP and violence against politicians (Krook in this volume).

Interviewees also noted the role of age, national origin, religion, and religiosity in abuse. Among them, a woman MP described the following:

> I have heard, "why is she opening her mouth on issues that are important to our homeland? It's not even her country. She was born elsewhere." Gender seems to trigger all of that. Because no such things seem to spread to my colleagues who came from the same region who are males.

Importantly, gender is not independent from comments related to ethnicity or age but interwoven into the discrimination that this MP is describing. For some, holding multiple marginalized identities contributes to greater sexism, while in this case, the MP is noting that she experiences national origin discrimination more acutely because of her gender.

In the text analysis of Twitter posts, I classified 2.3 percent of tweets as abusive, in line with other studies of online violence (Southern and Harmer 2019; Ward and McLoughlin 2020). Within the category of abusive tweets, I classified tweets as *harassment*, *hate*, and *threats*. *Threats* describes direct threats of death or rape; *hate* calls out the MP with a personal insult not critiquing a political position; and *harassment* describes a tweet that is generally insulting or goes beyond what is acceptable in democratic discourse. These names—harassment, hate, and threats—do not (and cannot) reflect the severity or intensity of the threat for the target or audience. VAWIP, as identity-based abuse, is captured in both hate and threats. Importantly, the violence in these tweets is not exclusively gender based.

Within the Twitter sample, I found that partisan identity was a factor in the violent tweets received by women MPs (see Figure 15.1). Israeli parties differ on economic policy, religiosity, and inclusion, particularly Palestinian equality and statehood. In Figure 15.1, these are combined to approximately order the 2018 parties in the Knesset from left to right.

This partisan split is consistent with big N findings from Chile (Rein Venegas 2019) as well anecdotal data in the United Kingdom. Seyi Akiwowo of Glitch U.K. notes that women on the left receive online hate from those on the far left, who think they are not left *enough*, and those from the right.

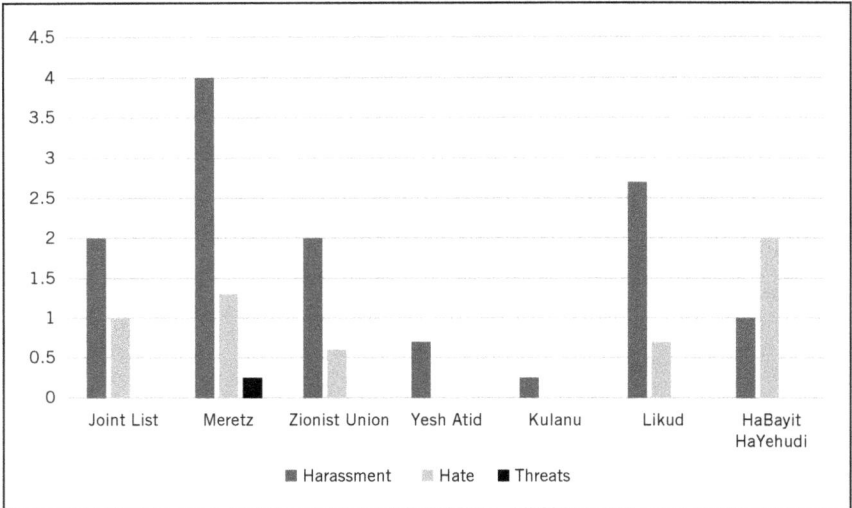

Figure 15.1 Percentage of abusive tweets by party

The same is true for women on the right. The U-shaped pattern of partisan violence, indicated in Figure 15.1, thus reflects patterns of violence in other cases.

In the Twitter portion of this study, I found less conclusive evidence that an MP's religion, race, national origin, or age impacted the number of violent tweets they received. However, the discourse of tweets included Islamophobic, racist, and sexist language. Even when discrimination is not directed at an MP who shares that identity, these public displays of hate attempt to dictate to representatives, constituents, and the general public what types of political activity, and which political actors, are welcome in the public space.

Future Research

There are many questions still to be answered by researchers interested in the juncture of online space, political violence, gender, and intersecting discriminations. Future research is needed on theoretical, methodological, and empirical questions.

An intersectional analysis asks that we are attuned to questions of power and difference. Much of the research on and theorizing of online violence has originated in the Global North, and many empirical analyses focus on a small group of languages. How is online violence understood in different contexts, where different internet and linguistic norms prevail? In addition, how can difference be probed more explicitly in our analyses of gender? By "anchoring" sexism in our analyses, we may be underemphasizing other discriminations. How can we balance both the need to study gendered political violence across difference while ensuring that gender reveals more than it obscures?

Methodologically, utilizing multiple methods allows us to map the complexities of intersectional online violence while still allowing for the uncovering of broader patterns. We cannot understand how oppressions are interconnected through machine learning algorithms alone.

Empirically, research on this topic has been relatively restricted in terms of the subjects of analysis. First, most research on online political violence has focused on national-level elected officials, as this chapter has. Other research on online abuse has profiled women who have high online visibility or have experienced significant abuse. These represent two types of political activity. There are fewer studies, and therefore less data, on how officials at the subnational or local level, voters, human rights defenders, and other political actors experience abuse online. Håkansson as well as Thomas and Herrick, both in this volume, are notable exceptions for their work on local political officials. Nonetheless, these represent a crucial direction for future research, especially as global elected officials hold relative privilege. LGBTQ, lower-class, and indigenous people—among many others—are underrepresented in elected political office around the world. Expanding the scope of the "political," as many authors in this volume have done, allows us to consider how sexism intersects with other discriminations.

Second, although some studies have compared men and women politicians online, and some have used an intracategorical model to study how abuse affects women at intersections of marginalization, there is limited research that centers men who hold marginalized or historically underrepresented identities. Third, though challenging methodologically, more research is needed on perpetrators of online abuse.

Finally, research that analyzes the implications of online abuse for elected officials, officials' staff and family members, political aspirants, constituents, and other members of the broader online public is necessary to underscore the importance of online violence as well as develop targeted solutions.

Online violence differs in form and impact across actors and geographic contexts. Being attuned to the nature and effects of violence can help us craft solutions that address the diversity of contemporary political actors and their experiences.

PART IV

Policy Responses

16

A Normative Foundation for Ending Violence against Women in Politics

Julie Ballington and
Gabriella Borovsky

This chapter examines how and where violence against women in politics (VAWIP)[1] is situated within the international normative women's rights framework and the multiple avenues it provides for states to initiate and act on policy responses to VAWIP. States have a duty to prevent, investigate, and punish all acts of violence against women, which are prohibited under international human rights standards (United Nations 2018b). As noted in the chapter by Krook, years of collective advocacy helped expand the scope of international norms and commitments on gender-based violence to include politics and those on political and electoral violence to include gender.

The United Nations has led efforts to address VAWIP, viewing it as a human rights violation that directly impedes its long-term objectives of helping states achieve sustainable peace and development. This chapter treats VAWIP as a specific form of violence against women that must be examined in its own right—as opposed to a dimension of political violence at large or violence occurring in conflict-affected contexts—and with a specific focus on women's experiences rather than on gender more widely.

A broad normative framework represents a relevant starting point for addressing all variations of the problem presented in this book, but offers states, as duty bearers in particular, specific actions for policy and program responses. While not exhaustive, this chapter examines key actions that can be taken by various state actors within this international normative framework to mitigate VAWIP. It will consider (1) international normative advancements articulating key action points for VAWIP prevention, (2) possible actions state actors can take to end VAWIP, and (3) areas for further research and action.

Normative Underpinnings

All states have an obligation to promote and protect all human rights and fundamental freedoms. Discrimination on the basis of sex is contrary to the Universal Declaration of Human Rights (1948), the International Covenant on Civil and Political Rights (1966), and the Convention on the Elimination of All Forms of Discrimination against Women (CEDAW) (1979), among others. In addition, 189 state parties agreed to the 1995 Beijing Declaration and Platform for Action, which established the international target of gender balance in decision-making. An extensive human rights–based framework demonstrates the commitment of the international community to prevent, respond to, and eliminate violence against women (VAW). The Declaration on the Elimination of Violence against Women (1993) provided a comprehensive definition of VAW, committed states and the international community to eliminate it, and provided a framework for national and international action.[2] The universal adoption of the 2030 Agenda for Sustainable Development (2015) provides further impetus to states to ensure full and effective political participation of women at all levels of decision-making (Target 5.5) and to eliminate all forms of violence against all women and girls in public and private spheres (Target 5.2).

While UN Security Council Resolution 1325 on women, peace, and security calls for special measures to protect women and girls from sexual and gender-based violence in situations of armed conflict (Krook in this volume), specific recognition in the international normative framework on ending VAWIP first appeared in UN General Assembly (GA) Resolution 66/130. Sponsored by the United States and adopted without a vote in 2012, the resolution urges all states to act, encouraging the UN system and other organizations to enhance their assistance to states in their efforts to investigate allegations of violence, assault, or harassment of women elected officials and candidates and create an environment of zero tolerance for such offenses (United Nations 2012). In its 2013 General Recommendation No. 30, the CEDAW Committee stated that substantive progress toward equal participation of women will be impossible without appropriate measures, such as ensuring that women voters and political candidates are not subject to violence either by state or private actors (para 72), and further recommended states to adopt zero-tolerance policies toward all forms of violence that undermine women's participation, including against women campaigning for public office or exercising their right to vote (para 73-f) (United Nations 2013).

Recognizing the need to address structural barriers to women's political participation, the GA in 2018 specifically called upon national legislative authorities and political parties to adopt codes of conduct and reporting mechanisms or revise existing ones, stating zero tolerance. GA Resolution 73/148 (para. 7) encourages legislative authorities and political parties within states to "adopt codes of conduct and reporting mechanisms, or revise existing ones, stating zero tolerance . . . for sexual harassment, intimidation and any other form of violence against women in politics" (United Nations 2018b).

More recently, the Agreed Conclusions of the Sixty-Fifth Commission on the Status of Women urged governments to protect women from all forms of violence and discrimination for engaging in public life, including in digital contexts, by taking practical steps and measures to create a safe and enabling environment, prevent and address violence, and promptly bringing perpetrators to justice (United Nations 2021).

The UN has issued public statements regarding acts of VAWIP in isolated cases and increasingly leverages its unique position as an intergovernmental body to prioritize action and systemwide approaches to VAWIP as a human rights violation. Independent human rights monitoring mechanisms and procedures have taken an active role in advancing the normative agenda on VAWIP. Noteworthy in this regard is a special, thematic report presented by the UN Special Rapporteur on Violence against Women (SRVAW), its causes, and consequences to the Seventy-Third Session of the UN General Assembly in 2018. The SRVAW's report notes the importance of designing, adopting, and enforcing laws and policies on gender equality and prevention of VAW consistent with international human rights law and lays out concrete actions that state and nonstate actors can take (United Nations 2018b).

Possible State Actor Responses to VAWIP

Viewing VAWIP as an impediment to women's equal contributions to long-term objectives of helping states achieve sustainable peace and development, UN Women has supported its national partners in stepping up efforts to identify possible policy responses to VAWIP based on the normative framework, including research and data collection, support to national institutions for monitoring and prevention, capacity building of national partners, strengthening complaints mechanisms, legislative and policy reform, and raising awareness. These are some examples of actions that may be considered by states and their institutions.

Parliaments

Parliaments, the chief legislative institution of the state, can adopt new legislation or adapt existing VAW legislation to define and protect against VAWIP and ensure implementation through oversight. While legal reform related to

VAWIP has been scant and uneven globally, developments in some countries provide a basis for reforms. Legal reforms related to VAWIP are largely pursued through three main channels: (1) adopting new, stand-alone laws to prohibit or criminalize VAWIP; (2) integrating adequate provisions on VAWIP into existing laws on eliminating VAW (including laws that prohibit sexual harassment), consistent with international and regional human rights standards (United Nations 2018b); or (3) introducing legislative reforms or expansions of electoral codes or penal codes (UN Women and UNDP 2017).

All *Latin American countries* are party to the *Inter-American Convention on the Prevention, Punishment and Eradication of Violence Against Women* (1994), which protects women's political rights (Article 5). After signing onto the convention, all countries in the region reformed their VAW laws, with some amending and expanding penal codes to include VAW crimes. Several countries went a step further by pursuing legal definitions on the scope of VAWIP and taking steps to punish offenders. *Bolivia* (see chapter by Restrepo Sanín) passed the world's first law on VAWIP in 2012. Laws and other instruments, including mechanisms, procedures, protocols, exist in *Argentina, Brazil, Colombia, Costa Rica, Ecuador, El Salvador, Mexico, Panama, Paraguay, Peru,* and *Uruguay,* among others.

Tunisia passed its first national law to combat VAW in 2017. The legislation includes a broad definition of violence, recognizing economic, sexual, political, and psychological forms of violence in addition to physical (UN Women 2017).

The right to live and work free from violence and harassment is universal, yet gender-based violence is present in all jobs, occupations, and sectors of the economy in all countries across the world (UN Women and ILO 2019), including in parliaments, which are also workplaces for elected officials and staff. As described in the chapter by Raney and Collier, parliaments can set examples, uphold standards and exemplify zero tolerance for gender-based violence in policy and practice by adopting new codes of conduct and reporting mechanisms, or revise existing ones, clearly stating zero tolerance for sexual harassment, intimidation, and any other form of VAWIP. They can also "conduct surveys and public debates periodically to raise awareness of the issue . . . and the crucial role that male parliamentarians can play in preventing [it]." Critically, this also must involve "addressing the impunity of [parliamentarians] with regard to [VAWIP] and examining immunity rules" (United Nations 2018b).

In *France*, the Senate amended its Rules of Procedure to include specific disciplinary sanctions for perpetrators of psychological or sexual harassment, whether they are senators or staff. It also adopted an anti-harassment plan, which focuses on prevention, complaints handling, victim support, and monitoring (IPU 2019).

The *United States* Senate and House of Representatives passed a bill to address sexual harassment in Congress following the momentum of the #MeToo movement. Under the bill, congressmembers are personally liable for financial settlements agreed with complainants, meaning taxpayers will no longer "foot the bill" for settling claims of misconduct (OHCHR and UN Women 2018).

Judiciary

As examined in the chapter by Restrepo Sanín, legal measures have been pursued by advocates. There is a range of responses through judicial action available to states. They may, for example, consider updating complaint mechanisms and response protocols, including for electoral courts, legislative chambers, or local administrations, to ensure enforcement mechanisms deal with VAWIP cases. This may require judges' training to raise their awareness of VAWIP and thereby ensure their ability to apply laws consistent with international human rights standards when investigating complaints and prosecuting perpetrators (United Nations 2018b).

The SRVAW has called for states to institute compensation for victims, reinstate officeholders forced to resign due to violence, provide adequate security measures to enable women officeholders to exercise their functions, and formally retract offenses or defamation leveled against women in politics. Even where specific laws or protocols on VAWIP are absent at the national level, when rulings issued by the judiciary (which may include electoral justice bodies) on cases that bear relevance to VAWIP are made public and include a gender perspective in line with international standards, the state must help carry out critical acts for ending impunity. To be effective, this requires state-backed efforts to build institutional capacity for promoting and protecting the human rights of women to live free from violence and participate in public affairs (United Nations 2018b).

In *Australia*, a federal judge ordered a senator to pay a fine of USD$80,000 plus costs for making sexist slurs toward a woman senator who took him to court. This was the first case of a sitting Australian politician to sue another for defamation. The judge ruled against the accused's lawyers' argument that media interviews should be covered by parliamentary privilege because the comments had originated in the Senate (BBC News 2019).

MESECVI, the follow-up mechanism to the Belém do Pará Convention,* relies on cooperation between state parties to the convention and a committee of experts. In 2015, they issued a declaration on *Violence and Political Harassment against Women*, which led to a "model law," defining VAWIP as a criminal act consistent with international norms and stipulates specific reparation measures and sanctions. The model law has stimulated additional actions toward policy responses, including a model protocol on VAWIP for political parties. As judges were unaware of basic gender concepts or VAWIP as a legal concept, a judges' guide for adjudicating electoral disputes from a gender perspective, and training curriculum for electoral courts on VAWIP, were created and are being carried out in cooperation with States (OHCHR and UN Women 2018).

---

* The 1994 Inter-American Convention on the Prevention, Punishment, and Eradication of Violence against Women, known as the Convention of Belém do Pará, defines VAW and establishes that women have the right to live a life free of violence.

Security Sector

States can support initiatives to train law enforcement officials to raise their awareness of VAWIP (United Nations 2018b). Security forces and police are critical for preventing and responding to VAWIP, as they have a duty to ensure public safety in political and electoral processes and carry out operational planning for electoral security. This is necessary for assessing and responding to security risks that may impede women's full participation in electoral processes, whether as voters, candidates, or polling staff (UN Women and UNDP 2017).

Specific training can strengthen security forces' awareness and capacity for ensuring public safety in accordance with national laws and international human rights and gender equality standards. Training ensures that operating practices and security arrangements protect women through various gender-sensitive measures. These may include respecting separated queues for women in polling stations; striving for gender balance in the police force to increase women's participation and ensure women police officers are available to respond to occurrences involving women; establishing appropriate mechanisms that will encourage women to report cases of VAWIP in a safe manner, such as setting up gender focal points or gender desks; detecting, investigating, and responding to incidents, which could include "subtle" forms of violence such as discrimination and family voting; bringing perpetrators to justice; and including gender perspectives in the research, policy, and practice of police, defense, and military institutions (UN Women and UNDP 2017).

Training and accountability are especially important where the security sector has been found to be a perpetrator itself. It can help raise awareness about types and frequency of VAW in elections, reinforce the sector's legal obligation to take the issue seriously, and provide guidance on how to respond to and report cases (UN Women 2021).

I n *Sierra Leone*, the national police (SLP) organized a series of countrywide trainings on gender, elections, and security for personnel from national Correctional Services and Fire Force, City Council Police, Chiefdom Police, and Road Safety Corps, who worked together with the SLP to provide 2018 general elections security. The training, jointly supported by UN agencies, covered gender sensitivity and VAW, human rights, election offenses, and relevant laws and regulations. Police training manuals were updated to include specific information on VAWIP and highlighted the importance of gender sensitivity across election security operations, particularly when responding to sexual violence incidents. Critically, the training was part of broader VAWIP-prevention programs and activities, including community mobilization, media monitoring, and advocacy campaigns in which police and security personnel also participated (UN Women 2018). Combined, these actions improved relationships between the security sector, civil society groups, and communities to collaborate on addressing VAWIP.

Electoral Management Bodies

While gender-based VAW is present in all political processes, elections are "hugely political," exposing social and political differences and increasing risk for violence; women, who comprise over half of most countries' eligible voters, are particularly at risk in some contexts (UN Women and UNDP 2017). Electoral management bodies (EMBs) are the principal state actors in electoral administration whose decisions and actions determine the credibility and security of elections. In administering the election law in preparation for an election, there are several points at which they can mitigate and respond to VAW, including the following: analyzing voter and candidate registration procedures to prevent barriers to women's participation; ensuring that registration and voting arrangements guarantee women's safety; ensuring candidates can campaign safely; integrating information about mitigation measures for gender-based violence into training programs for electoral administrators; ensuring that early-warning systems for electoral violence and security assessments are not gender blind; and reporting on incidents of VAW in elections (United Nations 2018b; UN Women and UNDP 2017).

EMBs can map out VAW in elections to identify "hot spots" and design appropriate mitigation and monitoring mechanisms. This, in conjunction with broader electoral security assessments, can help identify at-risk individuals and areas for gender-based violence and provide the EMB with information about effective ways to protect and include potentially vulnerable populations so they may exercise their rights (UN Women and UNDP 2017).

In some countries, EMBs and electoral tribunals have specific VAWIP prevention and enforcement roles, where EMBs use their mandate and authority to act in cases in alignment with the normative framework underpinning VAWIP in the country. This is an important strategy as, depending on the context, EMBs can have extensive jurisdiction over political party conduct, electoral processes, and enforcement of electoral laws, including gender quota laws. Where the terms of political party codes of conduct are legally mandated, EMBs can help enforce them through legal sanctions (UN Women and UNDP 2017).

Political parties are among the most common perpetrators of VAWIP. In some contexts, the EMB can help enforce laws, policies, and/or codes of conduct on political parties' treatment of gender-based violence. For example, in *Bolivia*, UN Women supported the electoral tribunal to convene a yearlong consultative process with a wide range of national stakeholders to draft the Political Organisations Law enacted in August 2018 (Observatorio de Paridad Democrática 2017). Under the new law, all political parties must ensure gender equality and parity within their own organizations, as well as prevent and mitigate violence against women.

Observatories

National observatories monitor various issues related to women's political participation, including VAWIP. Most known examples come from Latin America, where observatories conduct information-gathering and monitoring work to track states' compliance with gender quotas and parity laws, publicize missteps, and demand accountability (UN Women 2021). Some are state created and directed—modeled after "traditional" VAW observatories—while others are tied to electoral tribunals. Those founded and managed by civil society may cover other gender equality issues, such as health.

Reliable and systematic VAWIP repositories around the world are scarce; observatories help make data on women's political inclusion publicly accessible. State-managed observatories sometimes have authority on matters related to women's political participation and VAWIP, though they may depend heavily on the commitment of leaders and connections to other government stakeholders, political parties, and media. Such connections ensure collaboration, avoid duplication of efforts across different private and public sector agencies, and ensure the research and data have an impact beyond their web presence (UN Women 2021).

---

*U*N Women has supported the work of observatories in Latin America and Africa:

- *Mexico's* observatory monitors and evaluates progress on women's participation, generates and publishes available data for government and civil society, and collates good practice on women's political empowerment strategies and promotes alliances for implementing international normative frameworks on women's political participation. The observatory's web portal includes a dedicated section on VAWIP, which contains a case registry (UN Women 2019).
- *Bolivia's* observatory was established by the national EMB, Plurinational Electoral Organ (PEO), in 2017 to inter alia generate knowledge including sex-disaggregated data on women's political participation and rights, process VAWIP complaints, and monitor cases through legislative Councils or Assemblies (Observatorio de Paridad Democrática 2017).* The observatory uses a set of indicators covering electoral processes, political participation and representation (including rural, indigenous women), gender parity in public institutions, and VAWIP. This enabled the observatory to publish the country's first national dataset on political participation and support information-gathering for VAWIP research, all of which were used by the government to prepare 2018 CEDAW, Universal Periodic Review on Human Rights (UPR) and Beijing +25 reports (UN Women 2019).
- *Zimbabwe's* gender commission—in collaboration with the national EMB, Parliament, Human Rights, Peace and Reconciliation and Media Commissions, security sector, civil society organizations, women's peace committees, and academia—set up a gender observatory in 2017 to do the following: collect evidence and analyze trends on women's participation in elections; disseminate information through social media, political parties, and civil society; and respond to VAWIP incidents by issuing recommendations, referring cases to court, and encouraging political parties to adhere to the constitution or electoral code of conduct. The observatory is staffed through secondments from member institutions and compiles information gathered by women-led grassroots early-warning systems, election observation missions, situation rooms, media, community members and leaders, candidates, research, and courts.

---

* The electoral tribunal approved in 2017 the PEO's regulation to receive and process/manage complaints of harassment and political violence against women (candidates, elected, and/or in public office) as a prevention measure to stop forced resignations of women from office.

Conclusion

The international normative framework places states as the key actors responsible for addressing VAWIP, as they have a duty to prevent, investigate, and punish all acts of violence against women prohibited under human rights standards. It falls within the respective mandates of state actors to create and carry out normative, legislative, judicial, and institutional actions to enable, initiate, and implement VAWIP responses. The most crucial include parliamentary action to adopt and/or amend legislation, institutional reforms aimed at zero tolerance for VAWIP, strengthening justice mechanisms and reparation, developing security sector capacity to enforce laws and protections, and holding governments accountable through monitoring and data publicizing.

No actor alone, however, can eliminate VAWIP completely. The profiles of VAWIP's victims and perpetrators, forms and methods, locations and consequences are specific and distinct, yet often overlapping and cyclical in nature along the physical-psychological violence continuum, necessitating responses that are both tailored and holistic. Cooperation between state and nonstate stakeholders—including political parties, the media, independent human rights monitoring mechanisms, and civil society groups—is important and necessary given their interdependence and intersecting mandates. The normative framework is a critical starting point. It provides the justification and, to some extent, the road map that states and state institutions need to approach the problem. It also provides a framework for accountability and basis for advocacy by national and international actors.

Further research on the long-term efficacy of various policy responses called for within the international normative framework is needed. A top priority is strengthening the evidence base. National data on VAWIP is persistently lacking. Without it, it is difficult to assess the magnitude, types, or severity of VAWIP, risk and protective factors or consequences, or even the political or social climate in which appropriate and effective policy responses can be designed and implemented.

17

Policy Responses to Gender-Based Political Violence Online

GABRIELLE BARDALL

U nlike offline political violence where incidents of harm may be clearly defined in time and space and according to their intended victims and perpetrators, online harms are more complex and thus more challenging to respond to for mitigation and prevention purposes. Any given incident or event of gender-based political violence online may take place over a period of seconds, hours, days, or months. It may involve dozens, hundreds, or even thousands of diverse perpetrators from around the world, generating vast amounts of wide-ranging online vitriol across a multitude of platforms and fora, sometimes spilling into offline spaces.

This chapter looks at policy responses to a spectrum of forms of gender-based political violence in the online arena. Responses identified are based on the intensity of the harm, the identity of the perpetrator(s), and the medium/online location where the harm occurs. I argue that responses to these various manifestations of online violence should be grouped into three distinct sets of approaches: institutional and legal responses, platform responses, and community-based responses. Each approach should reflect the distinct nature and nuances of this problem. Responses to incivility and hate speech must be different than those targeted to criminal harassment and threats. Responses must reflect the fact that some kinds of harm can be codified and prosecuted, while others are embedded in cultural norms and require completely different strategies. All responses need to engage with the delicate conversation on free speech—protecting freedoms to express opinions and beliefs but also protecting the right to engage in civic and political activities free from fear of harm.

Problem Description

Under the broad umbrella of gender-based political violence on the online arena, distinctions about the nature of harm should be made according to its form and intensity, the actor(s) perpetrating the harm, and the medium used/cyber and physical world locations where it occurs.

Form and Intensity: Pinpointing the Spectrum of Online Violence

In crafting appropriate solutions, responders must evaluate where any given incident or harmful situation falls on the spectrum of online gender-based political violence as well as consider any spillover effects online violence has in offline spaces. Presented in Figure 17.1, this spectrum recognizes that direct criminal acts such as death or rape threats and criminal harassment are the most extreme form of gender-based political violence on the online arena and the least common. They are the tip of an iceberg of abuse that begins with *online incivility* and intensifies into *information disorder*. A third category on the spectrum of online violence—*gender-based hate speech*—bridges the gap into overt hostility. In turn, hate speech is the immediate predecessor to the final category on the spectrum: *overt, criminal acts of violence* including death and rape threats, criminal harassment, defamation, and stalking. All of these actions, when used to inhibit, control, coerce, or pressure a person's political

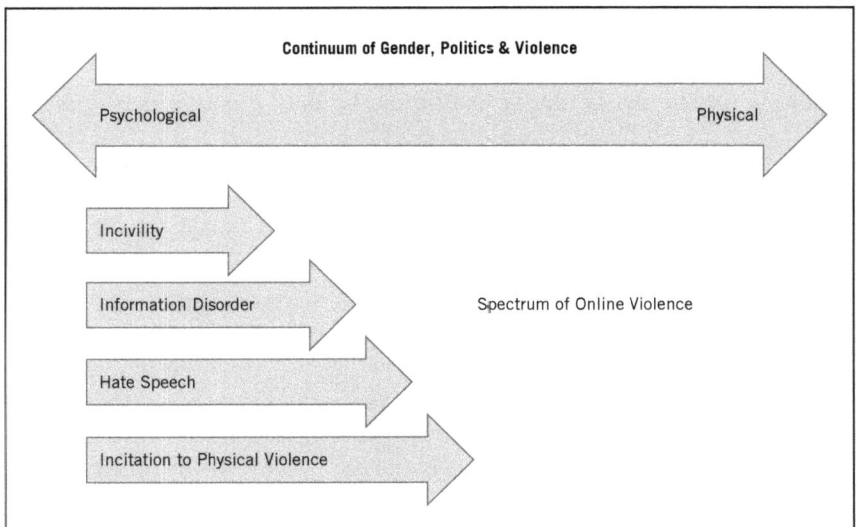

Figure 17.1 Spectrum of online political GBV

decisions and engagement on the basis of their gender, are forms of gender-based political violence on the online arena.

The different elements of this spectrum of violence can occur in a linear pattern, as part of an escalation of violence. Often these types interact, overlap, and/or reoccur during any given violent incident and may rise and fall in waves. In considering appropriate responses, it is necessary to define whether the harm is the result of a discrete and intense incident (e.g., a death threat) or the cumulative result of many incidents.

Appropriate Responses for a Multiplicity of Perpetrators

Offline gender-based political violence generally involves a single victim who is targeted by an identifiable perpetrator or group of perpetrators. Perpetrators of gender-based political violence online are much more complex. Instead of a single perpetrator, incidents of online gender-based political violence are often characterized by dozens or even thousands of actors contributing to a violent act. They engage with different degrees of intensity and malice.

Responses to mitigate, prevent, or prosecute acts of gender-based political violence on the online arena must be proportionate and adapted to the perpetrators' actions. If and when they can be identified, *direct perpetrators* (including toxic influencers) may be sanctioned under social media user guidelines or even under criminal law. Successful persecution requires collaboration on evidence collection from the social media platforms where the crime is committed and by educating at-risk targets of how to respond in the event of an incident, by documenting the evidence before deleting it from the web.

The vast majority of actors contributing to these incidents are not criminally liable. Instead, responses to *indirect perpetrators* must be driven by voluntary moral action within the community. This includes voluntary action by platforms to adopt algorithms to down-vote noncriminal abusive content and bystander intervention.

The widespread use of pseudonyms and hidden identities online often results in high levels of anonymity among perpetrators. This results in a particularly terrifying impact for victims of attacks and makes prosecution very difficult. On the other hand, perpetrators of gender-based political violence on the online arena may be well-known to the victim or even be intimate partners, for example, with so-called revenge porn.

Last but not least to recall, perpetrators of gender-based political violence on the online arena are not always humans. The automation of computational propaganda (the use of algorithms over social media in attempts to manipulate public opinion) allows malicious actors to scale their online offenses by using social media bots and automated profiles that look like real users (Woolley and Joseff 2018) as well as "cyborgs" and "soft puppets" (accounts partially managed by humans), or engaging in a combination of approaches ("inorganic coordinated activity") involving a group of social media accounts (human, automated, or a combination) to strategically amplify certain messages in an effort to manipulate the messaging (Woolley and Joseff 2018).

Digital Geography: Mediums and Online Locations

Cyberspace is multidimensional, and gender-based political violence on the online arena occurs across an ecosystem of platforms (Bardall 2019; Van Der Wilk 2018). Individuals (perpetrators and targets) share content both publicly and privately, retaining different degrees of control over content and what is said about them. Commentary and reporting on the internet appear in both more "formal" spaces, such as recognized commercial media and web-published journalism, as well as less regulated public, such as chatrooms, Twitter, YouTube, Instagram, blogs, and commentary spaces on media sites. These relationships are presented in Table 17.1.

Finally, the geography of gender-based political violence on the online arena is not constrained to different virtual spaces but also plays out at *distinct offline locations*, impacting possible responses. In many contexts in the Global South, gender-based political violence on the online arena initiates and is concentrated in urban centers (especially capital cities), and its messages spread into peripheral areas and across borders (Bardall 2019). High-density population centers are natural hubs for information and communications technology–facilitated abuse because they tend to have greater levels of access to technology, wealth, connectivity, and techno-literacy. Although most violent content originates in major cities, it spreads well beyond those cities in several ways. Violent or degrading themes and abusive messages that dominate urban-centric platforms (for example, Twitter or Instagram) fan out across WhatsApp and other messaging services. Traditional media plat-

TABLE 17.1 CONTENT ACCESS AND CONTENT MANAGEMENT			
		Content Access	
		Private	Public
Content Management	Private	Private conversations between individual users. Access and management limited to direct users (e.g., Facebook Private Messages, WhatsApp, Skype, Telegram).	Private user makes public posts on a self-managed web platform (e.g., making a public wall post on Facebook).
	Public	Formally published public media and journalism with some degree of regulation and recognized journalistic standards.	Weakly regulated or unregulated public fora (e.g., Twitter, Instagram, YouTube, blogs).

forms such as radio and print media pick up on online gossip and slander and echo it into rural areas where internet and data coverage is absent (ibid.).

Furthermore, this content does not respect national borders. Any given event may attract the involvement of perpetrators from *outside national borders*, including neighboring countries with an interest in regional politics and diaspora hubs. Diaspora hubs are frequent international hot spots (Bardall 2019). Gender-based political violence online is also employed as a strategy by some hostile foreign actors to disrupt democratic processes abroad (ibid.).

Precedent exists for regulating transnational cybercrime, including in the anti-terrorism sphere. These principles can be adapted and applied to fight the transnational dimension of online GBV, including politically motivated online GBV (Gercke 2012; Sofaer and Goodman 2001; Perloff-Giles 2018).

Adapted Responses to Online Violence against Women in Politics

The broad variety of forms, actors, and digital and physical geographies involved in gender-based political violence on the online arena make any single response approach impractical. Instead, current responses and recommended responses have adapted to reflect the defining factors presented above. In practice, we see these adapted responses falling into one of three spheres of interventions: institutional and legal responses, platform responses, and community/cultural responses.

Institutional and Legal Responses

Institutional and legal responses to gender-based political violence on the online arena seek to modify behavior by changing normative frameworks, sanctioning harmful behaviors, and restoring justice to survivors. While laws and institutions are the slowest to adapt to change, they can be the most powerful in driving lasting improvement due to their ability to penalize perpetrators and influence attitudes and behaviors at a national or even international level. Responses in this field focus on harms on the more intense end of the spectrum, primarily overt acts of violence, harassment, intimidation, and (to a lesser extent and dependent on the legal framework) on hate speech and disinformation. They do not address incivility. Legal and institutional responses rely on the presence of identifiable, individual perpetrator(s) and are especially sensitive to the issue of digital geography because they necessarily rely on defined jurisdictions.

Legal responses in this field suffer from a double gap: legal frameworks around gender-based violence are often inconsistent and underdeveloped in many parts of the world. At the same time, legal frameworks around online crime are still in their infancy. Online crime is challenging for many sub-national bodies to address, especially when crime involves actors or computers operating outside their jurisdiction, where laws may differ. Hence, online crime is generally left to national-level authorities to define, legislate, and prosecute.

National-level policymakers can take multiple actions to address gender-based political violence on the online arena. They may integrate online GBV (including political GBV) into relevant related criminal and civil frameworks (Australian Government n.d.) including but not limited to the following:

- Pornography laws (criminal distribution of nonconsensual pornography, child pornography laws)
- Harassment laws (general harassment, sexual cyber harassment, aggravated harassment, cyber-stalking, stalking)
- Privacy laws (invasion of privacy, posting a private image for harassment/pecuniary gain)
- Other areas (disorderly conduct, video voyeurism, unauthorized distribution of sensitive images, unlawful surveillance, dissemination of video and images obtained through unlawful surveillance, sexual assault, domestic violence, extortion, hacking) (Cyber Civil Rights Initiative 2022)

National policymakers can embed intolerance for online abuse in key national documents (declaration of rights, charter of rights and freedoms, national acts on broadcasting, immigration, anti-terrorism, etc.) (Media Smarts n.d.) and establish consistent, culturally sensitive definitions of "intimate images" that include images of a person without attire of religious or cultural significance if they normally wear such attire in public (Australian Government n.d.). National legal responses should balance legislating image-based harm with text-based abuses, which are more frequently overlooked but no less harmful. Policymakers and courts also need to grapple with challenging issues of free-expression rights for artificially intelligent communicators, which includes addressing the sensitive question of defining "journalist" as human and with fundamental essential qualities (Schroeder 2018). Importantly, legal frameworks should recognize social media platforms as publishers and hold them to the same rules, including liability for defamation and their responsibility for the presence of abusive and violence content from a variety of users. Fines and other sanctions measures may be placed on social media platforms that fail to meet standards, including a responsibility to remove abusive content.

Regional and international bodies can offer guidance in defining normative frameworks. The UN Charter of Human Rights and Principles for the

Internet (Internet Rights and Principles Coalition 2014) establishes rights-based principles for internet governance, including gender equality in learning, defining, accessing, using, and shaping the internet. International actors can also advance normative frameworks by establishing consistent definitions of the different forms of online gender-based violence and abuse across the spectrum, advocating and informing, and promoting states' commitment to action.[1]

Policy implementation and law enforcement are also essential components of responses in this area. Law enforcement actors, magistrates, judges, and juries need to be educated and informed. They require resources to investigate internet-based crimes and to train officers on how to recognize the various forms of gendered cybercrimes (including political) and how to collect and preserve evidence and establish burdens of proof. The emergence of solutions such as eSafety commissions[2] or dedicated cyber abuse ombudspeople are in their infancy.

Regional and international bodies as well as bi- and multilateral arrangements complete the picture on enforcement of legal frameworks on gendered cybercrimes (including political). Cooperation between agencies in different countries is often necessary and includes supranational actors such as the International Criminal Police Organization (Interpol) and the European Cybercrime Centre (EC3). However, international cooperation to date is mostly limited to financial cybercrime, attacks on information systems, and combating child sexual abuse and exploitation. Transnational hate speech, gender-based harassment, and direct online GBV are largely excluded. The absence of harmonized legal norms around online (P-)GBV and the low awareness of the transnational dimensions of online (P-)GBV exacerbate the situation.

Finally, legal frameworks also govern women's ability to respond to and defend themselves against these attacks. National law should protect the right of victims to block, mute, or hide abusive social media users as they deem necessary. Although the social media accounts of public figures are often regarded as public fora, the identity-based nature of online gender-based violence renders these attacks personal. As such, victims should always be able to protect themselves from exposure to violence, especially where other forms of recourse are absent.

Responses Involving Social Media Platforms

Social media platforms are positioned to stop much of the harm of gender-based political violence on the online arena at the source. While legal recourse can address the most egregious cases and create a deterrence effect, most cases of gender-based political violence on the online arena cannot be dealt with through formal legal systems for a plethora of reasons ranging from issues with perpetrators (i.e., being outside a jurisdiction, unidentifiable, bots, cases involving hundreds or thousands of social media users, etc.) to the nature of the act (i.e., not codified or acts of incivility that only constitute harm on a cumulative basis).

Solutions involving social media platforms seek to limit the amount of harmful content that appears on the web and to minimize the impact of harmful content by acting quickly to cut it off when it occurs. By taking appropriate measures, social media platforms can protect users from abuse and ensure more equal access. Solutions in this area address the full spectrum of harms, from incivility to criminal acts. These solutions generally operate regardless of the jurisdictional issues involved in legal responses, and they are more flexible in overcoming the challenges linked to perpetrator identity and multiplicities of perpetrators. While many possible responses are available, as described below, few are currently applied specifically to GBV, and almost none are used to address political GBV online. The fundamental challenge is thus related to raising awareness about the destructive presence of gender-based political violence on the online arena on social media platforms and advocating the platforms to integrate and elevate the topic within existing frameworks of responses.

First among responses, social media platforms can set the terms of engagement by prohibiting multiple forms of gendered harm (including political GBV) into their platform user agreements, terms of service, and codes of conduct. Terms of engagement should clearly state that the company's services may not be used to engage in hateful activity or used to facilitate hateful activities engaged elsewhere, either online or offline, and should define and provide examples of gendered hateful activity (Fernandez 2018). Platforms can establish transparent policies on their process for evaluating and resolving reported hate content as well as their appeals process.

One of the fastest-evolving responses today concerns the responsibility of social media platforms to manage and remove harmful content. Effective content moderation includes combined artificial intelligence (AI) and human intelligence. Automated content flagging and removal accounts for the majority of content policing for leading platforms. In its fourth quarter 2021 transparency report, YouTube reports 95 percent of nearly six million videos were removed through automated flagging (72 percent were removed before they had fewer than eleven views) (Google 2022).

Human flagging includes both content flagged by other public platform users (or watchdog NGOs) as well as content flagged by trained teams of experts employed by the platform. YouTube reports employing ten thousand people in content monitoring and removal and policy development; Facebook reports thirty-five thousand employees worldwide working on safety and security. The role of professional content management includes training and supporting programmers and content assessors, testing hate speech–identifying technology for bias, and ensuring teams in affected communities have appropriate cultural, social, political, and historical contexts. Of the nearly six million videos removed by YouTube in Q4 2021, only 4 percent were flagged by users, 1 percent was flagged by trusted individuals (trained experts), and less than 1 percent were removed following flagging by NGOs or government (ibid.).

Content management can also include providing fact-checking and alternative information or forbidding some topics (e.g., white nationalism [Ingram and Collins 2019] and anti-vax propaganda pre- and postpandemic [Wilson 2019; Heilweil 2021]). Platforms may develop repositories of multilingual hate-based language to facilitate the development of adapted algorithms (Hatebase 2022), mandatory labeling schemes for bot content (Williams 2019), and delays in content posting to slow the rapid spread of online hate and allow time to intervene. Sanctions must be consistently applied to violators. These emerging techniques have been increasingly used for content involving racist speech, extremist content, terrorism, and revenge pornography, but they are yet rarely applied to online GBV or political GBV.

Whereas responsibility for hate content has previously been almost exclusively the responsibility of the person who posted it, social media platforms are increasingly becoming legally accountable for the presence of hateful content on their sites. Germany now requires platforms to set procedures on complaint review, to remove illegal content within twenty-four hours, and to publish updates on their progress. Focusing on extremist content/terror videos, the European Union and Australia have placed steep fines on social media platforms who fail to remove content within twenty-four to forty-eight hours. In Australia, criminal penalties may include possible jail sentences for tech executives for up to three years and financial penalties worth up to 10 percent of a company's global turnover (BBC Reality Check 2020). Here again, existing solutions in related fields of online abuse have yet to systematically incorporate the forms of harm most common to gender-based political violence on the online arena.

Social media platforms are positioned to prevent and mitigate gender-based political violence on the online arena through targeted education and awareness raising among their users (including those who might be inclined to become indirect perpetrators). The platforms can offer user resources to recognize online abuse and guidance on how to effectively intervene to stop it, including de-escalation tactics, reporting up, and referral information. They can document abusive behavior from the earliest signs of incivility to track escalation and demonstrate patterned behavior. Further to this, platforms can encourage transparency, public awareness, and research by publishing this data on hateful activity occurring on the platform and their efforts to stop it so that users and researchers can better understand the scope of the problem and what is working (or not working) to address it (ibid.).

Finally, social media platforms can take a proactive stance on ending gender-based political violence on the online arena through strong leadership and public voice. Clear and strong messages stating platforms' commitments to gender equality and safe and equal access to the web should come from the highest levels of executive leadership and be incorporated in core governing documents. Members of senior management can be designated (or new positions can be introduced) to lead initiatives on ending hateful activity and report on the effectiveness of the company's efforts to end them. Executive committees and boards can form advisory groups of external experts to orient their actions.

Community Responses

The "community" of responders described in this group refers to both online and offline actors who may be affiliated with an organization or professional group (NGOs and other civil society groups, professional journalists) or independent citizens and bystanders to harmful behavior online. This collectively constitutes a community of human rights defenders, whether they formally identify themselves as activists or whether they are "ordinary people" who consciously adopt basic online behaviors and practices that reduce and mitigate online violence. Community actors may or may not work in coordination/collaboration with state institutions and/or social media corporations. Community-based solutions to gender-based political violence on the online arena go to the heart of the problem, dealing directly with victims and perpetrators, and involve immediate, real-time action.

Unlike responses in the other two categories, community-based responses focus less on systemic or institutional change and more on immediate care, harm reduction, damage control, and mitigation. They are the most flexible of all three categories of responses in that community responses can adapt to the different types and intensities of violence across the spectrum and are less constrained when faced with cases with a multiplicity of perpetrators (including extraterritorial), incidents occurring across multiple platforms, or in different regions or countries. As with the other two groups of response options, approaches are generally borrowed from related fields and applied to gender-based political violence on the online arena.

A first set of community responses are those that use direct intervention and service provision to stop gender-based political violence on the online arena in its tracks and to mitigate the harm it causes to its victims. Online bystander intervention tactics, such as those employed by groups like Hollaback! (iHollaback 2022), train people to recognize online harassment when it occurs and to constructively step in to diffuse, divert, and diminish harm through counter-speech strategies, including satire and comedy where appropriate (Anti-Defamation League 2022). Frontline activists and human rights defenders engage in a range of strategies from establishing helplines (Cyber Civil Rights Initiative 2022), online resources (pro bono "takedown guides" and services), and networks of law firms, attorneys, and other services that offer pro bono resources to victims (Cyber Civil Rights Initiative 2022). Activist groups and media use AI to react and respond. For example, ParityBot's AI model automatically sends a positive tweet every time their AI model detects an abusive tweet directed at women in politics (Areto Labs 2019). Fact-checking groups also rely on AI to detect potential disinformation online and flag it to users and/or platforms to request takedowns. App developers working with human rights defenders have made it increasingly accessible and secure to report and document incidents of harassment and abuse, including by integrating advanced security functions into pertinent apps (multilayer encryption, "quick exit" functions, etc.).

Activists advocate for cultures of zero tolerance and encourage social media users to push back and engage proactively against sexism and online violence and harassment. They provide feminist online security training for rights defenders that include coping mechanisms, support for trauma, and resilience tactics. Trainings are also increasingly available for political women and range from prevention tactics (i.e., setting up secure profiles and practices for online engagement with the public, personal data protection) to response strategies (i.e., how to deal with trolls, saving evidence of potentially criminally harassing activity, blocking and reporting online abusers, individual resilience story sharing and developing "psychological armor," and training and legal support in preparing to take cases to the police) (Australian Government n.d.; PEN America 2022).

Human rights activists and civil society groups are increasingly turning to work with media groups, both to ensure that media does not contribute to harmful behavior toward political women (intentionally or unintentionally) as well as to equip them to identify and accurately report on cases on gender-based political violence on the online arena. Efforts to hold media and journalists to account include both "carrots" and "sticks," such as awards for gender-sensitive journalism and gendered indicators for media monitoring (#ShePersisted 2022). Recognizing that gender-based political violence in the online arena includes violence targeted toward women in other civic roles, such as journalists and activists, increasing attention is paid to support women journalists against this kind of assault.

Finally, community-based responses to gender-based political violence on the online arena are also drawing on digital literacy and awareness-raising tactics. Civic education messaging addresses common misperceptions that gender-based political violence on the online arena is not "real" violence and informs target populations on the extent and impact of it. Digital literacy and accessible in-platform tools to combat online violence include nationally sponsored digital literacy centers (Media Smarts n.d.) and the promotion of social standards (personal and business) of "netiquette" (WebRoot–NZ 2022). Awareness raising should also be targeted at vulnerable populations, such as young girls and women in areas with low internet penetration. These women and girls may be especially vulnerable either to becoming targets of abuse as they begin using social media or to consuming disinformation and fake news. Awareness campaigns targeting these populations can use both traditional approaches (radio, face-to-face) as well as more high-tech outreach.

Conclusion

By recognizing the component parts of online political GBV, actors are able to define and target their solutions appropriately. The diversity of responses available reflects the complexity of the issue. These diverse responses are complementary, and when enacted strategically in combination with each other, they hold the promise of both providing immediate aid to those in harm's way and lasting normative change at policy and attitudinal levels. Many of the solutions discussed above have emerged in related fields but have yet to be fully incorporated into responses targeted specifically at political GBV online. Identifying common ground and mutual strategies between stakeholders in the areas of democracy promotion, women's rights, digital security, and gender-based violence will be a critical next step in transforming the potential of these innovations into reality.

18

Responses to Conflict-Related Sexual Violence

ROBERT U. NAGEL AND
ANNE-KATHRIN KREFT

S tate and nonstate armed actors (e.g., state armies, paramilitary groups, and insurgent groups) perpetrate conflict-related sexual violence (CRSV) as political violence in armed conflict. Figure 18.1 gives an indication of the occurrence of sexual violence in armed conflicts from 1989 until 2019, based on the updated Sexual Violence in Armed Conflict dataset (Cohen and Nordås 2014). CRSV is linked to gendered power imbalances existing in society and is a gendered form of political violence, as we discuss in Chapter 8. As such, CRSV elicits various political—and gendered—responses from the international community, from governments, and from civil society actors. These responses are the focus of this chapter.

International actors, governments, and civil society actors recognize CRSV as a severe human rights and security issue in armed conflict, and they respond to it in various ways. Just as gender is central to CRSV, so it is to these responses. This is because these actors operate in accordance with logics of gender differentiation. The vast majority of decision makers in political and state institutions have been male, which shapes institutional policies and practices (Acker 1992; Nagel 2021b). In the case of CRSV, this results in problematic dichotomies between female (or feminized) victims and male (or masculinized) perpetrators and protectors. The notion of the masculinist protector state is central to understanding responses to CRSV (Young 2003; Nagel 2019). Such gendered norms and hierarchies permeate the international system, where states and intergovernmental organizations composed of states are the primary actors. Within states, by contrast, civil society actors mobilizing in

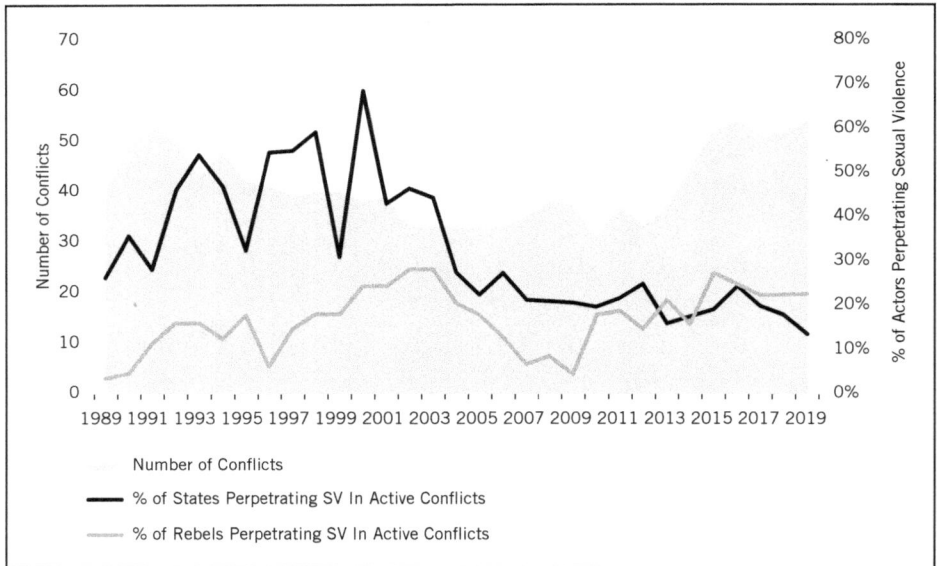

Figure 18.1 Share of state and rebel actors perpetrating sexual violence in active conflict years; SVAC data. (Cohen and Nordås 2014)

response to CRSV often challenge gendered hierarchies and their violent manifestations.

In this chapter, we first discuss the gendered nature of formal institutions such as governments and intergovernmental organizations. Second, we engage with the responses of the international community to CRSV in the context of the global Women, Peace and Security framework. Third, we discuss how governments respond to reports of CRSV by rebel groups. Fourth, we appraise the responses of civil society to CRSV before concluding the chapter.

Gendered Institutions

Formal institutions, like governments and international organizations such as the United Nations, are gendered because they "are symbolically and ideologically described and conceived in terms of a discourse that draws on masculinities and femininities" (Britton 2000, 420). As social creations, institutions reflect the preferences and values of their founders and members, which have been men for the majority of governments and most of history. These institutions thus reflect the behavior of people within them and under their control: distinctions between male and female, masculine and feminine, shape governments' identities and actions (Acker 1992). These gendered processes rely on patterns of sexual stratification that ensure men's power over women.

Second, governments and state-based intergovernmental institutions are tied to ideals of cis-hetero masculinity expressed through control over and subordination of women and their sexuality, for example, through policing women's reproductive rights. A pillar of the Weberian state is that the monopoly of force and the use of violence is the government's prerogative (Weber 2004, 33). Governments adopt and promote masculine behavior such as militarized posturing in defense of their citizens and territory, often framed in feminine terms (Yuval-Davis 1997; Sjoberg 2013). A concrete manifestation of this is governments seeking to justify violence and war by claims of fighting for and on behalf of women (Sjoberg and Peet 2011).

Third, these dynamics are intertwined with the gendered separation of combatants and civilians and the resulting gendered protection norm (Carpenter 2005; Sjoberg 2013). Men are conceived of as combatants, that is, legitimate targets of violence, whereas "women, children, and other vulnerable groups" are civilians who are deemed innocent and in need of protection (Carpenter 2005). These essentializing and subordinating notions manifest in governments' perception of women as literal and figurative reproducers of the nation (Peterson 1999). This makes women strategic centers of gravity that governments need to protect and fight for. In claiming the mantle of a just warrior purportedly protecting women, governments establish and entrench a gender hierarchy that prioritizes masculinity over femininity. Women and others who do not fit ideals of cis-hetero masculinity are gender subordinated. Women's presumed innocence spurs men to promise protection and take credit for supposedly providing it despite not actually doing so (Young 2003; Sjoberg and Peet 2011). This gendered protection norm undermines women's agency and puts them at the mercy of the men (government) tasked with protecting them. Sjoberg and Peet label this a protection racket (2011).

International Community

Since the authorization of the landmark Resolution 1325 on Women, Peace and Security (UNSCR 1325) in 2000, CRSV has received increased attention (Crawford 2017). The Security Council has since passed five other resolutions that have explicitly addressed CRSV. From 2008 to 2019, the resolutions evolve from first an oversimplified notion of sexual violence as a weapon of war (see UNSCR 1820, 1888, and 1960; Crawford 2017) to recently recognizing the role of structural gender inequality (UNSCR 2467). UNSCR 1325 and the Women, Peace and Security framework that emerged from it have transformed international responses to armed conflicts and CRSV.

The UN's attention to CRSV manifests in how it approaches peacekeeping operations. UN peace operations are more likely to have gender mainstreamed mandates in conflicts that are reported to have high levels of sexual violence

(Kreft 2017). Likewise, conflicts in which there are reports of CRSV attract more attention from the Security Council and other international actors (Agerberg and Kreft 2020; Benson and Gizelis 2020) and are more likely to receive peace operations (Hultman and Johansson 2017). The UN's approach reflects governments' adherence to a gendered protection norm rooted in the gendered separation of civilians and combatants (Carpenter 2005), as we discuss in greater detail in the next section.

Research suggests that peace operations can also play a role in reducing CRSV but that they are more effective at stopping lethal violence (Johansson and Hultman 2019; Kirschner and Miller 2019). Multidimensional peace operations with a protection mandate and police units can be effective in curtailing CRSV by rebel forces (Johansson and Hultman 2019). Another study finds that military peacekeepers in African conflicts reduce CRSV by both state and rebel forces (Kirschner and Miller 2019). These findings suggest that the international community nowadays pays attention to CRSV *and* seeks to counter it through peace operations. Yet, more work is necessary to understand how and when exactly peacekeepers might be best equipped to stop and prevent CRSV. For a comprehensive discussion of the potentials and challenges of peacekeeping to prevent CRSV, as well as persisting gaps in our knowledge, see the International Peacekeeping forum (Olsson et al. 2020).

International responses to CRSV also carry a risk. In treating CRSV as exceptional and elevating it above other types of violence, international interveners open themselves up to manipulation by local actors. For example, the UN mission in Mali mismanaged reports and rumors of sexual violence, incentivizing individuals to produce false reports (Sandor 2020, 925). Nonstate actors pay attention to these responses and know how to exploit them for their gains. In 2010, an armed group reportedly committed CRSV with the goal of seeking recognition and access to negotiations with the government of the Democratic Republic of Congo (Autesserre 2012, 217). Although confirmed reports of such an instrumental use of CRSV are rare, it nonetheless presents a stark warning about the dangers of fetishizing CRSV (Meger 2016a). Short-term funding needs can contribute to organizations repeating exaggerated claims and narratives of sexual violence as a weapon of war to solicit donations, knowing that CRSV catches people's attention (Cohen and Hoover Green 2012).

CRSV attracts the most attention, but it is not the only type of gender-based violence in armed conflict (see contributions from Kishi and Eriksson Baaz and Stern in this volume). The gendered responses by governments and intergovernmental organizations to CRSV expose their narrow conceptualization of women's safety and impede effective efforts to address other forms of gender-based violence (Meger 2016b, 32). The fetishization of CRSV reinforces the gendered hierarchy that subordinates women, diminishes their agency, and ignores their potential roles as perpetrators (Cohen 2013; Sjoberg 2016; Loken 2017). These patterns are mirrored by government responses to CRSV perpetrated by rebel groups within their borders, as we outline in the next section.

Governments

Governments' pervasive patriarchal nature means that they frequently co-opt citizens' imaginations and shape their preferences, leading to the entrenchment of patriarchal practices (Nagel 2021b). This means constituents want and expect masculine leaders that project strength and offer protection, and it helps explain why executive branches and defense ministries remain largely male dominated (Barnes and O'Brien 2018). Written and unwritten rules, daily interactions, and gendered language all perpetuate the gendering of these institutions (Cohn 1987). They legitimize and encourage the privileging of masculine conceptualizations of power. This pervasive gendering means its effects are not limited to men; women themselves are often co-opted and contribute to the entrenchment of this gender hierarchy that portrays men as protectors and women in need of protection. This in turn again feeds into governmental strategies.

Within their territorial boundaries, governments view themselves as holding a monopoly of violence. The combination of a government's masculine identity, its monopoly of violence, and the gendered protection racket means that any violence, and particularly sexual violence, by government actors such as police and military units can be seen as an expression of existing structural, social, and political power relations (Meger 2016b). Women's supposed protection by the government is frequently intertwined with government actors feeling entitled to women and their bodies. Governments' self-perception as sole legitimate wielders of violence and their masculine identity rooted in the gendered protection norm, shapes also how they respond to reports of nonstate actors perpetrating CRSV.

CRSV is political and gendered, as the literal and symbolic feminization and subordination of victims and their supposed protectors expresses a gender hierarchy in which violent masculinities sexually dominate subordinated masculinities and femininities (see Eriksson Baaz and Stern in Chapter 4 for a critical discussion of sexual violence as a gendered violence grounded in heteronormative norms). CRSV targets the direct victim *and* the supposed protector by exposing the inability to fulfill this protection role. For example, in Serbia, combatants raped Bosnian women in front of their men to shame and demoralize them by "demonstrating them to be incapable of fulfilling their responsibility to protect" (Benard 1994, 40).[1] Even when CRSV emerges as a group practice rather than a strategy or policy (Wood 2018), public reports of CRSV expose the supposed protector's, that is, the government's, failure. CRSV's gendered nature targeting and feminizing vulnerable groups triggers the gendered protection norm and presents a challenge to the masculinity of a government.

Research has shown that this can influence conflict management in intrastate conflicts (Nagel 2019). Nagel finds that governments are more likely to agree to mediation when rebels are reported to perpetrate CRSV in civil wars. This is notable because governments are usually hesitant to involve a mediator in intrastate conflicts because peace talks present reputational costs (Walter 2006). Opposition groups, domestic constituents, and international allies might perceive talks as a signal that the government has lost control and is unable or unwilling to win the conflict militarily (Melin and Svensson 2009; Kaplow 2016). This disincentivizes governments from negotiating. Involving an intermediary exacerbates the costs because it elevates the nonstate actors. When governments invite opposing nonstate actors to the peace table *and* include an intermediary, they explicitly recognize the opposition group and bestow legitimacy on them (Melin and Svensson 2009). International recognition and legitimacy incentivizes opposition groups to seek out mediation and disincentivizes governments to agree to it.

Governments weigh the costs of continued violence and the benefits of a military victory against the costs and benefits of a mediation process: as conflicts become costlier, the likelihood of mediation increases (Clayton and Gleditsch 2014). Reports of rebel-perpetrated sexual violence undermine a government's supposed role as masculine protector by publicly exposing its inability to protect vulnerable women. This presents a substantial cost to governments because the reports "emasculate" the government, demonstrating its "incapacity to fulfill the fundamental masculine function of protection" (Sjoberg 2013, 239). CRSV is not committed in a vacuum but in the context of a lethal conflict. The public humiliation of being exposed as incapable of providing protection from CRSV contributes to the costs of continuing conflict, outweighing the costs of legitimizing rebels through a mediation process. Hence, when rebels commit CRSV, it increases the likelihood of mediation.

This can have a substantial impact on the chances of mediation onset. An analysis of all intrastate conflict years between 1990 and 2009 reveals a 64 percent increase in the chances of mediation based on reports of rebel-perpetrated CRSV. This indicates that international actors looking to get involved in ending conflicts through mediation ought to pay close attention to whether rebels are reported to commit sexual violence.[2]

Although governments are masculine institutions constructed around gendered attributes, this does not mean that all governments necessarily share a uniform idea of masculinity. Masculinity is fluid—even when it is a government's masculinity, meaning the sociocultural and temporal context influences how a government practices its masculinity. Accountability and societal input from constituents also play a role in this (Nagel 2021b). Accordingly, governments exhibit different masculine traits at different times depending on how inclusive and representative they are. For example, military regimes subscribe to a more militarized notion of a warrior masculinity than democratic governments that represent inclusive societies (Nagel 2019).

Differing and changing gender identities entail the potential for differing responses to CRSV. For example, military regimes that adopt and perform a warrior masculinity rooted in notions of strength are more likely to interpret the gendered protection norm to mean continued fighting to demonstrate their strength. Such a militarized response is associated with a decreased probability of mediation. Other governments that are more accountable to their respective populations might adopt a protector identity that leads them to seek a way out of the conflict, such as mediated talks. For example, in Sierra Leone, it took civil society pressure and a democratic election in 1995 to replace the military-led National Provisional Ruling Council and have the democratic government sign a mediated agreement.

When governments follow a masculinist protection logic in responding to CRSV, they inadvertently put citizens and particular women at further risk. Doubling down on a military strategy means continued violence. Yet, engaging in mediated peace talks in response to CRSV carries risks too. It signals to other armed opposition actors that they can pressure governments into talks by targeting citizens through sexual violence, similar to terrorist acts (Thomas 2014). One way governments could balance the need to engage in talks with preventing future armed challengers from using CRSV to get to the negotiating table is to ensure that resulting peace agreements do not provide amnesty for perpetrators of sexual violence (Muvumba Sellström 2015).

Civil Society

We often observe a political response to CRSV in the form of (primarily) women's resistance and civil society mobilization (Kreft 2019). This may involve different forms of protest or the formation of self-help groups, social movements, or women's organizations, complementing and augmenting mobilization for women's rights and against war (Berry 2018; Tripp 2015; Zulver 2016). While women have mobilized in response to CRSV in contexts such as the Democratic Republic of Congo[3] or Bosnia,[4] Colombia is a particularly illustrative case.

Colombia has been affected by an armed conflict between the government, paramilitary forces, and left-wing rebel groups, primarily the Revolutionary Armed Forces of Colombia (FARC), since the 1960s. The SVAC dataset (Cohen and Nordås 2014) codes sexual violence as "widespread" for several years in the conflict (for a discussion of the dataset, see Chapter 8 on sexual violence in this volume). All armed actors have perpetrated sexual violence against civilians, although the paramilitary groups are particularly notorious. This section is based on author interviews carried out with women activists in Colombia (Kreft 2019, 2020).

Colombia boasts a vibrant civil society sector (Restrepo 2016; Zulver 2017). Women began mobilizing in response to the gendered nature of the armed conflict at least as early as the 1970s, when they came together in the movement Mujeres en la Lucha to challenge the large-scale victimization of women. This civil society mobilization gained momentum in the early 1990s, when conflict violence spiked once more. All major women's organizations and many smaller more locally based organizations now mobilize against CRSV in some form. Victims' associations specifically for CRSV have also formed, such as Red de Mujeres Víctimas y Profesionales, Corporación Mujer Sigue Mis Pasos, or the campaign No es Hora de Callar.

Several of these women's organizations and victims' associations work closely with victims and their families to mitigate the negative social and psychological consequences of CRSV, for example, through workshops or group therapy. They also provide psycho-legal assistance by giving victims a venue to report the crimes committed against them and by accompanying them in the courts. Such psycho-legal assistance is necessary, according to the activists, as the justice system generally lacks gender sensitivity, with victim blaming and dismissal of victim testimony constituting significant problems (see on this also the discussion in Restrepo Sanín's chapter). The result is rampant impunity.

Central to the processes of women's civil society mobilization is the understanding of CRSV as distinctly gendered, as targeting women *as women*, as emanating from and reasserting gender inequalities. As one interviewee reflected:

> Sexual violence is devastating in the lives of women, just as other crimes are devastating, but with one special characteristic and that is that it is a violence that affects directly the identity of women and the existence of women.

As elaborated elsewhere (Kreft 2019), many women in Colombia have mobilized in response to the *collective threat* that CRSV constitutes to their rights, their safety, and their identity as women. Many of the civil society organizations and activists in Colombia seek comprehensive structural transformations toward greater gender equality. Gender is, in other words, as central to civil society mobilization and resistance against CRSV as it is to the violence itself. In fact, gendered mobilization is a *direct response to* the gendered nature and origins of CRSV, but it has to contend also with masculinist state and government institutions, as discussed in the previous section.

Women's civil society mobilization in response to CRSV occurs in all regions of the world (Kreft 2019). And even though backlash against gains in women's rights and agency is a tragic reality in conflict-affected settings (Berry 2018), women's wartime civil society mobilization can effect tangible change. In Colombia, the pressure of women's organizations resulted in CRSV being exempted from amnesty provisions in the peace agreement signed between the government and the FARC in 2016. Sustained civil society pressure also played an important role in pushing the negotiating parties to integrate gender into all dimensions of the peace agreement.

Women's civil society mobilization for peace and structural transformations is particularly likely to be successful when it aligns with international actors' priorities (Tripp 2015). It is also conducive when—as was the case in Colombia—government and nonstate actors during peace negotiations are amenable to gender concerns and when the courts take gender dynamics seriously in their rulings. International actors, state institutions, and political leaders can thus jointly shape an environment conducive for women's civil society mobilization.

Conclusion

CRSV is a highly gendered form of violence in the dominant patterns of perpetration and victimization and also in terms of the gendered power relations and hierarchies that facilitate it (see Eriksson Baaz and Stern and Zetterberg and Bjarnegård in this volume for further discussions). The combination of gendered conflict violence and the inherently gendered nature of formal institutions means that CRSV elicits gendered political responses from actors operating at different levels: international organizations, governments, and civil society.

Although other forms of gender-based violence are more prevalent in conflict (see Kishi in this volume), CRSV plays an important role in activating the gendered protection norm. CRSV prompts international actors to give attention to, and to intervene in, armed conflicts at higher levels than other forms of violence against civilians and to do so with more gender-focused mandates. Other forms of gender-based violence in armed conflict, including against men, tend to fall by the wayside in the process.

Governments, aware of the political nature of CRSV and adhering to a masculinist understanding of their protector role, are likely to respond to rebel-perpetrated sexual violence with distinct policy choices. Depending on the predominant conceptualization of masculinity within the government, this can take diverging paths. Regardless of whether governments choose a violent or nonviolent policy response, the underlying motivation is the same. They do so out of concern that their failure to uphold their masculine protector role undermines their credibility and legitimacy. In contrast, civil society often contests gendered norms and practices, seeks justice and compensation for victims, and strives to change the legal landscape and safeguard women's rights. While the responses to CRSV emanating from the international sphere, from governments and from civil society, are all gendered, they differ in the extent to which they reinforce or challenge existing gender relations and hierarchies.

19

Measures to Address Violence against Women in Politics in Bolivia and Mexico

Juliana Restrepo Sanín

In March 2012, Juana Quispe, a councilwoman from a small town in Bolivia, was found murdered in La Paz. The death of Juana Quispe led to the approval of Law 243 against Political Violence and Harassment against Women, the first law of this type in the world. Before her murder, Mrs. Quispe had reported being the victim of harassment and violence. She was beaten in her town's plaza, her property was destroyed, and she was eventually forced to resign. A court ruled that her resignation was under duress and thus invalid and reinstated her as councillor; however, the harassment continued until she was murdered. The police investigation concluded that it was not related to her political activity despite evidence suggesting otherwise (Cabildeo Digital 2016; Restrepo Sanín 2018).[1]

Violence against women in politics (VAWIP) is a global phenomenon (Krook and Restrepo Sanín 2020). The terms *violence and harassment against women in politics* or *political violence against women* are used in Latin America instead of *gender-based violence against politically active women* or *gendered political violence* (Krook and Restrepo Sanín 2016a). In Latin America, violence and harassment against women politicians have been more evident than other forms of political violence such as violence against voters. Activists throughout the region have raised awareness and have proposed numerous civil society and state-centered solutions. Activists' preferred method for addressing VAWIP has been to promote the criminalization of VAWIP through the adoption of laws or electoral reforms (Albaine 2021; Restrepo Sanín 2022).

Mexico and Bolivia are at the vanguard in the advancement of state measures to address VAWIP and have set the example for other countries in the region. Although research on VAWIP is scarce, studies show that between 30 percent and 70 percent of elected women have faced some form of violence (JNE 2015; NIMD 2016).[2] The case of Juana Quispe represents the most extreme manifestation of VAWIP, but women in politics report physical and sexual violence, psychological abuse, harassment, economic, and semiotic violence (Krook and Restrepo Sanín 2020). Many of these behaviors are normalized as part of women's lives or "the cost of doing politics" and occur simultaneously, undermining women's performance and affecting their political and human rights (Restrepo Sanín 2018).

Law 243, approved in Bolivia in 2012, was the result of more than ten years of activism by the Association of Women Councilors and Mayors of Bolivia (ACOBOL). The discussion in Bolivia has influenced the debate in other parts of Latin America. Mexico, Costa Rica, and Peru have stand-alone laws criminalizing violence or harassment against women political actors, while eight other countries have included VAWIP in either their electoral or VAW laws (Albaine 2021; Restrepo Sanín 2021).[3] Besides laws criminalizing VAWIP, the Mexican "Protocol to Address Gender-Based Political Violence against Women,"[4] published in 2016 and updated in 2017, provides detailed guidelines to electoral authorities and other institutions to address VAWIP. This protocol was used as a reference for the 2020 law, and electoral authorities still use it. What can we learn from these policy responses? How can these strategies inform the global discussion to end violence against women politicians?

This chapter compares the Bolivian law and the Mexican electoral protocol to understand how these two different state responses can inform and complement other strategies used worldwide to address and end VAWIP (Krook and Restrepo Sanín 2016a). I argue that although state responses to address VAWIP are an important step in ending this problem, they are not enough, as they depend on the effectiveness of other state institutions and state actors that still hold patriarchal attitudes, complicating implementation. In making this argument, this chapter centers on women's experiences as political actors, recognizing that many manifestations of violence emanate from ideas about politics that exclude women in all their diversity. Additionally, this chapter focuses on violence against women in politics in democratic—if imperfect—contexts, adopting a comparative lens to analyze limitations and opportunities of state measures to address violence against women in politics.

Women and Politics in Bolivia and Mexico

Bolivia and Mexico currently have among the highest percentage of women in national legislatures. It is thus not surprising that they are leading the discussion of VAWIP in Latin America. Bolivia adopted its first quota law in 1997 and has since strengthened its electoral procedures to guarantee parity. Women are 46.2 percent[5] of the members of the Chamber of Deputies, 55.6 percent of senators, 51 percent of local councillors, and 51 percent of state-level deputies. Despite these impressive gains, the road to equality in decision-making is still long. A woman has never been elected as president,[6] and only 18 of 339 municipalities had a woman mayor in 2015. Around 30 percent of women in local and state politics have reported being victims of VAWIP.[7]

Similar to Bolivia, Mexico passed a quota law in 1996 and has since adopted a gender parity law. Women are 50 percent of the Chamber of Deputies and 49.2 percent of the senators. Since around 2015, all the Mexican states have had over 40 percent of women in their assemblies. However, at the local level, only 25 percent of councillors and 13 percent of mayors are women (Freidenberg 2017). The country has never had a woman president, and there is still resistance to women's inclusion (Schwindt-Bayer 2018). Electoral authorities have recognized VAWIP as an obstacle to women's full political participation.[8]

Different Responses: The Bolivian Law and the Mexican Protocol

Bolivia and Mexico offer important insights about the effectiveness and limitations of state policies to address VAWIP. As Ballington and Borovsky (this volume) explain, state responses to VAWIP vary in their type: they can be stand-alone laws, reforms to existing laws on gender-based violence, or reforms to electoral codes. The Bolivian law is a stand-alone law, while the Mexican protocol is an electoral approach.

The Bolivian law was proposed in the Chamber of Deputies in 2006, but it was never approved by the Senate (Salguero 2008). After a constitutional process and significant political changes, a similar bill was approved as Law 243 in 2012 (Restrepo Sanín 2022). Law 243 is grounded on the Convention of the Belém do Pará and the Convention for the Elimination of all Forms of Discrimination against Women (CEDAW). Law 243 emphasizes that violence and harassment are a violation of women's human rights. The law lists some of the actions that undermine women's presence in politics, including stereotyping, denial of resources, and giving false information. The formal recognition of the harm of these actions on women's political participation is necessary to demand that these behaviors stop. The law aims to protect women candidates and elected or appointed officials, along with women in social and political organizations. Women voters are not mentioned, but there is no evidence of widespread violence against them in Latin America.

Law 243 protects women from "acts of violence, persecution, or harassment" that have the purpose of "shortening, suspending, impeding, or hindering" their work or "force [them] to act against their will." A regulatory framework approved in 2016 clarifies the differences between harassment and violence, details the responsibilities of different actors, and expands the definition of *women in politics* by including women in social organizations.

The distinction between *violence* and *harassment* in the Bolivian law has influenced other proposals in Latin America. Rather than recognizing a continuum of violent acts from psychological to physical aggression, Law 243 separates different manifestations. Harassment against women in politics refers to "acts of pressure, persecution, harassment, or threats," and violence refers to "physical, sexual, or psychological aggression."[9] This separation means that there is no legal recognition of the continuum of violence because the law ignores how psychological violations of personal integrity are connected to physical violations (see Introduction). Instead, violence and harassment are sanctioned differently with real consequences as explained below.

The electoral protocol in Mexico was a response to VAWIP prior to the approval of the law in 2020. The protocol uses the Convention of Belém do Pará and CEDAW to justify the inclusion of VAWIP in domestic normative frameworks. This measure uses a gender perspective with existing electoral laws to address VAWIP. The electoral protocol defines VAWIP as the following: "Any action . . . that targets women *as women* (gender-based), has a differential impact or affects women disproportionately, [and] has the goal or outcome of undermining or nullifying women's politico-electoral rights, including in their [political or elected] positions" (TEPJF 2017, 41).

In addition to state-centered responses, civil society actors have created other initiatives to address VAWIP throughout Latin America. Bolivian activists created gender observatories to track cases of VAWIP and routinely denounce cases and demand action. In Ecuador, the Association of Women at the Municipal Level created a hotline to report cases and receive advice. In Colombia, the National Women's Network created a smartphone application that provides information about gender-based violence, including political violence. Associations of women at the local level provide training for women in local politics to recognize violence, while INGOs have designed campaigns and toolkits to collect data, raise awareness, and support victims (Krook 2019; Krook and Restrepo Sanín 2016a; Restrepo Sanín 2022).

Effects of State Responses

The measures created in Latin America make visible a problem that women politicians have faced for a long time and highlight how violence undermines women's rights to equality, political participation, and to live free from violence. They create sanctions for perpetrators of violence and mandate the creation of party rules to prevent VAWIP. The law and the protocol are a result of women's activism in civil society and the state.

The Bolivian law has criminalized VAWIP, giving victims a clear path to finding resolution and justice. Indeed, the law has been used to restitute the political rights of at least one councilwoman who was kidnapped and forced to resign (Bustillos 2014). In Mexico, the Specialized Attorney for Electoral Crimes (FEPADE) has received more than two hundred cases of VAWIP, formally opened 111, and is currently investigating around 11 percent of those (Martinez 2018; Miranda 2019). These examples show that state measures to address VAWIP can be used to protect women's political rights.

Limitations of State Responses

Although Law 243 and the protocol represent an advancement in the fight against VAWIP, they have limitations that are the result of their design and their interaction with other laws and state institutions. Law 243 has been insufficient as a mechanism for protecting women's political rights. The Bolivian criminal justice system in which Law 243 relies is crowded and inefficient,[10] making it hard for elected women to find justice in a reasonable timeframe. Judges, police officers, and party leaders still fail to recognize VAWIP and to decisively act when a woman is attacked.[11]

Although electoral authorities received 124 reports of VAWIP between 2016 and 2019, 28 percent resulted in the resignation of the woman. This shows that electoral authorities are not effective at preventing attacks. Moreover, the law has successfully recognized the use of harassment and violence to undermine women's political rights in one case. The mayor and members of the town council (all men) kidnapped and beat councillor Mrs. Magda Hasse until she resigned. These types of attacks target women but not men, and electoral authorities recognize them as a specific form of gender-based violence used to undermine women's rights to be elected and participate in equal conditions as men. This makes Mrs. Hasse's a case of VAWIP and not one of violence in politics.[12] A court ruled that her resignation was invalid and restituted her seat. However, this happened three years after the attacks. In a separate procedure, a court dismissed the case against the mayor and the councillors, who were never held accountable (ACOBOL 2020).

In addition, VAWIP is underreported. In 2018, electoral authorities received 87 reports, while ACOBOL received 117 cases. Between 2012 and 2018, ACOBOL received over five hundred complaints, but only Mrs. Hasse's case has been resolved using the criminal justice system. Based on the data collected by ACOBOL, electoral authorities only receive around 6 percent of the cases. Most victims attempt to use administrative means (85.8 percent), but it is unclear how many of these cases are resolved.[13]

Moreover, there are no independent oversight institutions, and victims have to report to party leaders or people in leadership positions who may be behind the attacks. In the case of Mrs. Hasse, the mayor and other councillors perpetrated the violence. In many cases, reporting a case of VAWIP results in political ostracism.[14]

The use of a gender lens for interpreting existing electoral procedures has facilitated the investigation of more cases of VAWIP in Mexico in comparison to Bolivia. Prior to the approval of the legal reform that criminalized VAWIP, the absence of such a law limited the ability of authorities to protect those rights. However, despite the approval of the law, some of these limitations remain.

First, the application of the protocol relied on the goodwill of electoral authorities. Silvia Alonso Felix from the FEPADE has expressed that electoral authorities "cannot act decisively [in cases of VAWIP] because there is no penal type establishing gender-based political violence as an electoral crime" (Miranda 2019). Although this is no longer the case, given the recent law, electoral tribunals have found that it is hard for victims to comply with the evidentiary standards required by courts.[15]

Second, electoral institutions have limited authority when cases of VAWIP involve criminal actions, such as with assassination or kidnapping. While electoral authorities can call attention to these incidents, and the Mexican protocol includes guidelines for the attorney general's office, they cannot initiate legal procedures, as these cases are handled by criminal courts that are inefficient. Third, even in favorable rulings, electoral courts do not have the capacity or authority to guarantee that further attacks will not occur (Hernández Estrada 2017). In a widely known case, the mayor of the town of San Pedro Chenalhó, Mrs. Rosa Pérez, resigned under pressure. Although electoral authorities restituted Mrs. Pérez as mayor, violence continued to be an obstacle to her administration.

Besides the issues with the Bolivian law and the Mexican protocol, there are other limitations to state responses. First, even in countries where the justice system is effective, cases take too long to be resolved.[16] This is especially problematic during elections. Electoral cycles last just a few months, which is not enough time for courts to resolve a case. The Mexican protocol relies on a specialized attorney, which is designed to address cases quickly. However, given the increase in electoral violence in recent years in Mexico, the FEPADE received in 2018 more cases than it could process.[17] Moreover, neither the law nor the protocol have the tools to assess the effects of VAWIP on electoral results and rule accordingly. Further, although electoral authorities can nullify elections, they cannot restitute the economic and human resources invested in the campaign, and even when new elections are convened, the perpetrators of violence are not always sanctioned (Miranda 2019).

Second, the law and the protocol are limited in how they define *women in politics*. The Bolivian law protects women candidates, elected or appointed officials, and any women in social and political organizations. Law 243 does not explicitly mention women voters, while the Mexican protocol leaves room for interpretation because its basis is the violation of women's politico-electoral rights. None of them explicitly protects women activists or human rights defenders.

Third, both strategies have very limited understandings of *gender* (as a synonym of *women*) and are inadequate in the protection they provide to people from marginalized groups. Indigenous women are not only attacked as women, but also suffer from racism. This is frequently compounded by attacks based on class and level of education (see Kuperberg in this volume). The Bolivian law includes aggravating factors that increase the penalties. However, as black feminists have noted, identities are not additive but interact with each other in complex ways, such that without explicit recognition of how power operates to exclude people at the intersections of multiple axes of marginalization, the addition of these aggravating factors is insufficient to address intersectional violence and its effects on different groups of women (Crenshaw 1991). Further, although the law includes sexual orientation, it does not mention gender identity, which leaves transgender people unprotected. Similarly, neither the protocol nor the law in Mexico mentions sexual orientation or gender identity. Although electoral authorities have recognized the rights of trans and nonbinary people, only transwomen are protected by the protocol. This omission is especially harmful, as LGBTQ groups are underrepresented in politics and are at higher risk of violence. Latin American countries do not have comprehensive hate crime laws that could protect LGBTQ communities, and many of the manifestations of violence against LGBTQ peoples and communities are normalized, justified, or accepted (Corrales 2012). In Mexico, for example, political parties unlawfully changed the sex of male candidates to appear to comply with the quota law (Animal Político 2018). This undermines the quota law and the rights and dignity of LGBTQ communities in Mexico.

Fourth, although electoral authorities, as well as the follow-up mechanism to the Belém do Pará Convention, have recognized the role of political parties in perpetrating or condoning VAWIP, neither the law nor the protocol sanction parties. In Bolivia, the law requires parties to update their rules to address VAWIP, but over eight years after the law was passed none of the major parties has recognized VAWIP (Restrepo Sanín 2018).

Finally, the law and the protocol list discrete actions as examples of VAWIP. This ignores the connection between seemingly "harmless" but systematic actions and much more pervasive and extreme forms of violence (Pain 2014). In other words, state mechanisms have failed to recognize the continuum of violence. This means that protection mechanisms are activated not when harassment occurs but once violence happens and it is too late to protect women.

Conclusions

The recognition of VAWIP as a crime is an important step in ending this problem, as it provides women with a tool to protect their rights. The Bolivian Law 243 and the Mexican electoral protocol focus their efforts on sanctioning the most visible manifestations of VAWIP. Although murder, rape, and other extreme forms of violence are of course unacceptable, they are the rarest. Research has found that most women in politics are victims of other forms of violence, including (sexual) harassment, psychological abuse, and online violence (Bardall 2013; IPU 2016; Kuperberg 2018). This chapter has shown that laws and electoral protocols are, by themselves, insufficient at stopping perpetrators.

State measures to address VAWIP require that criminal and electoral authorities take gender seriously when investigating cases. In Bolivia and Mexico, the reporting and prosecution of VAWIP is complicated by the pervasiveness of patriarchal attitudes among state authorities as well as overcrowded criminal justice systems. Although these reforms are an important advancement to end VAWIP, there is little we know about which measures are most effective, under what conditions legal or electoral measures work best, and how these measures impact women's political participation and electoral processes.

This chapter has shown that laws and protocols by themselves are not enough. Ending VAWIP requires strong state institutions that can effectively guarantee women's rights; it also requires a strong party system in which political parties are held accountable for using violence to avoid complying with electoral laws; it also requires robust judicial institutions that can sanction perpetrators in a reasonable timeframe. Finally, because VAWIP is an expression of gender hierarchies, ending VAWIP requires transforming social norms so that an inclusive political sphere is understood as a social good and not just as a bureaucratic requirement of gender quotas and parity laws.

20

Evaluating Violence and Sexual Harassment Rules in Canada's House of Commons

TRACEY RANEY AND
CHERYL N. COLLIER

This chapter considers how political leaders have addressed the problem of violence against women in politics (VAWIP) in the Canadian House of Commons (see Krook 2017, 2018; Krook and Restrepo Sanín 2020; Collier and Raney 2018). In 2014, Canada became one of the first countries in the world to tackle VAWIP by enacting a protection policy for political staffers. The next year, it adopted an MP-to-MP Code of Conduct on Sexual Harassment for elected members of Parliament, and in 2018, the legislature extended sexual harassment protections to all federal employees via Bill C-65. In early 2021, the House updated its staffing policy to align with the bill's provisions.[1]

As the Introduction to this volume lays out, this chapter uses gender, rather than women, as its primary lens to analyze Canada's staff policy and MP Code of Conduct. For Bacchi (1999), how policy problems are defined is an inherently gendered process and likely to produce particular gendered outcomes. Rather than tie in to the emerging international normative framework on VAWIP (identified by Ballington and Borovsky in this volume), Canada's Parliament has opted for a varied definition of violence. The 2021 staff policy covers harassment and violence, defining them as follows: "Any action, conduct or comment, including of a sexual nature, that can reasonably be expected to cause offence, humiliation or other physical or psychological injury or illness to an employee" (House of Commons 2021, 5). This definition captures the broader physical-psychological violence continuum that could in-

clude homophobic, transphobic, or racist remarks in addition to sexual in-
nuendos, sexist remarks, or aggressive, threatening, and rude gestures. The
MP Code of Conduct, however, is narrower in scope and only applies to instances of sexual harassment, including "unwelcome sexual comments or advances" (Krook and Restrepo Sanín 2020, 5). This is despite the fact that Canadian politicians experience violence in many forms. When Environment
Minister Catherine McKenna was referred to as "Climate Barbie" by fellow
MP Gerry Ritz in 2017, it was meant to demean and discredit her work. When
a vulgar, misogynistic term was spray-painted across her image on her constituency office window shortly after the 2019 federal election, McKenna said,
"I don't even have the words to describe what kind of person would do this.
It's the same as the trolls on Twitter. It needs to stop" (Glowacki and Foote
2019). This incident constitutes a gender bias event, which includes misogynistic language graffitied in a public place directed at a woman leader who
publicly identifies as a feminist (see Krook in this volume; Krook 2020). During the 2021 federal election, a variety of hate-based threats and attacks against
politicians were reported, ranging from racist graffiti and vandalism on lawn
signs to assault (Tunney 2021). Despite these and other ongoing incidents,
Canada's response to VAWIP does not address the full range of violence experienced by political actors in the country and that seems to be increasing
over time.[2]

In this chapter, we assess how the written rules—the staffing policy and
the MP Code of Conduct—are limited not only in scope but also in content.
To highlight some of these limitations, we consider how these rules are likely
to interact with the broader institutional context of Canada's Parliament, focusing in particular on *partisan patronage*. Patronage traditionally refers to
the ways in which "party politicians distribute jobs or special favors in exchange for electoral support" (Weingrod 1968, 379). Within legislatures, patronage norms work on an intraparty basis, with party elites able to leverage
institutional resources over their members in exchange for party loyalty. We
argue that partisan patronage has been embedded within Canada's VAWIP
rules, especially in the MP code, and is likely to reinforce masculine behavior
within Canada's Parliament, with (mostly male) party elites able to dilute or
override the new harassment and violence rules. Canada's approach to VAWIP
thus demonstrates how solutions to this problem must attend to the specific
institutional contexts within which they will be situated, including masculinized norms that may undermine their effectiveness.

The chapter begins with a brief review of feminist institutionalism (FI)
literature as it applies to different rule/norm types (formal/informal, non-
gendered/gendered). Our analysis is then presented in two parts. First, we
demonstrate how the informal norms and practices associated with partisan

patronage have been used historically in ways that have disadvantaged women. Second, we show how partisan patronage has been left intact in Canada's recent VAWIP rules, with anticipated negative gendered outcomes. The chapter concludes by suggesting that Canada's response to this problem is insufficient and unlikely to disrupt the dominant masculine norms within its Parliament.

Partisan (Male) Patronage in Canada's Parliament

FI research reveals the gendered nature and effects of rules, norms, and practices and the ways in which they reproduce or undermine patterns of status and domination (Chappell and Mackay 2017, 28). FI scholars have further examined the interplay between formal and informal institutional rules from a gendered perspective (Bjarnegård 2013; Freidenvall and Krook 2010). Formal institutions/rules are "official, visible and codified" and can be identified using state power or other official sources that enforce their provisions through various observable sanctioning mechanisms (Chappell and Mackay 2017, 26). In contrast, informal norms are generally not codified or enforced in observable ways; sanctions often include punishments like exclusion or shunning (Chappell and Galea 2017) or acts of violence.

The "hidden" dimensions of informal, seemingly nongendered norms are often key determinants of whether newly adopted gendered rules will "stick" and, thus, need to be "called out" in feminist research (Waylen 2014; Chappell and Mackay 2017). In this chapter, we seek to "call out" the hidden, gendered dimensions of partisan patronage in Canada's harassment/violence rules. We build on work by Verge and Claveria (2017), who argue that party patronage is underpinned by informal norms and practices that reinforce gendered power hierarchies. In Canada's parliamentary system of strong political parties and party discipline, party elites have control over how various institutional perks will be distributed within their parties (Kam 2009; Marland 2019). Gendered power imbalances may occur when parliamentary resources are leveraged through a system of "hidden" regulations and norms, with (mostly male) party elites able to act as the gatekeepers of what behavior best exemplifies loyalty and sufficient duty to their party.

We consider partisan patronage within Canada's House of Commons to be an informal—albeit important—norm, with no written guidelines, enforced through largely hidden channels. The chief stewards of partisan patronage within the House of Commons are party whips, who are appointed by their respective party leaders and are themselves (often senior) members of Parliament (MPs). The main responsibilities of whips are to ensure that their members show up to caucus meetings and vote in formal divisions along partisan lines; in other words, that they "toe the party line."[3] In addition to *whipping* votes, whips are further responsible for maintaining an array of informal dos and don'ts within their respective caucuses, operationalized through a range of sanctions that can be imposed on an errant MP. These might include the removal of speaking rights during debates, research fund clawbacks, denials of paid trips abroad, restricting access to the party leader, and even expulsion from cabinet/caucus or the withdrawal of the party's nomination in the next election. Members can be induced to abide by party wishes with promises of better committee assignments or, best of all, a coveted position in the cabinet within a governing party. Political staffers who behave in ways that bring the party's reputation into ill repute can be denied similar opportunities within the party or can be terminated. Informal norms can also be enforced with "positive" rewards (Chappell and Galea 2017, 69). Together, these informal aspects of partisan patronage give parties significant influence and leverage over their members, where whips in particular can use their powers of persuasion or dissuasion to enforce partisan loyalty.

We suggest that in Canada's Parliament, partisan patronage has its own "gendered logic of appropriateness" (Chappell 2014). One of the most observable displays of the gendered underpinnings of patronage is during the formal parliamentary debates. Officially, formal debates like Question Period are opportunities for the opposition to hold the government accountable. Unofficially, these debates serve as opportunities for members to demonstrate their party loyalty while under the close watch of their whip and the media. In this highly adversarial environment, hypermasculine performances are often equated with the fiercest displays of partisan loyalty. Combative, take-no-prisoners debates in Canada's Parliament often include shouting, jabs, and heckling. Women MPs have reported that these debates take on gendered overtones, with demeaning comments on their physical appearance, weight, intelligence, gender, and age (Samara Centre for Democracy 2016, 2). Partisan differences additionally heighten intersectional discrimination and sexism (Kuperberg in this volume). The gendered effect of these loyalty tests is that the actions of women and men are evaluated against a hypermasculine standard of behavior from which various rewards or punishments follow. During these formal debates, patronage norms thus work to reinforce the legitimacy of hegemonic male actors within the institution.

Control over party resources is also male dominated in Canada's Parliament. As the chief "enforcers" of patronage, the whips work alongside other party elites, including party leaders and the House leaders for each party. As Table 20.1 shows, these patronage enforcers are usually men, at an average rate of 92 percent since Confederation in 1867. Although supposedly gender neutral, Canada's informal patronage norms allow (mostly) white, cisgender men the ability to enforce partisan (male) norms within Parliament.

TABLE 20.1 PERCENTAGE OF MALE PARTY LEADERS (SINCE 1867)					
	Party Leaders*	Chief Government Whips	Chief Opposition Whips	House Leaders	Average
Historical % Men:	90% (55/61)	96% (46/48)	93% (37/40)	92% (69/75)	92% (207/224)
Current:	100% (5/5)	Man	Man	100% (4/4)	

* With seats in House only; as of September 2020. Data compiled by authors: https://lop.parl.ca/sites/Public Website/default/en_CA.

Entrenching Partisan (Male) Patronage in Canada's New Anti-Sexual Harassment Rules

Canada's 2014 staffing policy and the 2015 MP Code of Conduct emerged in response to public allegations that two women MPs had been sexually harassed/assaulted by two men MPs from an opposing party. In response, parliamentarians realized that they had no institutional rules to address noncriminal sexual harassment in the legislature. The 2021 staff policy was updated in response to Bill C-65, which in turn was introduced in response to the fall 2017 wave of the #MeToo movement. This legislation updates harassment provisions that apply to all federally regulated workplaces in Canada.

Both provide for informal processes to resolve cases, with the option of formal independent investigations (should mediation be unsuccessful). Despite their global novelty, however, our research suggests that Canada's harassment and violence rules are unlikely to fully curb abuse in Parliament and, in some cases, might help keep this problem hidden through the usage of partisan patronage, which is embedded within these rules. We see this phenomenon most directly with the involvement of whips in both the staff policy and the MP code. Below, we highlight three ways in which these rules empower institutional party elites to use patronage during a harassment claim against complainants or respondents. These include the powers of political parties to dissuade, persuade, and formally sanction members/staffers.

Power to Dissuade

Both the staff-based policy and the MP code allow for political parties (through the MPs or whips) to be involved at the earliest stages of a complaint of sexual harassment or violence. The staff-based policy requires an employee who has experienced violence first to report the behavior to their employing MP or to a "designated recipient."[4] Party whips are to be informed of any complaint concerning their caucus members or employees. While the identity of reporting employees is supposed to remain confidential from the whip, the policy permits their identities to be known if/when the whip is required to take any "appropriate measures" (House of Commons 2021, 10).[5] The MP-to-MP Code of Conduct similarly references the party whips (and/or the chief human resources officer—CHRO), both before and after a formal complaint is filed.

Our concern is that these processes afford party elites—using extensive patronage powers—opportunities to potentially "dissuade" complainants (either an employee or a member) from filing a formal claim or to encourage their MPs who receive complaints to handle issues quietly. As political actors operating in a highly partisan workplace, the primary job of a party whip is to ensure a strong and united party front. Whips are also not experts on sexual violence. These institutional dynamics are also potentially highly gendered, with junior employees or MPs (most of whom are women) having "informal" discussions behind closed doors with a senior, male member of their party leadership—someone who has considerable control over their career advancement.

Although it is impossible to know the contents of informal conversations between party elites and complainants, annual reports from the 2014 staffing policy are revealing. Table 20.2 shows the general statistics related to the policy over four years since being implemented (2015–2020). Since 2015, eighty cases have been filed with the CHRO; of those, fifty-eight, or close to three-quarters, were "enquiries" only.[6] In total, only 8 percent (six of eighty) of cases have led to formal investigations.[7] These statistics indicate that some element of "party protectionism" is occurring, with the overwhelming majority of enquiries not resulting in formal complaints moving forward. As women are disproportionately more likely to be targets of violence compared with men,

TABLE 20.2 ANNUAL REPORT STATISTICS ON STAFFING POLICY (2015–2020)

Year	Cases Resolved	Enquiries	Informal Resolutions	Formal Investigations
2015–16	10	7	2	0
2016–17	19	13	1	2
2017–18	35	28	0	3
2018–19	16	10	0	1
2019–20	0	5	unclear	1
Totals	80*	63	3	7

Sources: House of Commons (CHRO) Annual Report on the House of Commons Policy on Preventing and Addressing Harassment 2015–2020 inclusive.
* Excludes 13 cases deemed to have fallen outside the scope of the policy or were active and 36 enquiries handled through the *Respectful Workplace Program* in 2018/19. The 2019–2020 formal investigation had yet to be resolved at time of the report's publication.

any efforts to protect parties from time-consuming and potentially divisive formal claims may serve to preserve male privilege within the institution.

Power to Persuade

Canada's harassment and violence rules also provide opportunities for parties to have influence over rule interpreters. In the 2021 staffing policy, MPs are considered employers and therefore have substantial decision-making authority. The policy specifies that an employee may file a complaint with either their employing MP or with the designated recipient. In theory, this allows for an employee to report to someone outside their party. However, given that many employees hired by MPs often share political beliefs with their MP's party and may wish to move up the ladder within the party, a real question exists about whether such an employee would utilize channels outside of their party, which could be perceived as a sign of party disloyalty.

Party members are also decision makers in cases that move to formal investigations. In such instances, if the respondent is an employee, the MP is given the full report. If the respondent is an MP, the full report is provided to the CHRO, who is to provide the (redacted) report to the House's Board of Internal Economy, which is comprised entirely of MPs and often meets in secret, hidden from public view. The MP Code of Conduct also allows whips considerable leeway. Complainants may report directly to their whip in cases where the respondent is from the same party.[8] The MP code additionally permits whips to manage and facilitate discussions between a complainant and respondent. Should an independent investigation occur, the whip is to receive a copy of the final report.

Allowing MPs, a panel of politicians, or party whips to be involved in claims of harassment or violence is problematic, as it affords party leaders opportunities to persuade (or, informally, "whip") their members/employees to act in ways that protect the party rather than the targets of violence. In Canada, parties determine who serves on various legislative committees (proportionate to their share of House seats); whips and House leaders are also able to remove and replace their committee members at any time. Legislative behavior on committees is also whipped in Canada, meaning that members are expected to comply with their leaders' instructions.

Power to Sanction

Canada's VAWIP rules also give partisan actors power to decide on disciplinary actions. The 2021 staffing policy allows for MPs to decide upon any disciplinary actions to be taken against employees who have been found to have violated the policy. When a respondent is an MP, it is up to the Board of Internal Economy to determine whether "further action" may be required, and if it is, the board may "refer the matter to the appropriate parliamentary body for the consideration and imposition of remedial or disciplinary measures" (House of Commons 2021, 15). The MP-to-MP code similarly grants wide authority to party whips to propose and impose disciplinary actions, and it provides no guidelines, thus allowing whips to mete out sanctions—or decide against doing so at all—according to whatever criteria they choose. Allowing disciplinary decisions to remain in the hands of (mostly male) actors allows for the protection of "male insiders" across the institution irrespective of partisan stripes (Bjarnegård 2013). As harassment and violence are problems in every political party, (mostly male) party elites may have a shared interest in ensuring that these cases are handled quickly and quietly away from public view, thus reinforcing interparty male privilege across the institution.[9]

Further problematic is that both the staffing policy and MP code allow for a finding that a *complainant* has filed a claim in "bad faith" or that is "vexatious," which could be subject to potential disciplinary action. False-claims provisions are inherently problematic, as they rely upon a victim-stereotype myth that women are prone to falsely report violence and rape; they further reduce women's willingness to come forward and report a claim for fear of not being believed or of reprisals (Suarez and Gadalla 2010; Lonsway, Cortina, and Magley 2008). This provision may serve to further silence mainly women victims while protecting those in positions of power within the institution—party elites—in the process.

Policy Recommendations

In this chapter, we briefly evaluate Canada's policy response to addressing violence and harassment in politics. Although on paper these new rules appear as positive gendered change, their outcomes are likely to be quite different.[10] That Canada's new anti-harassment/violence rules allow for political parties, MPs, and/or whips to be involved in any way allows for political masculinity to remain embedded within its parliamentary system. Rather than consider the broader male-dominated institution as part of the problem that contributes to VAWIP, these informal gendered norms have not been acknowledged or addressed.

Foremost among our concerns is that in Canada, political parties (via whips and MPs) continue to play a role in harassment/violence claims to the disadvantage of mostly women complainants. To address this shortcoming, we suggest an independent Parliamentary Office of Workplace Rights be created to remove all partisan influence over the handling of violence and harassment claims. This office would ideally work with global actors (i.e., the UN) to develop and promote best practices on VAWIP prevention consistent with the international VAWIP normative framework and assist with data collection and an appropriate balance between privacy, confidentiality, and transparency. This office would improve the response to violence against political actors and open the door for a more fulsome approach to other areas of VAWIP in the Canadian context.

Political parties are key "critical actors" and also play a role in eliminating VAWIP alongside parliaments. As Ballington and Borovsky suggest in this volume, parties must adopt robust codes of conduct establishing zero-tolerance policies for this behavior within their own organizations. Party codes could help cement a broader norm that violence of any form will not be tolerated outside of, or within, Parliament. Elections Canada, which oversees Canada's election laws, could also monitor and track violence perpetrated against political candidates. Such observatories can help collect reliable data on VAWIP to raise public awareness about the scope of the problem (Ballington and Borovsky in this volume). To date, Canadian parties have not consistently adopted such codes, and Elections Canada does not collect data on violence in politics.

As mentioned, Canada's VAWIP strategy only partially addresses the physical-psychological violence continuum (i.e., the 2021 staffing policy); yet sexual harassment remains the only form of violence addressed in the MP Code of Conduct. Other forms of violence—including those motivated by racism, homophobia, or transphobia—are not addressed by the MP code. Given these and other limitations, we argue that global leaders and activists should be cautious in drawing upon Canada's policy responses as best practices, as they give political parties too much influence and oversight in addressing this problem in Parliament and are too narrow in scope. Rather than emulate the Canadian approach, successful solutions to VAWIP must be understood within specific local, institutional contexts and rules, which might appear on the surface to be gender neutral and positive for women, yet ultimately thwart or undermine positive gendered change. In Canada's highly partisan Parliament, foremost among our concerns is the power political parties continue to wield in its formal VAWIP rules.

21

Conclusion and Ways Forward

ELIN BJARNEGÅRD AND
PÄR ZETTERBERG

During the past few decades, various international agendas have highlighted the gendered dynamics of violence and politics. For instance, the UN Security Council Resolution 1325 on women, peace, and security, adopted in 2000, introduced the norm of including women and mainstreaming gender perspectives into the realm of conflict resolution and peace building. In addition, the United Nations General Assembly in 2011 called for zero tolerance of violence against female candidates and election officials (Resolution 66/130). These agendas have spurred significant scholarly activity, and various fields of research are now investigating the ways in which violence in politics is gendered.

Nonetheless, these research fields, although they all engage with gendered political violence, have rarely interacted with each other. There are clear disciplinary boundaries separating research fields. While they have all analyzed the three key concepts dealt with in this volume—politics, violence, and gender—they have had different definitions and foci, leading to different interpretations and analyses. Furthermore, and importantly, the gendered dynamics of violence in politics are significantly more diverse than what these international agendas would suggest. Therefore, this book has sought to acknowledge—and bring to light—this diversity by more broadly exploring how gender dynamics are manifested in violent acts against political actors. The book has aimed to build bridges across disciplines by initiating a discussion on gender and violence against political actors that builds on the insights of various research fields. By having a broad perspective on gender and violence in politics, and by engaging in interdisciplinary dialogue, the overall goal of the book has been to help create an agenda for studying gender, politics, and violence in a more holistic manner.

This concluding chapter has two ambitions. First, in an attempt to build bridges and create interdisciplinary intelligibility, the theoretical ambition of the chapter is to highlight and discuss points of agreement and ongoing discussions that will be important to keep in mind moving forward. Second, at a more empirical level, the chapter summarizes important insights from various research fields and highlights areas in which future research is needed.

Agreements and Controversies

One important goal of this book has been to try to initiate a process of overcoming the fragmentation of gendered research on political violence. By engaging scholars from various research fields, the volume has broadened the horizon and made it clear that concepts and phenomena that are taken for granted in one sphere may be seen very differently by someone working in another, neighboring field. By venturing out of our own silos of jargon, theories, and definitions, we can try to listen to other perspectives in an open way. This is an intellectual challenge and one in which scholars should lead the way. Unfortunately, academic silos encourage scholars to make narrow contributions to existing research fields, effectively limiting our openness to other perspectives. We hope this book can help to broaden perspectives and increase our opportunities to explain the issues we work with in relation to similar approaches. The workshops leading up to this book have taught us that trying to accomplish this is not easy. To adequately explain how and why your perspectives matter, you need to properly grasp other perspectives and the insights they offer. Because each of us situates our own perspective in relation to others,' we need to point out not only what our perspective entails, but also what its limitations are. This is not easy, but aiming for this kind of precision is a good thing.

Before delving into the empirical work, increased conceptual clarity is needed. Conceptual discussions have been at the core of the work with this book. In particular, we have discussed the distinction between the type of violence women encounter because they are politicians in contentious political settings and gender-based violence, that is, violence that women encounter because they are women. This is a question in relation to which different fields have chosen different starting points. The research on conflict-related violence has tended to start with the conflict lines, organized violence, and how it affects women and men differently. The research on violence against women in politics has used studies on misogyny and barriers to women's political influence as a starting point, emphasizing how and when such attitudes and behavior cross the line to become violence.

The book has shown us that gendered analyses of political violence can—and should—look different because they are applied for different reasons. A gender perspective can imply a long-neglected focus on women in political roles (see, e.g., the chapters by Olsson, Krook, Kishi, and Esposito), but it can also help us illuminate differences between women who have different political positions (Håkansson), have different ethnicity (Kuperberg), or simply operate in different political contexts (Zetterberg and Bjarnegård). Gender can also be used to illustrate the differences between women's and men's experiences of violence during peacetime (Thomas and Herrick), contentious elections (Schneider, and Haley and Baker) and wartime (Kreft and Nagel). Importantly, a focus on men as men is also a gendered focus, something that is sorely needed if we are to understand both the drivers and the implications of political violence (Eriksson Baaz and Stern).

Apart from being more explicit about our starting points, and about what our perspectives can and cannot add, this book has suggested a few lessons that could be applicable across research fields. From feminist literature on violence, the insight that there is a psychological-physical continuum of violence has structured much of the discussion in this book. Recognizing this continuum is important to discussions about gendered violence across the board and may be particularly relevant to scholarship on conflict, where psychological violence is often excluded from the conceptualization of violence (and is sometimes even seen as stretching the concept of violence too far). If scholars in this field of research could recognize the continuum of violence and justify which part of the continuum is relevant to the questions they ask, this would facilitate comparison with gendered political violence in other spheres as well as dialogue with other scholars and practitioners. The need to recognize the psychological end of the continuum of violence is even more evident given the rising political importance of the online sphere. Interactions taking place online cannot be ignored in the contemporary world, and incorporating online coercion and abuse implies a move toward the psychological end of the continuum of violence. Recognizing a continuum of violence does not mean everyone needs to study psychological forms of violence—it merely implies that there is increased pressure to argue for one's delimitations, also in relation to the continuum of violence.

The gender and politics literature has developed sophisticated ways of distinguishing between violence that is political because it disrupts the formal political process in some way and violence that is political in the broader sense of the word. Other fields can learn from this when they elaborate on the ways in which violence is political. Specifying why and how violence is political is important even though there are many different possible definitions.

The literature on armed conflict, on the other hand, has a long tradition of systematically categorizing violence and its perpetrators. Perhaps it is because of this focus on the origin of violent conflict that this field has also come relatively far in acknowledging the importance of recognizing men and masculinities as an important gendered perspective. The lesson we can learn from some contributions to this literature is that a gender perspective is not synonymous with women. Although this has been stated many times, it needs reiterating and is an important insight for all fields dealing with gender and violence against political actors. It is probably safe to say that a man is involved in most of the acts of violence that are studied under this wide umbrella, and a gendered perspective on men is thus needed for a complete gendered analysis of these acts. Again, this does not mean that all gender studies need to explicitly study men, but the chosen gendered focus should be justified by taking men into account.

Empirical Insights and Future Research

The empirical analyses and illustrations that have been presented in this book provide rich and nuanced information on how gender influences violence against political actors. While this brief concluding chapter does not aim to provide a detailed summary of the findings, we do want to highlight a few insights that have been generated through the empirical analyses. First, and perhaps most importantly, the case studies have provided strong empirical support for the usefulness of conceptualizing violence as a continuum that includes not only physical, but also psychological violence. Various chapters (e.g., Schneider, Collignon, Håkansson, Thomas and Herrick, and Zetterberg and Bjarnegård) have shown that psychological violence is more common than physical violence. Importantly, and in line with previous research analyzing both physical and psychological violence, the empirical analyses in this book have demonstrated that women are more likely to be exposed to psychological violence than men are. Thus, if we fail to take this form of violence into account, we run the risk of underestimating the prevalence of violence against women political actors. Because male political actors often experience more physical violence than women do, such an underestimation may cause us to draw the erroneous conclusion that men political actors experience more violence than women do, when they—in fact—simply experience a different type of violence than women do. If anything, also focusing on (the more frequent) psychological violence points in the opposite direction; that is, it indicates that women are exposed to more political violence than men are.

The empirical data used in this book, not least the survey data on political candidates and elected representatives, show that one specific type of psychological violence is most common (for both men and women political actors): online violence. This applies in particular to developed democracies in the Global North, as illustrated, for instance, by chapters on the United Kingdom (Collignon), Sweden (Håkansson), Israel (Kuperberg), and the United States (Thomas and Herrick). Importantly, the chapters have revealed that women in this part of the world tend to be more exposed to online violence than men are. Nonetheless, online political violence is also clearly gendered in the Global South, as illustrated, for instance, by Zetterberg and Bjarnegård, who found that online attacks on women politicians in the Maldives were often sexual in nature. Using techniques such as photoshopping (see also Esposito's chapter), perpetrators commonly attacked women's morality.

This brings us to a third important insight offered by the book: regardless of which types of political actors we investigate (voters, candidates, elected politicians, etc.), and regardless of context (peacetime or wartime, the Global North or Global South, democracies or hybrid regimes), sexual violence is clearly a gendered phenomenon. Importantly, this does not simply mean that men are always the perpetrators and women are always the victims of sexual violence. As the chapter by Eriksson Baaz and Stern highlighted, research on conflict-related sexual violence has increasingly recognized that men and boys are also victims of this type of violence. Yet what the book does suggest is that, overall, women are more vulnerable to this form of violence. For instance, Haley and Baker found that women citizens are coerced into sex work during election campaigns in Papua New Guinea to secure candidates' electoral support and political alliances. Similar election-related physical sexual violence (including rape) was reported in Schneider's chapter on Uganda. In other cases, the sexual violence is mainly psychological, such as when it is perpetrated online.

While all of the first three insights concern forms of violence, a fourth insight pays close attention to who the victims are. More specifically, the empirical analyses have demonstrated the importance of applying an intersectional perspective on gendered approaches to violence against political actors. Empirical analyses of different countries have emphasized that there is great variation within the group of women, as well as within the group of men, in the extent to which they experience violence. For instance, Thomas and Herrick's analysis of mayors and state senators in the United States showed that violence aimed at state senators has a racial component: black women senators experience most violence, whereas white men senators are least likely to be exposed to violence. Similarly, both religion and age intersect with gender in the Israeli Parliament: young women and Muslim women are more exposed to violence than others are. More broadly speaking, gender does not only intersect with sociodemographic characteristics, but also with individual roles in political bodies. For instance, in both Sweden and in the United States, women in executive positions (e.g., mayors) or in other leadership positions are more likely to be victims of violence. One explanation put forward is that these women are more visible than others, which puts them in a more vulnerable position.

Still, the book has also shown that intersectional approaches to gender and political violence are only in their infancy. Consequently, there are many unresolved issues that need to be addressed in future research. For instance, as emphasized by Kuperberg, we know little about how gender intersects with marginalized identities such as LGBTQI, working class, or indigeneity. Intersectional perspectives can be used to illuminate vulnerabilities as well as privileges, and it would be useful to compare the relative risk of being exposed to violence among different groups.

This brings us to the issue of unsettled questions that should be addressed in future research. While the emphasis of this book has mainly been on the victims of violence, the chapters on conflict-related violence are important exceptions (see, e.g., Kreft and Nagel). This mirrors the focus of this research field, which has a long tradition of categorizing the type of perpetrator who commits such acts. Research on "peacetime violence" could learn from this approach by paying more attention to the role of perpetrators as a way of distinguishing between the different types of risk political actors are facing. This would be useful in developing risk-reduction strategies in formal political settings as well and for developing comparisons between the type of violence that political actors face as a result of armed conflict and the violence they face as a result of being visible in predominantly peaceful political settings. This would also likely imply a gender perspective that puts a greater focus on men and masculinities. Rigid notions of masculinity, often associated with toughness, risk-taking, and group cohesion, have contributed to the fact that men are highly overrepresented as perpetrators of violence—in politics and in other spheres.

Another, and interrelated, question to address in future analyses in this topic area concerns the motives perpetrators have for using violence. While this issue has received significant attention in the theoretical section of the book (see, e.g., chapters by Eriksson Baaz and Stern and by Krook), it has generally played a smaller role in the empirical sections. Part of the reason for this is that it is challenging to observe motives empirically. How do we know whether a violence act is *motivated* by gender (e.g., sexism) or whether gender is mainly related to the *form* (i.e., perpetrators choose different types of violence for men and women even though the motive is the same)? While some chapters (e.g., Collignon's) have offered suggestions as to the answer to this question, future work should look more closely at the issue in an effort to better understand why women and men political actors are targets of violent acts. Again, the literature on conflict-related violence has generally put more effort into determining actors' motives by linking violent acts to declarations of intent (when they exist) or by inferring motive based on timing. A different continuum than the psychological-physical one we have stressed here is sometimes brought up in the conflict literature, namely, a continuum between violence during war and in peacetime. It is only when we have comparable data on the perpetrators of peacetime violence against political actors and their motives that we can fully investigate this type of continuum as well.

The book has also pointed to the unanswered question concerning the (gendered) consequences—or impact—of violence against political actors. Addressing this issue is key to understanding what this violence does to victims, but also to the societies in which it takes place. For instance, how do experiences of conflict-related sexual violence affect political gender relations during peacetime? Does exposure to election violence make voters less likely to vote in the next election and/or candidates less willing to run for office again? And are such consequences conditioned by the type of violence and/or by the gender of the victim? As discussed in Håkansson's chapter, there are indications that the impact of sexual violence on the victim's health is different from the impact of other forms of violence. If that is the case, the solutions—or responses—used to address the problem should be different too. It is clear that we need to explore the impact of violence if we are to design suitable responses.

One important contribution of this book has been to initiate a discussion about potential responses to gendered violence against political actors. In most cases, the responses addressed in the book are policy responses at the national (e.g., Restrepo Sanín; Raney and Collier) and international (see, e.g., Ballington and Borovsky) levels, targeting gender-motivated violence (e.g., Restrepo Sanín), online violence (Bardall), or conflict-related violence (Nagel and Kreft). Because policy responses have received limited attention in previous research, several questions should be addressed: To what extent are existing policy responses effective in combating (gendered) violence against political actors? What (state and nonstate) actors are involved in the work to address the problem of violence against political actors? What "bottom-up" initiatives (e.g., by citizens, organizations) have been taken to address the problem?

Finally, the most important way forward is to continue the dialogue between different fields of research and practice, with a view to identifying even more new and relevant questions that need to be addressed. What those steps should be, and exactly where they will take us, can only be determined if dialogue, conversations, controversies, and agreements continue to be explored among the researchers and practitioners representing different fields and agendas. We hope this book will contribute to this ongoing conversation.

Notes

CHAPTER 1

1. In certain publications, this has been referred to as direct violence against women, as opposed to indirect violence against women, or gender-differentiated violence against women (see, e.g., Ballington, Bardall, and Borovsky 2017).

CHAPTER 2

I would like to express my gratitude to Kristian Berg Harpviken, Anna Marie Ober-meier, and Gee Berry for great comments and suggestions when developing the chapter. I am also very grateful to the two editors, Elin Bjarnegård and Pär Zetterberg, and to the reviewers at Temple University Press for their productive feedback, helpful suggestions, and hard work in the production of the volume.

1. Both the terms *mainstream peace and conflict research* and *feminist research* are here used as ideal types to bring out and exemplify the influence of feminist theory on mainstream studies while recognizing the broad spectrum of approaches that exist in both fields and the multitude of their interactions (see Gizelis 2018, 2; Sjoberg et al. 2018).

2. That said, transferring knowledge between different standpoints on theory and epistemology carries its own challenges (see, for example, the debate in Bilgin 2004 and Caprioli 2004).

CHAPTER 3

1. It is not possible in this short chapter to include extensive references to the large and growing literature on violence against women in politics. For a continually updated list with full-text links, see https://www.vawpolitics.org/research.

CHAPTER 4

1. For instance, Belkin (2012, 36) argues that male rape in U.S. military settings is not necessarily emasculating, as the penetrated man can also demonstrate that he is man/tough enough to handle and "take it as a man." Schulz (2020) highlights how the notion of emasculation (and feminization and homosexualization) is problematic, as it conceptualizes masculinity as separate thing that exists and can be taken away and ignores contextual (cultural, temporal, etc.) factors and the meanings surrounding masculinity, femininity, heterosexuality, and homosexuality in specific contexts and by different audiences.

2. A similar process may be at play in relation to the lack of recognition of gendered and misogynistic motives in popular/media framings of mass violence committed by incels—given that such violence targets both men and women. See Bendfeldt 2021.

CHAPTER 5

The authors thank Gabriel Bardall, with whom they codeveloped the initial framework and who generously supported our further elaboration on this framework in this chapter. We also thank Pär Zetterberg for his detailed feedback and all the participants at multiple workshops over the years, including at Uppsala University and the Joint Sessions of the European Consortium of Political Research (ECPR), for their thoughtful and critical engagement with our work.

1. Though Krook disagrees with calling violence against women in politics "political violence."

CHAPTER 6

1. ACLED is a disaggregated data collection, analysis, and crisis mapping project tracking physical political violence and demonstrations around the world. Data capturing political violence *targeting women* is hence a subset of its larger mandate, with political violence targeting women *in politics* an even smaller subset therein.

2. Women are only coded as the main victims in events if the victim(s) are composed entirely of women, majority women, or if the primary target was a woman (e.g., a woman politician attacked alongside two male bodyguards). Events in which women are killed alongside men, for example, are not categorized as such.

3. Information at ACLED is coded by a team of researchers based around the world and goes through multiple rounds of review for intercoder, intracoder, and intercode reliability before being published each week. Data are regularly updated and supplemented as more information becomes available. For more on ACLED processes, see their guides and methodologies on the ACLED website.

4. Avoiding the inclusion of violence carried out by individuals with no external ties helps to avoid capturing interpersonal violence within this subset of information, in line with ACLED's mandate.

5. Following the fall of Kabul in August 2021, the Taliban are no longer coded by ACLED as a rebel group and are now considered to be the de facto state power in Afghanistan.

6. ACLED opts for a restrictive understanding of political violence, including gang violence only when it is used for overt political goals (i.e., the use of violence against political targets, e.g., a mayor or parliamentarian or those in the public domain, e.g., journalists or activists) or in rare contexts where gang violence fundamentally challenges public

safety and security (i.e., when a state's public security and safety is fundamentally challenged—e.g., when gang violence severely limits de facto control of the state over its territories or when gangs challenge the state's ability to enforce public security and safety by engaging in regular high-end and public violence).

7. For more on ACLED methodology around the coding of gangs and political violence in Latin America, see the ACLED gang methodology primer.

8. These factors are in addition to the underreporting by victims that is common when it comes to violence against women due to backlash or normative concerns. As is the same for all datasets, coverage within the ACLED dataset is limited to what has been reported in some capacity. ACLED makes every attempt to capture political violence accurately and thoroughly through various sources of reporting, including traditional media, new media, reports by international organizations, and information gathered by local partners. This fact should be considered when drawing conclusions from the data, as is the case when working with any data around violence against women.

9. For more on what users can and cannot do with these data, see ACLED's FAQs on "Political Violence Targeting Women (PVTW), Demonstrations Featuring Women (DFW), and Political Violence Targeting Women in Politics (PVTWIP)."

10. ACLED covers only physical, political violence (or an attempt at physical violence, such as a failed assassination attempt).

11. Analysis undertaken in this chapter accounts for these differences by not comparing trends across time across regions and rather comparing relative trends within each region.

12. While political violence perpetrated by women is included within the ACLED dataset in the sense that all reports of political violence are included, it is not known which events involve women as perpetrators specifically (with the small exception of women's units, such as the PKK-YJA STAR noted above, for example).

CHAPTER 7

The authors wish to acknowledge the contributions of Sandra Håkansson in the work on Sri Lanka. We also thank the Swedish Research Council for financial support.

CHAPTER 8

1. Such attitudes are not limited to Latin American countries; for example, a 2016 survey by the European Commission revealed that 27 percent of respondents in the European Union consider rape (sexual intercourse without consent) justifiable in certain situations. See https://ec.europa.eu/COMMFrontOffice/publicopinion/index.cfm/Survey/get SurveyDetail/instruments/SPECIAL/surveyKy/2115.

2. See also this report by Centro Nacional de Memoria Histórica: https://centrode memoriahistorica.gov.co/aniquilar-la-diferencia/.

3. See SVAC website (http://www.sexualviolencedata.org/bibliography/papers-in-prog ress/, accessed November 5, 2021).

CHAPTER 9

Eleonora Esposito's work was generously supported by the Marie Skłodowska-Curie actions (H2020-MSCA-IF-2017—Grant Agreement ID: 795937).

1. A useful list of more than fifty social media research tools is *The Social Media Research Toolkit*. Curated by the Social Media Lab at Ted Rogers School of Management, Toronto Metropolitan University it features software widely used in peer-reviewed academic studies, https://socialmedialab.ca/apps/social-media-research-toolkit-2/.

CHAPTER 10

This chapter draws primarily on data gathered during the ANU Election Observation Project for the 2017 Papua New Guinea general elections. The ANU observation was jointly funded by the ANU through the State, Society and Governance in Melanesia Program (now the Department of Pacific Affairs) and by the Australian government through the Papua New Guinea–Australia Partnership, the Pacific Research Program, and the core funding that preceded it.

CHAPTER 11

1. Focus group discussions (FDG): candidate, elected officials, agents, Soroti Hotel, Soroti, Uganda, July 27, 2018; women councilors LC3, UNWomen/UWONET Conference, Gulu, Uganda, August 2, 2018; Muslim women's group, Gulu, Uganda, July 30, 2019.

CHAPTER 12

I would like to thank the team behind the Representative Audit of Britain survey, especially Dr. Wolfgang Rüdig, for the fantastic dataset I am allowed to use in this chapter.

1. The survey obtained 1,495 responses, corresponding to a 53 percent overall response rate. The response rate was 57 percent women and 51 percent men candidates. More details on the survey and results are available at Collignon and Rüdig (2020).

2. The exact formulation of the question was the following: During the 2017 General Election campaign, there were several press reports about candidates experiencing harassment and even security threats. Did you personally experience any form of inappropriate behaviour, harassment or threats to your security in your position as a parliamentary candidate during the election campaign? Answer: Yes/No. This is a variation on the original questionnaire developed by David James and coauthors.

3. This response rate is in line with other similar surveys.

4. Exact wording of the question was the following: In politics, people sometimes talk of left and right. Using a scale from 0 to 10, where 0 means the most left-wing and 10 the most right-wing, where would you place . . . your views? . . . voters in your constituency?

CHAPTER 13

1. Every one of the fifty states except Nebraska has two legislative chambers. Nebraska has a unicameral legislature that is called a senate.

2. These definitions are inspired by a study from the Inter-Parliamentary Union (IPU 2016).

CHAPTER 14

1. In municipal politics, women occupy 43 percent of the rank-and-file positions and 37 percent of the chair and mayoral seats.

2. In addition, I use interview data to provide concrete examples violent events and their impacts. The interviews were carried out in 2017 and 2019 with former or present politicians in several Swedish municipalities.

3. Out of all respondents who reported having experienced violence in the KOLFU survey, 13 percent reported exposure to some form of physical violence (defined as violence against one's person or property damage). Out of all respondents who reported having experienced any form of violence in the PTU survey, 11 percent reported exposure to some form of physical violence (defined as violence with weapon; arson; punch, kick, or similar; theft; graffiti; push or similar; other physical violence or other damage).

4. Psychological violence is also found to be more common than physical in other contexts; see chapters by Collignon, Schneider, and Thomas and Herrick in this volume.

5. As a contrast, members of one's own party are found to be common perpetrators against political women in Uganda; see Schneider's chapter in this volume.

CHAPTER 15

Thanks to Elin Bjarnegård and Pär Zetterberg for their feedback and assistance.

1. Though I largely refer to social media applications here (Twitter, Facebook, Instagram), similar methods can be used to scrape website data.

2. This approach, "hashing" (anonymizing) data so that it cannot be tracked to the original author, is utilized by some social media scholars due to data and ethical guidelines.

CHAPTER 16

Julie Ballington is UN Women's Global Policy Advisor on Political Participation; Gabriella Borovsky is UN Women's Policy Specialist on Political Participation. The views expressed in this publication are those of the authors and do not necessarily represent the views of UN Women, the United Nations, or any of its affiliated organizations.

1. *Violence against women in politics* (VAWP) is the term largely used by the UN system; however, the term *VAWIP* is used here to be consistent with other chapters. Some content of this chapter is drawn from UN Women's internal Guidance Note on Violence against Women in Politics.

2. There is a vast regional framework beyond the scope of the chapter. For example, there have been many efforts to have comprehensive, consistent, and coherent regional approaches to responding to VAW, some being particularly notable for being legally binding instruments; these include the Inter-American Convention on the Prevention, Punishment and Eradication of Violence against Women (Belem do Para), the Protocol to the African Charter on Human and Peoples' Rights on the Rights of Women in Africa (the Maputo Protocol), and the Convention on Preventing and Combating Violence against Women and Domestic Violence (the Istanbul Convention), which came into force in August 2014.

CHAPTER 17

Thank you to the editors and chapter authors for a productive process through a challenging time.

1. See the agreed conclusions from the Sixty-Fifth Commission on the Status of Women (2020) as well as Report of the Special Rapporteur on violence against women, its causes

and consequences on online violence against women and girls from a human rights perspective (United Nations 2018a, report A/HRC/38/47) for examples.

2. Note the Australian model cited elsewhere is exemplary but is limited by geographic constraints. Specifically, the eComisson can only consider reports if the person in the image lives in Australia, the person who posted the image lives in Australia, or the intimate image is hosted in Australia.

CHAPTER 18

1. This example does not imply that CRSV is frequently used as a weapon of war. See Wood (2018) and Crawford (2017) for discussions on CRSV and the narrative of rape as weapon of war.

2. Numbers calculated using replication data for Nagel 2019.

3. See, for example, the *Synergie des Femmes pour les Victimes des Violences Sexuelles* (Women's Synergy for Victims of Sexual Violence, or SFVS), http://www.womensmedia center.com/news-features/a-champion-for-congolese-women.

4. See, for example, the Association of Women Victims of War, https://www.srebren ica.org.uk/survivor-stories/bakira-hasecic/.

CHAPTER 19

I would like to thank Elin Bjarnegård, Pär Zetterberg, and Paige Schneider for their thoughtful comments and suggestions to this chapter. I also want to thank Mona Lena Krook, Rebecca Kuperberg, and Jennifer Piscopo for their continuous support to my research.

1. During the 169th hearing of the Inter-American Court of Human Rights, Mrs. Quipe's family expressed their dissatisfaction with the resolution of the case. Electoral authorities were representing the Bolivian state, which suggests the state recognize her crime as VAWIP.

2. Observatorio de Género. Coordinadora de la Mujer. Bolivia.

3. Legislative proposals have been presented in Ecuador, Costa Rica, and Honduras.

4. In Spanish: Protocolo para la Atención de la Violencia Política contra las Mujeres en Razón de Género; from now on, *electoral protocol*.

5. Data about women in national congress is from the Interparliamentary Union Database, October 2021.

6. Two women have been *appointed* as presidents.

7. Observatorio de Género, Coordinadora de la Mujer, accessed March 13, 2020, http://www.coordinadoradelamujer.org.bo/observatorio/index.php/tematica/3/cifras/3 ?PageNum=7.

8. Phone interview with Mexican Electoral Magistrate, fall 2016.

9. The difference between harassment and violence is that harassment does not cause harm. However, the line between not causing harm and doing so is very thin according to the law and the regulatory framework. *Hostigamiento* (a type of harassment best translated as "harrying") is explained in the framework as "continuous attacks against a woman, causing concern and distress" (Art. 2. II.c), which, can be argued, cause harm. This highlights the importance of understanding VAWIP, not as discrete actions, but as a continuum of violence.

10. See, for example, the World Justice Project.

11. Interview with Bolivian activist, La Paz, Bolivia, summer 2015.

12. Interviews with women activists and electoral authorities, La Paz, Bolivia, summer 2016. Virtual interview with Bolivian electoral authorities, summer 2020.

13. Data from ACOBOL, http://www.acobol.org.bo/cuadros-estadisticos/, and the electoral authorities, http://observatorioparidaddemocratica.oep.org.bo/Eje-Tematico-04 -Datos/Indicadores-1-2-3/NAomero-de-denuncias-y-renuncias-por-acoso-y-violencia -polAstica-en-el-OEP,-por-gestiAsn.

14. Interview with Bolivian activist, La Paz, Bolivia, summer 2015.

15. Phone interview with Mexican electoral magistrate, fall 2016.

16. The World Justice Project estimates that 1.5 billion people worldwide cannot obtain justice for criminal, administrative, or civil problems.

17. In 2018, FEPADE was investigating 2,176 cases; by the end of the year, it had received an additional 1,484 cases and was only able to clear 1,571, leaving 2,089 cases still under investigation (FEPADE 2018).

CHAPTER 20

We would like to thank the editors of this volume and all the participants who attended the Gender and Violence against Political Actors Workshop in Uppsala, Sweden, on December 8–9, 2019, for their thoughtful suggestions for our chapter. This research is greatly improved from their input.

1. The 2021 policy, the Members of the House of Commons Workplace Harassment and Violence Prevention Policy, applies to employees hired by members of Parliament (MPs); employees of the House administration have their own, separate procedures and policies. Any employee who believes they have been subject to harassment and violence under the Canadian Human Rights Act may seek recourse under the act. We use *employee* to refer to political staff hired by MPs only.

2. For example, online harassment is not covered. See chapters by Bardall and Kuperberg.

3. "Toeing the party line" is an English idiom meaning to do what an authority figure tells you to do even though you may not want to.

4. If either the complainant or respondent is an MP, the complaint must be filed with a designated recipient (DR). In most cases, the DR is the chief human resources officer.

5. Appropriate measures might include interim or precautionary measures, although these are not specified and are left to a whip's discretion. Whips are given latitude to inform the MP of a complainant's identity.

6. Enquiries brought to members/whips that are resolved informally are not recorded; whips/members are obligated to report a claim to the CHRO to be officially recorded only when a complainant has indicated that they wish to file a formal complaint. The official statistics likely seriously underreport the total number of complainants who "enquire" about the procedures.

7. Records on formal investigation outcomes are not kept.

8. During the resolution process, a complainant who has reported to the whip may choose to have the matter dealt with by the CHRO instead.

9. Some complainants prefer their cases be handled informally and/or away from the public eye. Explicit preference for informal procedures, however, neglects the broader institutional context where male partisan elites have historically held a disproportionate amount of power and can wield influence behind the scenes.

10. See also Collier and Raney 2018.

References

Aaldering, Loes, and Daphne J. Van Der Pas. 2020. "Political Leadership in the Media: Gender Bias in Leader Stereotypes during Campaign and Routine Times." *British Journal of Political Science* 50, no. 3 (July): 911–31.

Acker, Joan. 1992. "From Sex Roles to Gendered Institutions." *Contemporary Sociology* 21, no. 5: 565–69.

ACOBOL. 2020. "ACOBOL manifiesta su preocupación por la impunidad de los casos de acoso y violencia política." Accessed March 26, 2020. Available at: http://www .acobol.org.bo/acobol-manifiesta-su-preocupacion-por-la-impunidad-de-los-casos -de-acoso-y-violencia-politica/.

Agerberg, Mattias, and Anne-Kathrin Kreft. 2020. "Gendered Conflict, Gendered Outcomes: The Politicization of Sexual Violence and Quota Adoption." *Journal of Conflict Resolution* 64, no. 2–3: 290–317.

Agger, Inger, and Søren Buus Jensen. 1993. "The Psychosexual Trauma of Torture." In *International Handbook of Traumatic Stress*, edited by John Wilson and Beverly Raphael, 685–701. New York: Plenum.

Ahikire, Josephine. 2015. "Gender Equality and Political Leadership in Uganda." Research paper, UN Women Uganda, Kampala, Uganda.

Akhtar, S., and C. M. Morrison. 2019. "The Prevalence and Impact of Online Trolling of UK Members Of Parliament." *Computers in Human Behavior* 99:322–27.

Albaine, Laura. 2016. "Paridad de género y violencia política en Bolivia, Costa Rica y Ecuador. Un análisis testimonia." *Ciencia Política* 11, no. 21: 335–62.

———. 2021. "Violencia política contra las mujeres por motivos de género en América Latina: Estrategias legales y el rol de los organismos electorales." *Elecciones* 20, no. 21: 163–87.

Alison, Miranda. 2007. "Wartime Sexual Violence: Women's Human Rights and Questions of Masculinity." *Review of International Studies* 33, no. 1: 75–90.

Amnesty International. 2018. "Toxic Twitter—Women's Experiences of Violence and Abuse on Twitter." Amnesty International. Available at: https://www.amnesty.org/en/latest /news/2018/03/online-violence-against-women-chapter-3-2/.

Animal Político. 2018. "Tribunal Electoral cancela 15 candidaturas de falsos trans en Oaxaca." Animal Político. Accessed June 22, 2018. Available at: https://www.animal politico.com/2018/06/candidatos-trans-oaxaca-tepjf/.

Anti-Defamation League. 2022. Best Practices for Responding to Cyberhate. Accessed October 2022. Available at: https://www.adl.org/best-practices-for-responding-to-cy berhate.

Areto Labs. 2019. Parity Bot. February. Accessed November 2019. Available at: https:// mobile.twitter.com/paritybot_ca.

Armbruster, Stefan. 2017. "Australia Praises 'Successful' Election as Death Toll Mounts." SBS News, August 5, 2017. Available at: https://www.sbs.com.au/news/article/australia -praises-successful-png-election-as-death-toll-mounts/gw4bfed5m.

Atalanta. 2018. "(Anti)Social Media: The Benefits and Pitfalls of Digital for Female Politicians." Accessed November 30, 2021. Available at: https://www.atalanta.co/antiso cial-media.

Auchter, Jessica. 2017. "Forced Male Circumcision: Gender-based Violence in Kenya." International Affairs 93, no. 6: 1339–56.

Australian Government. n.d. eSafety Commissioner. Accessed October 2019. Available at: https://www.esafety.gov.au/key-issues/image-based-abuse/take-action/civil-pen alties-scheme.

Autesserre, Severine. 2012. "Dangerous Tales: Dominant Narratives on the Congo and Their Unintended Consequences." African Affairs 111, no. 443: 202–22.

Awla News. 2020. "استهداف منزلين بعبوتين جنوبي ذي قار.. أحدهما منزل النائبة 'علا الناشي'." Awla News, February 16, 2020. Accessed October 2022. Available at: www.awla.news /استهداف-منزلين-بعبوتين-جنوبي-ذي-قار-أح/.

Bacchi, Carol. 1999. Women, Policy and Politics: The Construction of Policy Problems. London: SAGE.

———. 2009. Analysing Policy. New South Wales, AU: Pearson Higher Education.

Baker, Kerryn. 2018. "Great Expectations: Gender and Political Representation in the Pacific Islands." Government and Opposition 53, no. 3: 542–68.

Baker, Paul, and Jesse Egbert, eds. 2016. Triangulating Methodological Approaches in Corpus-Linguistic Research. London: Routledge.

Bakken, Ingrid Vik, and Halvard Buhaug. 2021. "Civil War and Female Empowerment." Journal of Conflict Resolution 65, no. 5: 982–1009.

Ballington, Julie. 2016. "Turning the Tide on Violence against Women in Politics: How Are We Measuring Up?" Paper presented at the 24th Annual Meeting for the International Political Science Association World Congress, Poznan, Poland, July 23–28, 2016.

Ballington, Julie, Gabrielle Bardall, and Gabriella Borovsky. 2017. Preventing Violence against Women in Elections: A Programming Guide. New York: UNDP and UN Women.

Bardall, Gabrielle. 2011. Breaking the Mold: Understanding Gender and Electoral Violence. Washington, DC: IFES.

———. 2013. "Gender-Specific Election Violence: The Role of Information and Communication Technologies." Stability: International Journal of Security and Development 2, no. 3: 1–11.

———. 2016. "Gender Based Distinctions and Motivations in Political Violence." In "Voices, Votes and Violence: Essays on Select Dynamics of Electoral Authoritarian Regimes."

Ph.D. diss., University of Montreal. Available at: https://papyrus.bib.umontreal.ca
/xmlui/bitstream/handle/1866/18513/Bardall_Gabrielle_2016_these.pdf?sequence=2
&isAllowed=y.

———. 2019. "Defending Democracy in Digital Spaces: Ending Violence against Women in Politics Online." Pre-American Political Science Association (APSA) event, Electoral Integrity Project Workshop, Washington, DC.

Bardall, Gabrielle, Elin Bjarnegård, and Jennifer M. Piscopo. 2020. "How Is Political Violence Gendered? Disentangling Motives, Forms, and Impacts." *Political Studies* 68, no. 4: 916–35.

Barker, Kim, and Olga Jurasz. 2018. *Online Misogyny as Hate Crime: A Challenge for Legal Regulation?* London: Routledge.

Barnello, Michelle A., and Kathleen A. Bratton. 2007. "Bridging the Gender Gap in Bill Sponsorship." *Legislative Studies Quarterly* 32, no. 3: 449–74.

Barnes, Tiffany, and Diana O'Brien. 2018. "Defending the Realm: The Appointment of Female Defense Ministers Worldwide." *American Journal of Political Science* 62, no. 2: 355–68.

Barrett, Edith J. 2001. "Black Women in State Legislatures: The Relationship of Race and Gender to the Legislative Experience." In *The Impact of Women in Public Office*, edited by Susan J. Carroll, 185–204. Bloomington: Indiana University Press.

Bassiouni, M. C. 1994. "The United Nations Commission of Experts Established Pursuant to Security Council Resolution 780 (1992)." *American Journal of International Law* 88, no. 4: 784–805.

BBC News. 2019. "Sarah Hanson-Young: Australia Senator Wins Defamation Case." November 25, 2019. Accessed October 2022. Available at: https://www.bbc.com/news/world-australia-50541277.

BBC Reality Check. 2020. "Social Media: How Do Other Governments Regulate It?" BBC, February 12, 2020. Accessed October 2022. Available at: https://www.bbc.com/news/technology-47135058.

Beckwith, Karen. 2005. "A Common Language of Gender?" *Politics and Gender* 1, no. 1 (March): 128–37. Accessed November 5, 2020. Available at: http://www.journals.cambridge.org/abstract_S1743923X05211017.

Bekoe, Dorina. 2012. *Voting In Fear.* Washington, DC: United States Institute of Peace.

Belkin, Aaron. 2012. *Bring Me Men: Military Masculinity and the Benign Facade of American Empire, 1898–2001.* New York: Columbia University Press.

Benard, Cheryl. 1994. "Rape as Terror: The Case of Bosnia." *Terrorism and Political Violence* 6, no. 1: 29–43.

Bendfeldt, Luise. 2021. "Gendered Tensions in the Portrayal of Incel Violence." Unpublished manuscript.

Beninger, Kelsey. 2017. "Social Media Users' Views on the Ethics of Social Media Research." In *The SAGE Handbook of Social Media Research Methods*, edited by Luke Sloan and Anabel Quan-Haase, 57–73. London: SAGE.

Benson, Michelle, and Theodora-Ismene Gizelis. 2020. "A Gendered Imperative: Does Sexual Violence Attract UN Attention in Civil Wars?" *Journal of Conflict Resolution* 64, no. 1: 167–98.

Berns, Nancy. 2001. "Degendering the Problem and Gendering the Blame: Political Discourse on Women and Violence." *Gender and Society* 15, no. 2: 262–81.

Berry, Marie. 2015. "From Violence to Mobilization: Women, War, and Threat in Rwanda." *International Quarterly* 20, no. 2:135–56.

———. 2018. *War, Women, and Power: From Violence to Mobilization in Rwanda and Bosnia-Herzegovina*. Cambridge: Cambridge University Press.

Berry, Marie, Yolande Bouka, and Marilyn Muthoni Kamuru. 2017. "Kenyan Women Just Fought One of the Most Violent Campaigns in History." *Foreign Policy*, August 7, 2017. Accessed October 2022. Available at: https://foreignpolicy.com/2017/08/07/kenyas-female-politicians-just-fought-the-one-of-the-most-violent-campaign-in-history-election/.

Bilgin, Pinar. 2004. "International Politics of Women's (In)Security: Rejoinder to Mary Caprioli." *Security Dialogue* 35, no. 4: 499–504.

Birch, Sarah, Ursula Daxecker, and Kristine Höglund. 2020. "Electoral Violence: An Introduction." *Journal of Peace Research* 57, no. 1: 3–14.

Birch, Sarah, and David Muchlinski. 2017a. "The Dataset of Countries at Risk of Electoral Violence." *Terrorism and Political Violence* 32, no. 2: 217–36. https://doi.org/10.1080/09546553.2017.1364636.

———. 2017b. "Electoral Violence: Patterns and Trends." In *Electoral Integrity and Political Regimes: Actors, Strategies and Consequences*, edited by Holly Ann Garnett and Margarita Zavadskaya, 100–12. New York: Routledge.

———. 2020. "The Dataset of Countries at Risk of Electoral Violence." *Terrorism and Political Violence* 32, no. 2: 217–36.

Biroli, Flávia. 2018. "Violence against Women and Reactions to Gender Equality in Politics." *Politics and Gender* 14, no. 4: 681–85.

Bjarnegård, Elin. 2013. *Gender, Informal Institutions and Political Recruitment: Explaining Male Dominance in Parliamentary Representation*. New York: Palgrave Macmillan.

———. 2018. "Making Gender Visible in Election Violence: Strategies for Data Collection." *Politics and Gender* 14, no. 4: 690–95.

———. 2021. "The Continuum of Election Violence: Gendered Candidate Experiences in the Maldives." *International Political Science Review* (forthcoming). https://doi.org/10.1177/0192512120977111.

Bjarnegård, Elin, Karen Brounéus, and Erik Melander. 2017. "Honor and Political Violence. Micro-Level Findings from a Survey in Thailand." *Journal of Peace Research* 54, no. 6: 748–61.

Bjarnegård, Elin, Sandra Håkansson, and Pär Zetterberg. 2022. "Gender and Violence against Political Candidates: Lessons from Sri Lanka." *Politics and Gender* 18, no. 1: 33–61. https://doi.org/10.1017/S1743923X20000471.

Bjarnegård, Elin, Erik Melander, Gabrielle Bardall, Karen Brounéus, Erika Forsberg, Karin Johansson, Angela Muvumba Sellström, and Louise Olsson. 2015. *Gender, Peace, and Armed Conflict. SIPRI Yearbook 2015: Armaments, Disarmament, and International Security*. Stockholm: SIPRI.

Blair, Graeme, Kosuke Imai, and Jason Lyall. 2014. "Comparing and Combining List and Endorsement Experiments: Evidence from Afghanistan." *American Journal of Political Science* 58, no. 4: 1043–63.

Boesten, Jelke. 2017. "Of Exceptions and Continuities: Theory and Methodology in Research on Conflict-Related Sexual Violence." *International Feminist Journal of Politics* 19, no. 4: 506–19.

Boesten, Jelke, and Marsha Henry. 2018. "Between Fatigue and Silence: The Challenges of Conducting Research on Sexual Violence in Conflict." *Social Politics: International Studies in Gender, State and Society* 25, no. 4: 568–88.

Bohnet, Iris. 2016. *What Works: Gender Equality by Design*. Cambridge: Belknap Press of Harvard University Press.

Boles, Janet. 2001. "Local Elected Women and Policy-Making: Movement Delegates or Feminist Trustees?" In *The Impact of Women in Public Office*, edited by Susan J. Carroll, 68–86. Bloomington: Indiana University Press.

Borzyskowski, Inken von, and Michael Wahman. 2021. "Systematic Measurement Error in Election Violence Data: Causes and Consequences." *British Journal of Political Science* 51, no. 1: 230–52.

Bottin, Aline, and Annette Young. 2021. "No Holding Back: Record Number of Female Candidates in Iraqi Elections." *France 24*, October 1, 2021. Accessed October 2022. Available at: https://www.france24.com/en/tv-shows/the-51/20211001-no-holding -back-record-number-of-female-candidates-in-iraqi-elections.

Bourke, Joanna. 2008. *Rape: A History from 1860 to the Present*. London: Virago Press.

Bowleg, Lisa. 2008. "When Black + Lesbian + Woman (Does Not Equal) Black Lesbian Woman: The Methodological Challenges of Qualitative and Quantitative Intersectionality Research." *Sex Roles* 59: 312–25. https://doi.org/10.1007/s11199-008-9400-z.

Boyle, Karen. 2019a. *#MeToo, Weinstein and Feminism*. London: Palgrave Pivot.

———. 2019b. "What's in a Name? Theorising the Inter-Relationships of Gender and Violence." *Feminist Theory* 20, no. 1: 19–36.

Boyle, Karen, and Chamil Rathnayake. 2019. "#HimToo and the Networking of Misogyny in the Age of #MeToo." *Feminist Media Studies* 20, no. 8: 1259–77. https://doi.org /10.1080/14680777.2019.1661868.

Britton, Dana. 2000. "The Epistemology of the Gendered Organization." *Gender and Society* 14, no. 3: 418–34.

Brounéus, Karen. 2010. "The Trauma of Truth-Telling: Effects of Witnessing in the Rwandan Gacaca Courts on Psychological Health." *Journal of Conflict Resolution* 54, no. 3: 408–37.

———. 2014. "The Women and Peace Hypothesis in Peacebuilding Settings: Attitudes of Women in the Wake of the Rwandan Genocide." *Signs: Journal of Women in Culture and Society* 40, no. 1: 125–51.

Brounéus, Karen, Erika Forsberg, Karin Dyrstad, and Helga Malmin Binningsbøl. 2017. "The Gendered Links between War-Related Trauma and Attitudes to Peace: Exploring Survey Data from Guatemala, Nepal, and Northern Ireland." Research paper, 58th Annual Convention of the International Studies Association, Baltimore, February 22–25, 2017.

Brownmiller, Susan. 1975. *Against Our Will: Men, Women, and Rape*. New York: Simon and Schuster.

Buchanan, NiCole T., and Carolyn M. West. 2009. "Sexual Harassment in the Lives of Women of Color." In *Handbook of Diversity in Feminist Psychology*, edited by Hope Landrine and Nancy Felipe Russo, 449–76. New York: Springer.

Bunch, Charlotte. 1990. "Women's Rights as Human Rights: Toward a Re-Vision of Human Rights." *Human Rights Quarterly* 12, no. 4: 486–98.

Bustillos, Iván. 2014. "De 221 Denuncias de Acoso Político, Una Llegó a Sentencia." *La Razón*, July 6, 2014. Accessed October 5, 2022. Available at: https://www.la-razon .com/politico/2014/07/06/de-221-denuncias-de-acoso-politico-una-llego-a-senten cia/.

Cabildeo Digital. 2016. "Juana Quispe sacrificada por el odio político." Accessed October 2022. Available at: https://www.youtube.com/watch?v=nxR5mjmggSI.

Caprioli, Mary. 2000. "Gendered Conflict." *Journal of Peace Research* 37, no. 1: 53–68.

———. 2004. "Multiple Pathways to Understanding: A Response to Bilgin." *Security Dialogue* 35, no. 4: 505–8.

———. 2005 "Primed for Violence: The Role of Gender Inequality in Predicting Internal Conflict." *International Studies Quarterly* 49, no. 2: 161–78.

Carli, Linda L., and Alice H. Eagly. 2001. "Gender, Hierarchy, and Leadership: An Introduction." *Journal of Social Issues* 57, no. 4: 629–36.

Carpenter, R. Charli. 2005. "'Women, Children, and Other Vulnerable Groups': Gender, Strategic Frames and the Protection of Civilians as a Transnational Issue." *International Studies Quarterly* 49, no. 2: 295–334.

———. 2006. "Recognizing Gender-Based Violence Against Civilian Men and Boys in Conflict Situations." *Security Dialogue* 37, no. 10: 83–103.

Castro, Carolina, Maria del Pilar Lopez Uribe, Fernando Posada, Bhavani Castro, and Roudabeh Kishi. 2020. "Understanding the Killing of Social Leaders in Colombia during COVID-19." Blog, LSE Latin America and Caribbean, October 6, 2020.

Ceballos, Joshua. 2021. "Transgender Protesters Allege Discrimination at Miami Jails." *Miami New Times*, May 18, 2021. Accessed October 2022. Available at: https://www.miaminewtimes.com/news/advocates-say-miami-jail-policies-hurt-transgender-inmates-12236803.

CEDAW Committee. 2017. *General Recommendation No. 35 on Gender Based Violence against Women, Updating General Recommendation No. 19.* Geneva: CEDAW Committee.

Centre for Monitoring Election Violence. 2018. "Local Authorities Election 2018. Media Communique 8 February 2018 in Colombo." Accessed October 19, 2022. Available at: https://cmev.org/wp-content/uploads/2018/02/communique-feb8.pdf.

Cerna, Daniela Cerva. 2014. "Political Participation and Gender Violence in Mexico." *Revista Mexicana de Ciencias Politicas y Sociales* 59, no. 222 (September–December): 117–40.

Chappell, Louise. 2014. "'New,' 'Old,' and 'Nested' Institutions and Gender Justice Outcomes: A View from the International Criminal Court." *Politics and Gender* 10:572–94.

Chappell, Louise, and Natalie Galea. 2017. "Excavating Informal Institutional Enforcement through 'Rapid' Ethnography: Lessons from the Australian Construction Industry." In *Gender and Informal Institutions*, edited by Georgina Waylen, 67–90. London: Rowman and Littlefield.

Chappell, Louise, and Fiona Mackay. 2017. "What's in a Name? Mapping the Terrain of Informal Institutions and Gender Politics." In *Gender and Informal Institutions*, edited by Georgina Waylen, 23–44. London: Rowman and Littlefield.

Chen, Gina Masullo. 2017. *Online Incivility and Public Debate.* New York: Palgrave Macmillan.

Chenoweth, Erica, and Zoe Marks. 2022. "Revenge of the Patriarchs—Why Autocrats Fear Women." *Foreign Affairs* (March/April).

Cho, Sumi, Kimberlé Crenshaw, and Leslie McCall. 2013. "Toward a Field of Intersectionality Studies: Theory, Applications, and Praxis." *Signs: Journal of Women in Culture and Society* 38, no. 4 (Summer): 785–810. https://doi.org/10.1086/669608.

Chynoweth, Sarah. 2018. "'It's Happening to Our Men as Well': Sexual Violence against Rohingya Men and Boys." Report, Women's Refugee Commission.

Citron, Danielle Keats. 2016. *Hate Crimes in Cyberspace.* Cambridge, MA: Harvard University Press.

Clayton, Govinda, and Kristian Gleditsch. 2014. "Will We See Helping Hands? Predicting Civil War Mediation and Likely Success." *Conflict Management and Peace Science* 31, no. 3: 265–84.

Cockburn, Cynthia. 2004. "The Continuum of Violence: A Gender Perspective on War and Peace." In *Sites of Violence: Gender and Conflict Zones*, edited by Wenona Mary Giles and Jennifer Hyndman, 24–44. Berkeley: University of California Press.

Cohen, Dara Kay. 2013. "Female Combatants and the Perpetration of Violence: Wartime Rape in the Sierra Leone Civil War." *World Politics* 65, no. 3: 383–415.

———. 2016. *Rape during Civil War.* Ithaca, NY: Cornell University Press.

———. 2017. "The Ties That Bind: How Armed Groups Use Violence to Socialize Fighters." *Journal of Peace Research* 54, no. 5: 701–14.

Cohen, Dara Kay, and Amelia Hoover Green. 2012. "Dueling Incentives: Sexual Violence in Liberia and the Politics of Human Rights Advocacy." *Journal of Peace Research* 49, no. 3: 445–58.

Cohen, Dara Kay, Amelia Hoover Green, and Elisabeth Jean Wood. 2013. "Wartime Sexual Violence: Misconceptions, Implications, and Ways Forward." Special Report, 617, United State Institute of Peace.

Cohen, Dara Kay, and Sabrina M. Karim. 2021. "Does More Equality for Women Mean Less War? Rethinking Sex and Gender Inequality and Political Violence." *International Organization* 76, no. 2: 414–44.

Cohen, Dara Kay, and Ragnhild Nordås. 2014. "Sexual Violence in Armed Conflict Introducing the SVAC Dataset, 1989–2009." *Journal of Peace Research* 51, no. 3: 418–28.

Cohen, Dara Kay, and Elisabeth Jean Wood. 2016. "Is Sexual Violence During War Exceptional—Or a Continuation of Everyday Violence?" International Studies Quarterly Online. Available at: http://www.isanet.org/Publications/ISQ/Posts/ID/5239/Is-sexual-violence-during-war-exceptional-or-a-continuation-of-everyday-violence.

Cohn, Carol. 1987. "Sex and Death in the Rational World of Defense Intellectuals." *Signs: Journal of Women in Culture and Society* 12, no. 4: 687–718.

Collier, Cheryl N., and Tracey Raney. 2018. "Canada's Member-to-Member Code of Conduct on Sexual Harassment." *Canadian Journal of Political Science* 51, no. 4: 795–815.

Collignon, Sofía, Rosie Campbell, and Wolfgang Rüdig. 2021. "The Gendered Harassment of Parliamentary Candidates in the UK." *Political Quarterly* 93, no. 1: 32–38.

Collignon, Sofía, and Wolfgang Rüdig. 2020. "Lessons on the Harassment and Intimidation of Parliamentary Candidates in the United Kingdom." *Political Quarterly* 91, no. 2: 422–29.

———. 2021. "Increasing the Cost of Female Representation? The Gendered Effects of Harassment, Abuse and Intimidation Towards Parliamentary Candidates in the UK." *Journal of Elections, Public Opinion and Parties*, 31, no. 4: 429–49.

Collignon Delmar, Sofía, Jennifer Hudson, Wolfgang Rüdig, and Rosie Campbell. 2017. "Inappropriate Behaviour: Experiences of 2017 Parliamentary Candidates Evidence from the Representative Audit of Britain Study (ESRC—ES/M500410/1)." Written submission.

Commonwealth Secretariat. 2017. *Papua New Guinea National Election, June–July 2017.* London: Commonwealth Secretariat.

Commonwealth Secretariat/Pacific Islands Forum Secretariat (CS/PIFS). 2007. *Papua New Guinea National Election, June–August 2007: Report of the Commonwealth-Pacific Islands Forum Election Assessment Team.* London: Commonwealth Secretariat and Pacific Islands Forum Secretariat.

Connell, Raewyn. 1995. *Masculinities.* Berkeley: University of California Press.

Corrales, Javier. 2012. "LGBT Rights in the Americas." *Americas Quarterly* 6, no. 2: 88–94.

Coulter, Chris. 2009. *Bush Wives and Girl Soldiers: Women's Lives through War and Peace in Sierra Leone.* Ithaca, NY: Cornell University Press.

Crawford, Kerry. 2017. *Wartime Sexual Violence: From Silence to Condemnation of a Weapon of War.* Washington, DC: Georgetown University Press.

Crenshaw, Kimberle. 1989. "Demarginalizing the Intersection of Race and Sex: A Black Feminist Critique of Antidiscrimination Doctrine, Feminist Theory and Antiracist Politics." *University of Chicago Legal Forum* 1: 139–67.

———. 1991. "Mapping the Margins: Intersectionality, Identity Politics, and Violence against Women of Color." *Stanford Law Review* 43, no. 6: 1241–99.

Crittenden, Courtney, and Christina Policastro. 2018. "Feminist Victimization Theories." Oxford Bibliographies: Criminology. Available at: https://www.oxfordbibliographies.com/view/document/obo-9780195396607/obo-9780195396607-0231.xml.

Crittenden, Courtney A., and Emily M. Wright. 2013. "Predicting Patriarchy: Using Individual and Contextual Factors to Examine Patriarchal Endorsement in Communities." *Journal of Interpersonal Violence* 28, no. 6: 1267–88.

CSPL. 2017. "Intimidation in Public Life—A Review by the Committee on Standards in Public Life." Report. Accessed October 2022. Available at: https://assets.publishing.service.gov.uk/government/uploads/system/uploads/attachment_data/file/666927/6.3637_CO_v6_061217_Web3.1__2_.pdf.

Cyber Civil Rights Initiative. 2022a. CCRI—Related Laws. Accessed January 2022. Available at: https://cybercivilrights.org/related-laws/.

———. 2022b. CCRI Crisis Hotline. Accessed January 2022. Available at: https://cybercivilrights.org/ccri-crisis-helpline/.

———. 2022c. Roster of Attorneys. Accessed January 2022. Available at: https://cybercivilrights.org/professionals-helping-victims/.

Cyr, Jennifer. 2016. "The Pitfalls and Promise of Focus Groups as a Data Collection Method." *Sociological Methods and Research* 45, no. 2: 231–59.

Dagens Nyheter. 2020. "KD-politiker misstänks ha utsatts för brandattentat." Dagens Nyheter, July 26, 2020. Available at: https://www.dn.se/nyheter/sverige/kd-politiker-misstanks-ha-utsatts-for-brandattentat/.

Dahlum, Sirianne, and Tore Wig. 2020. "Peace above the Glass Ceiling: The Historical Relationship between Female Political Empowerment and Civil Conflict." *International Studies Quarterly* 64, no. 4: 879–93.

Daigle, Leah E. 2017. "Introduction to Victimology." In *Victimology: A Text/Reader*, 1–13. Thousand Oaks, CA: SAGE.

Daniele, Gianmarco. 2017. "Strike One to Educate One Hundred: Organized Crime, Political Selection and Politicians' Ability." *Journal of Economic Behavior and Organization* 159 (March): 650–62.

Davies, Sara, and Jacqui True. 2015. "Reframing Conflict-Related Sexual and Gender-Based Violence: Bringing Gender Analysis Back In." *Security Dialogue* 46, no. 6: 495–512.

———, eds. 2019. *Oxford University Press Handbook on Women, Peace and Security.* Oxford: Oxford University Press.

Davis, Angela. 1971. "Reflections on the Black Woman's Role in the Community of Slaves." *Black Scholar* 3, no. 4: 2–15.

Daxecker, Ursula E., Elio Amicarelli, and Alexander Jung. 2019. "Electoral Contention and Violence (ECAV): A New Dataset." *Journal of Peace Research* 56, no. 5: 714–23.

DeKeseredy, Walter S. 2000. "Current Controversies on Defining Non-Lethal Violence against Women in Intimate Heterosexual Relationships: Empirical Implications." *Violence Against Women* 6, no. 7: 728–46.

Department of Foreign Affairs and Trade (DFAT). 2013. *Independent Evaluation of Australian Electoral Assistance in Papua New Guinea 2000–2012*. Canberra: DFAT.

Dhrodia, Azmina. 2017a. "Unsocial Media: Tracking Twitter Abuse against Women MPs." Medium, September 3, 2017. Accessed October 2022. Available at: https://medium.com/@AmnestyInsights/unsocial-media-tracking-twitter-abuse-against-women-mps-fc28aeca498a.

———. 2017b. "Unsocial Media: The Real Toll of Online Abuse against Women." Report, Amnesty International.

———. 2018. "Unsocial Media: A Toxic Place for Women." *IPPR Progressive Review* 24, no. 4: 380–87.

Dickson-Waiko, Anne. 2013. "Women, Nation and Decolonisation in Papua New Guinea." *Journal of Pacific History* 48, no. 2: 177–93.

Doerner, William, and Steven Lab. 2017. *Victimology*. London: Routledge.

Dolan, Chris. 2014. "Into the Mainstream: Addressing Sexual Violence Against Men and Boys in Conflict." Briefing paper prepared for the workshop held at the Overseas Development Institute, May 14, 2014.

Dolan, Chris, Maria Eriksson Baaz, and Maria Stern. 2020. "What Is Sexual about Conflict-Related Sexual Violence? Stories from Men and Women Survivors." *International Affairs* 96, no. 5: 1151–68.

Drumond, Paula. 2019. "What about Men? Towards a Critical Interrogation of Sexual Violence against Men in Global Politics." *International Affairs* 95, no. 6: 1271–87.

Eagly, Alice H., Mary C. Johannesen-Schmidt, and Marloes L. Van Engen. 2003. "Transformational, Transactional, and Laissez-Faire Leadership Styles: A Meta-Analysis Comparing Women and Men." *Psychological Bulletin* 129, no. 4: 569–91.

Eagly, Alice H., and Steven J. Karau. 2002. "Role Congruity Theory of Prejudice toward Female Leaders." *Psychological Review* 109, no. 3: 573–98.

Eck, Kristine, and Lisa Hultman. 2007. "One-Sided Violence against Civilians in War: Insights from New Fatality Data." *Journal of Peace Research* 44, no. 2: 233–46.

Eckert, Stine. 2018. "Fighting for Recognition: Online Abuse of Women Bloggers in Germany, Switzerland, the United Kingdom, and the United States." *New Media and Society* 20, no. 4: 1282–302. https://doi.org/10.1177/1461444816688457.

Edgell, Amanda B. 2018. "Vying for a Man Seat: Gender Quotas and Sustainable Representation in Africa." *African Studies Review* 61, no. 1: 185–214.

Edström, Jerker, Christopher Dolan, Thea Shahrokh, and Onen David. 2016. "Therapeutic Activism: Men of Hope Refugee Association Uganda Breaking the Silence over Male Rape in Conflict-Related Sexual Violence." Development report, International Development Studies.

Einstein, Katherine Levine, and David M. Glick. 2017. "Cities in American Federalism: Evidence on State-Local Government Conflict from a Survey of Mayors." *Publius: The Journal of Federalism* 47, no. 4: 599–621.

Enloe, Cynthia. 1989. *Bananas, Beaches and Bases: Making Feminist Sense of International Politics*. Berkley: University of California Press.

Epstein, Michael J., Richard G. Niemi, and Lynda W. Powell. 2005. "Do Women and Men State Legislators Differ?" In *Women and Elective Office: Past, Present, and Future*, edited by Sue Thomas and Clyde Wilcox, 94–109. New York: Oxford University Press.

Erikson, Josefina, Sandra Håkansson, and Cecilia Josefsson. 2021. "Three Dimensions of Gendered Online Abuse: Analyzing Swedish MPs' Experiences of Social Media." *Perspectives on Politics*: 1–17. https://doi.org/10.1017/S1537592721002048.

Erikson, Josefina, and Cecilia Josefsson. 2019. "Equal Playing Field? On the Intersection between Gender and Being Young in the Swedish Parliament." *Politics, Groups, and Identities* 9, no. 1:81–100. https://doi.org/10.1080/21565503.2018.1564055.

Eriksson Baaz, Maria, and Maria Stern. 2009. "Why Do Soldiers Rape? Masculinity, Violence, and Sexuality in the Armed Forces in the Congo (DRC)." *International Studies Quarterly* 53, no. 2: 495–518.

———. 2013. *Sexual Violence as a Weapon of War?: Perceptions, Prescriptions, Problems in the Congo and Beyond.* London: Zed Books.

———. 2018. "Curious Erasures: The Sexual in Wartime Sexual Violence." *International Feminist Journal of Politics* 20, no. 3, 295–314.

Esposito, Eleonora. 2022. "The Visual Semiotics of Digital Misogyny: Female Leaders in the Viewfinder." *Feminist Media Review.* https://doi.org/10.1080/14680777.2022.2139279.

Esposito, Eleonora, and Sole Alba Zollo. 2021. "'How Dare You Call Her a Pig, I Know Several Pigs Who Would Be Upset if They Knew': A Multimodal Critical Discursive Approach to Online Misogyny against UK MPs on YouTube." *Journal of Language Aggression and Conflict* 9, no. 1: 47–75.

Eves, Richard, and Angela Kelly-Hanku. 2014. "Witch-Hunts in Papua New Guinea's Eastern Highlands Province: A Fieldwork Report." State, Society and Governance in Melanesia In Brief 2014/4.

FEPADE. 2018. "Informe Anual de Actividades 2018." Mexico D.F., November 14, 2019. Accessed October 2022. Available at: https://pgrstastdgfepade020.blob.core.windows.net/fepade/informes/Informefinal2018.pdf.

Fernandez, Henry. 2018. "Curbing Hate Online: What Companies Should Do Now." Center for American Progress, October. Accessed November 2019. Available at: https://cdn.americanprogress.org/content/uploads/2018/10/24111621/ModelInternetCompanies-appendix.pdf.

Finkel, Michelle A. 2002. "Traumatic Injuries Caused by Hazing Practices." *American Journal of Emergency Medicine* 20, no. 3: 228–33.

Fischer, Jeff. 2002. "Electoral Conflict and Violence: A Strategy for Study and Prevention." IFES White paper, February 5, 2002.

Fitzgerald, Louise F., and Lilia M. Cortina. 2018. "Sexual Harassment in Work Organizations: A View from the 21st Century." In *APA Handbook of the Psychology of Women: Perspectives on Women's Private and Public Lives, vol. 2*, edited by Cheryl Brown Travis, Jacquelyn W. White, Alexandra Rutherford, Wendi S. Williams, Sarah L. Cook, and Karen Fraser Wyche, 215–34. Washington, DC: American Psychological Association.

Fitzpatrick, Kyle, and Jamie Grierson. 2019. "How Serious Are the Threats to UK MPs and Other Public Figures?" *Guardian*, September 26, 2019. Accessed November 30, 2021. Available at: https://www.theguardian.com/uk-news/2019/sep/26/how-serious-are-the-threats-to-uk-mps-and-other-public-figures.

Fjelde, Hanne, and Kristine Höglund. 2016. "Electoral Violence: The Emergence of a Research Field." *American Political Science Association Comparative Democratization Newsletter* 14, no. 2.

Folke, Olle, and Johanna Rickne. 2016. "The Glass Ceiling in Politics: Formalization and Empirical Tests." *Comparative Political Studies* 49, no. 5: 567–99.

Forsberg, Erika, and Louise Olsson. 2021. "Examining Gender Inequality and Armed Conflict at the Subnational Level." *Journal of Global Security Studies* 6, no. 2: ogaa023.

Forsyth, Miranda, and Richard Eves. 2015. "The Problems and Victims of Sorcery and Witchcraft Practices and Beliefs in Melanesia: An Introduction." In *Talking It Through:*

Responses to Sorcery and Witchcraft Beliefs and Practices in Melanesia, edited by Miranda Forsyth and Richard Eves, 1–19. Canberra: ANU Press.

Forum for Women in Democracy (FOWODE). 2018. "Deterred Not Barred: Unmasking Violence Against Women in the 2016 General Elections in Uganda." ISBN: 978-9970-14-019-0.

Frederick, John. 2010. "Sexual Abuse and Exploitation of Boys in South Asia: A Review of Research Findings, Legislation, Policy and Programme Responses." Working paper, UNICEF Innocenti Research Centre, April 30, 2010. Accessed October 2022. Available at: https://www.oecd-ilibrary.org/content/paper/f8e45fad-en.

Freedom House. 2021. *Freedom in the World 2021: Papua New Guinea*. Washington, DC: Freedom House.

Freidenberg, Flavia. 2017. *La Representación Política de Las Mujeres En México*. Mexico, D.F.: Instituto Nacional Electoral.

Freidenvall, Lenita, and Mona Lena Krook. 2011. "Gender Quotas in Sweden and France." In *Gender, Politics and Institutions*, edited by Mona Lena Krook and Fiona Mackay, 147–62. Basingstoke: Palgrave Macmillan.

Frenzel, Anna. 2017. *Politikernas Trygghetsundersökning 2017. Förtroendevaldas Utsatthet Och Oro För Trakasserier, Hot Och Våld 2016*. Stockholm: Bråttsförebyggande rådet.

Froio, Nicole. 2019. "Marielle, Presente!: A Movement Remembers." *Bitch Media*, March 14, 2019. Available at: https://www.bitchmedia.org/article/dispatch/remembering-marielle-franco.

Fulton, Sarah A., Cherie D. Maestas, L. Sandy Maisel, and Walter J. Stone. 2006. "The Sense of a Woman: Gender, Ambition, and the Decision to Run for Congress." *Political Research Quarterly* 59, no. 2: 235–48.

Fulu, Emma, Rachel Jewkes, Tim Roselli, and Claudia Garcia-Moreno. 2013a. "Prevalence of and Factors Associated with Male Perpetration of Intimate Partner Violence: Findings from the UN Multi-Country Cross-Sectional Study on Men and Violence in Asia and the Pacific." *Lancet Global Health* 1, no. 4: e187–e207.

Fulu, Emma, X. Warner, S. Miedema, Rachel Jewkes, Tim Roselli, and J. Lang. 2013b. "Why Do Some Men Use Violence against Women and How Can We Prevent It?" Quantitative findings from the United National multi-country study on men and violence in Asia and the Pacific, Partners for Prevention.

Funari, Renata. 2018. "Marielle Franco's Legacy Will Inspire Generations of Resistance in Rio." gal-dem, March 22, 2018.

Gallón, Natalie, and Matt Rivers. 2021. "At Least 88 Politicians Have Been Killed in Mexico since September." CNN, May 30, 2021. Accessed October 22, 2021. Available at: https://www.cnn.com/2021/05/30/americas/mexico-political-killings-intl/index.html.

Gavey, Nicola. 2005. *Just Sex? The Cultural Scaffolding of Rape*. New York: Routledge.

Gentry, Caron E., Laura J. Shepherd, and Laura Sjoberg, eds. 2019. *Routledge Handbook of Gender and Security*. London: Routledge.

Gercke, Marco. 2012. "Understanding Cybercrime: Phenomena, Challenges and Legal Response." International Telecommunication Union, September. Accessed November 2019. Available at: https://www.itu.int/ITU-D/cyb/cybersecurity/docs/Cybercrime%20legislation%20EV6.pdf.

Gibbs, Philip. 2012. "Engendered Violence and Witch-killing in Simbu." In *Engendering Violence in Papua New Guinea*, edited by Margaret Jolly, Christine Stewart, and Carolyn Brewer, 107–35. Canberra: ANU Press.

Gizelis, Theodora-Ismene. 2018. "Systematic Study of Gender, Conflict, and Peace." *Peace Economics, Peace Science and Public Policy* 24, no. 4: 20180038. https://doi.org/10.1515/peps-2018-0038.

Gizelis, Theodora-Ismene, and Louise Olsson, eds. 2015. *Gender, Peace and Security: Implementing UN Security Council Resolution 1325*. Abingdon: Routledge.

Glowacki, Laura, and Andrew Foote. 2019. "Vulgar Slur Painted across MP Catherine McKenna's Office." CBC News Online, October 24, 2019. Accessed October 2022. Available at: https://www.cbc.ca/news/canada/ottawa/catherine-mckenna-vandalism-office-1.5333420.

Goetz, Anne Marie, and Rob Jenkins. 2018. "Feminist Activism and the Politics of Reform: When and Why Do States Respond to Demands for Gender Equality Policies?" *Development and Change* 49, no. 3: 714–34.

Goldstein, Joshua. 2001. *War and Gender: How Gender Shapes the War System and Vice Versa*. Cambridge: Cambridge University Press.

Google. 2022. "Google Transparency Report." January. Accessed January 2022. Available at: https://transparencyreport.google.com/youtube-policy/removals.

Gorrell, Genevieve, Mark A. Greenwood, Ian Roberts, Diana Maynard, and Kalina Bontcheva. 2018. "Twits, Twats and Twaddle: Trends in Online Abuse towards UK Politicians." *Twelfth International AAAI Conference on Web and Social Media* 12, no. 1: 600–603.

Gottschall, Jonathan. 2004. "Explaining Wartime Rape." *Journal of Sex Research* 41, no. 2: 129–36.

Gray, Harriet. 2019. "The 'War'/'Not-War' Divide: Domestic Violence in the Preventing Sexual Violence Initiative." *British Journal of Politics and International Relations* 21, no. 1: 189–206.

Gray, Harriet, and Maria Stern. 2019. "Risky Dis/Entanglements: Torture and Sexual Violence in Conflict." *European Journal of International Relations* 25, no. 4: 1035–58.

Greiner, Ashley L., Katherine Albutt, Shada A. Rouhani, Jennifer Scott, Kirk Dombrowski, Michael J. VanRooyen, and Susan A. Bartels. 2014. "Respondent-Driven Sampling to Assess Outcomes of Sexual Violence: A Methodological Assessment." *American Journal of Epidemiology* 180, no. 5: 536–44.

Groves, Robert M. et al. 2009. *Survey Methodology*. 2nd ed. New Jersey: John Wiley & Sons Inc.

Guirola, Jamie. 2020. "Trans Women Say They Were Humiliated at Miami Jail After Getting Arrested at Protest," NBC Miami, September 8, 2020. Accessed October 2022. Available at: https://www.nbcmiami.com/news/local/trans-women-say-they-were-humiliated-at-miami-jail-after-getting-arrested-at-protest/2289766/.

Hafner-Burton, Emilie M., Susan D. Hyde, and Ryan S. Jablonski. 2014. "When Do Governments Resort to Election Violence?" *British Journal of Political Science* 44, no. 1: 149–79.

Håkansson, Sandra. 2021. "Do Women Pay a Higher Price for Power? Gender Bias in Political Violence in Sweden." *Journal of Politics* 83, no. 2: 515–31.

Halder, Debarati, and Karuppannan Jaishankar. 2011. "Cyber Gender Harassment and Secondary Victimization: A Comparative Analysis of the United States, the UK, and India." *Victims and Offenders* 6, no. 4: 386–98.

Haley, Nicole, and Ben Dierikx. 2013. "Guns, Money and Sex: Assessing the Impact of Electoral System Reform on Political Culture in Southern Highlands Province." In *Election 2007: The Shift to Limited Preferential Voting in Papua New Guinea*, edited by R. J. May, Ray Anere, Nicole Haley, and Katherine Wheen, 327–46. Canberra: ANU Press.

Haley, Nicole, and Robert Muggah. 2006. "Jumping the Gun? Reflections on Armed Violence in Papua New Guinea." *African Security Review* 15, no. 2: 38–56.

Haley, Nicole, and Kerry Zubrinich. 2013. "2012 Papua New Guinea General Elections Domestic Observation Report." Report prepared for Cardno Emerging Markets.

———. 2018. *2017 Papua New Guinea General Elections: Election Observation Report.* Canberra: Australian National University Department of Pacific Affairs.

Hardaker, Claire. 2013. "What Is Turning So Many Young Men into Trolls?" *Guardian*, August 3, 2013. Accessed November 30, 2021. Available at: http://www.theguardian.com/media/2013/aug/03/how-to-stop-trolls-social-media.

Harmer, Emily, and Karen Lumsden, eds. 2019. *Online Othering.* London: Palgrave Macmillan.

Harmon, Heidi. 2020. Interview by Sue Thomas and Rebekah Herrick. Telephone Interview. February 4, 2020.

———. n.d. Facebook page. Accessed February 19, 2020. Available at: https://www.facebook.com/permalink.php?story_fbid=10218414123997092&id=1013229765.

Hatebase. 2022. Hatebase. Accessed 2022. Available at: https://hatebase.org/.

Haynes, Suyin. 2018. "The Assassination of Brazilian Politician Marielle Franco Turned Her Into a Global Icon." *Time*, March 22, 2018.

Heilweil, Rebecca. 2021. "Facebook Is Finally Cracking Down Hard on Anti-Vaccine Content. It Is Facing an Uphill Battle." *Vox*, March 9, 2021. Accessed December 2021. Available at: https://www.vox.com/recode/22319681/vaccine-misinformation-facebook-instagram-spreading.

Hernández Estrada, Laura Lizbeth. 2017. "Rechazan Regreso de Alcaldesa de Chenalhó, Chiapas." *Televisa News*, March 13, 2017. Accessed March 13, 2017. Available at: http://noticieros.televisa.com/ultimas-noticias/estados/2017-03-16/rechazan-regreso-alcaldesa-chenalho-chiapas/.

Herrick, Rebekah, and Lori D. Franklin. 2019. "Is It Safe to Keep This Job? The Costs of Violence on the Psychological Health and Careers of U.S. Mayors." *Social Science Quarterly* 100, no. 6: 2047–58.

Herrick, Rebekah, and Sue Thomas. 2022. "Not Just Sticks and Stones: Psychological Abuse and Physical Violence among US State Senators." *Politics and Gender* 18, no. 2: 422–47.

Herrick, Rebekah, Sue Thomas, Lori Franklin, Marcia L. Godwin, Eveline Gnabasik, and Jean Reith Schroedel. 2019. "Physical Violence and Psychological Abuse against Female and Male Mayors in the United States." *Politics, Groups, and Identities* 9, no. 4: 681–98.

Hogan, Robert E. 2008. "Sex and the Statehouse: The Effects of Gender on Legislative Roll Call Voting." *Social Sciences Quarterly* 89, no. 4: 955–68.

Höglund, Kristine. 2009. "Electoral Violence in Conflict-Ridden Societies: Concepts, Causes, and Consequences." *Terrorism and Political Violence* 21, no. 3: 412–27.

Holman, Mirya R. 2014. "Sex and the City: Female Leaders and Spending on Social Welfare Programs in US Municipalities." *Journal of Urban Affairs* 36, no. 4: 701–15.

Hoover Green, Amelia. 2016. "The Commander's Dilemma: Creating and Controlling Armed Group Violence." *Journal of Peace Research* 53, no. 5: 619–32.

———. 2018. *The Commander's Dilemma. Violence and Restraint in Wartime.* Ithaca, NY: Cornell University Press.

House of Commons (Canada). 2014. *House of Commons Policy on Preventing and Addressing Harassment.* Accessed October 2022. Available at: https://www.ourcommons.ca/Content/Boie/pdf/policy_preventing_harassment-e.pdf.

———. 2016–2019. *Annual Report on the House of Commons Policy on Preventing and Addressing Harassment.*

———. 2021. "Members of the House of Commons Workplace Harassment and Violence Prevention Policy." January 28, 2021. Accessed October 2022. Available at: https://www.ourcommons.ca/content/boie/pdf/policy_preventing_harassment-e.pdf.

Hudson, Valerie M. 2012. *Sex and World Peace.* New York: Columbia University Press.

Hughes, Melanie M., Pamela Paxton, Amanda B. Clayton, and Pär Zetterberg. 2019. "Global Gender Quota Adoption, Implementation, and Reform." *Comparative Politics* 51, no. 2: 219–38.

Hultman, Lisa, and Karin Johansson. 2017. "Responding to Wartime Sexual Violence: UN Peacekeeping and the Protection Agenda." *Global Responsibility to Protect* 9, no. 2: 129–46.

Human Rights Watch. 2017. *World Report 2017: Events of 2016.* New York: Human Rights Watch.

iHollaback. 2022. iHollaback. Accessed 2022. Available at: https://www.ihollaback.org/.

Ingram, David, and Ben Collins. 2019. "Facebook Bans White Nationalism from Platform after Pressure from Civil Rights Groups." NBC News, March 27, 2019. Accessed November 2019. Available at: https://www.nbcnews.com/tech/tech-news/facebook-bans-white-nationalism-after-pressure-civil-rights-groups-n987991?cid=sm_npd_nn_tw_ma.

International Criminal Court. 2011. *Elements of Crimes.* The Hague: International Criminal Court.

International Foundation for Electoral Systems (IFES). 2017. *Violence against Women in Elections: A Framework for Assessment, Monitoring, and Response.* Arlington: IFES.

———. 2018. "Violence Against Women in Elections in Zimbabwe: An IFES Assessment." International Foundation for Electoral Systems. July 2018. Accessed December 2019. Available at: https://www.ifes.org/sites/default/files/vawie_in_zimbabwe_july_2018.pdf.

———. 2019. "Violence against Women in Elections." International Foundation for Electoral Systems.

Internet Rights and Principles Coalition. 2014. "The Charter of Human Rights and Principles for the Internet." Office of the United Nations High Commissioner for Human Rights (OHCHR), August 2014. Accessed November 2019. Available at: https://www.ohchr.org/Documents/Issues/Opinion/Communications/InternetPrinciplesAndRightsCoalition.pdf.

Inter-Parliamentary Union (IPU). 2016. "Sexism, Harassment, and Violence Against Women Parliamentarians." Brief, Accessed March 18, 2018. Available at: http://www.ipu.org/pdf/publications/ issuesbrief-e.pdf.

———. 2018. "Sexism, Harassment, and Violence against Women in Parliaments in Europe." Report. Accessed November 30, 2021. Available at: https://www.ipu.org/resources/publications/reports/2018-10/sexism-harassment-and-violence-against-women-in-parliaments-in-europe.

———. 2019. "Letter from the President of the French Senate to the President of the IPU on the Measures Taken to Combat Sexism, Harassment and Violence against Women in Parliament, 3 December 2018." In *Guidelines for the Elimination of Sexism, Harassment and Violence against Women in Parliament,* edited by Inter-Parliamentary Union (IPU), 23. Geneva: Inter-Parliamentary Union (IPU).

———. 2022. IPU Parline. "Global and Regional Averages of Women in National Parliaments." Interparliamentary Union Parline. Accessed October 2022. Available at: https://data.ipu.org/women-averages.

James, David V., Seema Sukhwal, Frank R. Farnham, Julie Evans, Claire Barrie, Alice Taylor, Simon P. Wilson. 2016. "Harassment and Stalking of Members of the United Kingdom Parliament: Associations and Consequences." *Journal of Forensic Psychiatry and Psychology* 27, no. 3: 309–30.

Jane, Emma A. 2014. "Your a Ugly, Whorish, Slut." *Feminist Media Studies* 14, no. 4: 531–46. https://doi.org/10.1080/14680777.2012.741073.

———. 2016. "Online Misogyny and Feminist Digilantism." *Continuum* 30, no. 3: 284–97.

JNE. 2015. *Reporte Sobre Resultados de La Encuesta de Acoso Político a Candidatas Regionales En Las Elecciones Regionales y Municipales 2014.* Lima, Perú: Jurado Nacional de Elecciones.

Johansson, Karin, and Lisa Hultman. 2019. "UN Peacekeeping and Protection from Sexual Violence." *Journal of Conflict Resolution* 63, no. 7: 1656–81.

Johnson, Kirsten, Jana Asher, Stephanie Kayden, Amisha Raja, Rajesh Panjabi, Charles Beadling, and Lynn Lawry. 2008. "Association of Combatant Status and Sexual Violence with Health and Mental Health Outcomes in Post-Conflict Liberia." *Journal of the American Medical Association* 300, no. 6: 676–90.

Johnson, Michael P. 1995. "Patriarchal Terrorism and Common Couple Violence: Two Forms of Violence against Women." *Journal of Marriage and Family* 57, no. 2: 283–94.

Johnston, Lisa G., and Keith Sabin. 2010. "Sampling Hard-to-Reach Populations with Respondent Driven Sampling." *Methodological Innovations Online* 5, no. 2: 38–48.

Joshi, Madhav, and Peter Krause, eds. 2018. *Understanding Quality Peace.* Milton Park: Routledge.

Joshi, Madhav, and Louise Olsson. 2021. "War Termination and Women's Political Rights." *Social Science Research* 94: 102523.

Kam, Christopher. 2009. *Party Discipline and Parliamentary Politics.* Cambridge: Cambridge University Press.

Kaplow, Jeffrey. 2016. "The Negotiation Calculus: Why Parties to Civil Conflict Refuse to Talk." *International Studies Quarterly* 60, no. 1: 38–46.

Karlsson, David. 2006. *Den Svenske Borgmästaren: Kommunstyrelsens Ordförande Och Den Lokala Demokratin / The Swedish Mayor.* Gothenburg, Sweden: School of Public Administration, Gothenburg University.

Karlsson, David, and Mikael Gilljam. 2014. *Kommun- Och Landstingsfullmäktigeundersökningen (KOLFU) 2012.* Stockholm: Santérus förlag.

Kauppinen, Antti. 2015. "Hate and Punishment." *Journal of Interpersonal Violence* 30, no. 10: 1719–37.

Keipi, Teo, Matti Näsi, Atte Oksanen, and Pekka Räsänen. 2017. *Online Hate and Harmful Content: Cross-National Perspectives.* London: Routledge.

Kellermann, A. L., and J. A. Mercy. 1992. "Men, Women, and Murder: Gender-Specific Differences in Rates of Fatal Violence and Victimization." *Journal of Trauma* 33, no. 1 (July): 1–5.

Kellow, Tim. 2010. *Women, Elections and Violence in West Africa: Assessing Women's Political Participation in Liberia and Sierra Leone.* London: International Alert.

Kelly, Liz. 1987. "The Continuum of Sexual Violence." In *Women, Violence and Social Control*, edited by J. Hanmer and M. Maynard, 46–60. Atlantic Highlands, NJ: Humanities Press International.

———. 1988a. "How Women Define Their Experiences of Violence." In *Feminist Perspectives on Wife Abuse*, edited by K. Yllö and M. Bograd, 114–32. New York: SAGE.

———. 1988b. *Surviving Sexual Violence.* Minneapolis: University of Minnesota Press.

———. 2012. "Preface: Standing the Test of Time? Reflections on the Concept of the Continuum of Sexual Violence." In *Handbook on Sexual Violence*, edited by Jennifer M. Brown and Sandra L. Walklate, 797–821. New York: Routledge.

Keohane, Robert O. 1998. "Beyond Dichotomy: Conversations Between International Relations and Feminist Theory." *International Studies Quarterly* 42, no. 2: 193–98.

KhosraviNik, Majid. 2017. "Social Media Critical Discourse Studies (SM–CDS)." In *Handbook of Critical Discourse Analysis*, edited by John Flowerdew and John E. Richardson, 583–96. London: Routledge.

KhosraviNik, Majid, and Eleonora Esposito. 2018. "Online Hate, Digital Discourse and Critique: Exploring Digitally Mediated Discursive Practices of Gender-Based Hostility." *Lodz Papers in Pragmatics* 14, no. 1: 45–68.

Kilger, Max. 2016. "Interventions, Policies, and Future Research Directions in Cybercrime." In *The Wiley Handbook on the Psychology of Violence*, edited by Carlos A. Cuevas and Callie Marie Rennison, 604–22. Chichester, UK: Wiley-Blackwell.

Kilpatrick, Dean G. 2004. "What Is Violence Against Women: Defining and Measuring the Problem." *Journal of Interpersonal Violence* 19, no. 11: 1209–34.

Kirschner, Shanna, and Adam Miller. 2019. "Does Peacekeeping Really Bring Peace? Peacekeepers and Combatant-Perpetrated Sexual Violence in Civil Wars." *Journal of Conflict Resolution* 63, no. 9: 2043–70.

Kishi, Roudabeh. 2015. "The Strategic Use of Unidentified Armed Groups in Conflict Zones." ACLED, April 9, 2015.

———. 2021. "Violence Targeting Women in Politics: Trends in Targets, Types, and Perpetrators of Political Violence." ACLED, December 8, 2021.

Kishi, Roudabeh, and Louise Olsson. 2019. "How Does Political Violence Target Women?" PRIO GPS Policy Brief, 2, February 2019.

———. 2022. "Violence Targeting Women in Politics: Implications for the UN Security Council." PRIO GPS Policy Brief, 2. February 2022.

Kishi, Roudabeh, Melissa Pavlik, and Hilary Matfess. 2019. "'Terribly and Terrifyingly Normal': Political Violence Targeting Women." ACLED, May 29, 2019.

Koos, Carlo. 2018. "Decay or Resilience? The Long-Term Social Consequences of Conflict-Related Sexual Violence in Sierra Leone." *World Politics* 70, no. 2: 194–238.

Krantz, Joakim, Lisa Wallin, and Sanna Wallin. 2012. *Politikernas trygghetsundersökning*. Stockholm: Brottsförebyggande rådet.

Krause, Jana, Werner Krause, and Piia Bränfors. 2018. "Women's Participation in Peace Negotiations and the Durability of Peace." *International Interactions* 44, no. 6: 985–1016.

Kreft, Anne-Kathrin. 2017. "The Gender Mainstreaming Gap: Security Council Resolution 1325 and UN Peacekeeping Mandates." *International Peacekeeping* 24, no. 1: 132–58.

———. 2019. "Responding to Sexual Violence: Women's Mobilization in War." *Journal of Peace Research* 56, no. 2: 220–33.

———. 2020. "Civil Society Perspectives on Sexual Violence in Conflict: Patriarchy and War Strategy in Colombia." *International Affairs* 96, no. 2: 457–78.

Krook, Mona Lena. 2016. "Contesting Gender Quotas: Dynamics of Resistance." *Politics, Groups, and Identities* 4, no. 2: 268–83.

———. 2017. "Violence against Women in Politics." *Journal of Democracy* 28, no. 1: 74–88.

———. 2018. "Violence against Women in Politics: A Rising Global Trend." *Politics and Gender* 14, no. 4: 673–76.

———. 2019. "Global Feminist Collaborations and the Concept of Violence against Women in Politics." *Journal of International Affairs* 72, no. 2: 77–94.

———. 2020. *Violence against Women in Politics*. New York: Oxford University Press.

Krook, Mona Lena, and Juliana Restrepo Sanín. 2016a. "Gender and Political Violence in Latin America: Concepts, Debates and Solutions." *Política y Gobierno* 23, no. 1: 127–62.

———. 2016b. "Violence against Women in Politics: A Defense of the Concept." *Política y Gobierno* 23, no. 2: 459–90.

———. 2020. "The Cost of Doing Politics? Analyzing Violence and Harassment against Female Politicians." *Perspectives on Politics* 18, no. 3: 740–55.

Krug, Etienne G., James A. Mercy, Linda L. Dahlberg, and Anthony B. Zwi. 2002. "The World Report on Violence and Health." *Lancet* 360, no. 9339: 1083–88.

Kuperberg, Rebecca. 2018. "Intersectional Violence against Women in Politics." *Politics and Gender* 14, no. 4: 685–90. https://doi.org/https://doi.org/10.1017/S1743923X18000612.

———. 2021. "Incongruous and Illegitimate: Antisemitic and Islamophobic Semiotic Violence against Women in Politics in the United Kingdom." *Journal of Language Aggression and Conflict* 9, no. 1: 100–26. https://doi.org/10.1075/jlac.00055.kup.

Lake, Milli, and Sarah Parkinson. 2017. "The Ethics of Fieldwork Preparedness." Political Violence at a Glance, June 5, 2017. Accessed October 2022. Available at: https://politicalviolenceataglance.org/2017/06/05/the-ethics-of-fieldwork-preparedness/.

Lange, Patricia. 2006. "What Is Your Claim to Flame?" First Monday 11, no. 9. Accessed November 30, 2021. Available at: http://firstmonday.org/ojs/index.php/fm/article/view/1393.

Langton, Rae. 2012. "Beyond Belief: Pragmatics in Hate Speech and Pornography." In *Speech and Harm. Controversies over Free Speech*, edited by Ishani Maitra and Mary Kate McGowan, 72–93. Oxford: Oxford University Press.

Lawless, Jennifer L. 2012. *Becoming a Candidate: Political Ambition and the Decision to Run for Office*. New York: Cambridge University Press.

Leatherman, Janie. 2011. *Sexual Violence and Armed Conflict*. Cambridge, MA: Polity.

Leiby, Michele. 2009. "Digging in the Archives: The Promise and Perils of Primary Documents." *Politics and Society* 37, no. 1: 75–99.

———. 2018. "Uncovering Men's Narratives of Conflict-Related Sexual Violence." In *Sexual Violence against Men and Boys in Global Politics*, edited by Marysia Zalewski, Paula Drumond, Elisabeth Prügl, and Maria Stern, 137–51. London: Routledge.

Levesley, David. 2017. "Diane Abbott's Staff Members Past and Present Share the Racism They See on a Daily Basis." Inews.co.uk, July 31, 2017. Accessed November 30, 2021. Available at: https://inews.co.uk/news/diane-abbotts-past-present-staff-members-share-racism-see-daily-basis-522195.

Lewis, Chloé. 2014. "Systemic Silencing: Addressing Sexual Violence against Men and Boys in Armed Conflict and its Aftermath." In *Rethinking Peacekeeping, Gender Equality and Collective Security*, edited by G. Heathcote and D. Otto, 203–23. London: Palgrave Macmillan.

Lewis, Ruth, Michael Rowe, and Clare Wiper. 2016. "Online Abuse of Feminists as an Emerging Form of Violence against Women and Girls." *British Journal of Criminology* 57, no. 6: 1462–81. https://doi.org/10.1093/bjc/azw073.

Liu, Bing. 2015. *Sentiment Analysis: Mining Opinions, Sentiments, and Emotions*. Cambridge: Cambridge University Press.

Loader, Brian D., and Dan Mercea. 2011. "Networking Democracy? Social Media Innovations and Participatory Politics." *Information, Communication and Society* 14, no. 6: 757–59.

Loken, Meredith. 2017. "Rethinking Rape: The Role of Women in Wartime Violence." *Security Studies* 26, no. 1: 60–92.

Lonsway, Kimberly, Lilia Cortina, and Vicki Magley. 2008. "Sexual Harassment Mythology: Definition, Conceptualization, and Measurement" *Sex Roles* 58, no. 9: 599–615.

Lumsden, Karen, and Heather Morgan. 2017. "Media Framing of Trolling and Online Abuse: Silencing Strategies, Symbolic Violence, and Victim Blaming." *Feminist Media Studies* 17, no. 6: 926–40.

Lundgren, Eva. 2002. *Captured Queen: Men's Violence Against Women in "Equal" Sweden: A Prevalence Study*. Stockholm: Fritzes Offtliga Publikationer.

Lupu, Noam, and Kristin Michelitch. 2018. "Advances in Survey Methods for the Developing World." *Annual Review of Political Science* 21: 195–214.

Maedl, Anna. 2011. "Rape as Weapon of War in the Eastern DRC?: The Victims' Perspective." *Human Rights Quarterly* 33, no. 1: 128–47.

Maestas, Cherie D., Sarah Fulton, L. Sandy Maisel, and Walter J. Stone. 2006. "When to Risk It? Institutions, Ambitions, and the Decision to Run for the US House." *American Political Science Review* 100, no. 2: 195–208.

Manne, Kate. 2017. *Down Girl: The Logic of Misogyny*. Oxford: Oxford University Press.

Mantilla, Karla. 2013. "Gendertrolling: Misogyny Adapts to New Media." *Feminist Studies* 39, no. 2: 563–70.

Marland, Alex. 2019. "The Stifling Conformity of Party Discipline." Policy Options Online, March 21, 2019. Accessed October 2022. Available at: https://policyoptions.irpp.org/magazines/march-2019/the-stifling-conformity-of-party-discipline/.

Martinez, Diana. 2018. "Suman 200 casos de violencia política de género: FEPADE." El Heraldo de México. Accessed November 12, 2019. Available at: https://heraldodemexico.com.mx/pais/suman-200-casos-de-violencia-politica-de-genero-fepade/.

Matfess, Hilary. 2020. "Part and Parcel? Examining Al Shabaab and Boko Haram's Violence Targeting Civilians and Violence Targeting Women." *Studies in Conflict and Terrorism* (June): 1–19.

Mazzoleni, Gianpietro, and Winfried Schulz. 1999. "Mediatization of Politics: A Challenge for Democracy?" *Political Communication* 16, no. 3: 247–61.

McCall, Leslie. 2005. "The Complexity of Intersectionality." *Signs: Journal of Women in Culture and Society* 30, no. 3: 1771–800.

McCarthy, John, Larissa Titarenko, Clark McPhail, Patrick Rafail, and Boguslaw Augustyn. 2008. "Assessing Stability in the Patterns of Selection Bias in Newspaper Coverage of Protest During the Transition from Communism in Belarus*." *Mobilization: An International Quarterly* 13, no. 2: 127–46.

McDoom, Omar S. 2013. "Who Killed in Rwanda's Genocide? Micro-Space, Social Influence and Individual Participation in Intergroup Violence." *Journal of Peace Research* 50, no. 4: 453–67.

McLoughlin, Liam, and Stephen Ward. 2017. "Turds, Traitors and Tossers: The Abuse of UK MPs via Twitter." ECPR Joint Sessions of Workshops. Available at: https://ecpr.eu/Filestore/PaperProposal/4f8bacf9-27a8-44b3-9132-dd5fa9fdf70f.pdf.

Media Smarts. n.d. Online Hate and Canadian Law. Accessed December 2019. Available at: https://mediasmarts.ca/digital-media-literacy/digital-issues/online-hate/online-hate-canadian-law.

Megarry, Jessica. 2014. "Online Incivility or Sexual Harassment? Conceptualising Women's Experiences in the Digital Age." *Women's Studies International Forum* 47, no. A: 46–55. https://doi.org/10.1016/j.wsif.2014.07.012.

Meger, Sara. 2016a. "The Fetishization of Sexual Violence in International Security." *International Studies Quarterly* 60, no. 1: 149–59.

———. 2016b. *Rape Loot Pillage: The Political Economy of Sexual Violence in Armed Conflict*. Oxford: Oxford University Press.

———. 2018. "The Political Economy of Sexual Violence against Men and Boys in Armed Conflict." In *Sexual Violence Against Men in Global Politics*, edited by Marysia Zalewski, Paula Drumond, Elisabeth Prügl, and Maria Stern, 118–32. London: Routledge.

Melander, Erik. 2005. "Gender Equality and Intrastate Armed Conflict." *International Studies Quarterly* 49, no. 4: 695–714.

———. 2016. "Gender and Civil War." In *What Do We Know about Civil Wars?*, edited by D. T. Mason and S. McLaughlin Mitchell, 197–214. Lanham, MD: Rowman and Littlefield.

Melin, Molly, and Isak Svensson. 2009. "Incentives for Talking: Accepting Mediation in International and Civil Wars." *International Interactions* 35, no. 3: 249–71.

Mendelsohn, Beniamin. 1976. "Victimology and Contemporary Society's Trends." *Victimology* 1, no. 1: 8–28.

Merriam-Webster. 2020. s.v. "violence." *Merriam-Webster.com Dictionary*. Accessed September 17, 2020. Available at: https://www.merriam-webster.com/dictionary/violence.

Miranda, Fernando. 2019. "Violencia política de género, ningún caso se ha resuelto." El Universal, August 3, 2019. Accessed November 12, 2019. Available at: https://www.eluniversal.com.mx/estados/violencia-politica-de-genero-ningun-caso-se-ha-resuelto.

Moldova.org. 2019. "Unei primare i s-ar fi tăiat intenționat frâna mașinei: 'Sunt cu piciorul frânt, dar în viață.'" Moldova.org, August 17, 2019. Accessed October 2022. Available at: https://www.moldova.org/unei-primare-s-ar-fi-taiat-intentionat-frana-masinei-sunt-cu-piciorul-frant-dar-viata/.

Monárrez Fragoso, Julia E. 2018. "Feminicide: Impunity for the Perpetrators and Injustice for the Victims." In *The Palgrave Handbook of Criminology and the Global South*, edited by Kerry Carrington, Russell Hogg, John Scott, and Máximo Sozzo, 913–29. Cham: Springer International.

Montin, Stig. 2014. "Municipalities, Regions and County Councils in Sweden: Actors and Institutions." Working paper, School of Public Administration, University of Gothenburg.

Moxley-Goldsmith, Taya. 2005. "Boys in the Basement: Male Victims of Commercial Sexual Exploitation." *American Prosecutors Research Institute* 2, no. 1: 83–84.

Musgrove, George Derek. 2012. *Rumor, Repression, and Racial Politics: How the Harassment of Black Elected Officials Shaped Post-Civil Rights America*. Athens: University of Georgia Press.

Muvumba Sellström, Angela. 2015. *Stronger than Justice: Armed Group Impunity for Sexual Violence*. Uppsala: Uppsala University.

Myrttinen, Henri. 2018. "Languages of Castration–Male Genital Mutilation in Conflict and its Embedded Messages." In *Sexual Violence Against Men in Global Politics*, edited by Marysia Zalewski, Paula Drumond, Elisabeth Prügl, and Maria Stern, 71–88. London: Routledge.

Nadim, Marjan, and Audun Fladmoe. 2019. "Silencing Women? Gender and Online Harassment." *Social Science Computer Review* 39, no. 2: 245–58.

Nagel, Robert. 2019. "Talking to the Shameless? Sexual Violence and Mediation in Intrastate Conflicts." *Journal of Conflict Resolution* 63, no. 8: 1832–59.

———. 2021a. "Conflict-Related Sexual violence and the Re-Escalation of Lethal Violence." *International Studies Quarterly* 65, no. 1: 56–68.

———. 2021b. "Gendered Preferences: How Women's Inclusion in Society Shapes Negotiation Occurrence in Intrastate Conflicts." *Journal of Peace Research* 58, no. 3: 433–48.

National Democratic Institute (NDI). 2018a. "#NotTheCost Programme Guidance for Stopping Violence Against Women in Politics." Report, Washington DC, NDI. Accessed November 30, 2021. Available at: https://www.ndi.org/sites/default/files/not-the-cost-program-guidance-final.pdf.

———. 2018b. "No Party to Violence: Analyzing Violence against Women in Political Parties." National Democratic Institute, March 19, 2018.

———. 2020. "#NotTheCost: Qualitative Research Report on Violence against Women in Politics in Fiji, Papua New Guinea and Solomon Islands." Report, Washington, DC, NDI.

NBC. 2019. "Lawmakers Condemn Online Threats Against State Senator." October 22, 2019. Accessed February 17, 2020. Available at: https://www.nbcconnecticut.com/news/local/lawmakers-condemn-online-threats-against-state-senator/1942113/.

News18.com. 2018. "Rape Threat to Daughter on Twitter, Cong's Priyanka Chaturvedi Files Complaint." News18.com, July 2, 2018. Accessed November 30, 2021. Available at: https://www.news18.com/news/india/congress-spokesperson-approaches-police-after-rape-threat-to-daughter-on-twitter-1798741.html.

Ní Aoláin, Fionnuala. 2000. "Rethinking the Concept of Harm and Legal Categorizations of Sexual Violence During War." *Theoretical Inquiries in Law* 1, no. 2: 307–40.

Nigam, Shalu. 2014. "Violence, Protest and Change: A Socio-Legal Analysis of Extraordinary Mobilization after the 2012 Delhi Gang Rape Case." SSRN Scholarly Paper, Rochester, NY, Social Science Research Network.

NIMD. 2016. *Mujeres y Participación Política En Colombia: El Fenómeno de La Violencia Contra Las Mujeres En Política.* Bogotá, Colombia: Netherlands Institute for Multiparty Democracy.

Nooraie, Yousefi Reza, Joanna E. M. Sale, Alexandra Marin, and Lori E. Ross. 2020. "Social Network Analysis: An Example of Fusion Between Quantitative and Qualitative Methods." *Journal of Mixed Methods Research* 14, no. 1: 110–24.

Norris, Pippa. 2013. "The New Research Agenda Studying Electoral Integrity." *Electoral Studies*, 32, no. 4: 563–75.

———. 2014. *Why Electoral Integrity Matters.* New York: Cambridge University Press.

Norris, Pippa, Richard W. Frank, and Ferran Martínez i Coma. 2015. *Contentious Elections: From Ballots to Barricades.* New York: Routledge University Press.

Nussbaum, Martha C. 2010. "Objectification and Internet Misogyny." In *The Offensive Internet*, edited by S. Levmore and M. C. Nussbaum, 68–87. Cambridge, MA: Harvard University Press.

O'Brien, Diana Z. 2015. "Rising to the Top: Gender, Political Performance, and Party Leadership in Parliamentary Democracies." *American Journal of Political Science* 59, no. 4: 1022–39.

Observatorio de Paridad Democrática. 2017. "Reglamento para El Trámite de Recepción de Renuncias y Denuncias Por Acoso y Violencia Política de Mujeres Candidatas, Electas o en Función Política Pública." Accessed October 2022. Available at: https://www.scribd.com/document/355465671/Reglamento-para-el-tramite-de-recepcion-de-renuncias-y-denuncias-por-acoso-y-violencia-politica-de-mujeres-candidatas-electas-o-en-funcion-politica-p.

OHCHR and UN Women. 2018. "Violence against Women in Politics: Expert Group Meeting Report and Recommendations." Report, United Nations Office of the High Commissioner on Human Rights (OHCHR) and United Nations Entity for Gender Equality and the Empowerment of Women (UN Women).

Okimoto, Tyler G., and Victoria L. Brescoll. 2010. "The Price of Power: Power Seeking and Backlash against Female Politicians." *Personality and Social Psychology Bulletin* 36, no. 7: 923–36.

Olsson, Louise. 1998. "Female Combatants." Department of Peace and Conflict Research, Uppsala University.

———. 2000. "Mainstreaming Gender in Multidimensional Peacekeeping: A Field Perspective." *International Peacekeeping* 7, no. 3: 1–16.

———. 2009. *Gender Equality and United Nations Peace Operations in Timor Leste.* Leiden: Brill.

Olsson, Louise, and Theodora-Ismene Gizelis. 2015. *Gender, Peace and Security: Implementing UN Security Council Resolution 1325.* London: Routledge.

Olsson, Louise, Angela Muvumba Sellström, Stephen Moncrief, Karin Johansson, Walter Lotze, Chiara Ruffa, Amelia Hoover Green, Ann-Kristin Sjöberg, Roudabeh Kishi, and Elisabeth J. Wood. 2020. "Peacekeeping Prevention: Strengthening Efforts to Preempt Conflict-related Sexual Violence." *International Peacekeeping* 27, no. 4: 517–85.

Omni. 2020. "Brandattentat mot KD-politiker: 'Känns otryggt,'" Omni, July 26, 2020. Accessed October 2022. Available at: https://omni.se/brandattentat-mot-kdpolitiker -kanns-otryggt/a/zGd9Lv.

O'Neill, Brenda, Scott Pruysers, and David K. Stewart. 2019. "Glass Cliffs or Partisan Pressure? Examining Gender and Party Leader Tenures and Exits." *Political Studies* 69, no. 2: 257–77.

Órgano Electoral Plurinacional (OEP). n.d. "Observatorio de Paridad Democrática." Accessed October 2022. Available at: http://observatorioparidaddemocratica.oep.org .bo/Destacados/El-TSE-presentAs-el-proyecto-de-Ley-de-Organizaciones-PolAsticas.

Østby, Gudrun, Michele Leiby, and Ragnhild Nordås. 2019. "The Legacy of Wartime Violence on Intimate-Partner Abuse: Microlevel Evidence from Peru, 1980–2009." *International Studies Quarterly* 63, no. 1: 1–14.

Pacific Islands Forum. 2017. *Pacific Islands Forum Election Observer Report: 2017 Papua New Guinea National Elections.* Suva: Pacific Islands Forum Secretariat.

Page, Benjamin I., and Robert Y. Shapiro. 1992. *The Rational Public: Fifty Years of Trends in Americans' Public Preferences.* Chicago: University of Chicago Press.

Pain, Rachel. 2014. "Everyday Terrorism." *Progress in Human Geography* 38, no. 4: 531–50.

Pantaleo, Diane, and Nate Chute. 2020. "'Anti-Feminist Lawyer' Identified as Primary Suspect in Shooting at Federal Judge Esther Salas' Home," *USA Today*, August 3, 2020. Accessed October 2022. Available at: https://www.usatoday.com/story/news/nation /2020/07/20/esther-salas-mark-anderl-shooting-new-jersey-home/5470802002/.

Patterson, Thomas E. 2016. Social "Media: Advancing Women in Politics? Women In Parliaments Global Forum." Accessed November 30, 2021. Available at: http://www .w20-germany.org/fileadmin/user_upload/documents/WIP-Harvard-Facebook-Study _Oct2016.pdf.

PEN America. 2022. "Online Harassment Field Manual." Accessed January 2022. Available at: https://onlineharassmentfieldmanual.pen.org/.

Penny, Laurie. 2014. *Unspeakable Things: Sex, Lies and Revolution.* New York: Bloomsbury.

Perloff-Giles, Alexandra. 2018. "Transnational Cyber Offenses: Overcoming Jurisdictional Challenges." *Yale Journal of International Law* 43: 191–227.

Person, Ethel Spector. 2006. "Masculinities, Plural." *Journal of the American Psychoanalytic Association* 54, no. 4: 1165–86.

Peterson, Spike. 1999. "Political Identities/Nationalism as Heterosexism." *International Feminist Journal of Politics* 1, no. 1: 34–65.

Phillips, Anne. 1995. *The Politics of Presence*. New York: Oxford University Press.

Picq, Manuela Lavinas, and Markus Thiel. 2015. *Sexualities in World Politics: How LGBTQ Claims Shape International Relations*. London: Routledge.

Piscopo, Jennifer M. 2016. "State Capacity, Criminal Justice, and Political Rights." *Política y Gobierno* 23, no. 2: 437–58.

Piscopo, Jennifer M., and Denise M. Walsh. 2019. "Introduction." *Signs: Journal of Women in Culture and Society* 45, no. 2: 265–78.

Pitkin, Hanna Fenichel. 1967. *The Concept of Representation*. Berkeley: University of California Press.

Plümper, Thomas, and Neumayer, Eric. 2006. "The Unequal Burden of War: The Effect of Armed Conflict on the Gender Gap in Life Expectancy." *International Organization* 60, no. 3: 723–54.

Porter, Holly. 2015. "After Rape: Comparing Civilian and Combatant Perpetrated Crime in Northern Uganda." *Women's Studies International Forum* 51 (July): 81–90.

Powell, Anastasia, and Nicola Henry. 2017. *Sexual Violence in a Digital Age*. New York: Springer.

Price, Melanye. 2016. "3 Ways to Tell if Your Distaste For Hillary Clinton Is Sexist." Ms. Blog, March 17, 2016. October 2022. Available at: https://msmagazine.com/2016/03/17/3-ways-to-tell-if-your-distaste-for-hillary-clinton-is-sexist/.

Puwar, Nirmal. 2004. *Space Invaders: Race, Gender and Bodies Out of Place*. Oxford: Berg.

Raleigh, Clionadh. 2014. "Political Hierarchies and Landscapes of Conflict across Africa." *Political Geography* 42 (September): 92–103.

Raleigh, Clionadh, Andrew Linke, Håvard Hegre, and Joakim Karlsen. 2010. "Introducing ACLED: An Armed Conflict Location and Event Dataset: Special Data Feature." *Journal of Peace Research* 47 no. 5: 651–60.

Rauschenbach, Mascha, and Katrin Paula. 2019. "Intimidating Voters with Violence and Mobilizing Them with Clientelism." *Journal of Peace Research* 56, no. 5: 682–96.

Rawlinson, Kevin. 2018. "Labour MP Calls for End to Online Anonymity after '600 Rape Threats.'" *Guardian*, June 11, 2018. Accessed November 30, 2021. Available at: https://www.theguardian.com/society/2018/jun/11/labour-mp-jess-phillips-calls-for-end-to-online-anonymity-after-600-threats.

Rein Venegas, Tatiana. 2019. "Violence Against Women in Politics: An Analysis from the Chilean Electoral Campaign in Twitter." European Conference of Politics and Gender, Amsterdam.

Restrepo, Elvira. 2016. "Leaders against All Odds: Women Victims of Conflict in Colombia." *Palgrave Communications* 2 (May): 16014.

Restrepo Sanín, Juliana. 2018. "Violence against Women in Politics in Latin America." Ph.D. diss., Rutgers University. Available at: https://rucore.libraries.rutgers.edu/rutgers-lib/59200/.

———. 2021. "Latin America Leads the Way in Fighting Violence and Harassment against Women in Politics." *European Journal of Politics and Gender* 4, no. 3: 463–65.

———. 2022. "Criminalizing Violence against Women in Politics: Innovation, Diffusion, and Transformation." *Politics and Gender* 18, no. 1: 1–32.

Rheault, Ludovic, Erica Rayment, and Andreea Musulan. 2019. "Politicians in the Line of Fire: Incivility and the Treatment of Women on Social Media." *Research and Politics* 6, no. 1: 1–7.

Rojas Valverde, María Eugenia. 2010. "Gender-Based Political Harassment and Violence: Effects on the Political Work and Public Roles of Women." *New Solutions* 230, no. 4: 527–35.

Romano, Stephen J., Micòl E. Levi-Minzi, Eugene A. Rugala, and Vincent B. Van Hasselt. 2011. "Workplace Violence Prevention: Readiness and Response." FBI, January 1, 2011. Accessed October 2022. Available at: https://leb.fbi.gov/articles/featured-articles /workplace-violence-prevention-readiness-and-response.

Rudman, Laurie A., and Kimberly Fairchild. 2004. "Reactions to Counterstereotypic Behavior: The Role of Backlash in Cultural Stereotype Maintenance." *Journal of Personality and Social Psychology* 87, no. 2: 157–76.

Rudman, Laurie A., and Peter Glick. 1999. "Feminized Management and Backlash toward Agentic Women: The Hidden Costs to Women of a Kinder, Gentler Image of Middle Managers." *Journal of Personality and Social Psychology* 77, no. 5: 1004–10.

Rudman, Laurie A., Corinne A. Moss-Racusin, Julie E. Phelan, and Sanne Nauts. 2012. "Status Incongruity and Backlash Effects: Defending the Gender Hierarchy Motivates Prejudice against Female Leaders." *Journal of Experimental Social Psychology* 48, no. 1: 165–79.

Ruiz, Damaris, and Belén Sobrino. 2018. "Breaking the Mould: Changing Belief Systems and Gender Norms to Eliminate Violence against Women." Oxfam. Accessed October 2022. Available at: https://oxfamilibrary.openrepository.com/bitstream/handle /10546/620524/rr-breaking-the-mould-250718-summ-en.pdf.

Russell, Suzanne. 2020. "Son of US District Judge Esther Salas Killed, Husband Shot in Their New Jersey Home; Suspect Found Dead." *USA Today*, July 21, 2020. Accessed October 2022. Available at: https://www.usatoday.com/story/news/nation/2020/07/20 /esther-salas-son-federal-judge-killed-husband-shot-new-jersey/5470403002/?utm _campaign=snd-autopilot.

Sabbagh, Dan. 2019. "'Death Threats Every Single Day': MPs on Effect of Brexit Vote." Guardian, March 5, 2019. Accessed November 30, 2021. Available at: https://www.the guardian.com/politics/2019/mar/05/death-threats-every-single-day-mps-on-effect-of -brexit-vote.

Salguero, Elizabeth. 2008. *Agenda Política Desde Las Mujeres 2008–2011*. La Paz, Bolivia: UN.

Samara Centre for Democracy. 2016. "Cheering or Jeering? Members of Parliament Open Up about Civility in the House of Commons." Report, Samara's Democracy 360: Leadership Series, Toronto, Canada.

Sanchez, Olga Amparo, Jose Nicholas Lopez Vivas, Diana Rubriche Cardenas, and Maria del Pilar Rengifo Cano. 2011. "First Survey on the Prevalence of Sexual Violence against Women in the Context of the Colombian Armed Conflict 2001–2009." Executive Summary. Accessed October 2022. Available at: http://www.peacewomen.org/assets/file /Resources/NGO/vaw_violenceagainstwomenincolombiaarmedconflict_2011.pdf.

Sandor, Adam. 2020. "The Power of Rumour(s) in International Interventions: MINUS-MA's Management of Mali's Rumour mill." *International Affairs* 96, no. 4: 913–34.

Sandvik, Kristin Bergtora. 2018. "Gendering Violent Pluralism: Women's Political Organising in Latin America." *Third World Thematics: A TWQ Journal* 3, no. 2: 244–59.

Saner, Emine. 2016. "Vile Online Abuse against Female MPs 'Needs to Be Challenged Now.'" *Guardian*, June 18, 2016. Accessed November 30, 2021. Available at: https://www .theguardian.com/technology/2016/jun/18/vile-online-abuse-against-women-mps -needs-to-be-challenged-now.

Sarkeesian, Anita. 2012. "Anita Sarkeesian at TEDxWomen 2012." Video, TEDxWomen.
———. 2015. "Stop the Trolls. Women Fight Back Online Harassment." Video, Women in the World. Accessed November 30, 2021. Available at: https://www.youtube.com /watch?v=BGrlk8_kevI.

Scarry, Elaine. 1985. *The Body in Pain: The Making and Unmaking of the World*. Oxford: Oxford University Press.

Schaftenaar, Susanne. 2017. "How (Wo)men Rebel: Exploring the Effect of Gender Equality on Nonviolent and Armed Conflict Onset." *Journal of Peace Research* 54, no. 6: 762–76.

Schedler, Andreas. 2006. *Electoral Authoritarianism*. Boulder, CO: Lynne Rienner.

Schneider, Paige L., and David Carroll. 2020. "Conceptualizing More Inclusive Elections: Violence against Women in Elections and Gendered Election Violence." *Policy Studies* 41, no. 2, 3: 172–89.

Schroeder, Jared. 2018. "Are Bots Entitled to Free Speech?" Columbia Journalism Review, May 24, 2018. Accessed October 2022. Available at: https://www.cjr.org/innovations /are-bots-entitled-to-free-speech.php.

Schulz, Philipp. 2018. "The 'Ethical Loneliness' of Male Sexual Violence Survivors in Northern Uganda: Gendered Reflections on Silencing." *International Feminist Journal of Politics* 20, no. 4: 583–601.

———. 2020. *Male Survivors of Wartime Sexual Violence: Perspectives from Northern Uganda*. Oakland: University of California Press.

Schulz, Philipp, and Heleen Touquet. 2020. "Queering Explanatory Frameworks for Wartime Sexual Violence against Men." *International Affairs* 96, no. 5: 1169–87.

Schwindt-Bayer, Leslie A., ed. 2018. *Gender and Representation in Latin America*. New York: Oxford University Press.

Scott, John, and Peter J. Carrington. 2011. *The SAGE Handbook of Social Network Analysis*. London: SAGE.

Shames, Shauna. 2017. *Out of the Running*. New York: New York University Press.

#ShePersisted. 2022. #ShePersisted. Accessed January 2022. Available at: https://www .she-persisted.org/.

Sivakumaran, Sandesh. 2007. "Sexual Violence against Men in Armed Conflict." *European Journal of International Law* 18, no. 2: 253–76.

Sjoberg, Laura. 2013. *Gendering Global Conflict: Toward a Feminist Theory of War*. New York: Columbia University Press.

———. 2016. *Women as Wartime Rapists*. New York: New York University Press.

Sjoberg, Laura, Kelly Kadera, and Cameron G. Thies. 2018. "Reevaluating Gender and IR Scholarship: Moving beyond Reiter's Dichotomies toward Effective Synergies." *Journal of Conflict Resolution* 62, no. 4: 848–70.

Sjoberg, Laura, and Jessica Peet. 2011. "A(nother) Dark Side of the Protection Racket: Targeting Women in Wars." *International Feminist Journal of Politics* 13, no. 2: 163–82.

Skjelsbæk, Inger. 2012. *The Political Psychology of War Rape: Studies from Bosnia and Herzegovina*. London: Routledge.

———. 2015. "The Military Perpetrator: A Narrative Analysis of Sentencing Judgments on Sexual Violence Offenders at the International Criminal Tribunal for the Former Yugoslavia (ICTY)." *Journal of Social and Political Psychology* 3, no. 1: 46–70.

———. 2018. "Silence Breakers in War and Peace: Research on Gender and Violence with an Ethics of Engagement." *Social Politics: International Studies in Gender, State and Society* 25, no. 4: 496–520.

Söderberg Kovacs, Mimmi, and Jesper Bjarnesen. 2018. *Violence in African Elections*. London: Zed Books.

Sofaer, Abraham D., and Seymour E. Goodman. 2001. *Cyber Crime and Security: The Transnational Dimension*. Stanford, CA: Hoover Institution Press. Accessed October 2022. Available at: https://www.hoover.org/sites/default/files/uploads/documents/081799 9825_1.pdf.

Solangon, Sarah, and Preeti Patel. 2012. "Sexual Violence against Men in Countries Affected by Armed Conflict." *Conflict, Security, and Development* 12, no. 4: 417–42.

Southern, Rosalynd, and Emily Harmer. 2019. "Othering Political Women: Online Misogyny, Racism and Ableism Towards Women in Public Life." In *Online Othering: Exploring Digital Violence and Discrimination on the Web*, edited by Karen Lumsden and Emily Harmer, 187–210. Cham, Switzerland: Palgrave Macmillan.

———. 2021. "Twitter, Incivility and 'Everyday' Gendered Othering: An Analysis of Tweets Sent to UK Members of Parliament." *Social Science Computer Review* 39, no. 2: 259–75.

Sporre, Tove, and Robeert Standar. 2006. *Konsten Att Läsa Statistik Om Brottslighet*. Stockholm: Brottsförebyggande rådet.

Stack, Liam. 2018. "Facing Threats and Bias, L.G.B.T. Candidates Are Running in Record Numbers." *New York Times*, November 5, 2018. Accessed November 30, 2021. Available at: https://www.nytimes.com/2018/11/05/us/politics/lgbt-candidates.html.

Stambolieva, Ekaterina. 2017. "Methodology: Detecting Online Abuse Against Women MPs on Twitter." Report, Amnesty International. Accessed October 2022. Available at: https://www.amnesty.org/en/latest/research/2018/03/online-violence-against -women-methodology/.

Stark, Lindsay, and Alastair Ager. 2011. "A Systematic Review of Prevalence Studies of Gender-Based Violence in Complex Emergencies." *Trauma, Violence, and Abuse* 12, no. 3: 127–34.

Straus, Scott, and Charlie Taylor. 2012. "Democratization and Electoral Violence in Sub-Saharan Africa, 1990–2008." In *Voting in Fear: Electoral Violence in Sub-Saharan Africa*, edited by Dorina A. Bekoe, 15–38. Washington, DC: United States Institute of Peace Press.

Stryker, Robyn, Bethany Anne Conway, and J. Taylor Danielson. 2016. "What Is Political Incivility?" *Communication Monographs* 83, no. 4: 535–56.

Suarez, Eliana, and Tahany M. Gadalla. 2010. "Stop Blaming the Victim: A Meta-Analysis on Rape Myths." *Journal of Interpersonal Violence* 25, no. 11: 2010–15.

Svensson, Isak. 2020. "Letter to the Editors: Emancipation and Critique in Peace and Conflict Research." *Journal of Global Security Studies* 0, no. 0: 1–5.

SVT. 2020. "Brandattentat mot KD-politiker i Karlskoga," SVT NYHETER, July 26, 2020. Accessed October 2022. Available at: https://www.svt.se/nyheter/snabbkollen/bran dattentat-mot-kd-politiker-i-karlskoga.

Swaine, Aisling. 2015. "Beyond Strategic Rape and Between the Public and Private: Violence Against Women in Armed Conflict." *Human Rights Quarterly* 37, no. 3: 755–86, 829.

Taylor, Charles Fernandes, Jon C. W. Pevehouse, and Scott Straus. 2017. "Perils of Pluralism: Electoral Violence and Incumbency in Sub-Saharan Africa." *Journal of Peace Research* 54, no. 3: 397–411.

TEPJF. 2017. "Protocolo Para Atender La Violencia Política Contra Las Mujeres." Accessed October 2022. Available at: https://www.gob.mx/cms/uploads/attachment/file /275255/Protocolo_para_la_Atencio_n_de_la_Violencia_Politica_23NOV17.pdf.

Thomas, Abdul Rashid. 2021. "Koinadugu District Council Bye-Elections Marred by Violence, Voter Intimidation and Fraud." *Sierra Leone Telegraph*, October 4, 2021.

Accessed October 23, 2021. Available at: https://www.thesierraleonetelegraph.com /koinadugu-district-council-bye-elections-marred-by-violence-voter-intimidation -and-fraud/.

Thomas, Jakana. 2014. "Rewarding Bad Behavior: How Governments Respond to Terrorism in Civil War." *American Journal of Political Science* 58, no. 4: 804–18.

Thomas, Jakana L., and Kanisha D. Bond. 2015. "Women's Participation in Violent Political Organizations." *American Political Science Review* 109, no. 3: 488–506.

Thomas, Sue. 1994. *How Women Legislate.* New York: Oxford University Press.

Thomas, Sue, Rebekah Herrick, Lori D. Franklin, Marcia L. Godwin, Eveline Gnabasik, and Jean R. Schroedel. 2019. "Not for the Faint of Heart: Assessing Physical Violence and Psychological Abuse against US Mayors." *State and Local Government Review* 51, no. 1: 57–67.

Tickner, Ann J. 1997. "You Just Don't Understand: Troubled Engagements between Feminists and IR Theorists." *International Studies Quarterly* 41, no.4: 611–32.

———. 2006. "On the Frontlines or Sidelines of Knowledge and Power? Feminist Practices of Responsible Scholarship." *International Studies Review* 8, no. 3: 383–39.

Tjaden, Patricia G., and Thoennes, Nancy. 2000. *Extent, Nature, and Consequences of Intimate Partner Violence.* Washington, DC: National Institute of Justice.

Tolleson-Rinehart, Sue. 2001. "Do Women Leaders Make a Difference? Substance, Style and Perceptions." In *The Impact of Women in Public Office,* edited by Susan Carroll, 149–65. Bloomington: Indiana University Press.

Tormos, Fernando. 2018. "Intersectional Solidarity." *Politics, Groups, and Identities* 5, no. 4: 707–20.

Touquet, Heleen. 2018. *Unsilenced: Male Victims of Sexual Violence in Sri Lanka.* Johannesburg: International Truth and Justice Project.

Touquet, Heleen, Sarah Chynoweth, Sarah, Martin, Chen Reis, Henri Myrttinen, Philipp Schulz, Lewis Turner, and David Duriesmith. 2020. "From 'It Rarely Happens' to 'It's Worse for Men': Dispelling Misconceptions about Sexual Violence against Men and Boys in Conflict and Displacement." *Journal of Humanitarian Affairs* 2 no. 3: 25–34.

Townsend-Bell, Erica. 2011. "What Is Relevance? Defining Intersectional Praxis in Uruguay." *Political Research Quarterly* 64, no. 1: 187–99. https://doi.org/https://doi.org/10 .1177/1065912910382301.

"#ToxicTwitter: Violence and Abuse against Women Online." 2018. Amnesty International. Accessed October 10, 2022. Available at: https://www.amnesty.org/download /Documents/ACT3080702018ENGLISH.PDF.

Transparency International Papua New Guinea (TIPNG). 2017. *TIPNG Observation Report, 10th National Parliamentary Elections 2017.* Port Moresby: TIPNG.

Tripp, Aili Mari. 2010. *Museveni's Uganda: Paradoxes of Power in a Hybrid Regime.* Boulder, CO: Lynne Rienner.

———. 2015. *Women and Power in Postconflict Africa.* New York: Cambridge University Press.

———. 2019. "Uganda: Achievements and Challenges for Women in Elected Office," in *The Palgrave Handbook of Women's Political Rights,* edited by Susan Franceschet, Mona Lena Krook, and Netina Tan, 577–90. London: Palgrave Macmillan.

True, Jaqui. 2012. *The Political Economy of Violence Against Women.* Oxford University Press.

Tucker, Duncan, and Thiago Camara. 2020. "Brazil: Two Years after Killing of Marielle Franco, Rio de Janeiro Authorities Must Solve Unanswered Questions." Amnesty International, March 14, 2020. Accessed October 2022. Available at: https://www.amnesty.org/en/latest/news/2020/03/brazil-two-years-after-killing-of-marielle-franco/.

Tunney, Catharine. 2021. "Between Violence and Vandalism, the Parties Are Experiencing a Very Ugly Campaign." CBC News Online, September 17, 2021. Accessed October 2022. Available at: https://www.cbc.ca/news/politics/violence-vandalism-campaign-rise-1.6177269.

Uganda SIGI Country Report. 2015. OECD Development Center. Available at: https://www.oecd.org/dev/development-gender/The%20Uganda%20SIGI%20Country%20Study.pdf.

UK-DCMS-Committee. 2019. "The Online Harms White Paper." House of Commons, April 8, 2019. Accessed October 2022. Available at: https://www.gov.uk/government/consultations/online-harms-white-paper.

UN Action. 2007. *UN Action against Sexual Violence in Conflict*. Information brochure: Stop Rape Now.

UN General Assembly. 2018. *Resolution 73/148: Intensification of Efforts to Prevent and Eliminate All Forms of Violence against Women and Girls: Sexual Harassment*. New York: United Nations.

United Nations. 2012. "Resolution Adopted by the General Assembly 66/130 on Women and Political Participation. A/RES/66/130." Resolution, United Nations.

———. 2013. "Committee on the Elimination of Discrimination against Women, General Recommendation No. 30 on Women in Conflict Prevention, Conflict and Post-Conflict Situations." Fifty-Sixth Session (CEDAW/C/GC/30), United Nations.

———. 2018a. "Report of the Special Rapporteur on violence against women, its causes and consequences on violence against women in politics. A/73/301." Report, United Nations.

———. 2018b. "Resolution Adopted by the General Assembly 73/148. Intensification of Efforts to Prevent and Eliminate All Forms of Violence against Women and Girls: Sexual Harassment. A/RES/73/148." Resolution, United Nations.

———. 2021. "Women's Full and Effective Participation and Decision-Making in Public Life, as Well as the Elimination of Violence, for Achieving Gender Equality and the Empowerment of All Women and Girls, Agreed Conclusions. E/CN.6/2021/L.3." Report, United Nations.

UNODC. 2018. "Home, the Most Dangerous Place for Women, with Majority of Female Homicide Victims Worldwide Killed by Partners or Family, UNODC Study Says." United Nations Office on Drugs and Crime, November 25, 2018.

UN Women. 2017. "Tunisia Passes Historic Law to End Violence against Women and Girls." August 10, 2017. Accessed October 2022. Available at: https://www.unwomen.org/en/news/stories/2017/8/news-tunisia-law-on-ending-violence-against-women.

———. 2018. "UN Women Internal Reporting." United Nations Entity for Gender Equality and the Empowerment of Women (UN Women).

———. 2019. "UN Women Internal Reporting." United Nations Entity for Gender Equality and the Empowerment of Women (UN Women).

———. 2021. "Guidance Note: Preventing Violence against Women in Politics." United Nations Entity for Gender Equality and the Empowerment of Women (UN Women).

UN Women and ILO. 2019. *Handbook: Addressing Violence and Harassment against Women in the World of Work*. New York: United Nations Entity for Gender Equality and the Empowerment of Women (UN Women) International Labour Organization (ILO).

UN Women and UNDP. 2017. *Preventing Violence against Women in Elections: A Programming Guide*. New York: United Nations Entity for Gender Equality and the Empowerment of Women (UN Women) and United Nations Development Programme (UNDP).

Urdal, Henrik, and Chi Primus Che. 2013. "War and Gender Inequalities in Health: The Impact of Armed Conflict on Fertility and Maternal Mortality." *International Interactions* 39, no. 4: 489–510.

Vaishnav, Milan. 2018. "Indian Women Are Voting More Than Ever. Will They Change Indian Society?" Carnegie Endowment for International Peace, November 8, 2018.

Van Der Wilk, Adriane. 2018. "Cyber Violence and Hate Speech Online against Women." Report, European Parliament, FEMM Committee, September 2018. Accessed December 2019. Available at: https://www.europarl.europa.eu/RegData/etudes/STUD/2018/604979/IPOL_STU(2018)604979_EN.pdf.

Van Zoonen, Liesbet. 2006. "The Personal, the Political and the Popular: A Woman's Guide to Celebrity Politics." *European Journal of Cultural Studies* 9, no. 3: 287–301.

Veilleux-Lepage, Yannick, and Emil Archambault. 2019. "Mapping Transnational Extremist Networks: An Exploratory Study of the Soldiers of Odin's Facebook Network, Using Integrated Social Network Analysis." *Perspectives on Terrorism* 13, no. 2: 21–38.

Verge, Tània, and Silvia Claveria. 2017. "Party Office, Male Homosocial Capital and Gendered Political Recruitment." In *Gender and Informal Institutions*, edited by Georgina Waylen, 91–114. London: Rowman and Littlefield.

Verma, Binita, and Ramjevaan Singh Thakur. 2018. "Sentiment Analysis Using Lexicon and Machine Learning-Based Approaches: A Survey." In *Proceedings of the International Conference on Recent Advancement on Computer and Communication*, edited by Basant Tiwari, Vivek Tiwari, Kinkar Chandra Das, Durgesh Kumar Mishra, and Jagdish C. Bansal, 441–47. Singapore: Springer.

von Borzyskowski, Inken, and Patrick M. Kuhn. 2020. "Dangerously Informed: Voter Information and Pre-Electoral Violence in Africa." *Journal of Peace Research* 57, no. 1: 15–29.

Von Clausewitz, Carl. 1976. *On War*. Translated by Peter Paret and Michael Eliot Howard. Princeton, NJ: Princeton University Press.

Wagner, Angelia. 2020. "Tolerating the Trolls? Gendered Perceptions of Online Harassment of Politicians in Canada." *Feminist Media Studies* 0, no. 0: 1–16.

Wahman, Michael, Jan Teorell, and Axel Hadenius. 2013. "Authoritarian Regime Types Revisited: Updated Data in Comparative Perspective." *Contemporary Politics* 19, no. 1: 19–34.

Walby, Sylvia. 1989. "Theorising Patriarchy." *Sociology* 23, no. 2: 213–34.

Waldron, Jeremy. 2012. *The Harm in Hate Speech*. Cambridge, MA: Harvard University Press.

Wallensteen, Peter. 2013. *Peace Research: Theory and Practice*. London: Routledge.

Walter, Barbara. 2006. "Building Reputation: Why Governments Fight Some Separatists but Not Others." *American Journal of Political Science* 50, no. 2: 313–30.

Ward, Stephen, and Liam McLoughlin. 2020. "Turds, Traitors and Tossers: The Abuse of UK MPs via Twitter." *Journal of Legislative Studies* 26, no. 1: 47–73. https://doi.org/10.1080/13572334.2020.1730502.

Waylen, Georgina. 2014. "Informal Institutions, Institutional Change, and Gender Equality." *Political Research Quarterly* 67, no. 1: 212–23.

Weber, Max. 2004. *The Vocation Lectures*. Translated by Rodney Livingstone. Edited by David Owen and Tracy Strong. Indianapolis: Hackett Publishing.

WebRoot–NZ. 2022. "What Is Netiquette? A Guide to Online Ethics and Etiquette." Accessed January 2022. Available at: https://www.webroot.com/nz/en/resources/tips-articles/netiquette-and-online-ethics-what-are-they.

Webster, Kaitlyn, Chong Chen, and Kyle Beardsley. 2019. "Conflict, Peace, and the Evolution of Women's Empowerment." *International Organization* 73, no. 2: 255–89.

Weingrod, Alex. 1968. "Patrons, Patronage, and Political Parties." *Comparative Studies in Society and History* 10, no. 4: 377–400.

Weldon, S. Laurel. 2006. "The Structure of Intersectionality: A Comparative Politics of Gender." *Politics and Gender* 2, no. 2: 235–48.

Westhead, Rick. 2020. "WHL Investigating Abuse Claims by Former Player." TSN, June 25. Available at: https://www.tsn.ca/whl-investigating-abuse-claims-by-former-player-1.1489379.

WHO. 2017. "Violence against Women." Report, World Health Organization, November 29, 2017.

Wick, Julia. 2020. "Newsletter: Facing Harassment as a Female Mayor." *Los Angeles Times*, January 16, 2020. Accessed November 1, 2021. Available at: https://www.latimes.com/california/story/2020-01-16/san-luis-obispo-mayor-heidi-harmon-harassment-essential-california-newsletter.

Williams, Jamie Lee. 2019. "Cavalier Bot Regulation and the First Amendment's Threat Model." Knight First Amendment Institute, August 21, 2019. Accessed November 2019. Available at: https://knightcolumbia.org/content/cavalier-bot-regulation-and-the-first-amendments-threat-model.

Williams, Matthew L., and Pete Burnap. 2015. "Cyberhate on Social Media in the Aftermath of Woolwich: A Case Study in Computational Criminology and Big Data." *British Journal of Criminology* 56, no. 2: 211–38.

Wilson, Mark. 2019. "The Tech Giant Fighting Anti-vaxxers Isn't Twitter or Facebook. It's Pinterest." Fast Company, February 26, 2019. Accessed November 2019. Available at: https://www.fastcompany.com/90310970/the-tech-giant-fighting-anti-vaxxers-isnt-twitter-or-facebook-its-pinterest.

Women in Local Government Baseline Statistics. 2018. "Uganda Bureau of Statistics." Kampala, Uganda.

Women's Refugee Commission (WRC). 2018. *It's Happening to Our Men as Well. Sexual Violence Against Rohingya Men and Boys*. New York: WRC.

Wong, Joon Ian. 2017. "Top Italian Politician Laura Boldrini Is Calling Out Mark Zuckerberg for Ignoring Hate Speech and Fake News." Quartz. Accessed November 30, 2021. Available at: https://qz.com/911293/top-italian-politician-laura-boldrini-is-calling-out-mark-zuckerberg-for-ignoring-hate-speech-and-fake-news/.

Wood, Elisabeth. 2006. "The Ethical Challenges of Field Research in Conflict Zones." *Qualitative Sociology* 29, no. 3: 373–86.

———. 2009. "Armed Groups and Sexual Violence: When Is Wartime Rape Rare?" *Politics and Society* 37, no. 1: 131–61.

———. 2018. "Rape as a Practice of War: Toward a Typology of Political Violence." *Politics and Society* 46, no. 4: 513–37.

Woolley, Samuel, and Katie Joseff. 2018. "Computational Propaganda, Jewish-Americans and the 2018 Midterms: The Amplification of Anti-Semitic Harassment Online." Anti-Defamation League, October 2018. Accessed October 2021. Available at: https://

www.adl.org/resources/reports/computational-propaganda-jewish-americans-and-the-2018-midterms-the-amplification.

World Health Organization. 1996. *Violence: A Public Health Priority: WHO Global Consultation on Violence and Health*. Chicago: World Health Organization.

Wrede, Magnus. 2017. "Hotrisken Hejdar Axén Olins Comeback." Dagens Samhälle, June 1, 2017. Accessed October 2022. Available at: https://www.dagenssamhalle.se/ny het/hotrisken-hejdar-axen-olins-comeback-17425?story=2547.

Wright, Melissa W. 2010. "Femicide, Mother-Activism, and the Geography of Protest in Northern Mexico." In *Making a Killing: Femicide, Free Trade, and la Frontera*, edited by Alicia Gaspar de Alba and Georgina Guzmán, 211–42. Austin: University of Texas Press.

Young, Iris. 2003. "The Logic of Masculinist Protection: Reflections on the Current Security State." *Signs: Journal of Women in Culture and Society* 29, no. 1: 1–25.

Yuval-Davis, Nira. 1997. *Gender and Nation*. London: SAGE.

———. 2006. "Intersectionality and Feminist Politics." *European Journal of Women's Studies* 13, no. 3: 193–209.

Zak, Michal. 2015. "Mizrahi Jews Remind Israel of its Hidden Other." Middle East Eye, September 22, 2015. Accessed October 2022. Available at: https://www.middleeasteye.net/opinion/mizrahi-jews-remind-israel-its-hidden-other.

Zalewski, Marysia, Paula Drumond, Elisabeth Prügl, and Maria Stern. 2018. *Sexual Violence against Men in Global Politics*. London: Routledge.

Zeiter, Kirsten, Sandra Pepera, Molly Middlehurst, and Derek Ruths. 2019. "Tweets that Chill: Analyzing Online Violence Against Women in Politics." Report, National Democratic Institute. Accessed October 2022. Available at: https://www.ndi.org/sites/de fault/files/NDI Tweets That Chill Report.pdf.

Zulver, Julia. 2016. "High-Risk Feminism in El Salvador: Women's Mobilisation in Violent Times." *Gender and Development* 24, no. 2: 171–85.

———. 2017. "Building the City of Women: Creating a Site of Feminist Resistance in a Northern Colombian Conflict Zone." *Gender, Place and Culture* 24, no. 10: 1498–516.

Contributors

Kerryn Baker is Fellow in the Department of Pacific Affairs at the Australian National University. She has published widely on gender, politics, and participation in the Pacific Islands region. Her book *Pacific Women in Politics: Gender Quota Campaigns in the Pacific Islands* was published by University of Hawaii Press in 2019, and she is the coeditor (with Marian Sawer) of *Gender Innovation in Political Science: New Norms, New Knowledge* (Palgrave, 2019).

Julie Ballington has been advancing global policy and research to increase women's political representation for more than twenty years. She is currently UN Women's Global Policy Advisor on Political Participation, overseeing technical assistance to field offices, programs to prevent violence against women, methodologies to measure women's representation in local government, and gender mainstreaming in UN Electoral Assistance.

Gabrielle Bardall specializes in feminist democratization processes. She has served as advisor and educator to parliamentarians and electoral commissions in more than sixty countries worldwide for nearly two decades. Dr. Bardall is Vice President of External Relations for the Parliamentary Centre and Nonresident Fellow with the Centre for Democracy and Technology. Her research on violence against women in politics has received numerous awards. She holds degrees from the Université de Montréal, Science Po Paris, and McGill University.

Elin Bjarnegård is Associate Professor of Political Science at Uppsala University. Her research interests are at the intersection of comparative politics, peace and conflict studies, and gender studies. Her publications have appeared in journals such as *Comparative Politics*, *Journal of Peace Research*, and *Politics and Gender*. She is author of *Gender, Informal Institutions and Political Recruitment* (Palgrave Macmillan, 2013).

Gabriella Borovsky is a gender specialist who has been working on initiatives to promote women's political empowerment with international organizations in more than a dozen countries for the past seventeen years. She is currently working in the Governance and Participation Policy Section of UN Women, leading on knowledge management and capacity development programs on political participation.

Cheryl N. Collier is Dean of the Faculty of Arts, Humanities, and Social Sciences and Professor, Political Science, at the University of Windsor. She researches in the areas of comparative women's movements, Canadian federal and provincial childcare and anti-violence against women policy, federalism, feminist institutionalism, and violence against women in politics. She has published in a variety of journals, including *Canadian Journal of Political Science, Politics and Gender, Social Politics*, and *Parliamentary Affairs*.

Sofia Collignon is Lecturer (Assistant Professor) in Comparative Politics at Queen Mary, University of London. Her research focuses on gendered political violence; the harassment, abuse, and intimidation of political elites; and the study of candidates, elections, and parties. Her articles have appeared in *Western European Politics, Party Politics, Electoral Studies, European Political Science Review*, and *Journal of Elections, Public Opinion and Parties*, among others.

Maria Eriksson Baaz is Professor in International Relations at the Department of Government, Uppsala University. Her research interests include gender and violence, postcolonial theory, civil-military relations, and research ethics and methodology. She is coauthor (with Maria Stern) of *Sexual Violence as a Weapon of War?: Perceptions, Prescriptions, Problems in the Congo and Beyond* (Zed Books, 2013). She has written and coedited several books, and her articles have appeared in leading international academic journals.

Eleonora Esposito is Researcher at the Institute for Culture and Society (ICS) of the University of Navarra and a Seconded National Expert at the European Institute for Gender Equality (EIGE). Her recent publications include the edited special issue of *Journal of Language, Aggression and Conflict* entitled "Critical Perspectives on Gender, Politics and Violence" (2021) and the monograph *Politics, Ethnicity and the Postcolonial Nation* (John Benjamins, 2021).

Sandra Håkansson is a Ph.D. candidate in political science at Uppsala University. Her thesis focuses on gender aspects of violence against politicians. Her research has appeared in *Journal of Politics, Perspectives on Politics*, and *Politics and Gender*.

Nicole Haley is a professor of political anthropology and a leading authority on elections in Melanesia. She leads the Pacific Research Program and was formerly head of the Australian National University Department of Pacific Affairs. Coeditor of two books, *Conflict and Resource Development in the Southern Highlands of Papua New Guinea* (2007) and *Election 2007: The Shift to Limited Preferential Voting in Papua New Guinea* (2013), she has led large-scale research-based election observations in Papua New Guinea (2007, 2012, 2017, 2022), Solomon Islands (2014), and Samoa (2016).

Rebekah Herrick is Professor of Political Science at Oklahoma State University. Her research interests concern issues of representation, particularly as they relate to gender and race in the United States. Presently, her research focuses on violence against women politicians and issues of voter turnout, including turnout of indigenous Americans. Her work has appeared in *Journal of Politics*, *Politics and Gender*, *Social Science Quarterly*, and *Political Research Quarterly*.

Roudabeh Kishi is Director of Research and Innovation at the Armed Conflict Location & Event Data Project (ACLED), the most widely used real-time data and analysis source on political violence and protest in the world. There she leads data collection, research, and analysis, including on political violence targeting women. Her work appears in numerous academic journals as well as media outlets. She holds a Ph.D. in government and politics from the University of Maryland.

Anne-Kathrin Kreft is Postdoctoral Fellow in Political Science at the University of Oslo. She obtained her Ph.D. at the University of Gothenburg in 2019. Her research interests include gender-based and political violence, armed conflict, civil society, public opinion, and the Women, Peace, and Security framework. Her work is published inter alia in *Comparative Political Studies*, *Journal of Conflict Resolution*, *Journal of Peace Research*, and *International Affairs*.

Mona Lena Krook is Professor of Political Science and Chair of the Women and Politics Ph.D. Program at Rutgers University. Since 2015, she has collaborated with the National Democratic Institute on its #NotTheCost campaign to stop violence against in women in politics. Her most recent book, *Violence against Women in Politics* (Oxford University Press, 2020), received the 2022 Grawemeyer Award for Ideas Improving World Order.

Rebecca Kuperberg received her Ph.D in the political science department at Rutgers University.

Robert U. Nagel is Research Fellow at Georgetown University's Institute for Women, Peace, and Security and a member of the Consultative Group of the Sexual Violence in Armed Conflict project. He obtained his Ph.D. from the University of Kent. A recipient of the Cedric Smith Prize and Dina Zinnes Award, he has published on the gendered dimensions of conflict in *International Studies Quarterly*, *Journal of Peace Research*, *Journal of Conflict Resolution*, and *Security Studies*, among other academic and policy-oriented outlets.

Louise Olsson is Research Director of the Department of Global Politics, Norms, and Society, and Coordinator of the Gender Research Group at the Peace Research Institute Oslo (PRIO). She has published on gendered dimensions of armed conflict and conflict resolution since 2000 and is the editor of three special issues and books, such as *Gender, Peace and Security: Implementing UN Resolution 1325* (Routledge, 2015), She has also served as Senior Advisor on Women, Peace, and Security at the Folke Bernadotte Academy, a government agency under the Ministry for Foreign Affairs in Sweden.

Jennifer M. Piscopo is Associate Professor of Politics and Director of the Center for Research and Scholarship at Occidental College in Los Angeles, California, and Honorary Fellow of the Gender Institute at Royal Holloway University of London. Her work on women, gender, elections, and representation has appeared in more than thirty peer-reviewed journals, including the *American Political Science Review*; *American Journal of Political Science*; *Comparative Political Studies*, *Politics and Gender*; and *Latin American*

Politics and Society. She coedits the journal *Politics, Groups, and Identities* and consults regularly for international organizations, including UN Women.

Tracey Raney is Professor in the Department of Politics and Public Administration at Toronto Metropolitan University (formerly Ryerson University). She studies women and politics, feminist institutionalism, sexual misconduct in legislatures, and gender-based violence in politics. Her research has been published in several leading journals and edited books, including *Parliamentary Affairs, Social Politics, Canadian Journal of Political Science*, and *Nations and Nationalism*.

Juliana Restrepo Sanín is Assistant Professor of Political Science at the University of Florida. Her research analyzes violence and harassment against women politicians in Latin America, women's activism to bring attention to this problem, and the development and effectiveness of state measures to end it. Her research has been published in *Comparative Political Studies, Perspectives on Politics, Politics & Gender, Signs, International Feminist Journal of Politics, European Journal of Politics and Gender, Política y Gobierno*, and *Revista de Ciencia Política*.

Paige Schneider has a joint appointment with the departments of Politics and Women's and Gender Studies at the University of the South (Sewanee). Her areas of scholarship include gender and politics, with a focus on gender and election violence, and gender and sport in the Global South. Most recently, her work has appeared in *Journal of Gender Studies, Policy Studies*, and the edited volume *Building Inclusive Elections* (edited by Toby S. James and Holly Ann Garnett).

Maria Stern is Professor in Peace and Development Studies at the School of Global Studies, University of Gothenburg. Her research interests include critical security studies, feminist theory, security development, the international political sociology of violence, and methodology. She is coauthor (with Maria Eriksson Baaz) of *Sexual Violence as a Weapon of War?: Perceptions, Prescriptions, Problems in the Congo and Beyond* (Zed Books, 2013). She has written and coedited several books, and her articles have appeared in leading international academic journals.

Sue Thomas is Senior Research Scientist at the Pacific Institute for Research and Evaluation. In addition to PIRE projects and publications, she has published books and journal articles, books chapters, encyclopedia entries, and book reviews on women, politics, and policy and American government. In 2020, she received the Malcolm Jewell Enduring Contribution Book Award from the State Politics and Policy Section of the American Political Science Association for her book *How Women Legislate*.

Pär Zetterberg is Associate Professor of Political Science at Uppsala University in Sweden. His main research interests lie in the area of comparative politics, with a focus on gender, and include issues such as candidate recruitment, political parties, electoral quotas, political violence, and political representation. His research has been published in *American Political Science Review, American Journal of Political Science, Journal of Politics, Comparative Politics, Politics and Gender*, and *Party Politics*, among other journals.

Index

Web 2.0, 93, 95–96, 102
Whitmer, Gretchen, 1
Women, Peace and Security, 4, 214–215;
   framework, 214–215
Women's organization, 219-221
Women's rights, 30, 32, 62t, 120, 157,
   219, 227; women's reproductive right,
   215

Working class, 45, 246
World Health Organization (WHO), 7, 95

YouTube, 102–103, 204, 208–209
Yugoslavia, 39, 42, 88

ZANU-PF, 67
Zimbabwe, 67, 199

www.ingramcontent.com/pod-product-compliance
Lightning Source LLC
Chambersburg PA
CBHW040144270326
41929CB00024B/3367